Copyright 2025 by Carol A Tebbs

No part of this book may be reproduced or transcribed in any form or by any means, electronic or mechanical, including photocopying or recording or by any information storage and retrieval system without written permission from the author and publisher, except in the case of brief quotations embodied in critical reviews and articles. Requests and inquiries may be mailed to: American Federation of Astrologers, Inc., 6535 S. Rural Road, Tempe, AZ 85283.

ISBN: 978-086690-687-9

Cover Design: Celeste Nash

Shutterstock: Stock Illustration ID: 2133106445

Illustration Contributor: Paolo Gallo

Published by:

American Federation of Astrologers, Inc.

6535 S. Rural Road

Tempe, AZ 85283

Printed in the United States of America

The New Complete Book of Chart Rectification

By Carol A. Tebbs, MA, CAP

© 2025 Carol Tebbs
All rights reserved
Third Edition

Dedication

To my rectification students, friends and colleagues at Kepler College who inspired me to update my out-of-print 2008 version of The Complete Book of Chart Rectification with new information, new format, and new examples. I especially owe a great thank you to my friend and colleague, Enid Newberg, who formatted the 2022 final pdf version of Rectification: Verify to Rectify for Accurate Forecasting. All of you have made me a better teacher.

About the Author

Carol Tebbs, MA, ISAR CAP, a practicing astrologer since 1971, is well recognized in the astrological community for over 50 years of community service: 3 terms as ISAR President and 23 years on the ISAR Board from 1979-2002; UAC co-founder and Board member 1984-1999; UAC Board Chair 1997-1999 and UAC '95 Conference Coordinator.

Ms. Tebbs specializes in all facets of natal chart and current patterns interpretation, as well as electional timing for important events and birth time rectification. Her publications include two E-books published in 2003 by Online College of Astrology (now IAA) entitled Beyond Basics: Moving the Chart in Time and Beyond Basics: Tools for the Consulting Astrologer.

With a master's degree in English and another in Education from Whittier College, Carol Tebbs successfully taught Advanced Placement English for 38 years in a California large urban school district. She worked for the College Board as an Advanced Placement "Writing Assessment Reader" and "Writing Assessment Teacher Trainer", 1997-2003, confirming college credit for student excellence in composition and writing. After serving on the Kepler College Board several years, she served as Kepler College President from 2003-2006 and lead Kepler's 1st graduation of BA Degree recipients and has continued to the present as Kepler College Director of Education and Instructor. Ms. Tebbs is noted in Who's Who in Education and Who's Who in the World.

TABLE OF CONTENTS

Dedication	iii
About the Author	iv
Contents	v
Introduction: The Importance Of Accurate Forecasting	xi
Chapter 1: Why Does Birth Time Matter?	1-1
• Know How Birth Time is Determined	1-1
• Understand Movement of the Chart Components	1-1
• The Lights and Nodes	1-1
• The Inner Planets	1-2
• The Outer Planets	1-2
• Understand the Complexity of the Rectification Task	1-3
• Birth Time Rectification Has Historical Roots	1-6
• Know the Pitfalls of Recorded Birth Time Accuracy	1-6
• Time Change Variance:	1-7
• Robin Williams – Daylight Savings Time vs Standard Time	1-8
• Cate Blanchett – Accurate Data for Public Figures vs Real People	1-8
• Sean Connery – Accurate Data for Public Figures vs Real People	1-8
Chapter 2: How Do I Verify A Given Birth Time?	2-11
• A Quick Test to Verify Birth Time	2-11
• A More Substantial Test of the Birth Time: "Event Hooks"	2-13
• A Method to Proceed with the Test: "Aspect Hooks"	2-14
• Narrow the Field for Midheaven Candidates	2-18
• Remember the Basics of Time	2-19
• Narrow the Field for Ascendant Candidates	2-21
• The Progressed Moon Gives "Second-Hand" Timing Accuracy	2-23

- The Progressed Sun and Inner Planets Can Mark Key Life Events — 2-25
- Progressed to Progressed Aspects Can Confirm Birth Time — 2-27
- Outer Transits Can Mark Potential Moon and Angle Positions — 2-28

Chapter 3: If The Quick Test Fails, Plan To Rectify! — 3-39
- Search Time Variances for the Birth Date and Birth Location — 3-39
- Find Resources for Further Birth Time Confirmation — 3-40
- Choose Astrology Software to Confirm or Rectify a Birth Time — 3-41
- Be Clear with Clients on What to Expect from the Rectification Process — 3-41
- Get a Comprehensive List of Life Events and Dates – "Event Hooks" — 3-42
- Develop a Case Theory from the Biography and Major Life Events — 3-46
- Find Planets in One-Degree Orb for "Aspect Hooks"– Beware the Moon — 3-47
- Establish a Working Chart for the Midpoint of the Search Time Range — 3-48
- Set A Procedure for the Rectification Search — 3-48
  - A Checklist for the Rectification Search — 3-50
- Align Astrological Descriptors "Aspect Hooks" to "Event Hooks" — 3-50
- Know the Search Time Range to Determine Where to Start — 3-51
  - Time Range within Fifteen Minutes – Angles Move Four Degrees — 3-54
    - Prince William — 3-54
  - Time Range within Three Hours – Angles Move One and a Half Signs — 3-55
    - Anna Nicole Smith — 3-55
  - Time Range within Six Hours – Angles Move Three Signs — 3-59
    - Princess Diana — 3-59
  - Time Range within Twelve Hours – Angles Move Six Signs — 3-62
    - Chris Costner Sizemore — 3-62
- Tally Some Preliminary Results — 3-65
- Go Out on a Limb: Experiment with the Short List of Birth times — 3-65
- Include the Client in Final Birth Time Choice: Ascendant Sign and Ruler — 3-66

Chapter 4: Why Is Case Theory So Important? — 4-67

- Study the Biography and Life Events to Build a "Case Theory" — 4-67
- Case Theory and Rectification Example: Female Client — 4-68
- Case Theory and Rectification Example: Televangelist Jimmy Swaggart — 4-71
- Death of two key women and mentors - mother and grandmother — 4-84
- Jimmy is Arrested with Prostitute — 4-85
    - Public Confession on Television/ Defrocked as Minister — 4-88
    - Jimmy Is Arrested Again with Prostitute — 4-90

Chapter 5: What Movement Techniques Work Best? — 5-99

- Know What Moves How Fast to Activate a One-Degree Orb — 5-99
- Software Settings Make a Difference — 5-102
- Assessing the Year with Solar Arc Directions — 5-104
    - Chelsea Clinton — 5-108
- Assessing the Year with Secondary Progressions — 5-109
- Prioritize What's Important in the Progression — 5-111
- Secondary Progressed Moon and Transiting Saturn Work as a Team — 5-113
- Assessing the Month with the Progressed Moon — 5-114
- Assessing Life Turning Points with Progressed New and Full Moons — 5-115
- Assessing the Year with Progressed Declination — 5-118
    - Declination: A Planet or Point at Crossover — 5-119
    - Declination: A Planet or Point at Maximum North or South — 5-119
    - Declination: A Planet or Point Out-of-Bounds North or South — 5-119
    - Declination: Personal Planets Out-of-Bounds North or South — 5-120
- Assessing a Month with Tertiary and Two-Weeks with Minor Progressions — 5-121
- Timing Months and Years with Outer Planet and Lunar Node Transits — 5-125
- A Transformative Two Years with Transiting Pluto — 5-127
    - A Pluto Transit — 5-130
- A Confusing Year and a Half with Transiting Neptune — 5-132
- A Surprising Year with Transiting Uranus — 5-134

- A Healing Half-Year with Transiting Chiron — 5-135
- A Responsible Season with Transiting Saturn — 5-136
- A Fruitful Period with Transiting Jupiter — 5-137
- Retrograde Periods Extend the Effect of Any Transit — 5-139
- Transiting Lunar Nodes are the Royalty of Retrograde — 5-139
- Timing a Half Year with Solar and Lunar Eclipses — 5-140
- Assessing the Degrees of Angles with Decans and Dwads — 5-143
- Assessing the Year with a Solar Return and a Correct Birthtime — 5-145
- A Final Birth Time Test: Relocation — 5-146

Chapter 6: How Do I Deal With Dirty Data? — 6-149
- Study the Resources for the Various Birth Time Claims — 6-149
- Establish a "Working Chart" for the Midpoint of Known Time Range — 6-150
- Michael Jackson, the King of Dirty Data, Must Start with a Case Theory — 6-151
- Software is Great, but A Trained Astrologer's Judgement is Better — 6-156
    - Filling the Blanks of Michael Jackson's Childhood That Built the Man — 6-157
    - DD Birth Time Results with Appropriate Movement to and from Angles — 6-159
- Taylor Swift has 3 Unverified Birth Times, so a 24-Hour Search is Needed — 6-166
- Without Birth Time, Set the Wheel with a Noon Time — 6-167
- Gather the Person's Comprehensive Biography and Major Life Events — 6-167
- Start With the Moon to Narrow the Search Time Range — 6-168

Chapter 7: How Do I Deal With No Birth Time? — 7-179
- Deriving Birth Time with Rectification Is Not Universally Accepted — 7-179
- Search the Recording Practice of Birth Country or State for Given Year — 7-180
    - Example 1: Client — 7-180
- Test the Narrowed List of Birth Times with Several Movement Methods — 7-187
- Decanates and Dwads are Another Tool to Test Birth Time — 7-188
- Example 2: Hillary Clinton — 7-190

- Example 3: Mike Tyson — 7-193

Chapter 8: Why Are Twins So Different?? — 8-197

- Rectification Example One – Actress Elizabeth Taylor — 8-197
  - Next, Search the Natal Chart for "One-Degree Hard Aspect Hooks" — 8-200
  - Time to List the Important Life Events for Elizabeth Taylor — 8-200
  - Once Background Work is Complete, Begin the Rectification Search — 8-202
  - Now Select the Most Dramatic Events in Close Time Proximity for the Initial Search — 8-204
- Back to Basics, Retrograde and Station Periods Greatly Extend the Effect of Any Transit — 8-219
  - Conclusions On Extenuating Circumstances on the Impact of Outer Transits — 8-221
  - Retrograde and Station Periods Mark Outer Transit "Shadows" for Elizabeth Taylor — 8-221
  - If You are Still Undecided on the Best Birth Time, Run Solar Eclipses for the Events — 8-223
- Rectification Example Two – Singer Johnny Cash — 8-225
  - Find the Dwad Placement of Johnny's Natal Moon — 8-231
  - Begin the Search to Derive the Birth Chart Angles from Life Events — 8-232
    - Tally the Preliminary Search Results to Narrow the Possible Birth Time Range — 8-236
    - Search the Secondary Progressions to Confirm Early Results — 8-237
    - Search Solar Eclipses for Key Events for Final Birth Time Confirmation — 8-243
- Chart Comparison of Time Twins: Liz Taylor and John Cash — 8-244
  - Recognize How Location and Date Can Affect the Angles — 8-244
  - Compare the Dwad Placements of Angles for John and Elizabeth — 8-246

- Outer Transits Activate John and Elizabeth's Close Natal
  Aspect Patterns Simultaneously   8-247
  - Solar Eclipses Activate John and Elizabeth's Close Natal
    Aspect Patterns Simultaneously   8-248
- Fraternal or Identical Twins are Very Different from "Time Twins"   8-248
- Rectification Example Three – Fraternal Twins, Barbara and
  Jenna Bush   8-249

Chapter 9: Why Are Some Charts Hard To Rectify?   9-253
- Easy to Rectify Example: Patsy Cline Has Close Hard Aspects   9-253
  - Patsy Cline Original Birth Information   9-253
  - Patsy Cline's Biography: 9-255
- Difficult to Rectify Example: Kobe Bryant Also Has Close Hard Aspects   9-258
  - Kobe's Capricorn Ascendant   9-265

Appendices
Appendix A: Frequently Asked Questions About Rectification   273
Appendix B: Frequently Asked Questions About Birth Time And Angles   277
Appendix C: Frequently Asked Questions About Transit Cycles   279
Appendix D: Frequently Asked Questions About Declination And Graphs   283

Bibliography   285

Introduction: The Importance of Accurate Forecasting

Most people know the date of their birth and the location but too many can only give a general birth time such as part of the day, morning, afternoon, evening, or a time rounded to the quarter-hour. Even the Birth Certificate time may vary up to a half-hour either way because the nurse and doctor are focused on care of the baby and mother first and foremost. The birthtime is well down the list of their priorities and it is often prepared well after the birth when the nurse fills out the paperwork for the doctor to sign. Memory fades, clocks run fast or slow, a few states in the US require births during daylight savings time or war time to be recorded in standard time – the list of variances is long. In astrology, four minutes of clock time equals one-degree on the chart angles and with some chart movement techniques an astrological forecast for a client may be off by a year or more. All birth times should be tested with a few prominent life events to confirm that the chart works with appropriate astrological descriptors aligning when the situation or event occurred. Bernadette Brady tells us that "Incorrect Birth Time…is probably one of the largest causes of errors in astrological work. Any change to the birth time can, of course, change the signs on the house cusps as well as the timing of movement to the angles."[1]

Astrologers have always relied upon their training to interpret the natal chart's planets, angles, signs houses and aspects to accurately translate astrology's symbolic language into a language the client can understand. Further, they rely upon their experience and preparation for the client consultation to provide an accurate forecast, not only of what is currently activated in the natal chart, but the timing of when the chart angles, planets and sensitive points are activated to fulfill the natal promise. Without a correct birth time, accurate forecasting is impossible. Basically, we rely on a variety of movement techniques that activate the natal chart to derive birth time from life events. The basic premise of all movement is to know:

1. What is moving to activate the natal chart?
2. How fast is it moving?
3. In what direction is it moving?
4. How long will it activate one-degree of the natal chart to activate a Light, Angle, planet or point?

A properly timed birth chart has planetary descriptors appropriately activated at the time

---

1. Brady, Bernadette, Predictive Astrology, The Eagle and the Lark; Weiser Inc., York Beach, Maine, 1992, pg. 83.

of a corresponding life event or situation, and it is often the case that the chart angles (ascendant, descendant, midheaven and imum coeli) are involved in the activated pattern. However, it is not unusual for the astrologer to encounter a client for whom the astrological symbolism does not appropriately align with life situations or events. Sometimes the astrologer may notice a consistently early or late activation of the natal chart patterns and may adjust the birth time by minutes to align events with appropriate astrological descriptors to improve interpretation and forecasting accuracy. That is the basis of chart rectification, pejoratively known in learned circles as, "Wrecktification." Nonetheless, it is important for astrologers to verify all client birth times by testing the alignment of astrological descriptors with three or four important life events provided by the client.

Further evidence for the disregard for the rectification process is that few astrologers in any tradition agree on a set of movement methods to confirm or rectify birth time. The compari-

A COMPARISON OF THE RECTIFICATION METHODS OF 10 MODERN AUTHORS

	Brady	Discepolo	Dobyns	Ely	Gillman	Meadows	Scofield	Tebbs	Tyl	Willner
1. Mars-Pluto Transits to Angles at Events	X									
2. Mars Transits to Houses to Test Planets in Houses	If dates are specific	X								Placidus houses
3. Jupiter-Pluto Transits to Angles at Events	X		X				X	X	X	
4. Eclipses or Lunations To Angles at Events							X Both	X Eclipses		
5. Questions Client - Birth Time Source and Situation		X						X	X	
6. Cayce Spiritual Birth times										X
7. Assess Planet Aspects in Known Time Range			X				X	X		
8. Start with Noon Chart in Unknown Birth Times			X			X		X	X	
9. Solar Returns – Natal and Relocated		X		Older systems weak			X			
10. Mars Transits to Relocated Solar Returns		X								
11. Experiment with Sun Sign Rulers in Time Range										
12. Astro*Carto*Graphy if events at various locations						X				
13. Decan and Septenary Time Lords - Clockwise				Needs more research	X Diurnal		X			
14. Inner Transits if Event Dates and Times Known							X	X		
15. Solar Arc Directions (or Naibod Average Arc)	X Solar Arc	X Solar Arc					X Solar Arc	X Solar Arc	X Solar Arc	X Naibod
16. Longitude/ Declination Secondary Progressions								X		X
17. Secondary Moon Progression			X					X	X	X
18. M.E. Jones Chart Patterns							X			
19. Midpoints of Known Natal Planets and Points							X			
20. Uranian Hypothetical Planets							X			

son chart below provides an overview of the diverse birth time rectification methods.

Clients may present rounded-off birthtimes, or only generally know their birthtime, or not know it at all. For any of these instances, the process of birthtime rectification becomes exceedingly complex. However, with the Internet, Zoom and Face Book, we are now a world community where rectification is even more in demand. Indeed, the rectification process within any time range provides a valuable confirmation of the birth chart for the new as well as the continuing client.

The fact that a birth time is rounded to the quarter-hour, or not known at all, poses a challenging range of problems for the astrologer. The degree of difficulty in deriving an accurate birth time, assuming that the date of birth and the geographical location are known, depends upon whether the client is able to narrow the birth time range from family memory and records with a specific hour and minutes. Working from the astrological premise that the activated birth chart should symbolically reflect actual life events, the astrologer can find a consistent pattern and derive the birth time. As defined by Nicholas Devore in The Encyclopedia of Astrology, rectification is, "The process of verification or correction of the birth moment or ascendant degree of the map, by reference to known events or characteristics pertaining to the native."[2] Therefore, the most reliable way to approach the complex puzzle is to first determine what is not going to move more than one-degree within the search time range. The answer is the ANGLES that move one-degree every four-minutes of clock time, and if the search range is more than two-hours, the MOON that moves about one-degree every two hours of clock time.

A properly timed birth chart should astrologically correspond with actual life events; however, it is not unusual to encounter a client for whom the astrological symbolism does not appropriately align with events. Sometimes the astrologer may see a consistently early or late activation of the natal chart planets or configurations and adjust the chart by a degree or two (4 to 8 minutes of clock time) to align events with appropriate astrological descriptors. Other times, clients may present birthtimes that are too general to test with events. For any of these instances, the process of birthtime rectification is useful for the astrologer's accuracy in continued forecasting for the client. Indeed, the process provides a valuable confirmation of birth data for the continuing client.

Getting the birth data from the client is only the beginning of the rectification task. Finding local time variances around the world can make a huge difference. For instance, we cannot assume that everyone in a country goes on Daylight Savings Time – they don't! Again, the Internet comes in handy to find that information for every country, every state and every region for the past century. The most common variances in birthtime come from earlier eras, where time is recorded only to a close approximation of time, but not exact. In United States births prior to the mid-twentieth century, the birthtime may have been rounded-off to sunrise, sunset, midnight or noon, a 6-hour span, or to the nearest hour, half-hour or quarter-hour. Fortunately, most hospitals in the United States have recorded exact birth times from the 1950's onward, that is, assuming that the clock in the hospital was correct. However, many countries, such as Japan, do not record birth time at all. So, even though most clients will have accurate or near accurate birth times, every astrologer should know rectification techniques to serve the clients who do not provide a birth certificate or verified birth time that is Rodden-rated

---

2. Devore, Nicholas, Encyclopedia of Astrology, Philosophical Library, New York, NY, 1947, p 329.

as "AA" data.

An explanation of the Rodden-rating system is in order, which provides the astrologer specific guidelines for evaluating the quality, or reliability, of birth data whether for consulting with clients or for research. The point is, accuracy of birth time to the minute provides more accurate forecasting and research results, and every astrologer should aspire to work with only "AA" quality data that is supported by an official birth record. Other less reliable data categories in the Rodden Rating system are described in greater detail on the www.astro.com website.

AA	Accurate data as recorded by the family or state
A	Accurate data as quoted by the person, kin, friend, or associate
B	Biography or autobiography
C	Caution: no source, or original source not known
DD	Dirty Data - two or more conflicting quotes that are unqualified
X	Data with no time of birth
XX	Data without a known or confirmed date

Table 1 The Rodden Rating system

"The AA, A and B data are fairly stable, but C and D data tend to change when Astro.com data is upgraded. Since data is always volatile, no rating system is infallible, and data is often updated when new information comes to light".[3]

Additionally, Ms. Rodden provides comment on some of the common problems with rectified charts for interpretation and feels most certainly that rectified charts are inappropriate for research, an opinion with which I heartily agree:

"All rectified data are also rated "C". Some astrologers consider rectified times more accurate than birth times. Unfortunately, there is no consensus on how to rectify birth times. Thus, one astrologer's ultra-accurate rectified time may contradict another astrologer's ultra-accurate rectified time. Until there is a standard and proven rectification method, you should treat all rectified data with caution."[4]

Lois Rodden's work in setting standards for chart data that astrologers now publish in articles, books, and other media, has transformed the astrology community around the world. Now a standard, all astrologers provide chart data resources and the Rodden Rating for all birth charts presented for publication.

---

3. Rodden, Lois, Rodden Rating system, www.astrodatabank.com, December 2007
4. IBID

1
Why Does Birth Time Matter?

Know How Birth Time is Determined

Before charging into a discussion of technique, awareness of the importance of birth time and its many variables is important. It is the combination of birth time, geographical location and birth date that determines the angles and house cusps of the natal chart, as well as positions of the planets within the chart. The key to verifying the birth time is in determining the most "time sensitive" chart factors, the Angles that move one-degree every four-minutes of clock time and, to a lesser extent, the Moon that averages one-degree every two-hours. House cusps, though fast moving like the Angles, are rarely useful in rectification work. More than a dozen house systems and methods for their calculation are in use, which creates many variations of the beginning degree, and sometimes sign, of each house. Therefore, house cusps are unreliable indicators of birthtime. However, the Angles (Ascendant, Descendant, Midheaven and Imum Coeli) are the same in most all house systems, and they are the key to unlock the precise birthtime for reliable delineation and forecasting for the client.

Understand Movement of the Chart Components

It is important to thoroughly understand the actual movement during the course of a day for each chart component: the planets, angles, and lunar nodes. Knowing their actual motion within the birth date and search time range, makes clear where to start – the Angles.

The Lights and Nodes

The Moon moves, on average, thirteen degrees eleven minutes (13:11) a day, or about 1-degree every two hours. So, the Moon is only useful for narrowing the time range beyond two hours. However, the elliptical orbit of the Moon and its five-degree axis tilt gives a movement variation from eleven to over fifteen degrees a day during certain times of the year. In most cases, clients give the astrologer a birth time that is reasonably accurate – within a few minutes either way. In that case, the Moon will not move enough to confirm the birthtime. The Moon's daily average is 13-degrees 11-minutes, but in its apogee the Moon moves faster up to 15- degrees a day, while at its Perigee moves slower to 11-degrees a day.

The Moon is important for interpretation, but only the accurate birth time determines the chart Angles based on the birth latitude. Since the average daily rotation of the Earth is 361-degrees a day, every sign rises daily, or about 4-minutes of clock time for each degree.

The Lunar Nodes on average move 3-minutes a day clockwise in a 18.6-year cycle to span 360-degrees. The Lunar Nodes are an important chart feature for interpretation, but they do not move fast enough to confirm or derive birth time.

The Sun moves, on average, one-degree a day. However, the Sun moves fifty-seven minutes (:57) a day in the northern and southern hemisphere winters, and over one-degree (1:02) during the summers of each hemisphere. The Sun's movement variation is created by the tilt of the Earth's axis by over twenty-three degrees (23.27), and that same axis tilt is what creates our planet's seasons. In terms of verifying the natal chart's alignment of life experience with appropriate astrological descriptors into a consistent pattern to establish birthtime, the one-degree movement of the Sun in a day is not enough to confirm birthtime.

The Inner Planets

Mercury moves about one degree a day like the Sun, however, because we view its motion from our position on Earth, three times a year is appears to move backwards in the sky, or retrograde. Mercury sometimes moves very slowly, or even appears to stop in place, or moves extremely fast up to two degrees a day. The important thing to know is that variation of movement is over the course of the year. During the course of one day, Mercury does not move enough to verify birth time.

Venus, like Mercury, moves about one degree a day like the Sun, and it also has a period during the year when it appears to stand still and go retrograde. The range of Venus's movement during the year varies from zero-degrees a day to one and a half-degrees (0-1 ½) per day.

Mars moves about forty-five minutes (:45) a day and, like Mercury and Venus, during its two-year cycle it appears to stand still and go retrograde for all the same reasons: its elliptical orbit that brings it closer and then farther from Earth in its apparent motion of direct- stationary- retrograde- stationary- then direct again from our Earth vantage point. The movement range of Mars is from 0-degrees a day to 1 ¼-degrees a day. None of the inner planets can verify birth time.

The Outer Planets

Jupiter moves through one sign each year averaging about a half a degree per day, though like the inner planets, it goes through a retrograde period every three years. Therefore, Jupiter's motion on any given day can be from zero to half a degree (0- ½), not useful to verify birth time.

Saturn moves through a little less than a half a sign per year with the same conditions of retrograde and elliptical orbit that gives wide movement variation within the planet's cycle. However, Saturn's whole cycle is twenty-nine and a half years, so its movement for one day could vary from zero to fifteen minutes (0- ¼ degrees) a day – again, not useful to verify birth time.

Uranus, Neptune, and Pluto all move very slowly over the course of one year and their movement is barely noticeable in one day. They also go through a retrograde cycle of varying lengths that retraces every single degree as they move forward in a zig-zag pattern of varying lengths. The complete cycle of Uranus is eighty-four years, or about four and a half degrees per year. The complete cycle of Neptune is 165 years, or about two degree per year and the complete cycle of Pluto is 248 years, or about one to two degrees per year – again not useful to verify birth time.

Outer Planet	Transit Average	3 Hits in Shadow Area	Retrograde Only
Years in Sign	Travel in 1 Year	Full Retrograde Cycle	Retrograde Period
1 Jupiter:	1 sign	9 ½ months	4 months
2 ½ Saturn:	2 ½ signs	11 months	4 ½ months
4+ Chiron:	7.2 degrees	11 ½ months	5 months
7 Uranus:	+8 / - 4.3 degrees	1 year	5 months
14 Neptune:	+4 / -2.2 degrees	1 ¼-1 ¾ years	6 ½ months
20 Pluto:	+ 3 / -1.5 degrees	1 ½-2 years	6 months

Table 2 Average Planetary Movement and Duration of Activation of One-Degree

The major point is that all of the planets give excellent interpretive information once we have the birthtime, which defines the angles and houses where the planets reside.

Understand the Complexity of the Rectification Task

To give some understanding of the complexity of finding an unknown, or a known but general birth time, the search for position of the Angles (Ascendant, Descendant, Midheaven and Imum Coeli) of a quarter-day can span up to 90 degrees; of a half-day up to 180 degrees; and of a full day 360 degrees. To confirm the average amount of clock time it takes for an Angle to move 1-degree, divide 360 degrees by 24 hours. First, one must convert the 24 hours to minutes. Since an hour is 60 minutes, multiply 24 hours by 60 minutes to arrive at 1440 minutes of clock time in a day. Then divide the 1440 minutes by the 360 degrees in the wheel to arrive at the desired result: 4-minutes of clock time equals 1-degree of movement in the 360-degree chart wheel. Therefore, rectification on such wide time ranges as 24-hours is quite difficult. Table 2 of time comparisons may be helpful to keep in mind.

Table 3 Clock Time to Average Calendar Time Comparisons

Birth Chart Degrees	to	Clock Time	Calendar Time	to	Clock Time
360 degrees	=	24 hours	1 year (12 months)	=	1 day (24 hours)
180 degrees	=	12 hours	1 month (30 days)	=	2 hours (120 minutes)
150 degrees	=	10 hours	½ a month (15 days)	=	1 hour (60 minutes)
135 degrees	=	9 hours	1 day	=	4 minutes
120 degrees	=	8 hours		=	
90 degrees	=	6 hours		=	
60 degrees	=			=	
45 degrees	=			=	
30 degrees	=			=	
15 degrees	=			=	
1 degree	=			=	
½ degree or 30 minutes	=			=	
¼ degree or 15 minutes	=			=	

Rectification is much easier with birth times narrowed to a half-hour or less making the search range for the Angles no more than 8 degrees. Remember that the Angles are consistent in most systems of chart calculation, which makes them the best candidates to search and match with events. The Solar Arc Method of movement is a preferred start because of its regularity and no planets ever retrograde.

Another issue to be aware of that our computer software easily provides the ascension time of the signs at different latitudes. For instance, at 45-degrees North Latitude Pisces and Aries rise very fast in just over an hour, whereas Virgo and Libra at the same latitude rise very slowly in nearly three hours. The reverse is true at 45-degrees South Latitude where Virgo and Libra rise fast in just over an hour and at the same South Latitude, Pisces and Aries rise very slowly in nearly three hours.

Figure 2 Table of Ascensional Arcs At Different Latitudes

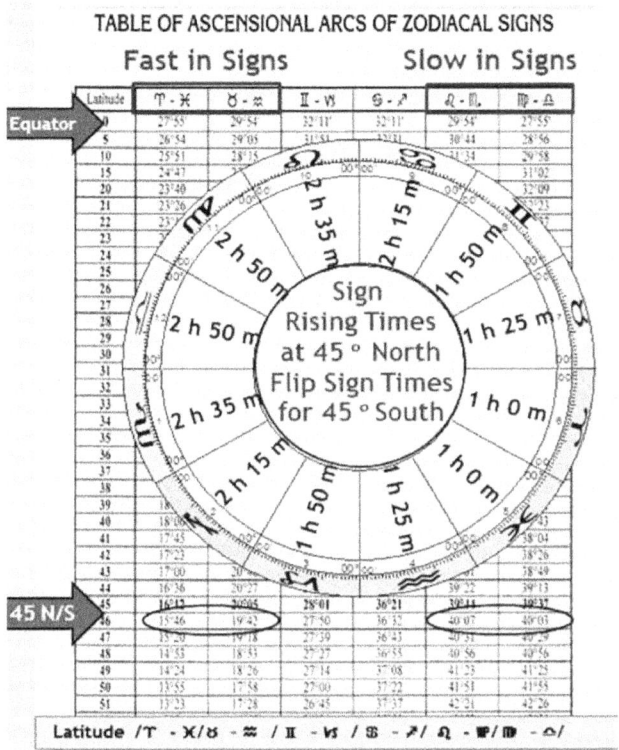

Because the Earth's axis is tilted relative to the ecliptic, the twelve signs do not take the same amount of time to cross the eastern horizon. Therefore, fewer people in the Northern hemisphere have Aries or Pisces rising and very many people have Virgo or Libra rising. The reverse is true in the Southern hemisphere.

Narrow birth time parameters are unquestionably easier for the astrologer to "rectify" or "align" known dates of life events with appropriate astrological indicators. The astrologer aims for consistency of a match-up between the two. Noted astrologer and researcher, Dr. Zip Dobyns, describes the process thus, "Rather than using the character of the natal chart to deduce the destiny which will follow, it is possible [through rectification] to deduce the natal chart from the destiny."[5] Nonetheless, it is in the best interests of all to first exhaust every resource to find some documentation of the birth time to narrow the search to as small a range as possible. British astrologer R.C. Davison concludes that:

---

5. Dobyns, Zipporah, Progressions, Directions and Rectification, T.I.A. Publications, a division of CCRS Inc., Los Angeles, California, 1975, p 7.

"The prime importance of the angles of the birth chart has been repeatedly stressed. It is absolutely necessary that the birth chart should be as accurate in this respect as the most careful rectification can make it. It is useless to expect satisfactory results from Secondary Directions [Progressions] unless the angles of the horoscope under consideration have been carefully checked with reference to past events. Even a "stop-watch timed" birth must not be regarded as above suspicion until two or three major events in the life have occurred either to corroborate or to confound the prevailing angular directions." [6]

Birth Time Rectification Has Historical Roots

The first reference to birth time rectification is found in Claudius Ptolemy's, The Tetrabiblios, Book 3, in the first century of the Common Era. Ptolemy sets out a complicated formula for rectifying the Ascendant to the sign and degree of a planetary ruler; if the native's character doesn't match the influence, then the same strategy was applied to the MC to find a match. Ptolemy's method prevailed into the early 1700's until timepieces became more accurate and available.

In the first century CE Dorotheus of Sidon used the Greek "terms" and "Dodecatamoria", similar to the Arabic "Dwadashamsas" (Dwads), to rectify birth time within two and a half degrees or ten-minutes of clock time to get more specificity from the thirty-degree signs that describe two-hours of clock time.

Since the seventeenth century Johannes Kepler considered the number of days after birth that the Sun took to reach a natal planet was equal to the number of years of life before the influence would manifest, still true in Secondary Progression and Solar Arc Direction movement of the Sun.

Transits of Jupiter and Saturn were commonly used for timing but the nineteenth and twentieth centuries brought the discovery of Uranus, Neptune and Pluto, dwarf bodies, thousands of asteroids and new interpretive techniques that complicated old traditions. Then and today, doctors and nurses focus on care of mother and baby, NOT on recording accurate birth time.

Know the Pitfalls of Recorded Birth Time Accuracy

The most common variances in the birth time come from earlier eras, or states and countries, where time is recorded only to a close approximation of time, but not exact. In births prior to the mid-twentieth century, the birth time may have been rounded-off to sunrise, sunset, midnight, or noon, a 6-hour span; or to the nearest hour, half-hour, or quarter-hour. For-

---

6. Davison, R. C., The Technique of Prediction, published by L. N. Fowler & Co. Ltd. 1201/3 High Road, Chadwell Heath, Romford Essex RM6 4DH, 1979, p 137. [Directions does not refer to Solar Arc, but Secondary Progressions]

tunately, most hospitals in the United States have recorded exact birth times from the 1950's onward, that is, assuming that the clock in the hospital was correct. However, many countries of the world, such as Japan, do not record birth time at all, and others may record birth dates from the Lunar calendar. Even though most clients will have an accurate or near accurate birth time on a birth certificate, every astrologer should know rectification technique to verify or rectify birth time to serve the clients who do not provide verified evidence of birth time that fits the Rodden-rating of "AA" data.

Attempting to verify birth time for public figures can often be a "fool's errand" because events rarely have specific dates and the biography focuses on the years of their fame, often omitting the struggling years to make their career mark. Verifying or rectifying birth time for friends, family or clients, the real people who can provide feedback are the best candidates for this task. In a birth time search of several hours, often two or three times look promising. At that point, it is helpful for the astrologer to ask the client which Ascendant sign, and possibly the degree, feels most descriptive of their personality. Most people have a good feel for how others see them and can reject the signs that don't fit and affirm the Ascending sign that does.

Daylight Savings time has been a problem worldwide, since the standards are very uneven because every country, and in the US, every state sets its own rules – and some choose not to observe Daylight Time at all. The confusion surrounding Daylight Saving Time impacts international as well as interstate travel and commerce. Fortunately, our digital devices now automatically adjust to the correct time wherever we are in the world from the "Universal Atomic Clock" in Colorado, USA.

Time Change Variance:

❖ The Worst Offender Is Illinois, "State law required all birth times to be recorded in CST until July 1, 1959, except during WWII when CWT was recorded officially. But this law was not always observed, leading to considerable confusion about actual time of birth for summer births… Small towns are assumed to follow nearby larger towns, which may not always be correct." Tom Shanks, The American Atlas

❖ Indiana gets second place with 345-time variations: According to Tom Shanks, The American Atlas,[7] "This state has a very complex time zone picture and not all of the time shifts are documented. Even newspaper reports present contradictory information…As a general rule the CST portions of Indiana observe daylight time in the summer, while the EST portions do not observe daylight time. The exceptions are 1969 and 1970 when the entire state observed daylight time…"

---

7. Shanks, Tom quote from The American Atlas by Neil Michelsen, 1990?

Robin Williams – Daylight Savings Time vs Standard Time

Solar Fire gives Milwaukee, WI as Robin's birthplace, but www.astro.com gives Chicago, IL

Both locations are in the same time zone, so should be virtually the same. HOWEVER, Illinois recorded birth times in Standard time even though Daylight time was in effect. Are we sure that the nurse remembered to follow the odd distortion of recording birth time? So which is the correct birth time for Robin Williams, 1:34 PM CDT or 1:34 PM CST?

Cate Blanchett – Accurate Data for Public Figures vs Real People

"Sy Scholfield quotes her birth notice and two statements from her to speculate an approximate time of birth. The birth notice gives the date and place…without birth time. Blanchett has stated, 'I like the heroines. I'm a bull. I'm a Taurus. She has also reportedly stated, 'Apparently, I'm Taurus Moon, Taurus Sun and Taurus Rising. That's pretty Taurus, eh? Which explains a lot, doesn't it?" (2/20/2014)

It is not possible for Cate to have Taurus rising and a Taurus Moon.

"The birth announcement appeared the day after her birth which usually indicates a time of birth early in the day. The moon did not move into Taurus until about 5:30 pm and it is unlikely that her birth would have been phoned through to the newspaper that late in the day. A speculative time of 6:40 a.m. puts mid Taurus (15 degrees) on the Ascendant which seems the best approximation considering the info given. Scholfield emailed a family member on 7, April 2001 requesting her time of birth but did not receive a reply. Previously: LMR quotes Biography magazine 6/2001 for date; time unknown."

Sean Connery – Accurate Data for Public Figures vs Real People

Though many students work with public charts that are readily available on the Internet, they are missing a most important component to rectify birth time, which is personal interaction with a friend or family member who clarifies the event or situation and how they felt about it. Another drawback of public charts is that their biographies often focus only on the period of their fame or notoriety, rather than their full span of life. The rectification process needs such detail. Further, many biographies that do cover the full life are vague about the events, noting only the year. Astrologers need specific dates of events for the life span to rectify the birth time. The more vague the biography, the more difficult the birth time search.

"Sean Connery was awarded the Academy Award in 1987 for "Best Supporting Actor" in the film, "The Untouchables." Connery's over 50-film career has not slowed. Known on movie sets as a hard-working actor, he demands and expects professionalism from every actor, director, and crew member.

He lived in an Edinburgh tenement flat as a child where the lower dresser drawer served as his crib when he was a baby. At nine, he helped supplement his van driver father's income by delivering milk. Once he left school he tried his luck at brick laying, coal mining, usher at the cinemas and posing nude as a model at the Edinburgh Art School. He joined the Royal Navy but was discharged for stomach ulcers. He began to sculpt his imposing lean 6'2 body to compete for the Mr. Universe title representing Scotland. In 1951, he auditioned for a part in the male chorus in the London West End version of South Pacific. At the age of 20, he began his acting training. He went to the public library and taught himself the classics with the encouragement of a theater manager-actor friend. His first staring film role was in "Requiem for a Heavyweight" in 1957.

Connery garnered bit parts until 1962 when he was chosen to play super-agent 007 in the "James Bond" series. The movies triggered an immediate notoriety, fame, and high acclaim. Unhappy with the Bond franchise, he tried other roles but found his career limited by his Bond Adonis image. He continued to work in films but ran into little success in the late '70s and early '80s. After appearing in one more Bond film, "Never Say Never" in 1982, his career turned around. He won a British Best Actor Academy Award for his role in "The Name of the Rose" in 1986. He was honored by the American Academy when he won "Best Supporting Actor" Oscar for his role as an Irish beat cop in Brian DePalma's 1987 film, "The Untouchables." As a mature actor, he continued to work, often in roles where he was cast as a seasoned mentor teamed with another noted actor. In 1969, he attempted directing but the film was never released.

In November 1962, Connery married actress Diane Cilento and they had a son Jason, born 1/11/1963. While married to Cilento, Connery met Micheline Roquebrune at a golf tournament in Morocco in 1970, a painter and a fierce golf competitor with a young son. He divorced in 1973 and married Micheline in March 1975. He prefered an unpretentious lifestyle without the trappings of celebrity status symbols and did not employ an agent. He made his own travel arrangements and when in London, he preferred to walk to his appointments by himself. When he drove, he preferred his fuel-efficient Toyota Land Cruiser to his Mercedes.

In a 1965 Playboy interview he quipped that slapping a woman was justified if she was a bitch. His reputation as a male chauvinist haunted him as he rallied against the female encroachment into traditional all-male enclaves like clubs and bars. Women, however, were always a part of his life, as evidenced by the loss of his virginity at age 14 to an older woman, who seduced him. Connery had no qualms about taking movie productions to litigation if he felt his financial earnings were hidden under clever accounting skills. As a philanthropist and co-founder, he donated millions to the Scottish International Education Trust since 1970. He lent his rich voice to Scottish politics by doing voice-over advertisements for the Scottish Nationalist party for an independent Scotland."

Connery's biography, posted with his chart in Astro.com, contains only one specific event date given out of eighteen event references for some seventy years of life. Even if we wanted to rectify his birth time, there is not enough biographical information tied to specific dates to go forward. On the other hand, adjusting birth time to consistently align appropriate astrological descriptors with life events brings a willing partner to clarify situations and how intensely they felt about each event. Interaction with the client saves much time and adds client confidence in the rectified birth time to get reliable interpretation of current situations.

2

How Do I Verify a Given Birth Time?

At a pivotal time in life, I was confused and searching for a new direction. My good friend and neighbor had been attending astrology classes in Los Angeles and urged me to see an astrologer for a reading of my chart and a forecast of the current situation and possible outcome. Strongly identified as an academic at the time, I was very dismissive about astrology to say the least. After a while, my curiosity got the upper hand, and I contacted the American Federation of Astrologers for an astrologer reference in my area. When I made the appointment the astrologer, Elaine, asked for my birth data: Carol Tebbs born September 9, 1939, in Columbus, Ohio 39N38, 83W01 at 8:18 am EST, and if the source was a birth certificate – that's all!

A Quick Test to Verify Birth Time

When I arrived for the consultation, Elaine simply asked me three questions before reading my chart. First, she asked, "When you were seven did you receive close care from your mother for an illness or a situation where you needed her comfort? I answered, "Yes, I had my tonsils out." (Figure 3) She continued asking, "When you were twelve, was there a separation from your father related to some problematic family issue?" In amazement, I answered, "Yes! Dad had gotten into some minor trouble with the law, then went to California to get a job and later bring the family there." (Figure 4) She finally asked, "Was age seventeen a very difficult time for you when a relationship brought hardship and grown-up reality? I gasped, stunned, and just nodded to indicate yes! I had been an unmarried pregnant teenager whose premature child died after five months. (Figure 5) Elaine had my full attention! She had never met me before and all she had was my birth data. I was hooked! I wanted to know how she looked into my past so accurately with so little information, which has turned into a fifty-year journey of astrological exploration.

After dipping into studying astrology the first few years after the 1971 consultation, I learned that birth time is the key component to determine the chart Angles. Finally, I understood the simplicity of my astrologer's technique to test my birth time accuracy before

Figure 3 Tebbs Event: Tonsils Out

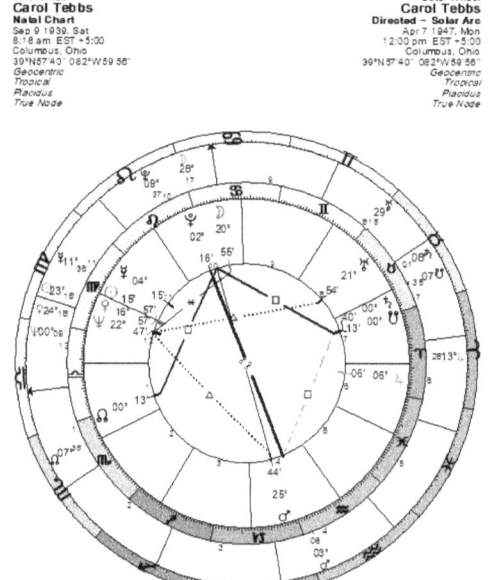

Figure 4 Tebbs Event: Dad Trouble, Move to CA

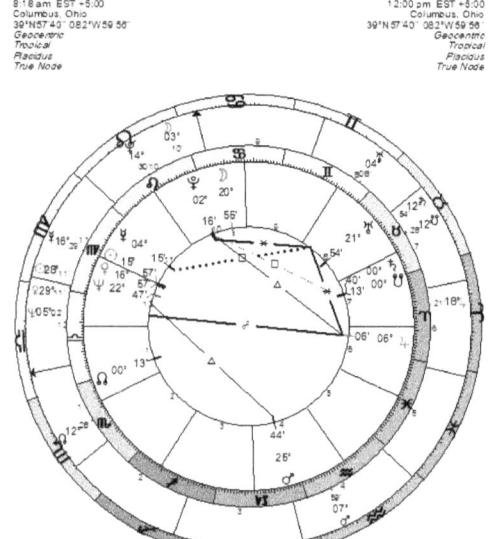

Figure 5 Tebbs Event: Severe Depression, Child Died

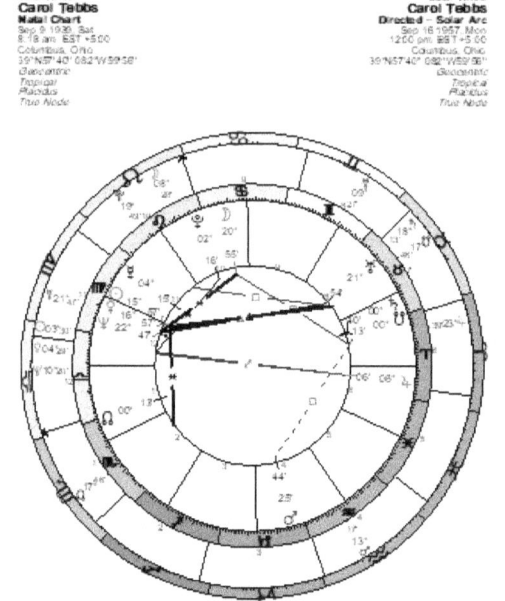

Event 1: April 7, 1947, Directed to Natal Chart Tonsils removed, surgery, mother's care

Event 2: April 10, 1952, Directed to Natal Chart Father left family to find a new job and home for us

Event 3: Sept 16, 1957, Directed to Natal Chart Severe depression after sudden death of child continuing with delineation of the current chart activation. Elaine simply tested my birth time by moving the chart Midheaven by Solar Arc Direction one-degree per year to align in appropriate aspect to natal planets: At seven, my 13 Cancer Midheaven arced to conjunct the 20 Cancer Moon in the tenth house; at twelve my Midheaven arced to oppose 25 Capricorn Mars in the fourth house; and at seventeen the Midheaven arced to 0-Leo square Saturn and South Node in the seventh house. She didn't even need the list of important life events that I had carefully prepared – she already knew that my birth time worked.

Remember that verifying the birth time is most reliable by moving the Midheaven/Imum Coeli axis rather than the Ascendant/Descendant axis. The MC/IC axis is calculated at the regular movement of the Sun and the ASC/DES axis is dependent on the birth location latitude which varies incrementally as the birth location is farther away from the Equator, so it is a less reliable source to quickly estimate movement.

A More Substantial Test of the Birth Time: "Event Hooks"

Most astrologers use three to four movement methods to confirm a birth time. My birth data is September 9, 1939 in Columbus, Ohio, 39°N38', 83W01 at 8:18 am EST. The following list of life event dates provide the "Event Hooks" to align with appropriate astrological indicators. Event times are not essential, since they only become useful for determining the birth time once narrowed to within a minute or two.

Table 4 Notable Life Events for Carol Tebbs (Important events are in bold type)

	Event	Place	Age	Date	Time
1	Many moves during WWII	OH/CA	3-5	1943-5	
2	**Tonsils removed**	Columbus, OH	7	4-1947	
3	Finalist in Ohio State Spelling Bee	Columbus, OH	11	4-1951	
4	**Father trouble/Sudden move**	Columbus, OH	12	7-1952	
5	Valedictorian at jr. high graduation	Whittier, CA	13	6-1953	
6	**Break-up with first boyfriend**	Whittier, CA	14	2-1954	
7	**Premature birth of first child**	Whittier, CA	17	2-21-1957	12:01 AM
8	**Marriage**	Whittier, CA	17	3-31-1957	2:00 AM
9	**Death of first child**	Whittier, CA	18-	7-25-1957	1:00 AM
10	Birth of second child	Whittier, CA	18	5-4-1958	6:03 AM
11	Birth of third child	Whittier, CA	19	4-10-1959	6:29 AM
12	Returned to college full-time	Whittier, CA	19	7-1-1959	
13	College graduation	Whittier, CA	23	6-1-1963	2:00 PM

Table 4 Cont'd: Notable Life Events for Carol Tebbs (Important events are in bold type)

	Event	Place	Age	Date	Time
14	Began career as art teacher	Whittier, CA	23	9-1-1963	
15	**Marriage difficulty**	Whittier, CA	25	9-25-1965	
16	Moved to new house	Whittier, CA	25	9-6-1966	
17	**Left family suddenly**	Whittier, CA	31	4-16-1971	
18	Graduated with MA degree	Whittier, CA	32	6-1-1972	
19	**Reunited with family**	Whittier, CA	32	8-25-1972	
20	Both children moved out on own	Whittier, CA	37	8-1977	
21	Death of grandmother	Columbus, OH	43	1-29-1983	
22	**Job Change**	Whittier, CA	44	8-25-1984	
23	**Estrangement from godson**	Whittier, CA	49	3-3-1989	
24	**Father trouble revealed in family**	Whittier, CA	52	10-1991	
25	Conference Coordinator	Whittier, CA	54	12-5-1993	
26	Suddenly bought 2nd home	La Quinta, CA	54	3-31-1994	
27	Elected Head of Organization	Whittier, CA	56	5-1996	
28	**Sold 2 homes/moved new home**	La Quinta, CA	58	5-15-1998	
29	Honored "Teacher of the Year"	Whittier, CA	59	4-1999	
30	Retirement from teaching	Whittier, CA	59	6-21-2000	
31	**Aunt murdered**	Columbus, OH	61	2-16-2001	
32	**Kepler College President**	Whittier, CA	63	7-12-2003	
33	Death of father	Whittier, CA	67-	7-7-2006	9:00 AM
34	Bought vacation home	Cleora, OK		5-12-2012	
35	**Death of mother**	Whittier, CA	73	10-13-2012	
36	Built new house / moved in	Disney, OK	78	2-13-2017	
37	**Death of husband**	Disney, OK	78	6-19-2017	12:31 PM

A Method to Proceed with the Test: "Aspect Hooks"

1. Lock onto a planetary pair or network of planets in one-degree aspect orb as "Aspect Hooks". If there are no one-degree aspects, consider those within a two-degree orb. Of course, the closer the orb of aspect to exact, the more important the contact and easier to search. Consider all planets, the Sun through Pluto and the Moon's Nodes, to begin the search for the synchronicity of dramatic life events appropriate to the astrological symbolism. Remember, one or more of the Angles is almost always involved at major

life events – either moving into aspect with a planet or its close planetary network; or a planet and its close planetary network moving into aspect with the Angle. Simply put, test planet to angle and angle to planet. It is tempting to include planet to planet aspects at the event, but regardless of birth time, those aspects are true all day long – they do not give information relevant to birth time. Only the Angles can confirm birth time.

2. Scan the client's list of life events and note the handful of most important events as "Event Hooks", that span the life. It is especially helpful to get client input in deciding the most important events and their emotional impact they had on their life. For instance, I did not rate my retirement from teaching public high school students as a major life event, because I had already transitioned to teaching adults online in the Kepler College Bachelor of Arts program. The client is the best judge of the impact of major events, that the astrologer may assume incorrectly.

3. Be aware of important events occurring in close time proximity. They may be either the easiest or the most difficult to sort out. Why such equivocation? In closely aspected networks involving two or more planets, the difficulty may come in sorting out which planetary influences describe which events; or whether they all worked together to describe facets of one event that unfolded within a close range of time. If the client has many major events occurring in close time proximity, the astrologer may assume that a close natal network of planets, and possibly Angles, were triggered by the slow-moving factors of Directions, Secondary Progressions and/or Outer Planet Transits. It is possible, however, that several planets or Angles might be independently activated at the same time. In either situation, the "stacking up" of several chart factors activated simultaneously symbolically accounts for the heightened importance of the dramatic life events.

4. Experimenting with moving the Angles to a planet or connected planets symbolic of the event is a good place to begin the search. And if two planets, or more, form a close one-degree major aspect network in the birth chart, the astrologer finds a much easier task of finding when the network was activated and aligning the activated planet(s) to actual life events. For example, a planet at 6 Aries in natal square aspect to another at 6 Cancer may be directed by Solar Arc to a third planet or Angle at 15 Libra at age 9 (6 + 9 = 15) to form a T-square. Three points activated suggests a more prominent event than two, and so on with more planets or points in the pattern. The more points simultaneously involved at the time of activation, the more prominent the event or action. By the same token, the 6 Aries and 6 Cancer planetary pair are an "Aspect Hook" that travels together in Solar Arc Direction to other planets that may have their own cluster, such as a close degree stellium which would ignite the energy of the whole group. Any planets in natal close 1-degree aspect is forever activated as a pair.

Though planets networked in close aspect are often associated with multiple events in close succession, many of the astrology software programs that contain a research function actually eliminate dates in close time proximity as invalid for the search. This computer search "breakdown" is precisely where the trained astrologer may harvest a wealth of information through study of the natal chart's close aspect patterns to develop a "Case Theory". Study the Tebbs chart in Figure 6, for close natal one-degree aspects. Close hard aspects between planets or nodes (conjunction, opposition, square and possibly quincunx) suggest painful events when activated. However, it is also true that hard aspects do motivate people to address a difficult situation in their lives by doing something about it that may ultimately lead to some degree of contentment and success.

Figure 6 Natal Chart for Carol Tebbs RR-AA

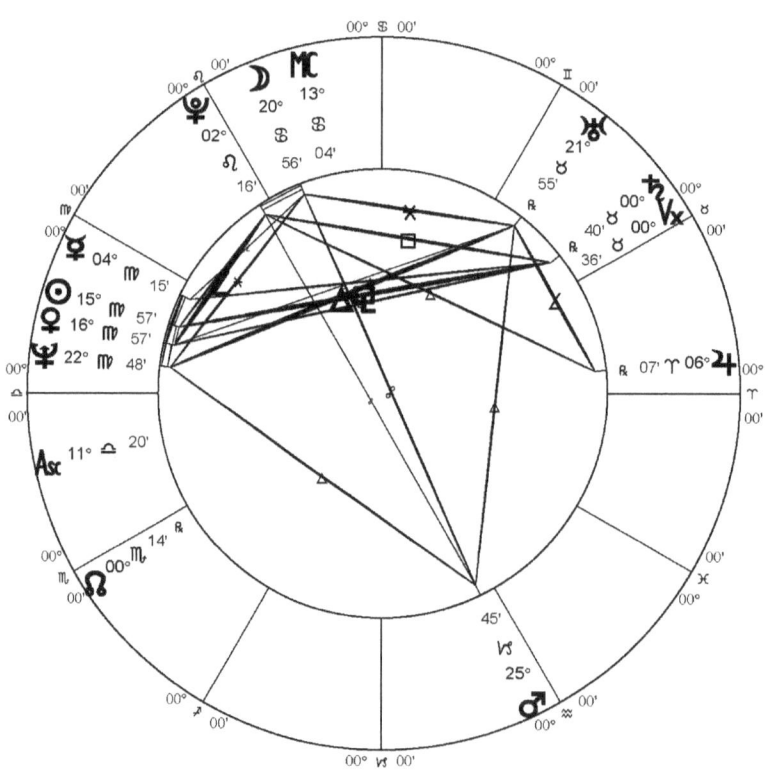

Carol Tebbs natal: September 9, 1939 8:18 AM (Standard time) Columbus, OH 39N57'40" 82W59'56" 5 Hours west; Geocentric, Tropical Whole Sign

Examine the Significant Natal Close Aspect Networks

There are three prominent major natal aspect networks within one-degree orb:

1. A 21 – 26 degrees of an earth/water Kite pattern with the Moon at the apex, Mars at the tail, and Uranus and Neptune forming the arms sextile to the Moon and trine Mars, but the orb range of the Moon/Mars opposition is a bit wide for rectification;

2. A 21 – 26 degrees Cancer/Capricorn cardinal T-square of Moon/ Mars to the one-degree Taurus Saturn/South Node that spans 10 degrees in all, way too wide an orb for rectification; and

3. A tight one-degree close orb network of the lunar nodes and five planets, including a light. Astrologically, we have "struck gold" for birth time verification. The close Sun/Venus conjunction in Virgo is semi-square to Pluto in Leo and sesqui-square the Saturn/South Node closely conjunct in Taurus.

4. Of course, in this last configuration, Pluto is also in one-degree orb of square to the Saturn/South Node conjunction. Bingo! This close 1-degree hard aspect network should provide an easy "hook" for a rectification search, even if the birth time is unknown. One can safely assume that this network is the key to the most dramatic life events.

It is true that when one leg of the important 6-point configuration is triggered by slow moving factors such as Solar Arc Directions, Secondary Progressions or Outer Transits, the other points are activated within a year or less because of their tight orb of natal aspect. Assuming the average motion of a Solar Arc Direction or Secondary Progression is one-degree a year and knowing that one-degree translates to 4-minutes of birth time, the astrologer may then successfully determine the birth time from life events. In the Solar Arc Direction method, a one-degree natal aspect between planets is measured in time at the rate of one-day of the Sun's arc equal to one year of life. Just in calculating the Solar Arc for the client's age for a dramatic life event and subtracting that increment from each leg of the configuration, the astrologer may arrive at a few potential Midheaven positions to narrow the birth time search. The closest planets in natal aspect or in an aspect configuration provide the very important "hook" for beginning the rectification search.

In this example, death of a child at a very young age is one of the most dramatic life events and astrologically best described by the native's strong natal hard aspect pattern at 1-2 degrees of fixed signs involving Pluto square the Moon's Nodes and Saturn – also semi-square and sesqui-square Sun and Venus. From the list of life events, we know the native experienced such a traumatic event just a few weeks short of age 18. By counting back 18 degrees from any of the planets or points involved in the aspect configuration, one can fairly assume four possible Midheaven degrees at 13-14 degrees of cardinal signs, accounting for the legs of the T-Square, and to a lesser extent 29 Leo, accounting for the minor aspects of semi-square and sesqui-square of the Sun and Venus. For such a dramatic event, one may further assume that the strongest aspect, a conjunction, formed to one of the planets in the network at the time of the tragic event, narrowing the possible Midheaven degrees to two: 13-14 Cancer conjunct Pluto at age 18, or 13-14 Aries conjunct Saturn and the South Node at age 18. (Note that the event occurred 6 weeks prior to the 18th birthday, so we have rounded to 18). Always seize upon the most dramatic life event to begin the search, even if only rectifying a few minutes of birth time.

Secondary Progressions of planets and Transits of Outer Planets should help to further narrow the time for activation of the already determined critical degrees noted above. Outer transits mark time in various ranges from two weeks (a Jupiter transit) to two years (a Pluto transit), not including any stationary or retrograde periods that may lengthen the influence. All of these methods are useful in attempting to find an unknown birth time or to rectify an approximate time to one that consistently corresponds with life events. In addition to outer planets transiting a natal planet or network, one must also consider the entire time span of the transit's multiple contacts through retrograde and direct motion. For instance, a transit of Uranus takes 12 months to complete its movement across one planet, or network of planets in the natal chart – crossing first in direct motion, then retrograding back over, and turning direct to make a final pass.

To offer a word of caution, one must be careful when including the Moon or "working Angle" in the assessment of the close aspect patterns in the natal chart, because a few minutes of birth time changes the Angle degree, and two hours changes the Moon degree. Therefore, one should first consider only the planets (from the Sun out) and/or Nodes involved in the network. Since the Moon moves about one degree every two hours and a bit more than 13 degrees in 24 hours, the close orb exactitude of the pattern may be in question unless the client can reliably narrow the birth time range to a couple of hours or keeping the Moon within 1 degree of change. Similarly, if one suspects that an Angle is also involved in the network, first narrow the search so the birth time range is less than 16 minutes or within a four-degree orb of exact. Remember, the Angles sweep the entire zodiac in the course of a day, moving one-degree every four-minutes of clock time. Therefore, locating the position of the Moon and the Angles are the keys to determining the rectified birth time. The converse is true as well; it is the birth time that determines the Angles at a given location on a given date.

Narrow the Field for Midheaven Candidates

From examining the example chart and the key life events, the time period of 1957 was extremely dramatic because several life-defining events occurred in close succession. Close sequence of major life events suggests the activation of a close aspect natal pattern involving several planets, or simultaneous activation of multiple close natal aspects. In this case, the actual drama began in July of 1956 at the onset of teen pregnancy, but the chain of external events commenced from the premature birth of a son on February 21, 1957, to a shotgun marriage on March 31, 1957, to the death of the child on July 25, 1957. This period of a year, including the 7 months of fear and anxiety prior to the birth and the many months in shock after the child's death, describes the most important of the "life-defining" events. Since these events spanned from near age seventeen to age eighteen as noted earlier, the initial search should set the Midheaven 17-18 degrees prior to each of the legs of the close one-degree natal aspect configuration to allow for the activation of applying hard aspects. Rather than search a whole year of stressful events, one can make a very good case to zero in on the most dramatic event, the death of the child just a few weeks short of age 18, which would give a Midheaven at 13+ degrees of cardinal signs, rather than moving the Midheaven to the Sun/Venus conjunction.

Table 5 lists each of the networked planets with the possible Midheaven placement 17 to 18 degrees before contact with each planet or point, as potential starting points against which to test the other important life events. Since the Sun and Venus are only connected closely to Pluto and Saturn by minor aspect, one may reasonably eliminate them from the search and zero in on the obvious suspects for the dramatic event described by, the natal Pluto and the Saturn/South Node in close square and conjunction positions.

Table 5 Working from Major Event at 18 to Close Natal Configuration in the Tebbs Chart

Natal Planet	Natal Placement	Event Age/ Degreees to Subtract	Potential Natal Midheaven	Aspect At Event	Potential Birth Time
Sun	15:57 Virgo	-17 to 18 Degrees	28-29 Leo	conjunction	11:22 AM
Venus	16:57 Virgo	-17 to 18 Degrees	29 Leo--0 Virgo	conjunction	11:26 AM
Pluto	2:16 Leo	-17 to 18 Degrees	14 to 15 Cancer	conjunction	8:22 AM
Saturn	0:40 Taurus	-17 to 18 Degrees	13 to 14 Aries	conjunction	2:16 AM
S Node	0:14 Taurus	-17 to 18 Degrees	12 to 13 Aries	conjunction	2:08 AM
N Node	0:14 Scorpio	-17 to 18 Degrees	12 to 13 Libra	conjunction	2:08 PM

Check each of the possible birth times in the same manner using Solar Arc Direction or Secondary Progression, since the Midheaven moves at the same rate in both systems. Your results should closely match the estimated positions given in Table 5.

Remember the Basics of Time

Back to our example of possible birth times derived from moving the Midheaven to each of the planets and points in the 1-degree natal aspect network for the target year of 1957 at age 17 – 18. Notice that 6 hours, or one-quarter of a day, separates the 2:08 – 2:16 AM and PM times from the 8:22 AM time. Six hours of clock time represents the distance of the natal square between Pluto, Saturn and the Moon's Nodes, or 90 degrees x 4 minutes = 360 minutes or 6 hours of clock time. Any potential birth times that are opposite, 12 hours earlier or later, such as 2:08 AM and 2:08 PM; or square to it as 8:22 AM or semi-square and sesqui-square to it as 11:22 – 11:26 AM, would also trigger the same hard aspect configuration at age 17 to 18. Preference is given to the conjunction aspect for any moving factor to one of the configuration legs, rather than the opposition or square, because it carries much more potential to describe so powerful a life period. In fact, the timing of conjunctions of possible chart Angles to natal planets from each of the potential birth times should constitute the first line of the search.

Further, notice that the 11:22 – 11:26 AM times are only 3 hours and 9 hours from 8:22 AM and 2:08 AM, the other times which represent when the Midheaven activated the semi-square natal aspect of Pluto to the Sun/Venus conjunction and the Saturn/South Node sesqui-square to it. It might be helpful to remember that 360 degrees equals 24 hours of clock time; 180 degrees equals 12 hours of clock time; 150 degrees equals 10 hours of clock time; 135 degrees equals 9 hours of clock time; 90 degrees equals 6 hours of clock time; 45 degrees equals 3 hours of clock time; 30 degrees, or 1 sign, equals 2 hours of clock time; and 1 degree equals 4 minutes of clock time. So, from any of the derived potential birth times, the Midheaven progresses at the average Solar Arc rate of one degree per day (year) to activate this important configuration.

Table 6 Degrees to Clock Time and Calendar Time to Clock Time

Degrees to Clock Time			Calendar Time to	Clock Time
360 degrees	=	24 hours	1 year (12 months)	1 day (24 hours)
180 degrees	=	12 hours	1 month (30 days)	2 hours
150 degrees	=	10 hours	½ a month (15 days)	1 hour (60 minutes)
135 degrees	=	9 hours	1 day	4 minutes
120 degrees	=	8 hours		
90 degrees	=	6 hours		
60 degrees	=	4 hours		
45 degrees	=	3 hours		
30 degrees	=	2 hours		
15 degrees	=	1 hour		
1 degree	=	4 minutes		
30 minutes or ½ degree	=	2 minutes		
15 minutes or ¼ degree	=	1 minute		

Note: The word, "minutes" denotes portions of a degree as well as clock time; it is easy to confuse which meaning is intended. Since the same word "minutes" is used differently in each system and can represent large variances, the reader must always be alert to the appropriate application of the term.

We are searching for the appropriate Midheaven to correspond with actual events from a possible 360 degrees of a 24- hour day. Since one sign equals approximately 2 hours of clock time, and 1 degree equals 4 minutes, we can use inductive reasoning to work backward from the planetary configuration degrees by subtracting the client's age at the event(s) to arrive at the potential natal Midheaven placement. Each potential Midheaven placement corresponds to a specific birth time. For births in the six months of Standard Time, as in this case, the 11:22 and 11:26 AM times place the Sun/Venus conjunction in the 10th house near the Midheaven. The 8:22 AM birth time places the Sun/Venus conjunction on the 12th house cusp (Placidus), and the 2:16 and 2:08 AM times place the Sun/Venus conjunction on the 3rd house cusp (Placidus). In all cases, the planets involved in this network remain in the same relationship since none of them moves more than one-degree in the course of the day. However, if the Moon is part of the close aspect configuration, be sure to reserve judgment until other indicators provide enough evidence to set the time of birth within an hour, so the potential Moon error is not more than a half-degree.

Other factors such as Midheaven or Ascendant Ingresses into a new sign or house, and Eclipses or Synodic Returns to the Angles, can help in the search if the birth time is narrowed to only a few minutes. Of course, these additional astronomical events can activate the native's inner planets to provide further confirmation or rejection of potential times, but the real time markers of importance in rectification are the Angles and the Moon. The other planetary contacts will occur within one degree for the given event year regardless of the birth time – especially if the search is initially set for Noon for an unknown birth time.

Narrow the Field for Ascendant Candidates

Once the Midheaven possibilities have been narrowed, use the Table of Houses, or appropriate computer software, to determine the correct Ascendant for the geographical latitude of the birthplace. Some astrologers move the Ascendant at the Solar Arc rate as well as the Midheaven, but many prefer the traditional method of applying the Solar Arc rate only to the Midheaven and deriving the Ascendant (and cusps) from the birth location latitude using the Secondary Progressed method. For beginning a rectification search, directing the Ascendant at the Solar Arc rate is best, at least until the birth time is determined within a few minutes. Table 7 gives all of the possible Ascendants for birth times derived from the potential Midheaven search:

Table 7 Potential Ascendant Times for Major Event at Age 18 for the Tebbs Example

Potential Birth Time	Potential ASC	ASC Placement at Events (age 17-18)	Aspected Planets at Events
11:22 AM	17 Scorpio 48	5 Sagittarius	Square N Mercury
11:26 AM	18 Scorpio 36	6 Sagittarius	Trine Jupiter
8:22 AM	12 Libra 08	0 Scorpio	Conjunct N Node; Opposition Saturn/SN
2:11 AM	28 Cancer 20	17 Leo	no major aspect
2:08 AM	27 Cancer 44	16 Leo	no major aspect
2:08 AM	21 Sagittarius 38	9 Capricorn 30	no major aspect

Of the most likely Midheaven and Ascendant combinations appropriate to describe the actual life-altering events of 1957, the three birth times with no major aspect involving the progressed Ascendant can reasonably be eliminated. Further, at the final event very near age 18, the death of a child is not adequately described by the late square to natal Mercury, unless the time might be adjusted several minutes earlier. Clearly the Ascendant trine Jupiter of the 11:26 AM time does not describe so tragic an event. Remaining, then, as possible times for the birth to correspond with these major life events are 8:22 AM and 11:22 AM EST. The fact that the client was early recognized as an artist and taught art for the first twenty one years of her teaching career might give more credence to the 8:22 AM time that places the important Sun/Venus conjunction right on the 12th house cusp in the Placidus house system. Of course, the time must be tested against other major life events to be certain, but it is apparent that some of the potential birth times not producing consistent results may be easily eliminated.

To fine tune the confirmed birth time, a more time-specific test is found in the Arabic tradition of Decanantes that divide 10-degrees of each sign equaling 40-minutes of clock time and Dwadashamsas that divide 2 ½ degree segments of each sign equaling 10-minutes of clock time. In this case, we know that she was a career teacher of both art and literature, then as a consulting astrologer and teacher of astrology. The natal Moon is in Cancer, but the biography is most consistent with the Moon in the more empathetic Pisces dwad of the 8:10-8:20 AM range.

Table 8 Signs, Decanantes and Dwadashamsas – Fine-tuning of Degrees

MOST USED MODERN TRIPLICITY DWAD SYSTEM												
	0°-2°29	2°30-4°59	5°-7°29	7°30-9°59	10°-12°29	12°30-14°59	15°-17°29	17°30-19°59	20°-22°29	22°30-24°59	25°-27°29	27°30-29°59
AR	♈	♉	♊	♋	♌	♍	♎	♏	♐	♑	♒	♓
TA	♉	♊	♋	♌	♍	♎	♏	♐	♑	♒	♓	♈
GE	♊	♋	♌	♍	♎	♏	♐	♑	♒	♓	♈	♉
CN	♋	♌	♍	♎	♏	♐	♑	♒	♓	♈	♉	♊
LE	♌	♍	♎	♏	♐	♑	♒	♓	♈	♉	♊	♋
VI	♍	♎	♏	♐	♑	♒	♓	♈	♉	♊	♋	♌
LI	♎	♏	♐	♑	♒	♓	♈	♉	♊	♋	♌	♍
SC	♏	♐	♑	♒	♓	♈	♉	♊	♋	♌	♍	♎
SG	♐	♑	♒	♓	♈	♉	♊	♋	♌	♍	♎	♏
CP	♑	♒	♓	♈	♉	♊	♋	♌	♍	♎	♏	♐
AQ	♒	♓	♈	♉	♊	♋	♌	♍	♎	♏	♐	♑
PI	♓	♈	♉	♊	♋	♌	♍	♎	♏	♐	♑	♒
	Decan				Decan				Decan			

The Progressed Moon Gives "Second-Hand" Timing Accuracy

At an average movement of 1 degree 6 minutes per month, and 13-degrees 11-minutes per year, the Progressed Moon ticks by the planets and angles much faster than Progressions or Directions of the other planets, therefore, it is more effective as a "fine-tuning" timing device. To convert the Moon's Progressed motion from calendar time to clock time, its 13-degrees 11-minutes annual motion equals slightly less than one-half a sign per year, or in clock time, a bit less than 2 hours.

Begin by looking in the ephemeris to determine the range of the Progressed Moon for the year of several prominent life events. In our example chart, the natal Moon ranged from 12:58 to 27:25 Cancer on September 9, 1939 or movement of 14 degrees 27 minutes, a bit faster than the average motion. Allowing for each degree of the Progressed Moon motion to approximate 2 hours of clock time, allowing for the birth in Eastern Standard Time in Columbus, Ohio to be adjusted by adding 5 hours of Greenwich Mean Time correction, the natal Moon possibilities range from about 20:58 to 22:47 Cancer for the two potential birth times we are considering, 8:22 AM and 11:22 AM. Now that the natal position of the Moon is narrowed to 2 degrees, it is possible to experiment with progressing it to various planets and points to align with key life events.

If you have been able to narrow the birth range to one or two possible times by other methods, then begin searching for the Progressed Moon alignments for the key dates. If slightly less than two hours of birth time equals just over one degree, or one month of calendar time for the Progressed Moon, we should be able to approximate the timing for the Progressed Moon aspects to activate any Angles, planets or aspect networks at the times of important events.

Creating a table may be helpful to track the Progressed Moon results. Solar Fire 9 software provides a good example to confirm the 8:22 am birth time that can still be tweaked plus or minus 3 or 4 minutes of clock time.

Major events according to possible Progressed Moon positions are sorted by the most dramatic events using only the 4th harmonic aspects, conjunction, opposition, and square. The 8:22 AM possible birth time on 9/9/1939 with a birth location of +5 hours from Greenwich. Table 9 may be helpful in aligning events to appropriate Progressed Moon positions:

Table 9 Tracking the Progressed Moon for Life Events in Tebbs Example

Age	Event Date	Event Description	Prog Date	Moon Range	Aspects	Est Time
8	Fall 1947	Tonsils surgery	9/17/39	11-25 Scorpio	opp Uranus	8:00 AM
13	July 1952	Father trouble-Sudden move	9/22/39	16-28 Capric	opp Moon conj Mars	8:00 AM 6:00 PM
15	Feb 1954	Break-up first love	9/24/39	10-22 Aquar	sq Uranus	8:00 AM
18	Feb 21, 1957	Birth of son, unwed	9/27/39	15-28 Pisces	opp Sun opp Venus opp Neptune	8:00 AM 10:00 AM 10:00 PM
18	Mar 31, 1957	Shotgun marriage	9/27/39	15-28 Pisces	opp Sun opp Venus opp Neptune	6:00 AM 8:00 AM 8:00 AM
18	July 25, 1957	Death of son	9/27/39	15-28 Pisces	opp Sun opp Venus opp Neptune	6:00 PM 8:00 PM 8:00 PM
25	Sep 25, 1965	Marriage near end	10/4/39	12-25 Gemini	sq Sun sq Venus sq Neptune	6:00 PM 8:00 AM 8:00 PM
31	Apr 14, 1971	Suddenly left family	10/10/39	6-21 Virgo	conj Sun conj Venus	12:00 AM 2:00 AM
32	Mar, 1972	Break down	10/11/39	21 Vir-6 Libra	conj Neptune	8:00 AM
32+	Aug 25, 1972	Returned home	10/11/39	21 Vir-6 Libra	opp Jupiter	8:00 AM

44+	Aug 25, 1984	Upset / job change	10/23/39	6-18 Pisces	opp Sun opp Venus	8:00 PM 10:00 PM
50	Mar 3, 1989	Godson estranged	10/29/39	13-26 Taurus	conj Uranus	8:00 PM
52	Fall 1991	Father's secret life revealed in family	10/31/39	9-22 Gemini	sq Sun sq Venus sq Neptune	10:00 AM 12:00 PM 12:00 AM
58	Apr/May 98	Sold 2 homes moved	11/6/39	2-16 Virgo	conj Merc conj Sun	8:00 AM 12:00 AM
60	Jun 21, 2000	Teaching retirement	11/8/39	0-15 Libra	sq Moon	8:00 AM
62	Feb 16, 2001	Aunt murdered	11/10/39	29 Lib-14 Scorpio	conj NN sq Pluto	2:00 AM 4:00 AM
64	July 12, 2003	Appointed college president	11/12/39	27 Sco-11 Sag	sq Merc	8:00 AM
66+	July 1, 2006	Retired again suddenly	11/14/39	5 Cap-18 Cap	opp working MC	8:00 AM
66+	July 7, 2006	Father's death	11/14/39	5 Cap-18 Cap	opp working MC	8:00 AM
74	Oct 13, 2013	Mother's death	11/17/39	0 Aqu- 3 Aqu	opp Pluto	8:00 AM

Of course, the Progressed Moon search can as well be narrowed to activate only the planets in the close aspect network that we used for the Midheaven and Ascendant search. In this case, only the Progressed Moon aspects to the Sun, Venus, Saturn, Pluto, and the Moon's Nodes should be considered for this chart since they are the planets of the close aspect natal pattern.

The Progressed Moon contacts reinforce the 8:22 AM time rather than the later 11:22 AM time. But even with known birth times, a multiple of other factors overlap to make the exact timing of any Progressed Moon aspect more complicated, such as its movement to a Progressed Planet or Angle yet undetermined.

The Progressed Sun and Inner Planets Can Mark Key Life Events

Other reliable indicators for a rectification search, are planet-to-planet contacts established by Solar Arc Direction, Secondary Progression and/or Transits of outer planets. As you may recall from earlier study, inner planet contacts are the most revealing as personal event descriptors. Assuming that the possible Angle choices have been narrowed to two or three, Progression or Direction of the Sun and the personal planets, Mercury through Mars, may provide confirmation to select one birth time over the other.

The movement of the Sun is always the same in either the Directed or the Progressed systems because both are based upon the Solar Arc, or the Sun's motion from one day to the next as recorded in the ephemeris. It is important to remember that the Solar Arc moves faster at 1:01 minutes per day during the Winter months of January and February, and slower at :57 minutes per day during the summer months of July and August; therefore, the average motion of the Sun is :59 minutes per day. The temptation is to "guestimate" planetary contacts by applying the average 1-degree Solar Arc rate, but the surer course is to rely upon good computer software for progressing possible birth times to key life events.

The planetary contacts of the moving Sun, either by Progression or Direction, are also useful for assessing important life periods, though it does not give adequate information to confirm or establish the birth time. The Sun moves at about 5-minutes per month and about 1-degree per year in either system. Ideally the Sun, or any planet, should make exact contact very close to the event date. In this example, the client's natal Sun makes many contacts to other planets during the course of the listed events. In your search, list the major aspects made by the Progressed or Directed Sun and see how they align with actual life events. A synchronicity should be evident if enough events related to individual identity are provided and the birth time is narrowed to a range of an hour, making the Sun's variance relatively small.

Table 10 Progressed Sun Positions at Life Events for the Tebbs Chart

Progressed Sun Position	Aspect Contacts of Progressed Sun	Approx Age at event	Corresponding Life Events
16 Virgo 57	Conjunct Venus	1	Adored first child
21-23 Virgo	Sextile Moon*	5-7	Excelled early in school
21 Virgo 54	Trine Uranus	6	Early artistic talent
22 Virgo 48	Conjunct Neptune	7-8	Severe throat infection/surgery
25 Virgo 54	Trine Mars	11	State Spelling Bee Finalist
0 Libra 0	Ingress into Libra	14	Gained recognition as an artist
0 Libra 14	Quincunx S Node	14	Break-up with long-term beau
0 Libra 40	Quincunx Saturn	14	Father trouble with law
2 Libra 16	Sextile Pluto	16	Met future husband
6 Libra 07	Trine Jupiter	21	Honors at entry/4 year college
12 Libra 08	Conjunct 8:22 AM ASC	27	Moved to new house
13 Libra 59	Square 8:22 AM MC	29	Discontent period beginning
21-23 Libra	Square Moon*	35	Talk of divorce
21 Libra 54	Quincunx Uranus	36	Both children moved out of town

25 Libra 54	Square Mars	**40**	Talk of divorce
28 Libra 09	Sextile 11:22 AM MC	**42**	
0 Scorpio 0	Ingress into Scorpio	**44**	Focus on organization work
0 Scorpio 14	Conjunct N Node	**44**	Traumatic change of job
0 Scorpio 40	Opposition Saturn	**44**	Still traumatic change of job
0 Scorpio 40	Opposition Saturn	44	Still traumatic change of job
2 Scorpio 16	Square Pluto	46	Hard work- 1st Major Conference
4 Scorpio 16-21	Sextile Mercury	48	Appointed Mentor Teacher
6 Scorpio 07	Quincunx Jupiter	50	Estranged from godson
15:57-16:03 Sco	Sextile Sun	60 ¾	Retirement
16:57-17:03 Sco	Sextile Venus	62	Life is good
17 Scorpio 48	Conjunct 11:22 AM ASC	63	Cruise to Mexico
19 Scorpio	Trine Moon*	63 ¾	Named College Administrator
21 Scorpio 54	Opposite Uranus	66 ¾	Second Retirement
21 Scorpio	Opposite Uranus	66 ¾	Death of father
28 Scorpio		74	Death of Mother

*Note that we strongly suspect the Moon position to favor the 8:22 AM birth time derived from the appropriate Progressed timing of Midheaven and Ascendant contacts as well as the Progressed Moon 4th harmonic contacts to describe most major life events. Also, the Sun range has been narrowed to 6-minutes of arc using the same process of elimination.

In a similar manner, the Progressions or Directions of the other planets to key event dates can reveal timing through the "stacking up" of similar event indicators. The outer planets reveal very little about the most important features of the rectification search until close approximation of the Moon and Angle positions are derived, thereby giving a close estimate of a birth time that matches actual life events, feelings, or situations. Progression or Direction of outer planets is particularly evident when moved to contact an Angle or an inner planet, but such a search is useless until the Angles are established. Any Progression of an outer planet is so slow as to be useless for a rectification search. To reiterate, the rectification search must initially be concentrated upon establishing the Angles for the chart that appropriately align with life events.

Progressed to Progressed Aspects Can Confirm Birth Time

In some cases, progressed planets and Angles may make a one-degree aspect to another progressed planetary position. Often such contact provides important supplementary information according to the nature of the planets, aspects, and house position of the contacted bodies. It is not uncommon to find that an outer planet that has progressed only a degree or two from its natal position is just as sensitive to contact from another progressing body as it is in the natal position. For instance, in the example above, the natal retrograde Saturn of 0 Taurus 40 Progressed to 28 Aries 45 at age 31, which made no new aspect to the natal chart. However, during that same year Progressed Mercury moved to 28 Libra 45 to oppose the Progressed Saturn when I moved away from the family. The Progressed Mercury made no other aspect to the natal chart at that time, so clearly, it was responding to its opposition to Progressed Saturn.

The other progressed to progressed position commonly evident in forecasting or rectification is the Progressed Moon activating a progressed planet or Angle. The Progressed Moon is an important timing trigger and moves between the natal and progressed positions of outer planets in a few months highlighting the period between awareness of an issue at natal contact and its resolution at progressed planet contact. Similarly, the Progressed Moon moves from its contact to an inner planet natal position to the planet's progressed position anywhere from several months to years later for full resolution of the issue signified by the activation. For instance, if at age 31 Venus progressed 32-degrees from its natal position, it may take decades for the activating planet to reach the planet's progressed position, from natal Venus to progressed Venus. The nature of the issue activated at contact with natal Venus may extend beneath the surface for inner planet to inner planet is a long period if the person is in mid-life or older.

Generally, progressed positions of outer planets to a natal planet are less revealing because they move so slowly that they may never activate another planet, not useful for determining the birth time nor for interpretation. I can't emphasize strongly enough that the Angles and the position of the Moon are the key determiners in searching for birth times with appropriate descriptors that correlate at the right month and year of major life events.

Outer Transits Can Mark Potential Moon and Angle Positions

Finally, the outer transits (Jupiter through Pluto) mark key periods and events by their transiting contacts to the Sun, Moon and the Angles. The slowest transiting planets such as Saturn, Uranus, Neptune and Pluto activate a 1-degree area of the chart from a few months to two years including their retrograde cycles, and therefore, any one of those planets moving to contact an Angle by conjunction, or other major aspect, should give noticeable results. Uranus, Neptune and Pluto transits to the Sun, Moon and Angles also provide important life event markers, especially in narrowing the active degree range of the uncertain factors. Transiting Mars and Jupiter activate a one-degree area from a few weeks to a couple of months including retrograde cycles, so their transits to the Sun, Moon or Angles are not such major indicators of life events, unless they occur together with several other indicators. However, they are invaluable for activating the Angles of the chart at appropriate event times. Search the positions of transiting Saturn, Uranus, Neptune, and Pluto in close hard aspect to the "working Angles" at the dates of major events for a repeated pattern of degree or sign emphasis.

Table 11 Angles for 8:22 AM Birth   Table 12 Angles for 11:22 AM Birth

Table 11	8:22 AM MC: 13 Cancer 59	8:22 AM ASC: 12 Libra 08	Table 12	11:22 AM MC: 28 Leo 09	11:22 AM ASC:
T Pluto	Square at 37 Square at 37 ½ Square at 38 InConj at 61	Conj at 36 Conj at 36 ½ Conj at 37	**T Pluto**	Conj at 16 Conj at 16 ½ Conj at 17 Square at 55	Square at 10 Square at 11 Square at 11 ¾ Conj at 51
T Nept	Square at 9 Square at 9 ½ Square at 9 ¾ Oppos at 50 ¼ Oppos at 50 ½ Oppos at 51	Conj at 7 ½ Conj at 8 Conj at 8 ½ Square at 49 ½ Square at 49 ¾ Square at 50	**T Nept**	Square at 29 Square at 29 ½ Square at 30 Square at 30 ¾	Conj at 24 ½ Conj at 25 Conj at 25 ¾ Conj at 26 Square at 66 ½ Square at 67
T Uranus	Conj at 12 Conj at 12 Conj at 12 ¾ Square at 31 Square at 31 ½ Square at 32 Oppos at 51 Oppos at 51 ½ Oppos at 52 Onconj at 60 ¾	Square at 11 ¾ Square at 12 ½ Square at 12 ¾ Conj at 31 Conj at 32 Square at 51 Square at 51 ½ Square at 52 Inconj at 67	**T Uranus**	Square at 1 ½ Square at 2 Square at 2 ½ Conj at 22 Conj at 22 ½ Conj at 22 ¾ Square at 41 Square at 41 ½ Square at 42 Oppos at 62 ½ Oppos at 62 ¾ Oppos at 63 ½	Square at 20 Square at 20 ½ Square at 20 ¾ Conj at 39 Conj at 39 ½ Conj at 40 Square at 60 ½ Square at 61 Square at 61 ¼
T Saturn	Conj at 6 Square at 12 Square at 12 ½ Square at 12 ¾ Oppos at 20 Oppos at 20 ¾ Oppos at 21 Square at 28 Conj at 34 Conj at 35 Conj at 35 ½ Square at 43 Oppos at 49 ½	Square at 6 Conj at 12 Conj at 12 ½ Conj at 12 ¾ Square at 20 Oppos at 27 ½ Oppos at 27 ¾ Oppos at 28 Square at 34 Conj at 42 Square at 49 ½ Square at 49 ¾ Square at 50	**T Saturn**	Square at 1 ½ Square at 2 Square at 2 ½ Conj at 9 Square at 16 Square at 16 ¼ Square at 16 ¾ Oppos at 25 ½ Square at 31 ¾ Conj at 38 ½ Conj at 38 ¾ Square at 45	Oppos at 1 ½ Square at 8 Square at 8 ½ Square at 8 ¾ Conj at 15 Conj at 16 Square at 24 Square at 25 Square at 25 ¼ Oppos at 30 ½ Oppos at 31 Oppos at 31 ½ Square at 37 ¾

	Table 11	8:22 AM MC: 13 Cancer 59	8:22 AM ASC: 12 Libra 08	Table 12	11:22 AM MC: 28 Leo 09	11:22 AM ASC:
	T Pluto	Oppos at 49 ¾ Square at 57 Conj at 63 Conj at 63 ½ Conj at 64	Oppos at 50 Oppos at 57 Square at 63 Square at 63 ½ Square at 64	T Pluto	Oppos at 53 ½ Oppos at 54 ½ Square at 60 ½ Square at 61 Square at 61 ½	Conj at 45 Square at 51 ½ Square at 51 ¾ Square at 52 Oppos at 60 ½

An outer transit search using an ephemeris or computer software should provide the necessary detail to select the correct birth time for the example chart. Recall that we narrowed the possible times to two, 8:22 AM and 11:22 AM EST with a strong bias so far for the 8:22 AM time. Tables 11 and 12 provide transiting major aspects to the Midheaven and Ascendant for both times and the age at events. See if you can discern which set of angles best fits with actual events.

In Table 11, the Midheaven or Ascendant aligns with key events at ages 12, 31-32 and 49-50. In Table 12, few ages at key events align with the "working birth time". So, the 8:22 AM birth time is the best result of the rectification search. Finally, a search of Solar Eclipses at key life events may help to confirm one time over another if the Angles or the Moon are involved.

Table 12 Solar Eclipse Contacts at Key Life Events for 8:22 AM Birth

	Event	Eclipse	Age	Date	Aspect
1	Father trouble/Sudden move	6 Pisces	12	1/1952	Oppos Mercury
2	Break-up with serious boyfriend	14 Capricorn	14	2/1954	Conj 4th
3	Premature birth of first child	10 Sag	17	2/21/1957	Sextile ASC
4	Shotgun marriage	9 Taurus	17	3/31/1957	Conj 8th
5	Death of first child	9 Taurus	18-	7/25/1957	Conj 8th
6	Left family suddenly	6 Pisces	31	4/16/1971	Oppos Mercury
7	Break-down/returned to family	19 Cancer	32	8/25/1972	Conj Moon
8	Estrangement from godson	17 Pisces	49	3/3/1989	Oppos Sun/Venus
9	Retirement from 38 yrs teaching	10 Cancer	60	6/21/2000	Conj MC
10	Aunt murdered	4 Capricorn	61	2/16/2001	Trine Mercury
11	Appointed college President	9 Gemini	63	7/12/2003	Conj 9th
12	Death of father	8 Aries	67-	7/7/2006	Conj 7th

Table 13: Jigsaw 2.2 Rectification Search for 9-9-1939 CarolTebbs

Time	Midheaven	Ascendant	Solar Arc	Sec Prog	Outer Trans	Overall
0:18 AM	11° Pisc 15'	2° Canc 56'	4/8	4/8	3/9	47%
8:22 AM	13° Canc 59'	12° Lib 08'	3/9	5/9	6/9	61%
9:40 AM	2°Leo 00'	27° Lib 31'	5/6	4/6	3/9	64%
1:17 AM	28° Virg 00'	10° sag 38'	5/7	4/7	3/8	58%
6:03 AM	11° Sag 15'	27° Aqu 12'	5/10	1/3	4/9	47%
10:19 PM	11° Aqu 15'	3° Gem 42'	2/8	4/8	5/10	47%

The Tebbs chart has an actual Ohio birth certificate recorded time of 8:18 AM EST, pretty close to the derived time of the rectification search. Actually, the 8:22 AM birth time seems to correspond better to life events, in which case the astrologer may wish to make this working adjustment to rectify the chart.

Remember, the main point of any rectification search is to adjust the birth time so that the astrological descriptors consistently align with actual life events. It is not uncommon for a minor time adjustment from a recorded birth time to be necessary. In any software search based on events, several potential birth times will emerge and the birth certificate time, or a close match, will be in the list – and it may not be at the top of the list. The trained astrologer's judgement trumps the limit of information put into the software.

Narrow the time range with the Moon

In any birth time search within 4-hours the Moon moves about 2-degrees. And if the birth time is not known and the search is 24-hours, the Moon moves 12 to 15 degrees staying in one sign or straddling two signs which is a benefit because one of the signs will clearly not fit the client and many hours can be lopped off of the birth time search before testing any events.

My client asking for a 24-hour search is a good example to illustrate the point. She provided me with about 500 words describing her personality, emotions, early childhood, interests, work, relationships, etc., plus a list of a dozen most dramatic life events with dates to the year, month and day, including how she felt about each event. Though the Moon could be in one sign for 24-hours, my client's Moon straddled two signs, one fixed water and the other mutable fire - very different emotional backdrops.

An ephemeris is a great tool for finding planetary positions for any date, but not enough for the fast-moving Moon. The birth location is also important for precision and can vary the Moon house placement significantly, though retaining its sign and degree. The house position of the Moon provides information about how the person engages with others. For instance, in the CST zone, a dignified Cancer Moon in the 10th house suggests recognition for diplomacy in working with others, but the same Moon in the JST zone is in the 2nd house suggesting good handling of finances and personal values.

For the important life events, I always start with the most challenging events where the client had little to no choice. Hard events narrow the birth time quickly, and most often, the Ease events fall into place with appropriate descriptors.

Major Life Events spanning the life feelings about each event:	Personality, childhood, interests, work, values, relationships, education:
Age 5 Molested by grandfather	1. Set in her ways, deliberate and slow to face change
Age 13 Parents separated	
Age 19 Gang Raped	2. Shy and private demeanor
Age 29 Shot-gun marriage	3. Thoughtful and kind
Age 31-45 Spousal abuse	4. Excellent in crafts, sewing and cooking
Age 45 Divorce	5. A daddy's girl
Age 50 Bankruptcy	6. Loves shopping and nice clothes
Age 59 Death of father	7. A good camper and making do when in need
Age 63 Scammed, lost money	8. Her nickname is "Nita Neat", everything is organized and in order

In a 24-hour search, I set the chart for Noon and use the 0-Aries ascendant wheel, or the Sun as the ascendant wheel. I chose the latter for my client. At this point it is important to remember that during 24-hours none of the planets other than the MOON rarely move more than 1-degree but her Moon is fast moving 14-degrees, 37-minutes on May 4, 1958, in Whittier, California.

Looking at her Noon chart, it is evident that in 24-hours, her Moon straddles from mid-Scorpio into early Sagittarius. With the personal information she provided in the list, there is no way that a Moon in Sagittarius fits this person and her biography. Immediately, I knew that she must be born before Noon on May 4th, 1958, and actually before 9:30 AM for a Scorpio Moon. The shoe fits, and I have lopped off 14-hours of the 24-hour search.

Chart for 12:00 pm PDT, May 4, 1958, Whittier, California (mid 12:00 am 11:59 pm)

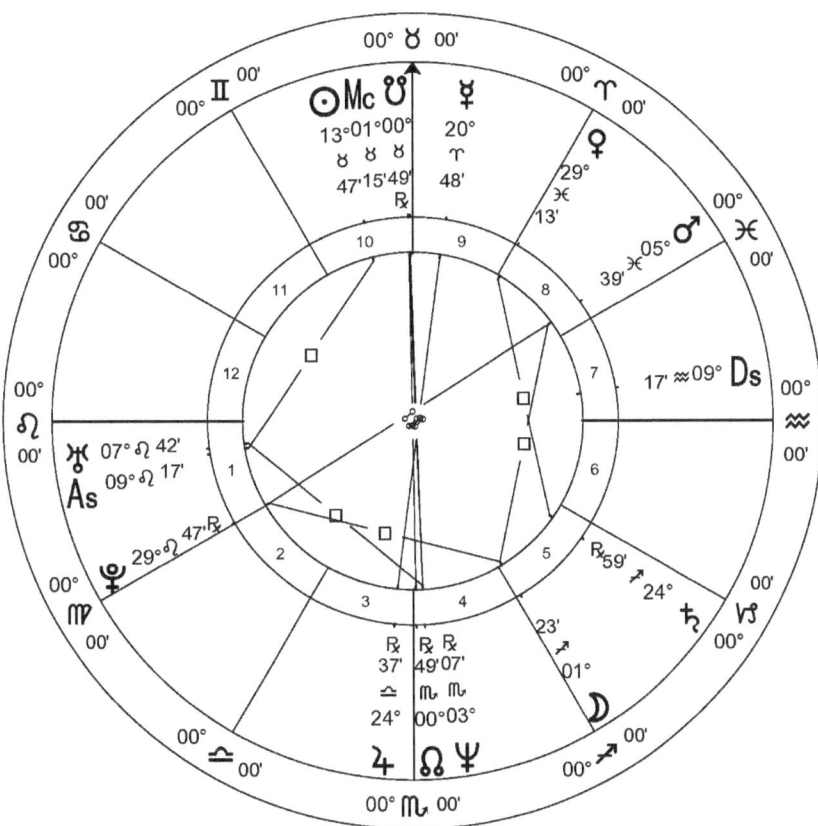

    Still looking at the Noon chart, I look to assess the condition of her Moon and what close aspects could occur in the remaining time range of 9 -hours, from 12:00 am to 9:30 am. In that new time range, the Moon spans about 6:50 degrees from 23:04 Scorpio at midnight to 29:54 Scorpio at 9:30 am. With that information, I know not only that the Moon is in Scorpio, but the time range is shortened by hours. In 9 hours the Moon moved only 6-degrees 50-minutes which is much easier than testing 24-hours of the total Moon range of 14-degrees and 37-minutes!

How Do I Verify a Given Birth Time?

Chart for 4:45 am PDT, May 4, 1958, Whittier, California (mid 12:00 am 9:30 am)

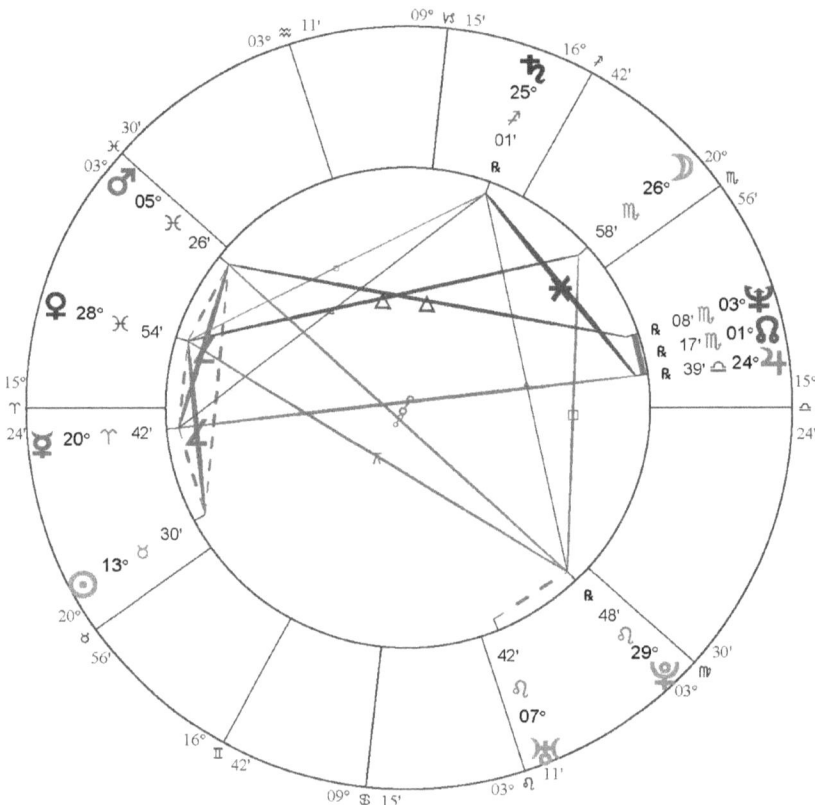

Now that I have confirmed the Moon in Scorpio and narrowed its range of aspect possibilities, I can look for the close 1-degree aspects to her Moon to confirm the childhood issues, her personality description and her fixity in life and her chart with her already abundance of planets in fixed signs.

At this point, I set the time range for halfway between midnight and 9:30 am on May 4, 1958, which is 4:45 am PDT. Not only can I find the close aspects to her Moon, but to also start thinking about the appropriate Ascendant that fits her personality. In the 9 hour time range, the Ascendant can only be in one of five signs, Aries, Taurus, Gemini, Cancer or a few degrees of Leo. Clearly, I am not going with Aries or Leo rising for her, therefore she has to be born later than 4:45 am to about 9:15 am. Wow! I have now lopped off more hours of the time range search, from midnight to 4:45 am. Now, I am only searching from 4:45 am to 9:30 am. In this range, the Moon moves from 26:58 Scorpio to 29:54 Scorpio, but the Ascendant can still move between two signs and part of a third. The next step is to divide the time range in half again and confirm the close 1- degree aspects to the Moon and the Ascendant sign and ruler that fits the client's personality and traits. Certainly, one or two of those signs will not fit the personal traits of the person. Once you have determined the best sign that fits the client's personal traits, you can build a case theory and begin testing events.

Chart for 7:08 am PDT, May 4, 1958, Whittier, California (mid 4:45 am 9:30 am)

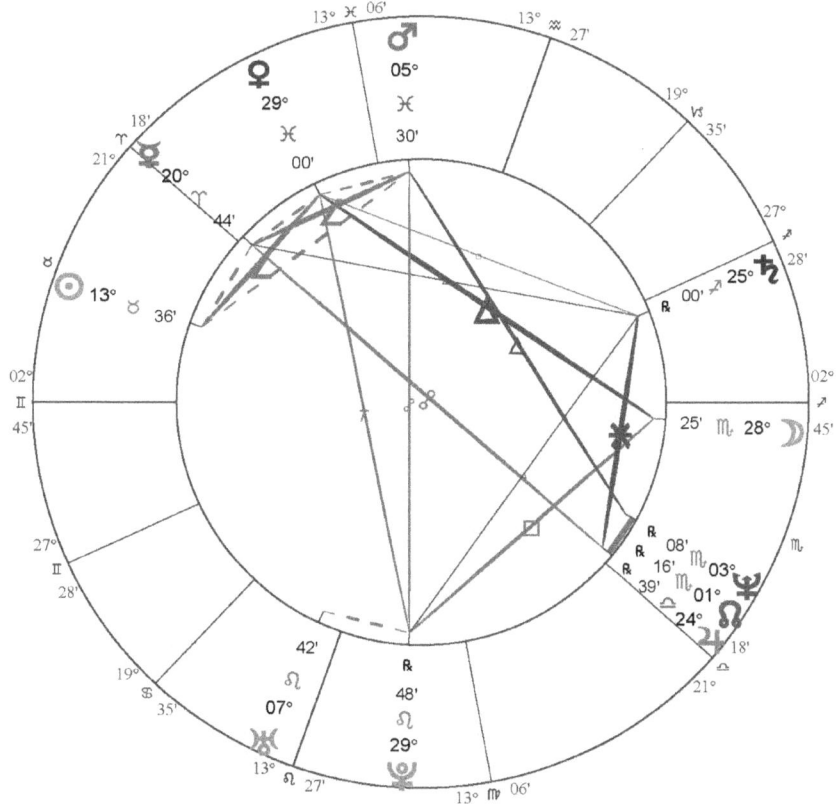

In this narrowed time range set the time at the midpoint between 4:45 and 9:30 am, and the Moon will move plus or minus a little over 1-degree. In this case, the Moon would still be in a close square aspect to Pluto. Also, Gemini rising with the Mercury ruler in the Mars sign Aries does not fit. Of the possible Ascendants left, only Taurus (a few minutes up to -2 hours earlier than 7:08 am) or Cancer (about 2-hours later than 7:08 am) which we have already cancelled. Taurus rising with a dignified Venus as ruler for an earlier time between 4:08 am and 6:08 am does fit the client's biography.

Chart for 5:38 am PDT, May 4, 1958, Whittier, California (mid 4:45 am 7:08 am)

Now that we are certain within 2-hour 20-minutes of Moon's sign and the Ascendant sign, it is time to start testing events with basic movement techniques such as outer transits or solar arc directions that activate natal planets or angles and provide appropriate astrological descriptors that fit events. Always consider the message the moving planet brings to the natal planet or angle, and how does it fit the event?

Rectification is easier to start with Solar Arc Directions and leave Secondary Progressions for later when the time is narrow, within a half hour or so. Remember, in Secondary Progression movement, only the inner planets and lights progress enough in a lifetime for meaningful information, AND except the Sun and Moon, planets can go retrograde to complicate your search.

I tested all of the major hard events for my client and the movement activation of the natal chart at each event consistently led to an earlier birth time near 6:00 am PDT. The example below, for the recent scam and loss of money, confirms what all of the other event tests confirmed, that my 6:03 am PDT is the correct rectified birth time. The client acknowledged the results that explained so many of her questions and concerns.

Rectified birth time 6:03 am PDT, May 4, 1958, Whittier, California
Outer Planet Transits for event April 22, 2022

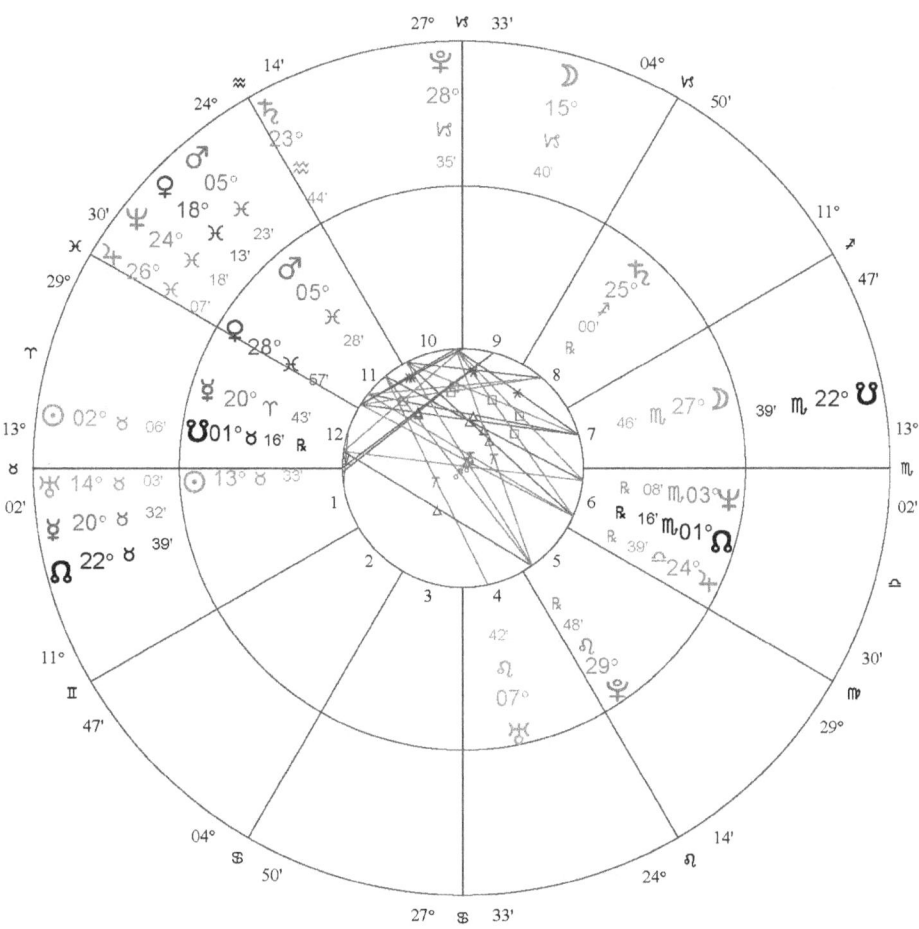

The slow moving Uranus activated her Ascendant with sudden light and hope that got dashed in seconds and deeply left damage to her self-worth, conjunct both Ascendant and Sun together. Concurrently, transiting Pluto had a power play on her public image for over 2-years.

How Do I Verify a Given Birth Time?

Eventually, she shared her hopes with some family members about her plans with her Facebook old friend to travel with him during his upcoming concert tour. At first, she was doubtful and cautious, but after several months of regular chats, she gave in and provided her personal information so he could have his secretary prepare the international travel papers for her. She has been hurt a lot in her life, and the 6:03 am birth time confirms each event with appropriate chart activation by moving planets bringing their messages to the trusting and vulnerable person's natal planets and angles. Now with a rectified birth time, accurate forecasting can identify the periods for caution as well as building a fulfilling path to the future.

The scam event lasted for over 9 months where the Facebook "friend" posed as a famous member of the Van Halen Band that she briefly met at an "after concert party" in the 1970's over 40 years ago. Having been divorced for 30 years, with only one or two short relationships since, she basically lives alone and is lonely — a prime target. The Facebook "friend" not only hurt her pocketbook, but more deeply her pride.

3

If the Quick Test Fails, Plan to Rectify!

Search Time Variances for the Birth Date and Birth Location

Even though births in the United States from the mid-20th century are reliably recorded, one cannot assume the same accuracy in birth records from other countries. At the dawn of the 21st century, many countries still do not record birth times precisely, if at all, so the astrologer's work still can be quite difficult. Many states and countries that do record specific birth times also have laws regulating to whom access is granted - most often restricted to immediate family members. Therefore, in the absence of a timed birth certificate, it is much more efficient if the client does the initial groundwork by searching though family records such as letters, baby books, or the family bible.

Other complications can impede the search for birth records. Early in the 20th century some states did not record birth times, but later legislation required them to do so. Knowing the local recording procedures and dates of any changes is quite important. The Doris Chase Doane reference works, Time Changes in the U.S.A. and Time Changes in the World published by The American Federation of Astrologers in Tempe, Arizona, are important books to own for astrologers still doing hand-calculations. Fortunately for computer users, U.S. and World time variances have been incorporated into all of the major chart calculation programs, saving a huge amount of search time and possibility for error.

Of course, accurate clock time is dependent upon a reasonably good timepiece accurately set in the first place – a huge assumption. We all know of the infinite variations of consistent time from communities refusing to observe Daylight Savings Time, to clocks and watches running too slow or too fast. Just experiment by asking the time in a group of people and you will likely get as many variances. Of course, atomic clocks commonly in use at the turn of the 21st century may narrow the time variables for future generations. Even the cell phone that most everyone carries is set to atomic time and changes itself automatically as one travels across time zones or time changes from "standard" to "daylight" or "war time". Accurate birth time is a major concern for all astrology forecasting work whether researching, consulting with clients, or writing for the astrology market. Even though rectified charts are not proper to use for research, or publication without appropriate disclaimers, knowing the principles of rectification may make the difference in accurate forecasting for the client – especially for clients returning each year for an update as is usually the case.

Find Resources for Further Birth Time Confirmation

People must be aware of the variety of resources for locating a birth time, or at least an approximate birth time, to make the rectification task easier and more affordable. Assuming that the client does not know his birth time, others who were present or notified of the birth may remember or made record of the birth in some way. It is important to contact with relatives, friends, and community connections to determine if some sort of record exists to narrow the search. The following list provides some suggestions for good resources to check:

1. Relatives and friends who were present at the birth may remember the time, or if they received an announcement, may have saved it
2. The family Bible often has birth time listed
3. Family correspondence at the time frequently mentions the birth details
4. Local newspapers list all hospital births from the previous day, and some list the birth time
5. Baptism records may be found at the family's church
6. Baby book entries by the mother very often reveal birth details
7. Even saved hospital ID bracelets may have the birth time recorded
8. An official birth certificate from the state or country of birth usually will have the time.

Having completed the survey of family members for the birth data (month, day, year, city, state, country and birth time), one must be advised not to proceed unless all variables are known except the time. "If more than one factor in the needed data is missing, the variations become staggering, and the task [of rectification] is almost impossible."[1] Dr. Dobyns recognizes the importance of birth time in setting a chart, but implies that if one has the birth time, but is missing the birth date or the birth location that either of those may be inferred by working from the other two. That is not the case. The birth time provides the Angles at any given location in the world, but even with the birth time, the Angles cannot be determined without knowing the location and the date. Dobyns is correct that the birth time is critical, but with any other factor missing the rectification task is impossible.

---

1. Dobyns, Zipporah, Progressions, Directions and Rectification, T.I.A. Publications, A division of CRCS Inc, California, 1975, p 18

Choose Astrology Software to Confirm or Rectify a Birth Time

For an example, a client is unable to provide a birth time but is certain only of the birth date and place. Therefore, the search must be for the full 24 hours of the day. Even with an adequate list of important life events with specific dates, the alignment task grows exponentially difficult as the search time range expands. From this point there are several ways to proceed, depending upon the available technology and astrology software with the appropriate search features. Some of the current best software programs for PC format are "Solar Fire 9" from www.Alabe.com and "Sirius 4.1" from www.CosmicPatterns.com. The current best software programs for MAC format are "Astro Gold" from www.astroproductsinc.com and "Time Passages" from www.AstroGraph.com available in both PC and MAC format.

More serious searchers of unknown birth times may prefer to invest in one of the research-based astrology software programs such as Jigsaw 2.2 from Astrolabe in Massachusetts, Sirius 4.1 from Cosmic Patterns in Florida, or Alphee LaVoie's Time Tunnel rectification program at www.alphee.com which greatly reduces possible birth times within the given time range using various techniques. Always be on the alert for newer versions of software that provide even more "bells and whistles". But these, and other astrological software pioneers, have now made rectification a reasonable undertaking, rather than the nearly impossible task of only a few years ago.

Be Clear with Clients on What to Expect from the Rectification Process

Few people understand the rectification process and the time it takes for the astrologer to derive the birth time from the client's life events. Basically, the wider the time range for the search, the more work for the astrologer. There are several ways to address this problem, but first, ask the client to do some homework. By following the strategies from the prior list, the client can narrow the birth time range and it is easier for the astrologer to derive the correct birth time. The client doing some homework before starting the rectification process saves time for the astrologer and money for the client. All professional astrologers are within a market standard for their services, but many price their rectification service by the search time range. A search to confirm a rounded birthtime is relatively easy and may take an hour, so the fee is quite reasonable. However, each additional hour of the search time range adds equally to the time the astrologer needs to derive the birth time. Most astrologers solve that issue by simply not accepting rectification work beyond the easy time adjustment of a few minutes. Now that we are a world community through the Internet, astrologers are getting many more requests for natal chart interpretation from clients without birth time, or only an approximation of it. I suggest to my students that even though rectification is hard work and often not profitable, if they offer the rectification service, they will most likely have that client for life.

With knowledge and practice of rectification, a 1 to 2 hour search takes about the time you prep for a consultation, about 2 hours. Of course, as your search time range expands, so does your prep time. Going forward, there are several steps to narrow the time range substantially before testing any events to derive the birth time. Most astrologers would argue that rectifying an unknown birth time is impossible within those limits; however, at least one of the suggested software programs with rectification function, Sirius 4.1 or Jigsaw 2.2, makes it possible. A rectification function in any advanced software weights the list of events to derive a few, or a handful, of possible birth times to be tested. Years ago, I beta-tested David Cochrane's early version of the Sirius rectification module with timed charts from my files. The actual birth time was always prominent in the list, though it often was not the first. Once I have tested the few promising birth times that appropriately align with the life events and personal interests and traits, the client can usually identify with the descriptors of the rising sign, the Ascendant, and its ruler, to make the final choice. Examples of the Sirius 4.1 and Jigsaw 2.2 program results follow later in this chapter.

Get a Comprehensive List of Life Events and Dates – "Event Hooks"

Once other resources are exhausted and rectification of the birth time becomes necessary, the next step is to gather a list of specific life events with dates and times, as many as possible. To begin a rectification search of any range, one must ideally start with a dozen or more dates of major life events to make the search reasonably reliable and worthwhile. Major challenging events provide the most prominent indicators for a search because many personal planets and angles are activated for the major events. It is much easier to detect a high peak of several long and short-term moving factors to natal chart planetary positions when they simultaneously activate the chart by "stacking up", rather than wading through the more ordinary life events described by fewer activated chart factors. Some astrology software is specifically designed for research and rectification searches. Bernadette Brady and Graham Dawson's Jigsaw 2.2 program marketed by Astrolabe in Massachusetts is one very good rectification search program, though the Kepler 6.0 program, Solar Fire Deluxe and WinStar 2.0 programs include good search features as well.

The major life events most useful in the rectification search are the most painful and dramatic losses in life and may include:

1. Death of a child
2. Separation from a loved one: death, break-up, etc.
3. Death of a parent
4. Surgery or major illness
5. Loss of job or job change
6. Accident with serious injury
7. Abuse of any sort

8. Victim of serious crime
9. Arrest or incarceration
10. Bankruptcy or major financial loss
11. Extreme stress from any source

Events important to note, but generally less useful in the rectification search:

1. Moving to a new location
2. Job promotion or sudden financial gain
3. Marriage
4. Birth of a child or grandchild
5. Honors or recognition
6. Retirement
7. Spiritual milestones marked by intense preparation
8. Travel
9. Purchase of a home or vehicle

The more painful events rate a much higher priority than the generally pleasant or joyful events. How much more? Some may differ, but the first list of events may be 4 or 5 times as helpful in the rectification search, for a reasonable estimate. In the case of an unusually dramatic loss at a young age, the impact may be more than 10 times more prominent than a pleasant event. For instance, the loss of a parent is a very powerful loss for anyone, but the individual is affected differently by the loss at various times of life. If the parent dies at age 95 and the client accepts the natural transition, the loss is not nearly as powerful as the loss of a parent for a young child who is scared and confused, even traumatized, by the loss. Hopefully, the list the client provides for the birth rectification search has many combinations of these events to provide a dozen or more with specific dates, and where possible, specific times. Certainly, the search may be attempted with fewer than a dozen events, but the result may not be as reliable. Also, rectification is an extremely difficult task to attempt for young people without several challenging and/or life-changing events to use as time markers.

It is helpful to have a "Rectification Questionnaire" for the client to list important life events and rate their emotional impact, from 1 highest to 10 lowest. I do not share the information about painful events being easier rectification "event hooks". I encourage the client to include as many events across the lifetime, especially where specific dates are known. Their rating of the event, as they were affected by it, is my guideline to which events I select to begin the rectification search. The following "Rectification Questionnaire" is a suggested format.

Figure 7 Sample for a Rectification Questionnaire

Client Questionnaire for Birth Time Rectification

1. Name_____ Birth Location/City/State/Country_____

   Birth Date/Mo/Yr_____ Birth Time _____AM/PM Birth Time Source_____

   Range of birth time search – Number of hours from _____ to _____AM/PM

2. Describe your work or career_____ Education level_____

   Hobbies/Interests_____

3. Family/Children_____

4. Describe your personality/How do others see you_____

5. Describe your most significant relationship_____

6. List important life events (Dy/Mo/Yr): marriage, recognition, births, accident, surgery, deaths, divorces, etc.

DATE	EVENT OR SITUATION	RATE THEIR IMPORTANCE – from 1 low to 10 high
1. _____	_____	_____
2. _____	_____	_____
3. _____	_____	_____
4. _____	_____	_____
5. _____	_____	_____
6. _____	_____	_____
7. _____	_____	_____
8. _____	_____	_____
9. _____	_____	_____
10. _____	_____	_____
11. _____	_____	_____
12. _____	_____	_____
13. _____	_____	_____
14. _____	_____	_____
15. _____	_____	_____
16. _____	_____	_____
17. _____	_____	_____
18. _____	_____	_____
19. _____	_____	_____
20. _____	_____	_____

Client Information Needed for Birth Time Rectification

1. Birth Information:

    a. date, month and year _____

    b. city, state, country _____

    c. birth time and source _____

    d. If uncertain birth time, what is the time range to search? from _____ to _____

2. Biography and Background:

    a. Personality traits _____
    _____

    b. Hobbies & interests _____
    _____

    c. Education & training _____
    _____

    d. Career or Work_____
    _____

    e. Relationship history_____
    _____

    f. Family situation and history_____
    _____

    g. Early childhood history_____
    _____

3. List Major Life Events from Childhood to Now with Date, Month and Year

4. Rate Events 1-low to 5-high Impact and List Events in Chronicle Order:

    a. Accident(s) or Surgery

    b. Births

    c. Marriage(s)

    d. Divorce or Separation

    e. Deaths

    f. Failure, Loss or Victim

    g. Success, Benefit or Honor

    h. Relocation

If the Quick Test Fails, Plan to Rectify!

Develop a Case Theory from the Biography and Major Life Events

Once the client provides the biography and list of important life events, it is time well spent to think about what features of the natal chart might support a case theory. For instance, hard situations early in life suggest that the Moon may be in close hard aspect to another planet that appropriately describes the situation. A controlling and distant father, with no praise for his talented son, may suggest that the natal Moon is in close hard aspect to Saturn or possibly Pluto. Are we then surprised to find the Moon in partile square to Pluto in Elton John's chart, who suffered a lifetime of his father's neglect amid the approval he sought and never got? The Moon is a reliable key to the emotional foundation of a person, much of which is grounded in the early family life.

Figure 8 Elton John Birth Chart, Possible Rounded Birth Time

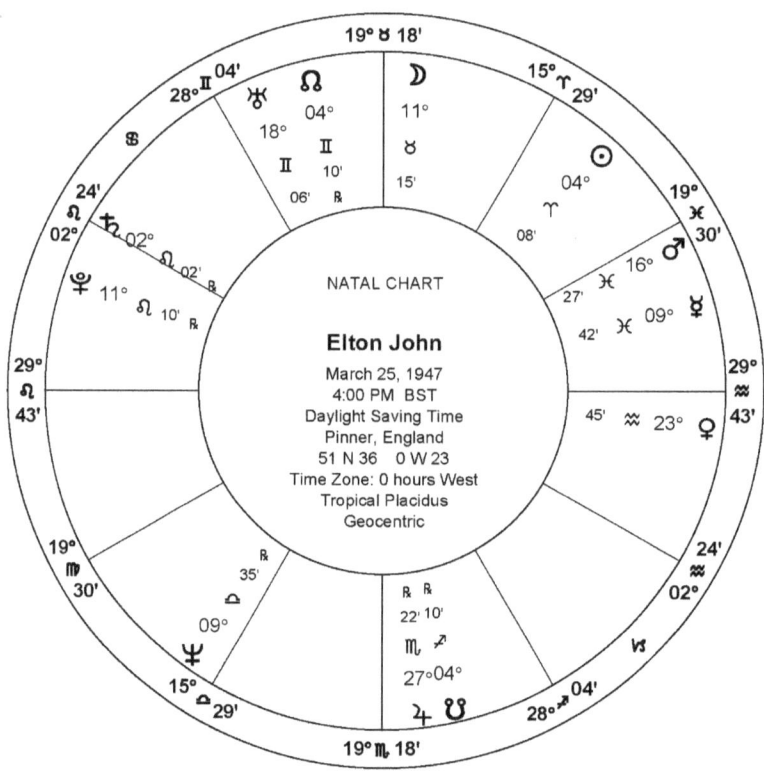

I have found other useful "tells" to build a case theory. If the person seems to have low self-esteem, the Sun is often in hard aspect to the Ascendant, particularly the square from the fourth house. In Elton's case, I would expect the Aries Sun identity to be strong, based on his decades of composing and performing his music. That assumption is confirmed by his Sun in a close kite pattern of trines and sextiles with the North Node at the apex. Of course, we cannot create the whole chart by case theory, but with close study of the biography, we can glean the possible natal chart descriptors of the life situation. The Moon's close natal connections are the best "tells" for building a "case theory".

It is easiest to start with the five or six most important events to test. Testing only these events with several movement methods, they most easily align with appropriate astrological descriptors to narrow the birthtime to one or more good choices for further testing. In an hour time range, it is common to find two possible times to test; in a three-hour range three or four possible times to test, and so on. The point is, the wider the birthtime search range, the more times that show possibility. How to narrow the time range is another chapter, but for now, know that once you have the major events aligned with appropriate astrological descriptors on or near the event date, all of the other events should also align appropriately on or very near the event date.

Find Planets in One-Degree Orb for "Aspect Hooks"- Beware the Moon

In modern astrology, the techniques commonly used for the process of rectification provide varying degrees of success. Indeed, the process is so complex that few astrologers attempt the task because the time involved is extensive and few clients want to pay the fee for an extended search. As a practical result, very little is written on the topic, and therefore, few astrologers feel well enough schooled in the art to offer birth time rectification as a service.

Now that the groundwork of listing the dates of important life events is done, the next step is to search the natal planetary placements for close aspect connections within one-degree. The premise is that when planets or the Moon's nodes are in close natal aspect, or when one of them is activated by Solar Arc Direction, Progression or Transit, so are the other planets or points in the configuration. Think of the Richter Scale that measure earthquake intensity. – close aspects provide just such a measure for the astrologer to easily "Hook" to important events and life situations. Therefore, we should list all of the one to two-degree close-aspect networks of the chart in order of closeness of orb. Orbs beyond two-degrees are less helpful as the "hook" upon which to begin the rectification search. Of course, it is possible that the natal Moon or an Angle may also be involved in the close aspect network, but that cannot be determined with reasonable certainty until the birth time range is narrowed to a few minutes.

If the chart has no planets connected within one or two degrees of a major hard aspect (conjunction, opposition, square, or quincunx) then start experimenting with the next closest aspect, even if it is a harmonious trine or sextile, or a minor hard aspect. Using a computer and appropriate software greatly facilitates close aspect searches and experimentation with "age-arcs" for timing of their activation. Of course, set the "working chart" for a time midway of the search time range. In a 24-hour search, 12:00 pm, a Noon "working chart" time is a reasonable starting point.

Establish a Working Chart for the Midpoint of the Search Time Range

A good place to start is to set the "working birth time" to a point half-way between the ranges of known time. If the birth time is not known or narrowed, set the chart for Noon. If mother says the birth occurred at 4:30 AM and an aunt recalls that the birth was after the Sun was up at 6:00 AM, set the chart for 5:15 AM. One may safely assume that at least one pair of the Angles will nearly always be involved for major events. Most astrologers agree that one or both pair of the chart Angles are activated by movement in one-degree orb at major life events. Personal issues such as health, and relationships will show involvement of the Ascendant / Descendant axis (1st and 7th); and status, career and home issues will show involvement of the Midheaven / Imum Coeli axis (10th and 4th).

The process of rectification must begin by establishing a "working birth time" to begin testing the key life events for appropriate astrological descriptors when the event occurred. Since the Angles are so time sensitive, moving approximately 1-degree every 4-minutes of clock time, they are the key to any rectification search. Set the chart for the midpoint of the search time range. If the birthtime search is between 6:00 am and 11:00 am for the birth date at the given location, 8:30 am is the time midpoint that narrows the Moon range by half. In a 5-hour range, the Moon moves 2 ½ -degrees, and by starting from the midpoint of the time range, we have cut the Moon range by half, a bit more than 1-degree. Whatever the time range of the rectification search, this method provides a set of "working Angles" to which planets can be moved to experiment and determine when each Angle is activated for selected life events. Of course, the converse is true; the Angles may move to activate planets but since we have not yet determined the Angles by rectification, it is better to reserve that search as a final confirmation of our rectified Angles and birth time.

The position of the natal Moon is another important timing factor in rectification work. Since the Moon moves approximately 1-degree every 2 hours, the Moon's position might range from a small fraction of 1 degree for births less than 1 hour of exact, to as many as 3-degrees for births rounded to a quarter of a day; and 6 to 7 degrees for a half-day. One need not allow for greater range for the natal Moon position in totally unknown birth times because setting the chart for Noon means that the Moon is, at most, within 6-7 degrees of exact, plus, or minus.

Set A Procedure for the Rectification Search

The more commonly used rectification techniques are: Solar Arc Directions, Secondary Progressions and Transits of outer planets. To a lesser extent, Eclipses, Decanantes and Dwads are useful. Solar Arc Directions provide a distinct advantage for the initial search because the Angles and the planets move consistently at the rate of the Sun, varying from 57 minutes per

---

2. Tyl, Noel, Solar Arcs, Astrology's Most Successful Predictive System, Llewellyn Publishing Co., St. Paul, MN, 2001; pg 290

day in the summer, to 61 minutes per day in the winter. Noel Tyl states, "Direct Solar Arc aspects from and to the Midheaven and Ascendant are extremely important in preparing and testing rectification, as well as for analysis of developments in the past and projections into the future."[2] To quickly estimate the Solar Arc movement for ease of hand-calculation, one may reasonably use the rounded average of 1 degree per day of solar movement and apply it to all planets and speculative angles for the various ages at life events. It is called the Radix method, less in favor now that astrology software is so far advanced from the earlier "short-cuts" to calculation. For most others, the computer readily calculates the Solar Arc for any date of birth to any event date, and moves each planet and chart point the exact Solar Arc distance. According to Dr. Dobyns, "…the most effective [of the Directed systems] in my experience is to move the whole chart the same distance which the Sun has moved in the Day-for-a-Year system; that is, the distance called the solar arc."[3]

Secondary Progressions of planetary motion, or "Day for a Year" in the ephemeris, moves each planet at its own speed, rather than the uniform motion of the Solar Arc. "In this system, each day after birth is equated with a day actually lived, so that to understand the developments in the life of a person who is twenty years old, one looks in the ephemeris at the date twenty days after birth."[4] The system works well for planet-to-planet aspect connections at the various ages of events, but it is much less effective for determining the time of sensitive Angles. The Ascendant is particularly variable in the Secondary Progressed method, moving from 47 minutes per day while passing through Virgo and Libra, to nearly 2 degrees per day while passing though Pisces and Aries – and locations of high latitude can produce even wider variances. However, if one wishes to use the Secondary Progressed method for movement of the planets, and the Solar Arc method for movement of the Angles, the search may produce more reliable results with fewer variables.

Once the initial search is completed and the possible birth times narrowed to just a few, transits of the slow-moving outer planets serve well as timing indicators when in aspect to natal planets. It is relatively easy to search an ephemeris for the positions of Mars, Jupiter, Saturn, Uranus, Neptune, and Pluto for the dates of important life events to see what natal planets or configurations are activated, and even easier in a computer search. Once the Solar Arc Directions to planets appropriate to life events are determined and the search narrowed, Outer Planet Transits are useful to fine-tune the birth time and determine the "good candidate" Angles.

Less reliable methods for rectification are Eclipses, Planetary Returns, Pre-Natal Epoch, Physical Appearance, Character Traits and Degree Meanings, though the Hindu 2 ½ degree subdivisions of each sign called Dwadashamsas, dwads for short, are sometimes helpful in determining the Ascendant degree once other techniques have been used to narrow the birth

---

3. Dobyns, Zipporah, Progressions, Directions and Rectification, TIA Publications, a division of CRCS Inc, Los Angeles, CA; 1975, pg 34.

4. IBID

time search to less than 15 minutes.[5]

An important caveat of Dr. Dobyns: "One crucial rule to remember is that there must be an appropriate aspect for each event in each system of current patterns. That is, the event must show in Secondary Progressions, Solar Arc Directions and in Transits."[6] If systems are selectively "mixed and matched", then it is possible to make a case for most any birth time. Always keep in mind that in the course of one day, twenty-four hours, planet to planet movement will not move enough to distinguish birth time. Only the Angles that move one-degree every four-minutes of clock time can align appropriate astrological descriptors with life events. However, for searches more than two hours, the Moon moves one-degree which may move into or away from a close "aspect hook" that may modify your "case theory"

A Checklist for the Rectification Search

- Begin by getting a list of important life events with dates and a complete biography from the client
- Run a "working chart" set for noon, or a point halfway between the widest range of disputed or reported times
- Search the list of life events for a few "event hooks" to begin: choose the 5 to 6 most dramatic and painful events, or search a year where multiple major life events occurred
- Create a table for the possible Moon position for each hour of 24 hours
- Create a table for the possible dwad position of the Moon for each hour of 24 hours
- Search the chart for close major hard aspect patterns within a 1-2-degree orb at most, omitting the Moon and Angles, to find the "hard aspect hooks" for a starting point
- Search the "apex point(s)" of all of the 1-2-degree hard aspects hooks

Align Astrological Descriptors "Aspect Hooks" to "Event Hooks"

Now that we have gleaned what we can from the "working natal chart", we need to systematically apply the astrological techniques to move the chart in time in our attempt to align actual life events with appropriate astrological signatures that occur with regularity and that may be accurately forecast. Restated, we are using both the "aspect hook(s)" and the "event hook(s)" to begin the search. Again, the order is not as important as searching without prejudice for a birth time that reliably matches events.

- Create a table for each of the most dramatic few life events whereby the directed Midheaven is moved to conjunct each of the planets or Moon's nodes involved in a

---

4. Dobyns, Zipporah, Progressions, Directions and Rectification, p 15.

5. Dobyns, Zipporah, Progressions, Directions and Rectification, p 19.

1-2-degree hard aspect pattern. Count backward from a point equal to the number of degrees of the person's age at the event

- EXAMPLE: If the Sun and South Node at 15 Scorpio are square Jupiter at 15 Leo, and an important event occurred that damaged the client's career or reputation when he was 35, then subtract 35 degrees from each planet in the configuration to derive a "working Midheaven" that would active that close natal hard aspect at age 35. By subtracting 35-degrees from the planets, the "working Midheaven" would be 10-degrees of a cardinal sign. If the planets are moved ahead 35-degrees by solar arc direction to activate the "working Midheaven" it would be at 20-degrees of a mutable sign at 35 years. Continue the same process for each leg of the close aspect networks identified earlier.

- Create a table for the same most dramatic few life events whereby the directed Ascendant is moved to conjunct each of the planets or nodes involved in a 1-2-degree hard aspect pattern. Count backwards from a point equal to the number of degrees of the person's age at the event

- Create a table for the same most dramatic few life events whereby the directed Midheaven and Ascendant are moved to conjunct each of the "apex points" or open points opposite the planets or nodes involved in the same 1-2-degree hard aspect pattern(s). Count backwards from a point equal to the number of degrees of the person's age at the event

- For those of you who own the Jigsaw 2.2 research and rectification software, consult the "Help" feature in the program for directions on how to enter the life event data and select the techniques you will use to sort for the program to provide a list of possible birth times and a percentage of accuracy. Note that even with the Jigsaw program, such searches of known birth times, though helpful, did include the approximate range of the recorded birth time but often not the first choice. Software is wonderful for the rectification task, but it is the astrologer's trained eye and astrological judgment that produces a good, rectified birth time.

Know the Search Time Range to Determine Where to Start

Of course, the specific order that one proceeds in the rectification search is not as important as beginning with chart elements that are known within one-degree or less. In establishing one or more "Aspect Hooks" and aligning them with important "Event Hooks" we are better able to search for the important unknowns – the position of the Moon and the Angles.

The search time range dictates the rectification process and the time it takes to test all of the options. It follows that a 24-hour birth time search is greatly more difficult than a one-hour search, so our first task is to narrow the time range. If the time range is 2-hours, the

Moon may have moved 1-degree; in 6-hours 3-degrees, in 12-hours 6-degrees, and so on. For the wider time search, the Moon should be aligned first before attending to the more precise confirmation of birthtime by aligning the Angles. In the wider time search, it is common to find peaks at twelve-hour internals that mimic a pair of Angles, ASC/DES or MC/IC. Testing will confirm which, but in my experience, the most prominent peak is the ascendant, and the lesser peak 12-hours later is the descendant. The Sirius 4.1 program by David Cochrane, www.CosmicPatterns.com, is a helpful tool to narrow the large time range to a handful of possible birth times.

Figure 9 Graph is a Sirius 4.1 24-hour Birthtime Search for Cate Blanchette

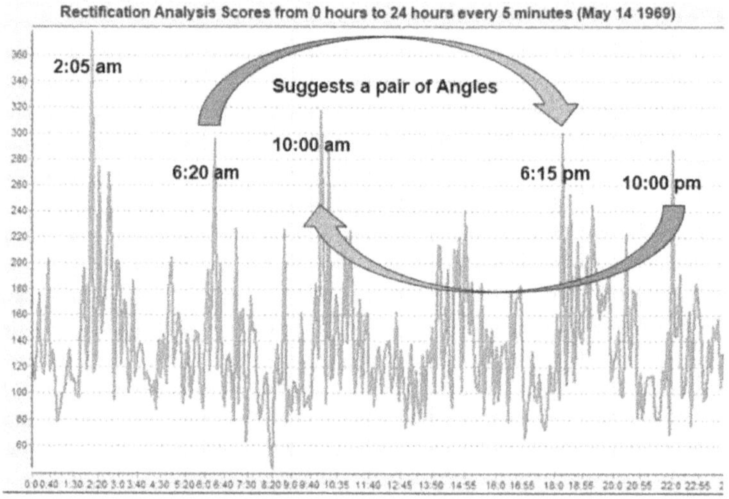

Figure 10 Graph is a Jigsaw 2.2 24-hour Birthtime Search for Cate Blanchette

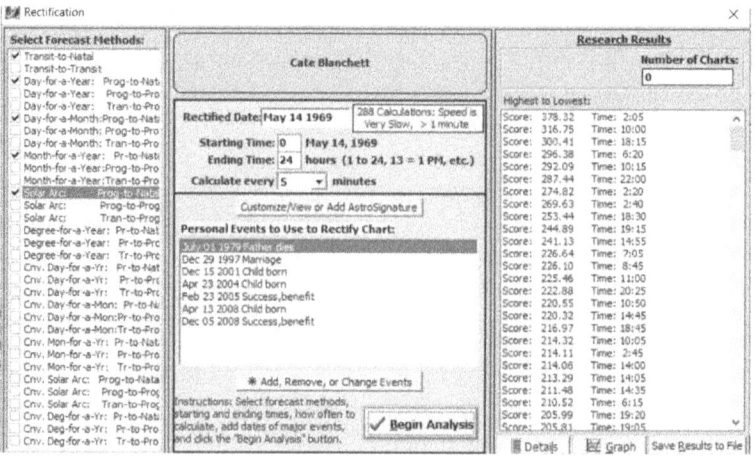

The graphs are based only on a few event dates for Cate Blanchette. More events would provide even better results for the birthtime search, which again reminds us that celebrity or historical charts are not good rectification candidates. Rectification works best with interaction with someone who will provide feedback.

For wide time searches, twelve hours or more, I first narrow the range by posting major life events in the software and choosing the movement techniques for the test. In this case, I chose, outer planet transits, secondary progressions, tertiary progressions, minor progressions, and solar arc directions. The programming is based on many astrological signatures or descriptors, such as Moon trine Venus for a romantic situation. As you can see, I could have chosen more movement techniques, but the purpose is achieved – the 24-hour time range is narrowed to a small handful of possible times to test.

Figure 11 graph is a Jigsaw 2.2 2-Hour Birthtime Search for Paul McCartney

Time	Asc	MC	Trans	S.Progs	S.Arcs	Overall
1:01 am	08°♒47'-10°♒39'	09°♐00'-10°♐00'	5/5	2/3	3/3	100%
2:45 am	09°♈14'-12°♈02'	03°♑15'-04°♑15'	3/4	0/1	2/4	63%
3:23 am	02°♉15'-04°♉01'	12°♑00'-12°♑45'	2/3	2/2	3/3	67%
4:33 am	03°♊32'-04°♊38'	28°♑30'-29°♑15'	4/5	2/3	3/4	78%
6:51 am	09°♋26'-10°♋13'	03°♓15'-04°♓15'	1/5	0/1	1/1	60%
9:03 am	04°♌01'-04°♌39'	09°♈00'-10°♈00'	2/5	2/2	3/4	71%
2:22 pm	28°♍52'-29°♍26'	28°♊30'-29°♊15'	1/4	1/2	1/3	33%

Figure 12 Graph is a Sirius 4.1 2-hour Birthtime Search for Paul McCartney

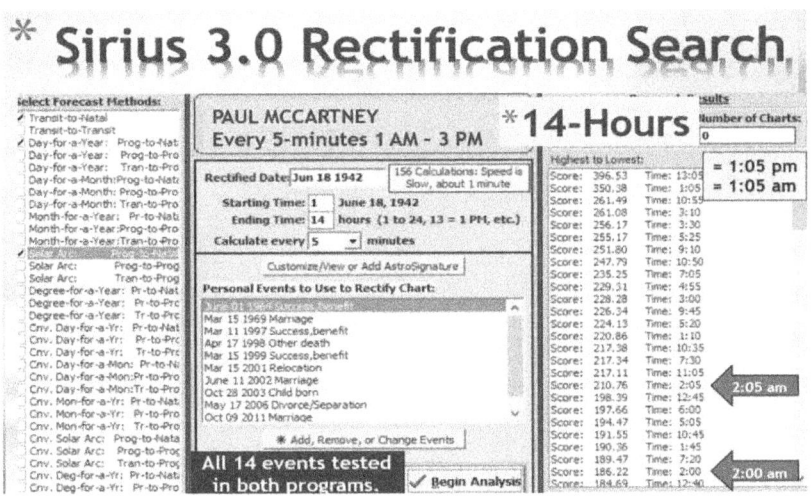

If the Quick Test Fails, Plan to Rectify!

I also use Jigsaw 2.2 by Bernadette Brady and Graham Dawson, sold by Astrolabe www.alabe.com, that is very different than Sirius 4.1. In Jigsaw, the event dates are entered but the movement techniques are limited to solar arc direction, secondary progression, tertiary progression, and outer planet transits.

Most often, the results are similar but not the same. Jigsaw is programmed to count planet, angle, and nodal aspect hits by 8th harmonic (conjunctions, oppositions, squares, semi-squares, and sesqui-squares) and 12th harmonic (conjunctions, oppositions, squares trines, sextiles, quincunxes, and semi-sextiles). The more major the event, the more hits occur to derive the chart angles, Midheaven/Imum Coeli and the Ascendant/Descendant. By comparing the search program results, the birthtimes echoed in both systems are where I start testing, particularly those most near my case theory.

In the test of Paul McCartney's 14-hour birth time search, both Sirius 4.1 and Jigsaw 2.2 gave nearly identical results and yet, the disputed birth records say 2:00 am and 2:00 pm. He was born during the summer when Daylight Savings Time was in force, but because his birth was in the midst of World War II and England was observing Double Daylight Time (War Time), could it be that they continued to record birth time in regular Daylight Savings Time? The problems we might face with time reporting around the world are endless and difficult to resolve for some locations, especially for births prior to WWII. To emphasize the point, no one else cares about precise birth time except the astrologer

Time Range within Fifteen Minutes – Angles Move Four Degrees

- **Prince William**

Figure 13 A Birth Certificate Quick Test with Solar Arc Direction for Prince William

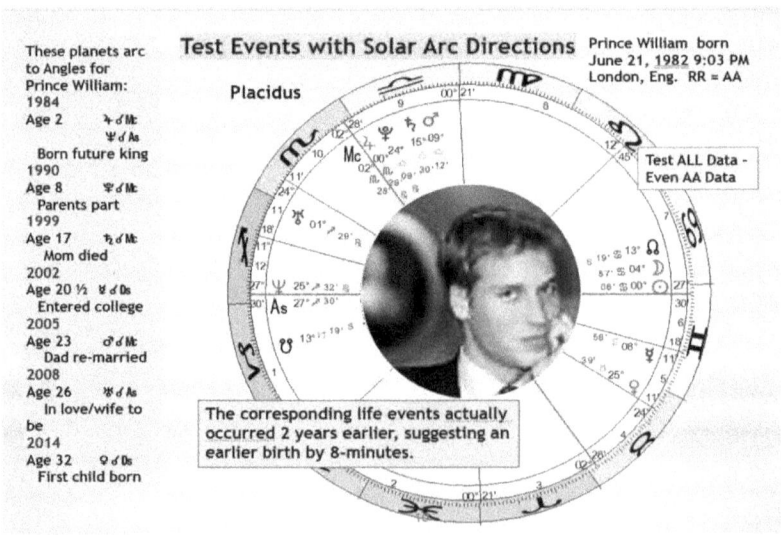

Prince William appears to have an exact birth time; however, with a simple test with Solar Arc Direction the age at which the natal chart is activated is two years later suggesting that his birth time is 7 to 8-minutes earlier. By adjusting his birth time 8-minutes earlier, the major life events align.

Figure 14 A Rectified Birth Time Quick Test with Solar Arc Direction for Prince William

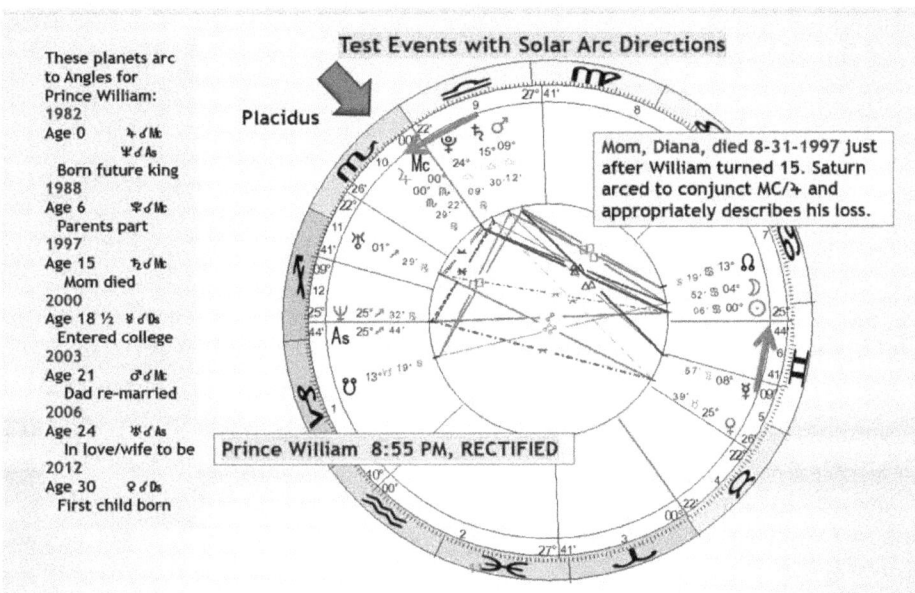

Prince William's chart is another example of how astrologers make small adjustments to birth time for appropriate astrological descriptors to consistently align with the life events. It is when the small time adjustment does not align events with the activated planets and aspects that the rectification process begins by testing for confirmation with several movement techniques.

Time Range within Three Hours – Angles Move One and a Half Signs

- **Anna Nicole Smith**

Many astrologers refer to www.Astro.com, previously known as Astro-Data-Bank, for free and well-resourced birth time information for thousands of public and historical figures. For Anna Nicole Smith, Lois M. Rodden quotes media for date; time unknown = X (spec 5:30 AM). Later Sy Scholfield quotes an article "Britney's Downfall In The Stars" by Nadine Linge, Sept 22, 2007 in the Daily Star: "Anna was born on November 28th … Sagittarius, Libra rising." Approximate time gives mid-Libra rising based on article.

Figure 15 A Quick Test with Solar Arc Direction for Anna Nicole Smith

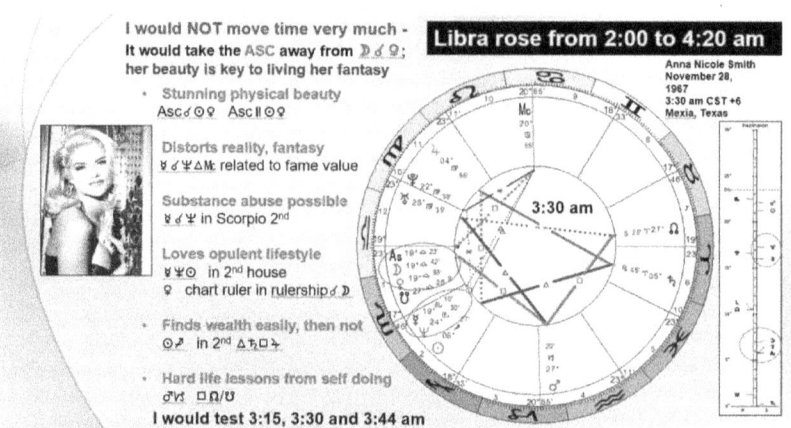

I created a 3-hour search from 1:30 am to 4:30 am for Anna and developed a case theory from her traits and biographical events. Since Libra only rose from 2:00 am to 4:20 am and her Moon and Venus are closely conjunct in Libra, my case theory was based on her compelling beauty. By aligning the natal Moon and Venus conjunct the Libra Ascendant, 3:30 am was where the search began.

I then tested the birth time range with Jigsaw 2.2 software, particularly looking for times with a high percentage that fit my case theory. In using software to narrow the search range or to confirm the case theory, the more events with specific dates that span the life, the higher percentage. Not only did Astro.com have just thirteen events, but they were all within thirteen years – not the whole life span.

Biography: www.AstroDataBank.com

Figure 16 A Jigsaw 2.2 24-Hour Test for Anna Nicole Smith with Solar Arc, Progressions, Transits

Anna Nicole Smith ith

Jigsaw 2.2

Finished - Best Scoring Birth Time: 3:44 am

Time	Asc	MC	Trans	S.Progs	S.Arcs	Overall
3:13 am	14°♎12'-17°♎11'	15°♋15'-18°♋30'	0/2	1/1	1/2	42%
3:44 am	21°♎03'-23°♎31'	22°♋45'-25°♋30'	2/2	1/2	2/3	83%
5:45 am	16°♏47'-19°♏00'	22°♌45'-25°♌30'	1/2	2/3	2/3	67%
1:32 pm	18°♓17'-22°♓42'	22°♐45'-25°♐30'	1/2	1/1	2/4	50%
3:11 pm	24°♈11'-29°♈04'	15°♑15'-18°♑30'	0/2	0/1	2/2	0%

3:44

Times 12-hours apart are chart flipped on MC axis
Only 3:44 am and 3:13 am give
Libra Ascendant

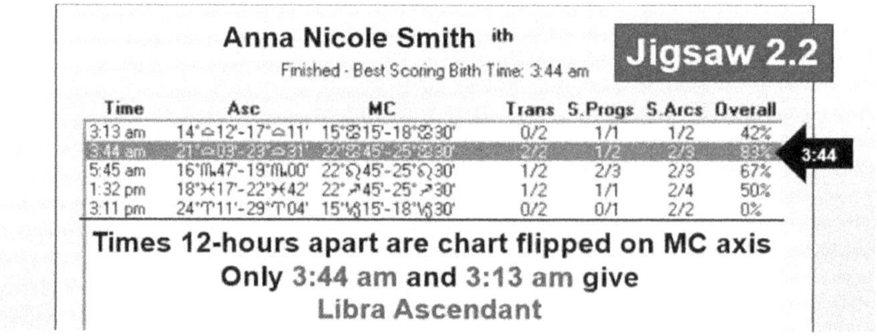

April 1994	Married multi-millionaire	Age 26
June 1994	Broke two ribs by falling	Age 26 ½
Spring 1995	Rich husband died, age 90	Age 27 (serious drug use)
March 7, 2002	Court awarded $88 m	Age 34 ½
December 30, 2004	Lost in Court $88 million	Age 37
September 7, 2006	Baby girl born	Age 38 ¾
September 10, 2006	Death of son	Age 38 ¾
February 8, 2007	Own death, Drug overdose	Age 39 1/6

Once the time range has been narrowed to a few good times for more intensive testing, software provides several ways to see what is activated in the natal chart at the time of the event. Since we are seeking the correct birth time, it follows that we test movement of the Angles to Planets, and Planets to Angles with at least three or four movement techniques. For Ana, I tested 3:15 am and 3:44 am with the "Time Map" in Solar Fire 9 plus the Angles to Planets and Planets to Angles listing in the twelfth harmonic in both Solar Arc Directions and Secondary Progressions. The 3:15 am chart for Anna Nicole was too early to properly align with events and the 3:44 am chart was too late for consistent alignment to events. The 3:30 am chart will serve well as the "working chart" for the final fine-tuning of plus or minus a couple of clock time minutes to adjust the Angles a half-degree.

Figure 17 Solar Fire 9-Solar Arc Directions, Angles to Planets for Anna Nicole Smith 3:44 am

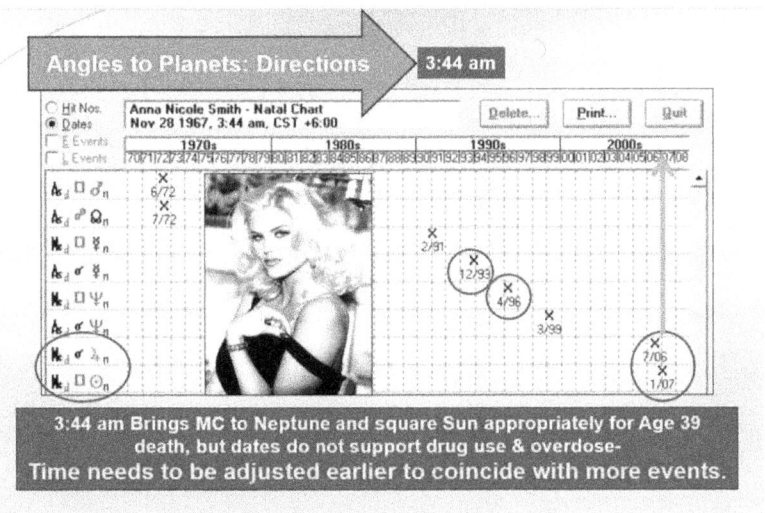

If the Quick Test Fails, Plan to Rectify!

Figure 18 Solar Fire 9-Solar Arc Directions, Angles to Planets for Anna Nicole Smith 3:15 am

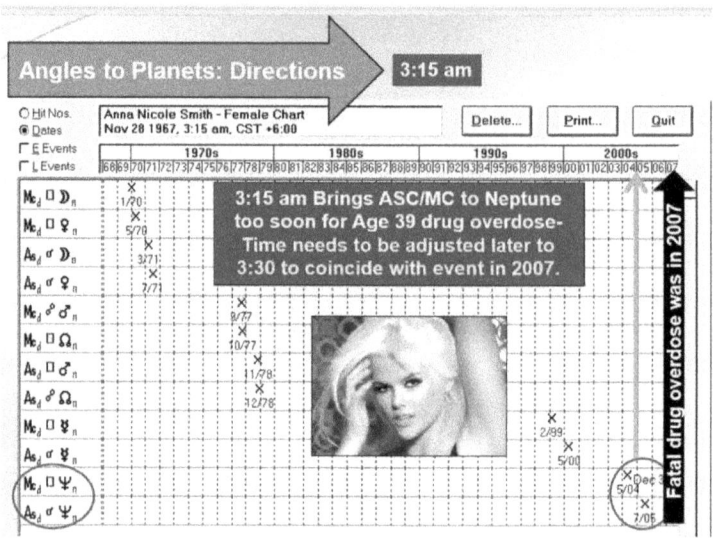

Figure 19 Solar Fire 9-Solar Arc and Progressed Planets to Angles for Anna Nicole Smith 3:44 & 3:15 am

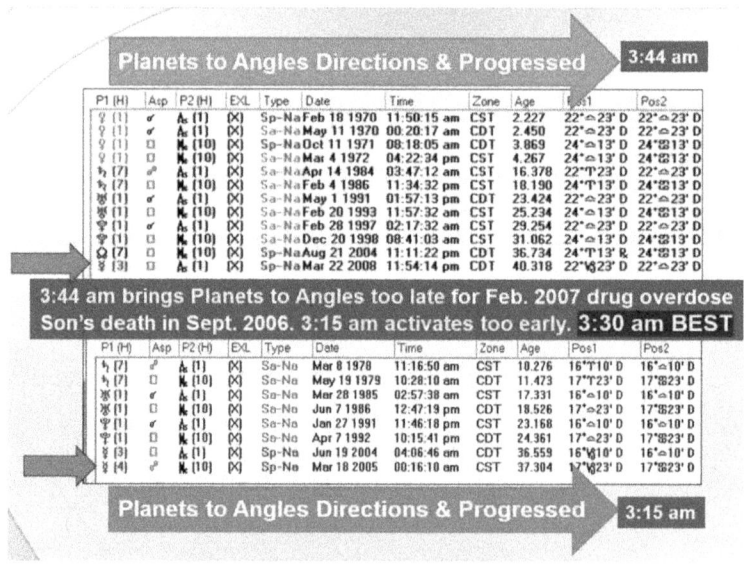

The New Complete Book of Chart Rectification

Figure 20 Solar Fire 9-Transits with Relocated Chart Angles for Anna Nicole Smith

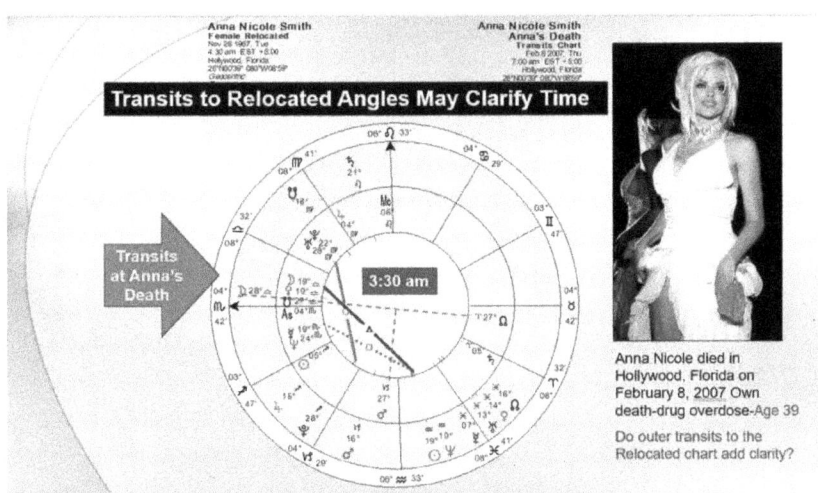

Time Range within Six Hours – Angles Move Three Signs

- **Princess Diana**

According to Astro.com, Princess Diana has used two very different birth times with astrologers creating some confusion. The time range varies by six hours for our confirmation search. Astro.com tells us that one of Diana's British astrologers, Penny Thornton, gives 2:10 PM, "just before the start of play at Wimbledon."

"Separate and various reports have confirmed the birth time of 7:45 PM. In the Nov/Dec 1997 Astrological Journal, Vol. 39, No. 5, Nick Campion writes, 'When Diana's engagement to Charles was announced, her birth time was given as 2:00 pm on 1 July 1961, Sandringham. The time was then corrected to 7:45 pm and confirmed in a letter to Charles Harvey from the Queen's assistant press secretary as being from Diana's mother (note 15, p 168). 7:45 pm is the time used by Debbie Frank, Diana's astrologer for the last eight years, and I would recommend that it remain the Princess's officially recognized birth time…' Debbie Frank told me that in the eighteen months before Diana died, she raised the question of Diana's birth time with her, and Diana was insistent that she was born in the evening." Charles Harvey

Major difficulties in childhood are most often described in the natal chart with the Moon in close hard aspect. Is it clear which birth time fits Diana's childhood experience?

Figure 21 Solar Fire 9-Two Birth Times for Princess Diana

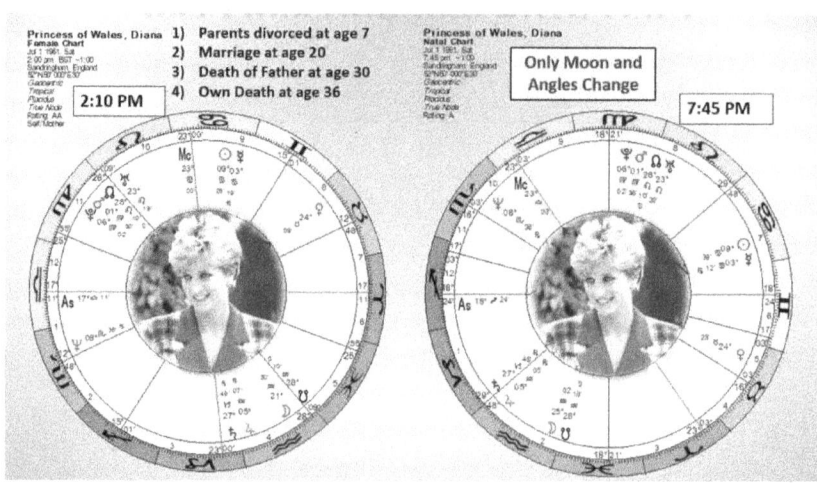

Astro.com listed only a few events for Diana, so more information is needed for a definitive rectification, however, we can test with the life events that we have.

- Parents divorced Jan 1969
- Inherited money 1 July 1979
- Engagement 24 February 1981
- Marriage 29 July 1981
- Prince William born 21 June 1982
- Prince Harry born 15 September 1984
- Book came out 15 June 1992
- Met Dr. Khan September 1995
- $26 million settled August 1996
- Divorce dates 28 August 1996
- Dr. Khan left her 11 July 1997
- Met Dodi Fayed 14 July 1997
- Death accident 31 August 1997

Simply testing Angles to Planets and Planets to Angles with Solar Arc Directions we can easily see which birth time appropriately allows activation of the natal chart on, or very near, the event date. Compare the Tables 16 and 17 of Solar Arc Direction for both birth times, 2:10 pm and 7:45 pm.

60   The New Complete Book of Chart Rectification

Use Basic Astrology and Start with the Biography

(Image credit: Central Press)
Marie Claire, by Emily Dixon,
Published September 14, 2020.

In 1969, the family unit ruptured when Diana's mother reportedly abruptly left her father for Peter Shand Kydd, an Australian wallpaper tycoon (no known connection to Camilla Shand). What ensued was a courtroom and custody battle that resulted in what her brother called an "unhappy childhood."

"Diana and I had two older sisters who were away at school, so she and I were very much in it together and I did talk to her about it," Spencer explained in a revealing 2020 interview in The Sunday Times. "Our father was a quiet and constant source of love, but our mother wasn't cut out for maternity. Not her fault, she couldn't do it. She was in love with someone else—infatuated, really."

Following an intense custody battle (in which Frances's mother, Ruth, testified against her), the Spencer children lived with their father permanently. According to her brother, Diana felt abandoned by their mother. "While she was packing her stuff to leave, she promised Diana she'd come back to see her. Diana used to wait on the doorstep for her, but she never came," Charles, Diana's brother, told The Sunday Times.

Table 16: Planets to Angles / Angles to Planets for Princess Diana for 2:10 pm Birth Time

Table 17: Planets to Angles / Angles to Planets for Princess Diana 7:45 pm Birth Time

P1 (H)	Asp	P2 (H)	EXL	Type	Date
♄ (1)	⚻	☊ (8)	(X)	Sa-Na	Nov 17 1961
☽ (2)	☍	☊ (8)	(X)	Sa-Na	Oct 19 1964
♀ (5)	□	☊ (8)	(X)	Sa-Na	Jun 21 1965
As (1)	⚹	Mc (10)	(X)	Sa-Na	May 22 1966
♅ (8)	☌	☊ (8)	(X)	Sa-Na	Aug 3 1966
Mc (10)	⚹	☊ (8)	(X)	Sa-Na	Nov 20 1966
☉ (7)	⚻	As (1)	(X)	Sa-Na	Sep 11 1970
As (1)	△	☊ (8)	(X)	Sa-Na	Oct 9 1971
♇ (9)	□	As (1)	(X)	Sa-Na	Jul 1 1974
♃ (2)	⚹	As (1)	(X)	Sa-Na	Jun 30 1975
☉ (7)	□	Mc (10)	(X)	Sa-Na	Jul 31 1975
☿ (7)	⚻	As (1)	(X)	Sa-Na	Jun 26 1977
♂ (9)	□	As (1)	(X)	Sa-Na	Feb 13 1979
♃ (2)	△	Mc (10)	(X)	Sa-Na	May 17 1980
~~♆ (11)~~	~~□~~	~~☊ (8)~~	~~(X)~~	~~Sa-Na~~	~~Jan 14 1982~~
☿ (7)	□	Mc (10)	(X)	Sa-Na	May 15 1982
☊ (9)	□	As (1)	(X)	Sa-Na	Oct 7 1982
♄ (2)	⚹	As (1)	(X)	Sa-Na	Feb 22 1983
♃ (2)	☍	☊ (8)	(X)	Sa-Na	Oct 3 1985
☽ (3)	□	As (1)	(X)	Sa-Na	Jan 22 1986
♀ (7)	☍	As (1)	(X)	Sa-Na	Sep 24 1986
♅ (9)	□	As (1)	(X)	Sa-Na	Nov 6 1987
♄ (2)	△	Mc (10)	(X)	Sa-Na	Jan 10 1988
☽ (3)	⚻	Mc (10)	(X)	Sa-Na	Dec 8 1990
♀ (7)	△	Mc (10)	(X)	Sa-Na	Aug 10 1991
♄ (2)	☍	☊ (8)	(X)	Sa-Na	May 24 1993
☽ (3)	⚻	☊ (8)	(X)	Sa-Na	Apr 20 1996
♀ (7)	⚹	☊ (8)	(X)	Sa-Na	Dec 20 1996
~~As (1)~~	~~□~~	~~Mc (10)~~	~~(X)~~	~~Sa-Na~~	~~Nov 18 1997~~
~~Mc (11)~~	~~□~~	~~☊ (8)~~	~~(X)~~	~~Sa-Na~~	~~May 18 1998~~

P1 (H)	Asp	P2 (H)	EXL	Type	Date
As (1)	⚻	♀ (5)	(X)	Sa-Na	Oct 21 1967
As (1)	⚹	☽ (2)	(X)	Sa-Na	Jun 22 1968
☊ (8)	⚻	♃ (2)	(X)	Sa-Na	Oct 12 1968
☊ (8)	☌	♇ (8)	(X)	Sa-Na	Oct 10 1969
Mc (10)	⚹	♂ (8)	(X)	Sa-Na	Jul 14 1970
As (1)	⚹	☋ (2)	(X)	Sa-Na	Oct 9 1971
As (1)	△	☊ (8)	(X)	Sa-Na	Oct 9 1971
Mc (10)	△	☿ (7)	(X)	Sa-Na	Mar 3 1972
☊ (8)	⚹	♆ (10)	(X)	Sa-Na	Jul 2 1972
☊ (8)	⚹	☉ (7)	(X)	Sa-Na	Jul 31 1973
Mc (10)	□	♃ (2)	(X)	Sa-Na	Feb 28 1974
Mc (10)	⚹	♇ (8)	(X)	Sa-Na	Feb 27 1975
As (1)	△	♂ (8)	(X)	Sa-Na	Jun 3 1975
As (1)	☍	☿ (7)	(X)	Sa-Na	Jan 20 1977
Mc (10)	☌	♆ (10)	(X)	Sa-Na	Nov 18 1977
Mc (10)	△	☉ (7)	(X)	Sa-Na	Dec 17 1978
As (1)	△	♇ (8)	(X)	Sa-Na	Jan 16 1980
As (1)	⚹	♆ (10)	(X)	Sa-Na	Oct 6 1982
☊ (9)	□	As (1)	(X)	Sa-Na	Oct 7 1982
As (1)	☍	☉ (7)	(X)	Sa-Na	Nov 4 1983
☊ (9)	△	♀ (5)	(X)	Sa-Na	Jan 21 1989
☊ (9)	⚻	☽ (2)	(X)	Sa-Na	Sep 23 1989
☊ (9)	△	♄ (1)	(X)	Sa-Na	Aug 21 1992
☊ (9)	⚻	☋ (2)	(X)	Sa-Na	Jan 6 1993
Mc (11)	□	♅ (8)	(X)	Sa-Na	Apr 24 1993
Mc (11)	☍	♀ (5)	(X)	Sa-Na	Jun 5 1994
Mc (11)	□	☽ (2)	(X)	Sa-Na	Feb 4 1995
As (1)	□	Mc (10)	(X)	Sa-Na	Nov 18 1997
Mc (11)	⚹	♄ (1)	(X)	Sa-Na	Dec 31 1997
As (1)	⚻	♅ (8)	(X)	Sa-Na	Mar 6 1998

Just by testing with one movement method, it is clear that the 7:45 pm birth time is more accurate in aligning appropriate astrological descriptors that activate the natal chart at the time of the event. Obviously, we would test the same events with other movement methods to gain confirmation of the 7:45 pm birth time for Princess Diana.

Time Range within Twelve Hours – Angles Move Six Signs

- **Chris Costner Sizemore**

Let's not forget our astrological training to question a client of birth time and its source if something doesn't align with astrological logic. We have learned the Moon is often associated with childhood and relationship with the mother. If a client or public figure experienced a traumatic event or situation early in life, we may expect that the Moon is involved in a close hard aspect to one or more planets or angles. Chris Costner Sizemore was the subject of the Academy Award winning move, "Three Faces of Eve", played by Joanne Woodward as the psychotic housewife with three different personalities. Lois Rodden questioned the birth time listed in her biography, "I'm Eve ", and wrote a letter to Ms. Sizemore asking for birthtime confirmation.

Biography – Chris Costner Sizemore

"American schizophrenic whose multiple-personality disorder was portrayed by Joanne Woodward in the movie 'The Three Faces of Eve.' She had 22 personalities which she finally integrated into one. **Early traumas of childhood, including the witnessing of two violent deaths before age two, are believed to be the causes of her disorder.**

After overcoming the fear of being rejected by others, she now lectures on mental illness and the plight of the mentally ill. The demure, petite, and soft-spoken Sizemore has, for most of her life, had her mind and body inhabited by three personalities at a time in what is known as multiple-personality disorder.

Source Notes

LMR quotes her by letter dated 4/03/1978 from her B.C. (Her autobiography "I'm Eve" gives 3:00 AM in error. Rodden wrote to question the time in the bio and Chris checked to find the accurate time and confirmed Rodden's PM time.)"

Study the 3:00 am chart for Ms. Sizemore to understand why Lois Rodden thought it was wrong – that her biography did not fit the chart. The Moon was not giving a message of emotional trouble.

Figure 22 Solar Fire 9-Published Birth Chart for Chris Costner Sizemore
True Node, Rodden Rating: C

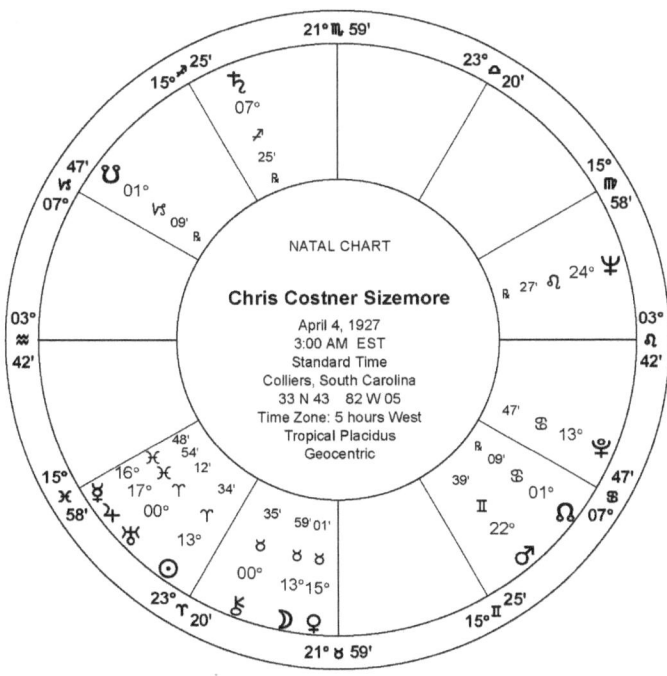

6. https://www.astro.com/astro-databank/Sizemore,_Chris_Costner

Indeed, the 3:00 am Moon had no hard aspects at all, resting comfortably in the third house conjunct Venus. Yes, the Sun is square Pluto suggesting that her identity may be controlled by others or possibly connected to fear of death – but the Sun is square Pluto all day long, and even into the next day. The Moon must align appropriately with the biography.

In the 3:00 pm chart for Ms. Sizemore, the Moon resoundingly confirms the lifelong emotional trauma with the Moon conjunct the Midheaven square Neptune and the Ascendant. And the Sun is now in the 8th house still square Pluto now in the 11th house. The 3:00 pm chart fits the astrological case theory like a glove. Always trust your astrological training and question birth times that produce charts that do not fit the person and the life story. In fact, I would rectify the Costner time to 2:52 PM bringing the Moon closer to the Midheaven and closer to square the Ascendant and Neptune.

Figure 23 Solar Fire 9-Rectified Birth Chart for Chris Costner Sizemore

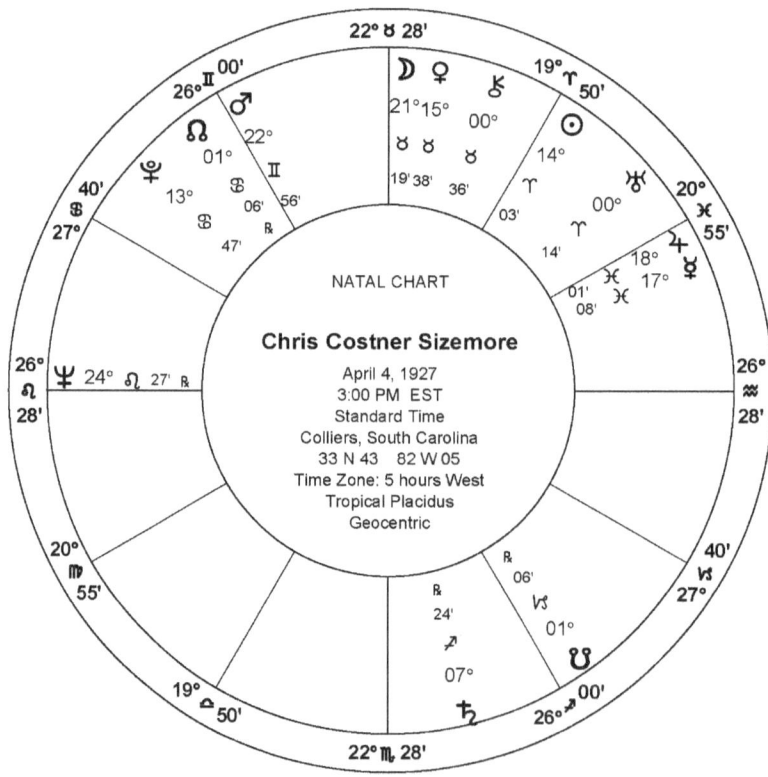

Always trust your astrological training and logic to question any birth time that derives a chart that does not match the story of the person's life. As for the twenty-four hour search, the process of narrowing the time range is the same – it just takes much more time to test the many more possibilities with at least three for four movement techniques. Before delving into testing the many possibilities with software, further narrow the field even more. Study each chart with your "astrologer's eye" that can more easily spot the charts that do not fit the life story of the person who has lived it, then test the birth times that are left. By this time you may understand why most astrologers will not take rectification work. Most don't know how and others feel that the service is not profitable. Both are true, but this text serves to amend the first issue, and with a good rectification and workable birth time, in most cases, the astrologer has a client for life. That's a pretty good payback!

Tally Some Preliminary Results

So far, we have only experimented with possible Midheaven and Ascendant positions that would activate the close aspect natal patterns and their "apex points" at the various ages of corresponding life events. Now it is time to tally the preliminary results and narrow the search to the few (2 or 3) birth times that emerge as more prominent than the others.

- Create a table of AM and PM times for the 24 hours of the day and tally the number of Midheaven hits at each hour from the Midheaven search for contact to the close 1-2-degree natal aspects at key life events
- Continue the same process for tallying the Ascendant hits at each hour for contact to the close 1-2-degree natal aspects at key life events
- Continue the same process for tallying the number of Midheaven and Ascendant hits each hour to the apex points that activate the close natal aspects at key life events
- Note that one may combine the tally for all of these in one table with the final results highlighting the most prominent birth time possibilities

Go Out on a Limb: Experiment with the Short List of Birth times

By this time, a clear pattern should emerge of a few possible birth times that stand out from the rest. Remember, the key to our search is to determine the natal position of the Moon and the Angles. We now have enough information to see if the Moon is possibly involved in any of the close natal aspect networks. If no clear evidence suggests that the natal Moon is involved, move on to search the secondary progressions of the Sun and the Moon to key life events and conclude with a transit search of outer planets to the list of close 1–2-degree aspect natal patterns.

- Run charts for the few narrowed birth times to see if the Moon might be involved in a close natal aspect network
- Create a table of the Progressed Sun to conjunct planets and the Moon's nodes at major life events (Note that the Sun position will not appreciably change from one working chart to the other)

- Create a table of the Progressed Moon from the 2 or 3 most likely birth times to conjunct planets and the Moon's nodes at major life events (Note that the Progressed Moon position may noticeably change from one working chart to the other)
- Create a table of Outer Planet transits at the same major life events of prior searches (Saturn through Pluto transits are sufficient, though one may reasonably add Jupiter and even Mars to the search)
- Create a table of Solar Eclipses at the same key life events of earlier searches
- Tally the hits for Secondary Progression of the Lights and outer planet transits to each of the "working birth times"

It is time to put your reputation on the line and choose the birth time that produces the best results. After all of the hard work and methodical searching with many of the techniques of ancient and modern astrology, the other life events may be added to the list to align activated planets and point to life events to confirmation the final birth time. Indeed, consistent, and accurate forecasting with the rectified birth time is the whole point of the rectification exercise.

Include the Client in Final Birth Time Choice: Ascendant Sign and Ruler

Particularly for the wider time range search of several hours, a handful of times show possibility, and the astrologer must not only rely upon software to test each time, but even more, their astrological judgement to fit the right chart to the real person. It is common for time ranges beyond one hour to provide two birth times that appropriately describe the events on or near the event dates. This situation is multiplied by the increase of the search time range. A 3-hour search may reveal three or four possible birth times; a 6-hour search may reveal even more possible birth times, and so forth. However, once we have finished testing the handful of birth time contenders, it is important to get feedback from the client by describing the traits suggested by each Ascendant sign and its planetary ruler. Invariably, the client knows without a doubt which Ascendant and ruler description fits best. One birth time may have Sagittarius rising with Jupiter in the 10th house conjunct the Sun, describing one who is outgoing and sociable, and the identity is fulfilled by work with a broad reach such as politics, foreign relations or show business. The other birth time may have Capricorn rising with Saturn conjunct the Moon in the 4th house, describing one who is reserved and shy with much family responsibility that limits expression of feelings. After the astrologer has narrowed the wide time range to just one or two birth times, almost always, the client knows "what shoe fits" and can aptly choose the appropriate rising sign connected to the birth time that created it.

4
Why is Case Theory so Important?

Study the Biography and Life Events to Build a "Case Theory"

Case Theory is based on the astrologer's understanding of appropriate astrological descriptors to represent the client's life narrative. For instance, if one has devoted a lifetime to caring for others, we suspect that the Sun may be a mutable house or in a house ruled by a water sign. If one is intense and very private, we suspect that Scorpio may be rising. If a person had a life-threatening birth, we suspect a very close hard aspect to the Ascendant from a planet or point known for such challenge. Saturn through Pluto come to mind, and possibly the South Node. If several events occur in a close range of time, we suspect that the chart has several planets in close 1 to 2-degree aspect in some sort of configuration.

Other ways to build a "Case Theory" is considering what part of life the major events occurred.

For instance, we know that:

Angles arc to planets in ANGULAR houses (1, 4, 7, 10) early in life, but

Planets in ANGULAR houses (1, 4, 7, 10) arc to Angles late in life.

Angles arc to planets in SUCCEDENT houses (2, 5, 8, 11) in mid-life.

Planets in SUCCEDENT houses arc to Angles in mid-life.

Angles arc to planets in CADENT houses (3, 6, 9, 12) late in life.

Planets in cadent houses (3, 6, 9, 12) arc to Angles early in life.

But there is much more to building the case theory. Just knowing an event date and what it was about leaves a gulf of information untapped that can lead the astrologer to inaccurate assumptions. In addition to the questionnaire, the next step requires a probing conversation with the client about the event situation and relevant feelings. For instance, if the event on the list is a marriage, it is helpful to know the conditions. We can't assume that all marriages start out as happy occasions. Not too long ago, many Asian marriages were arranged by the parents and the couple may not have had an affectionate relationship at all. More often than is confessed, many more marriages are forced because the woman is pregnant, and the parents want their daughter's reputation intact as well as legitimacy for the child. Other times, parents or family may object to the marriage for status, religious or cultural reasons. This sort of information can change the sort of aspects the astrologer would consider as descriptive of such a traditionally happy event.

Case Theory and Rectification Example: Female Client

This female client born in Moscow, Russia on 13 November 1985 sometime between 3:00 am and 7:00 am started life with a compelling biography. Within the 4-hour search range for birth time, the Moon stays in Scorpio. At 3:00 am in Moscow, the Moon is at 26:18 Scorpio, and by 7:00 pm the Moon has moved to 28:52 Scorpio. She was born several months premature weighing just two and a half pounds and was hospitalized for five months to gain appropriate weight and life stability. Right off, the dramatic situation of birth suggests that the Ascendant and/or its ruler may be significantly distressed by hard aspect from one or more planets descriptive of the threat to life. In my mind that leaves two choices: the Lunar Nodes across the Ascendant/Descendant axis or Pluto conjunct the Ascendant. Of course, Saturn, Uranus or Neptune could also bring trouble to the Ascendant given their condition in the Noon "Working Chart". Other important issues to consider are listed below:

- Difficult birth circumstances – premature 2.5 lbs – in hospital 5 months
- The Lunar Nodes are exactly square Jupiter, and could be closely connected to the Angles in hard aspect to describe danger at birth
- Pluto conjunct Ascendant may describe a life-threatening birth
- Born before daylight – between 1:00 AM -7:30 AM
- Doctors and nurses too busy saving her life to record birth time.
- Birth time is not recorded in Russia.

Case Theory Suggests Searching:

6:52 am 1. SNode conjunct ASC/NNode conjunct DES/Jupiter square all

6:34 am 2. Pluto conjunct ASC, with Nodes/Jupiter T-square close by

6:41-6:52 am 3. Times near top in both Sirius 4.1 and Jigsaw 2.2 Searches

Advanced Software Suggests Searching:

4:36 am Sirius 4.1 top choice

4:39 am Jigsaw 2.2 top choice

The search range is 4-hours, 3:00 am to 7:00 am, so the "Working Chart" is set for 5:00 am.

Figure 24- 5:00 AM Chart for Client

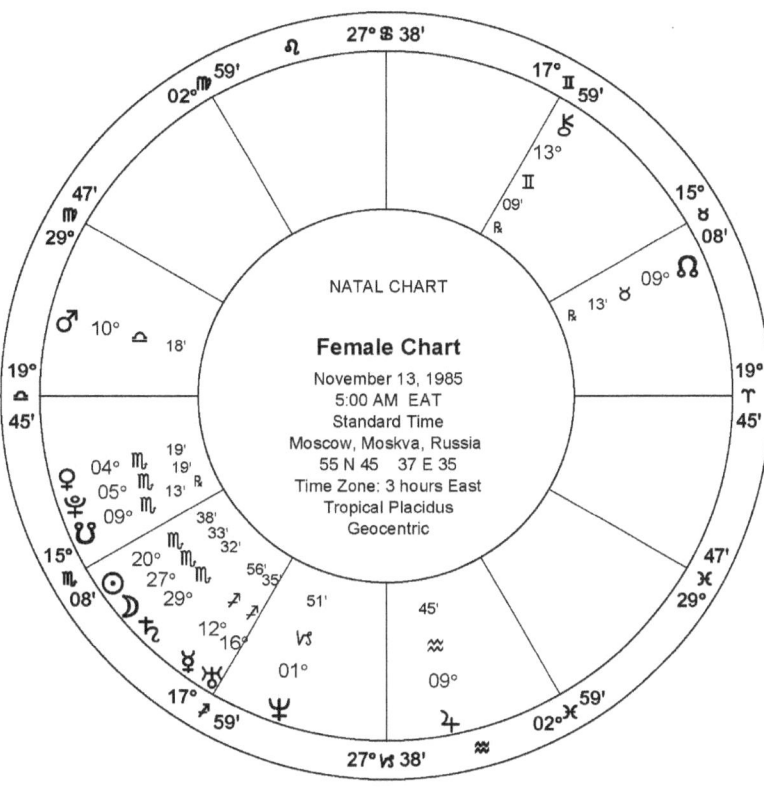

Studying the Chart for the midpoint of the birth time search, 5:00 AM, I see that Pluto and the South Node are conjunct with both square Jupiter. However, the Nodal axis is square Jupiter at the same degree, whereas Pluto is 4-degrees away. Jupiter can give a boost for life, but square the Lunar Nodes suggests a struggle for it. Pluto alone on the Ascendant is a wide square to Jupiter and just not strong enough for the dire circumstance of her birth and struggle to survive. Therefore, I chose to start testing later than the time range midpoint and started testing nearer to the time that fit the quite dramatic biography, 7:00 am. From my case theory, I began testing the major life events to align with appropriate astrological descriptors to derive the specific birth time.

Figure 25- Rectified Birth Time Chart for Client

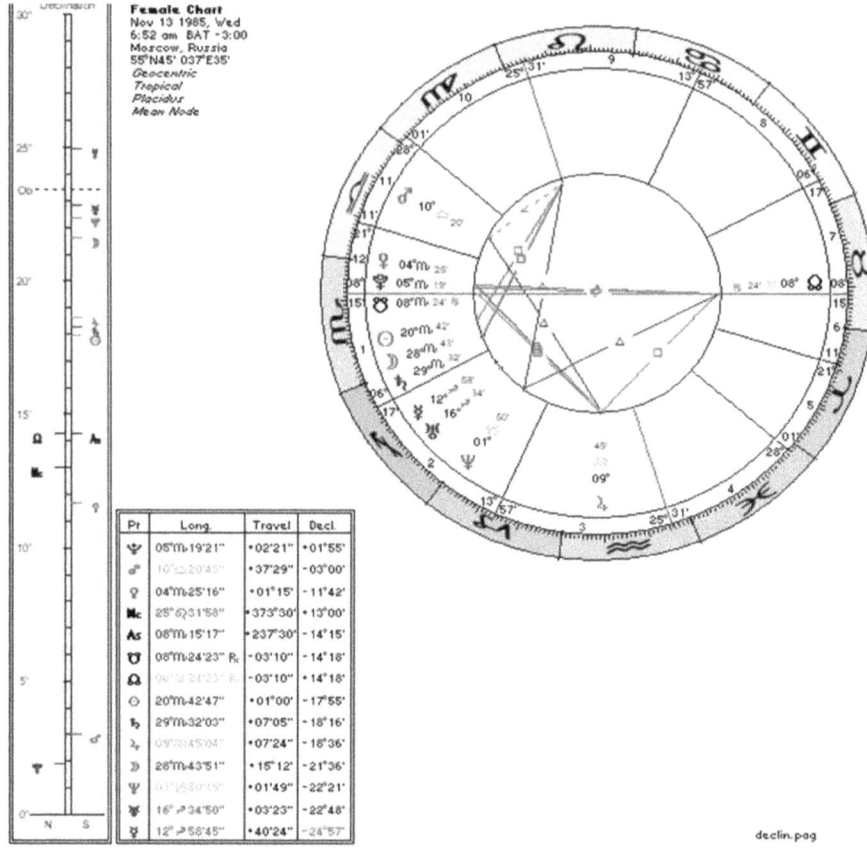

Other evidence that supports this birth time are the Lunar Nodes with both conjunct and parallel the Ascendant/Descendant axis. Additionally, it is the South Node conjunct and parallel the Ascendant emphasizing the life struggle, though the North Node conjunct and parallel the Descendant emphasizes looking forward to building a good relationship to fulfill the purpose of that struggle for life.

Pluto does have a role in this 6:52 am chart as the modern Ascendant ruler of Scorpio. Pluto in close conjunction with Venus moves to the 12th house and describes her several serious health issues as well as her beauty and intensity in giving and receiving love. The Sun/Moon/Saturn conjunct in the 1st house for the 6:52 am birth time describes her intense need for security and privacy and interest in psychology.

Figure 36 Female Client Lifetime Declination Graphic

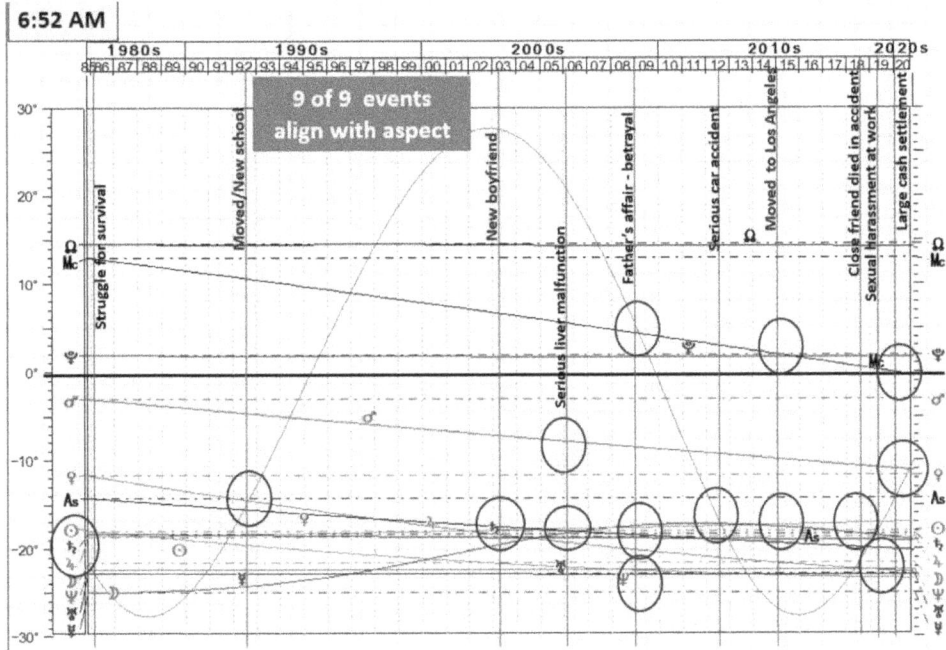

After our consultation for the rectification result, the client told me that another astrologer had rectified the time to put Pluto rising at 6:34 am conjunct ASC. Nonetheless, Jupiter closely square the Lunar Nodes across the Ascendant/Descendant axis is a much stronger statement for the dramatic and serious birth situation. Our astrological training and logic is the best check on astrology software that provides everything but the kitchen sink. It is up to us to sort it all out to serve our clients.

Build Your Case Theory Before Testing Major Life Events: Jimmy Swaggart

Let's continue with the well-known televangelist, Jimmy Swaggart. We know a great deal of his biography from the news and his written biography, and he does have a timed birth certificate that we can compare how well we did with the rectification starting with only a list of major life events and a solid biography.

First of all, for a 24-hour search start with by finding the possible range of the Moon from midnight to midnight with Whole Sign houses and no angles.

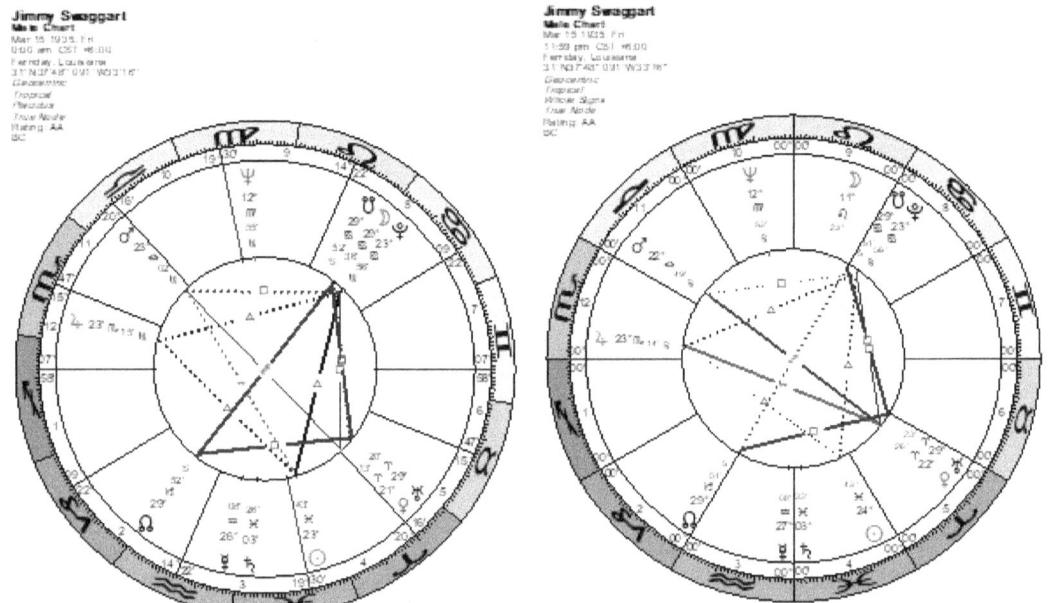

In 24-hours, Jimmy's Moon moves from 29:36 Cancer to 11:23 Leo. From the biography, a Leo Moon fits his need to be seen. Through his television ministry and showmanship, he taught the gospel to millions of people, many of whom were ill or incapacitated and unable to go to church. On Jimmy's birthday, the Moon went into Leo at 0:48 am CST, so we only cut the search range by just seconds. But don't stop there, look for the possible Ascendant signs in the time range and see if the biography confirms one, or even two.

Can you see the problem here? In 24-hours, minus only 48 seconds, you still have 12 possible Ascendant signs making it very risky to choose one at this point. That said, start with a working chart set for noon, or put the Sun or 0-Aries on the Ascendant – your choice. The next step is to know the biography, especially the early years and the family dynamics. If there was childhood trauma of any sort, it is very likely that the natal Moon is in a close hard aspect to a limiting planet such as Mars, Saturn, Uranus, Neptune, Pluto or the Lunar Nodes. Jimmy's biography reveals the serious abuse by his father until he left home at 20. From living in poverty and daily beatings from his drunken father, Jimmy found a safe haven in the Pentecostal Church and the encouragement of his grandmother. With this difficult childhood, I immediately search for the nearest hard aspect to the Moon within the 23:12 time range which is easiest to see by setting the chart to the midpoint of the time range.

The closest hard aspect to Jimmy's Moon is conjunct the South Node and square Uranus that brings the birth time very early in the morning. Now narrow the time range from 12:48 am to 2:00 am and now select the appropriate Ascendant sign that fits the biography.

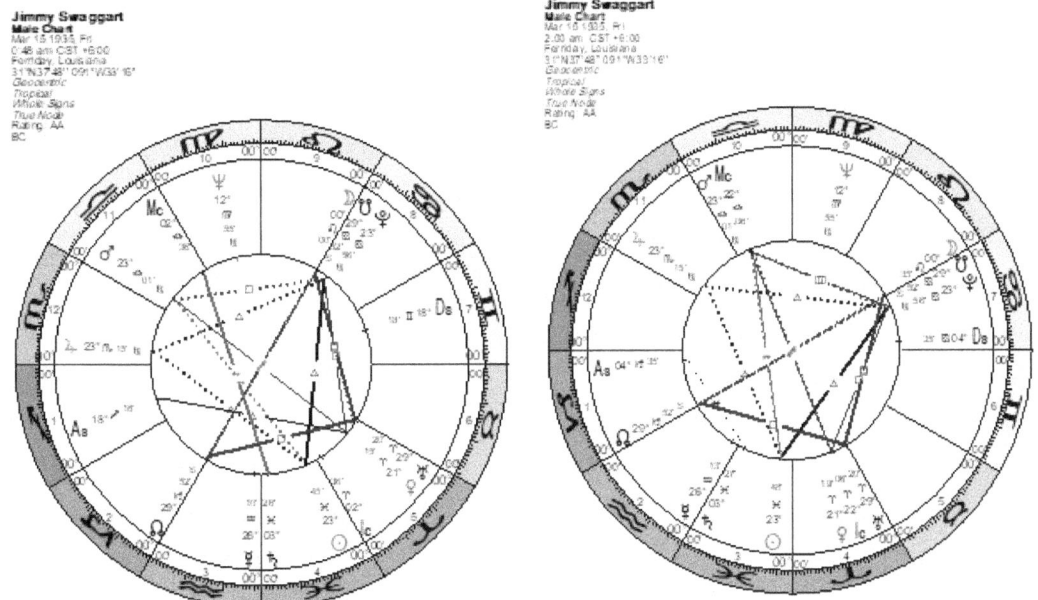

Now decide which Ascendant sign fits the biography. Certainly, Jimmy's outgoing personality does not fit Capricorn rising, so once again we can narrow the search range before testing his major life events for the exact birth time. At this point, I choose to set the chart to Placidus because I like to see the angles on the cardinal house cusps.

Why is Case Theory so Important?

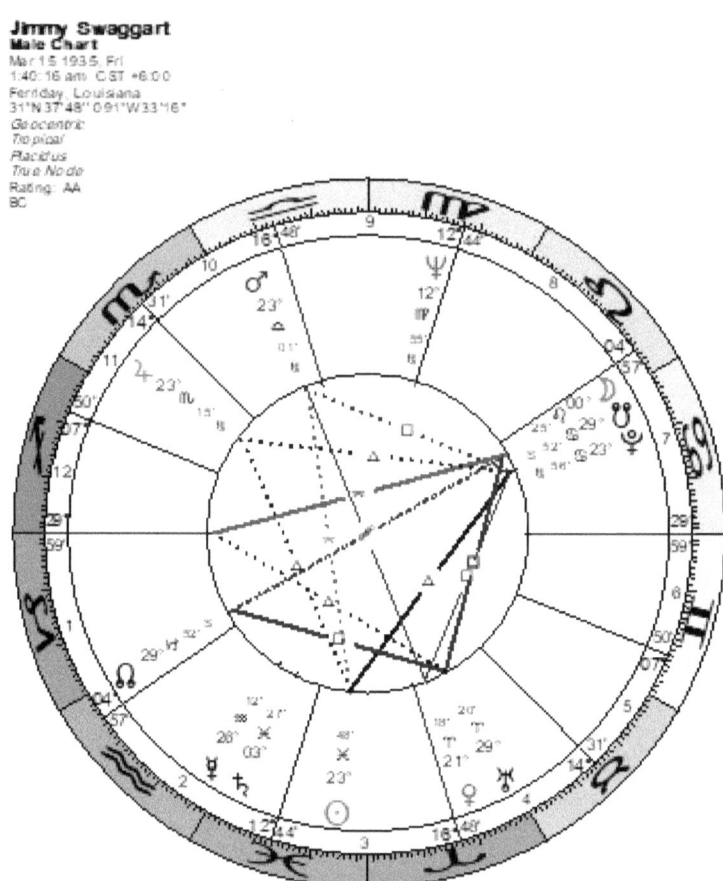

Since 1:40 am brings the Moon closest to the South Node and square Uranus in the 4th house of family we are ready to go forward with 1:40 am as our "Case Theory" and start testing the major life events to derive the actual birth time.

First TV show at 35, MC arcs to Jupiter 1-degree over, so remove 4-minutes from 1:40 am to 1:36 am.

Defrocked at 53, ASC arcs to Mercury 1-degree over, so remove 4-minutes from 1:40 am to 1:36 am.

Heart Attack at 67, Pluto arcs to MC 1-degree over, so remove 4-minutes from 1:40 am to 1:36 am.

Here is Jimmy's Birth Certificate birth time found in his biography and also in www.astro.com rated as AA Birth Certificate data.

It is easy to see that close aspect configurations are very important. When one planet arcs to an angle, the other planets must also be included in the interpretation.

Now with the rectified birth time of 1:36 am CST is very close to the actual birth time of 1:35 am CST, so now the chart aligns appropriately to astrological descriptors at all major life events.

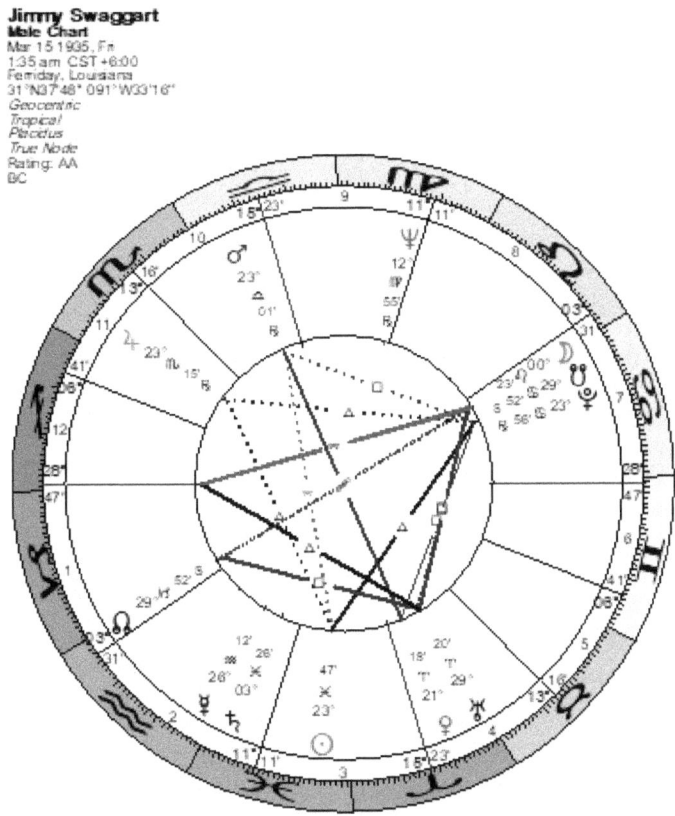

At age 35 Swaggart's Jupiter arced to his ASC, and at the same time the Sun arced to Uranus, trine the ASC and Pluto also arced trine the ASC.

No wonder at age 35, Jimmy's broadcasting ministry became immediately very successful.

Be sure to do the easy work to narrow the birth time range and building a "Case Theory" before testing the major life events. These beginning steps apply to any birth time range. It is helpful to start the search with Whole Signs without Angles, just planets and Lunar Nodes set for midpoint of the time range. Software is a great help in birth time rectification but

Table 18 Swaggart Possible Natal Moon 1-Degree Aspects for 24 Hours

Aspects	AM Moon	Dwad	Time	Dwad	PM Moon	Aspects
Conjunct SNode Square Uranus	29:36 Cancer	Gemini	0:00			
Conjunct SNode Square Uranus	00:05 Leo	Leo	1:00	Libra	06:00 Leo	Trine MC
Square Uranus	00:35 Leo	Leo	2:00	Libra	06:29 Leo	
	01:05 Leo	Leo	3:00	Libra	06:59 Leo	Square MC
	01:34 Leo	Leo	4:00	Libra	07:28 Leo	
Inconjunct Saturn	02:04 Leo	Leo	5:00	Scorpio	07:58 Leo	Sesqui-squa Sun Sextile MC
Inconjunct Saturn Sesqui-squa ASC	02:33 Leo	Virgo	6:00	Scorpio	08:27 Leo	Sesqui-squa Sun Semi-squar MC
Inconjunct Saturn	03:03 Leo	Virgo	7:00	Scorpio	08:56 Leo	Sesqui-squa Sun
Inconjunct Saturn	03:32 Leo	Virgo	8:00	Scorpio	09:26 Leo	Sesqui-squa Sun
Inconjunct Saturn Opposite MC	04:02 Leo	Virgo	9:00	Scorpio	09:55 Leo	Sesqui-squa Sun
Inconjunct Saturn	04:31 Leo	Virgo	10:00	Sagittar	10:25 Leo	Sesqui-squa Sun
Inconjunct Saturn Inconjunct MC	05:01 Leo	Libra	11:00	Sagittar	10:54 Leo	Sesqui-squa Sun
Sesqui-squa MC	05:30 Leo	Libra	12:00	Sagittar	11:24 Leo	

Again, knowing the dwad, or 2 ½ degree sub-section of each sign, may be helpful if one knows enough of the character and personality of the individual to use this handy fine-tuning device. The Table 8 may serve as a handy reminder.

For example, if Swaggart's natal Moon is in the last couple of degrees of Cancer, the "home-body" and sensitive Cancer Moon has a Gemini's eclectic interests and need to communicate. If, however, Jimmy's natal Moon is in the first couple of degrees of Leo, he doubly exhibits the need to be seen and perform because the first 2 ½ degrees of any sign is repeated in the dwad – hence a double emphasis of the traits of the sign. One may analyze the other possible degree positions for his natal Moon, but seeing Jimmy Swaggart on television and knowing his biography, the 0 – 2 ½ degree Leo Moon does seem to fit well and place the birth time in the 1:00 – 5:00 AM range. When considered with the possible natal 1-degree aspects to the Moon in Table 40, the time between 1 and 2 AM is reinforced.

In case the Moon does not have any natal close 1-degree aspects, the Noon chart is always safe. Figure 13 is Jimmy Swaggart's chart set for Noon as a "working birth time", which does still bring the Moon close to the South Node and the suspect T-square configuration. Of course, this possibility must be tested further against life events, but at this point the conjecture looks promising enough to pursue.

Study all of the closely aspected planets in the natal chart, especially those within 1-degree orb, and take note of any networks of three or more closely aspected planets. For starters, this chart has a close Nodal axis T-square to Uranus, and the Moon may well turn out to be part of that configuration. Further, Jimmy Swaggart's chart has a very close water Grand Trine between Jupiter, Pluto and the Sun, no matter what time of day he was born. Notice, too, that Mars is part of that closely aspected 23-degree network and makes major hard aspect, square and quincunx, to two legs of the Grand Trine. In addition, Venus opposes Mars and squares Pluto, so Pluto is not only the apex of yet another T-square, but also the apex of the Grand Trine. It is rather like "all roads lead to Rome", and in this case, to Pluto. These very close natal patterns provide a multiple of one-degree natal aspects and a good beginning point for a birth time search. Of course if a chart provides the semi-square and the sesqui-square aspects in the closest one-degree natal pattern(s) then by all means include them too.

Use the computer search capabilities or ephemeris to match actual life events to the appropriate planetary patterns when life events correspond. Appropriate Directed Angles to planets and Progressed Moon and planet contacts at important life events are the most important tools to arrive at a reasonable selection of birth times from placement of the Midheaven. Narrow the search by the process of elimination using the additional techniques described in the first example to arrive at the best time for birth.

The Jimmy Swaggart biographical information comes from an unauthorized biography, Swaggart, by Anne Rowe Seaman, that not only provides specific situations and formative events in Jimmy's life, but traces the history of a whole family from the early 1930's to the turn of the 21st century. Though no specific date is attached, Jimmy's parents fought constantly until he was about 16, and he was scared to death of his father who disciplined him frequently with the belt. Everything enjoyable in life always had "Pentecostal Sin" attached to it from the strong influence of his mother and grandmother – except for his enjoyment of singing church hymns. So, talented Jimmy chose a different path than his equally talented first cousins, Jerry Lee Lewis of Rock and Roll and "Great Balls of Fire" fame, and Mickey Leroy Gilley of Country and Western music fame. Jimmy Swaggart became the most famous televangelist in American history, who like most of the other televangelists, dramatically fell from grace through a "weakness of the flesh". Here is an extensive list of important events in the life of Jimmy Swaggart to begin the birth time search:

Table 19 Jimmy Swaggart Important Life Events

	Event	Date	Age	Location
1	**Brother died of pneumonia/Jimmy also ill**	Feb, 1940	4+	Rio Hondo, TX
2	**Spoke in tongues/ "Saved" in the church**	July, 1943	8	Ferriday, LA
3	**Preached of several bomb/flood prophecies**	July, 1944	9	Ferriday, LA
4	Performed at churches/contests w/ Jerry Lee	1947-1949	12/14	Ferriday, LA
5	Started stealing/no sports/first prostitute exp	early 1949	13	Ferriday, LA
6	2nd in high school talent show/ Jerry Lee 1st	Jan, 1950	14	Ferriday, LA
7	Dropped out of school 10th grade	June, 1951	16	Ferriday, LA
8	**Married against parents' wishes/Never dated**	Oct 10, 1952	17	Ferriday, LA
9	Got fired for stealing	Winter, 1952	17	Ferriday, LA
10	Suicidal despair/son Donnie born	Summer, 1954	19	Ferriday, LA
11	**Pneumonia/Made ministry his career**	Jan 1, 1958	22	Ferriday, LA
12	Ordination- Assembly of God minister denied	Spring, 1959	24	Ferriday, LA
13	**Ordination given Assembly of God minister**	June 23, 1960	25	Ferriday, LA
14	**Mother, Minnie Bell, died in hospital**	July 9, 1960	25	Ferriday, LA
15	**Grandma Ada Died of stroke-Jim devastated**	Feb 19, 1961	25	Ferriday, LA
16	Jerry Lee's son drowned in family pool	Easter, 1962	27	Ferriday, LA
17	**1st recording/help from cousin, Jerry Lee**	July, 1962	27	Memphis, TN
18	5 gospel records doing well/ built 1st home	1967	32	B. Rouge, LA
19	**1st radio broadcast of "Camp Meeting Hour"**	Jan 1, 1969	33	B. Rouge, LA
20	Aunt Mamie died, Jerry Lee's mom	April 21, 1971	36	Ferriday, LA
21	<u>Best selling</u> gospel album in country	1971	36	B. Rouge, LA
22	grandfather W. H. Swaggart died	May, 1971	36	Ferriday, LA
23	**Bought radio station – paid cash**	March, 1973	38	B. Rouge, LA
24	Got license for radio broadcasting	June, 1973	38	B. Rouge, LA
25	Jerry Lee's son killed in auto accident	Nov 13, 1973	38	Ferriday, LA
26	**Began televising "Camp Meeting Hour"**	Spring, 1973	38	B. Rouge, LA

Table 19 continues

27	World's largest daily radio and TV gospel show	1975	40	B. Rouge, LA
28	Expand ministry world travel/Time magazine	Fall, 1977	42	B. Rouge, LA
29	Major rift between Jerry Lee and Jimmy	July, 1979	44	Ferriday, LA
30	Trouble with other televangelists-scandal starts	1980 – 1981	45/46	B. Rouge, LA
31	**Found daughter-in-law in affair w/ guitarist**	June, 1982	47	B. Rouge, LA
32	"Frontline" aired documentary on Jim's ministry	May 19, 1983	48	National news
33	**Dropped by several stations over insensitive Holocaust comments**	Nov 1983-Feb 1984	48	B. Rouge, LA
34	Swaggart Bible College opened	Sept, 1985	49	B. Rouge, LA
35	**Arrested with prostitute by cop, son of rival**	Oct 17, 1987	52	B. Rouge, LA
36	**Swaggart hedged on confession/Gorman released photos/made public confession**	Feb 21, 1988	52	B. Rouge, LA
37	**Defrocked by Assemblies of God**	April 8, 1988	53	B. Rouge, LA
38	Lost Supreme Court case	Feb 21, 1989	53+	Wash. DC
39	CNN Broadcast prostitute/Jimmy photos	June 25, 1991	56	Atlanta, GA
40	Lost $10 million dollar lawsuit to Gorman	Sept 13, 1991	56	B. Rouge, LA
41	Walking pneumonia – very sick	Sept 15-Oct 15, 1991	56	San Diego, CA
42	**Arrested with prostitute**	Oct 11, 1991	56	Indio, CA
43	**News of 2nd arrest hit the national news**	Oct 12, 1991	56	Nationwide
44	Almost lost tax-exempt status/big fine	Spring, 1992	57	B. Rouge, LA

Concentrating on the bolded events should be the first line of search, since they are life-defining events. The un-bolded events are more useful for fine-tuning of the final few possible birth times, best left for later. By scanning the list of important life events for Jimmy Swaggart, one sees an obvious concentration at ages 8-9; 25; 38; 52 and 56 which are obvious "hooks" for beginning the search. Since he experienced dramatically happy and sad events at age 25, one might be drawn to the interlocking network of the Grand Trine (Sun, Jupiter, Pluto) and the T-square (Pluto, Mars, Venus). Of course, one must experiment with Directing the Midheaven as well as the Ascendant to the dates of other key life events to determine if the assumption is correct.

Since we see 3 major life events occurring at age 25 for Jimmy Swaggart, searching from that key year is a good place to begin. Particularly important dates are June 23 and July 9, 1960 and February 19, 1961. Working from a Noon birth time for Swaggart, the following Table 42 gives possible birth times that could trigger (by conjunction) any of the two close hard aspect networks, the first of which includes an interlocked Grand Trine. The first configuration includes the Venus, Mars, Pluto natal T-square interlocked with the natal Sun, Jupiter Pluto Grand Trine; and the second is the close square of Uranus to the Moon's Nodes. Keep in mind that we are reserving judgment of the Angles and the Moon's position until we can establish a consistent pattern of the Solar Arc Directed Angles contacting any of these networks at key life events.

Table 20 Directed Midheaven Times Conjunct Aspect Network at Age 25

Planet Contacted by Conjunction	Ordained Minister June 23, 1960	Mother's Death July 9, 1960	Grandmother's Death Feb 19, 1961
Grand Trine:			
Jupiter 23:14 Scorpio	2:21 AM MC 27:41 Libra	2:21:30 AM MC 27:45 Libra	2:19 AM MC 27:09 Libra
Pluto 23:56 Cancer	6:30 PM MC 28:42 Gemini	6:29:30 PM MC 28:36 Gemini	6:28 PM MC 28:01 Gemini
Sun 24:13 Pisces	10:41:10 AM MC 28:57 Aquarius	10:40:40 AM MC 28:53 Aquarius	10:38 AM MC 28:18 Aquarius
T-Square:			
Venus 21:49 Aries	12:23:30 PM MC 26:27 Pisces	12:23 PM MC 26:31 Pisces	12:21:30 PM MC 25:54 Pisces
Mars 22:55 Libra	12:30 AM MC 27:39 Virgo	12:29:30 AM MC 27:35 Virgo	12:27:30 AM MC 27:00 Virgo
Pluto 23:56 Cancer	6:30 PM MC 28:42 Gemini	6:29:30 PM MC 28:36 Gemini	6:28 PM MC 28:01 Gemini
T-Square			
N Node 28:20 Capric	6:51 AM MC 3:05 Capricorn	6:50:30 AM MC 3:01 Capricorn	6:48 AM MC 2:22 Capricorn
S Node 28:20 Cancer	6:49 PM MC 3:05 Cancer	6:48:30 PM MC 3:01 Cancer	6:46 PM MC 2:25 Cancer
(Moon possible) 29:45 Cancer+ if very early birth	(12:00 – 2:00 AM)	(12:00 – 2:00 AM)	(12:00 – 2:00 AM)
Uranus 29:21 Aries	12:52 PM MC 4:09 Aries	12:51:30 PM MC 4:05 Aries	12:49 PM MC 3:26 Aries

At this point, it may be helpful to discuss the nature of the sensitive points in a T-Square configuration. We have charted the Directed Angles, Midheaven and Ascendant, to each leg of the two T-squares and Grand Trine in the Jimmy Swaggart chart, but we would be remiss not to consider the sensitive point opposite the T-square apex planets that, when activated, would form a Grand Cross, a highly dynamic configuration. The point in opposition to the apex planet of each T-Square is plotted in the Table below.

Table 21 Directed Ascendant Times Conjunct Aspect Network at Age 25

Planet Contacted by Conjunction	Ordained Minister June 23, 1960	Mother's Death July 9, 1960	Grandmother's Death Feb 19, 1961
Grand Trine:			
Jupiter 23:14 Scorpio	2:21 AM MC 27:41 Libra	2:21:30 AM MC 27:45 Libra	2:19 AM MC 27:09 Libra
Pluto 23:56 Cancer	11:29 AM ASC 28:41 Gemini	11:28:30 AM ASC 28:36 Gemini	11:26 AM ASC 28:01 Gemini
Sun 24:13 Pisces	10:41:10 AM MC 28:57 Aquarius	10:40:40 AM MC 28:53 Aquarius	10:38 AM MC 28:18 Aquarius
T-Square:			
Venus 21:49 Aries	6:28 AM ASC 26:27 Pisces	6:27:30 AM ASC 26:31 Pisces	6:26:30 AM ASC 25:54 Pisces
Mars 22:55 Libra	6:24:30 PM ASC 27:39 Virgo	6:24 PM ASC 27:35 Virgo	6:21:30 PM ASC 27:00 Virgo
Pluto 23:56 Cancer	11:29 AM ASC 28:41 Gemini	11:28:30 AM ASC 28:36 Gemini	11:26 AM ASC 28:01 Gemini
T-Square:			
N Node 28:20 Capr	1:53:30 AM ASC 3:05 Capricorn	1:53:17 AM ASC 3:01 Capricorn	1:50:43 AM ASC 2:25 Capricorn
S Node 28:20 Canc	11:48 PM ASC 3:05 Cancer	11:47:30 PM ASC 3:01 Cancer	11:45 PM ASC 2:25 Cancer
(Moon possible) 29:45 Cancer+ if	(12:00 – 2:00 AM) very early birth	(12:00 – 2:00 AM)	(12:00 – 2:00 AM)
Uranus 29:21 Aries	6:49 AM ASC 4:09 Aries	6:48:30 AM ASC 4:05 Aries	6:46:41 AM ASC 3:26 Aries

Table 22 Times Directed Opposite the T-Square Apex Planets at Age 25

T-Square Apex Planet Opposition	Ordained Minister 6-23-1960	Mother's Death 7-9-1960	Grandmother's Death 2-21-1961
Opposed Pluto 23:56 Capricorn	6:31 AM MC 28:41 Sagittarius	6:30:30 AM MC 28:36 Sagittarius	6:29 AM MC 28:01 Sagittarius
	1:34 AM ASC 28:41 Sagittarius	1:33:30 AM ASC 28:36 Sagittarius	1:31 AM ASC 28:01 Sagittarius
Opposed Uranus 29:21 Libra	12:51:30 PM MC 4:05 Aries	12:51 PM MC 4:01 Aries	12:49 PM MC 3:26 Aries
	6:48:30 AM ASC 4:05 Aries	6:48 AM ASC 4:01 Aries	6:46:30 AM ASC 3:26 Aries

By arranging all of the times into AM or PM columns according to each hour, one can easily see where the best few times stack up to narrow the detailed search. Looking at Table 22, it appears that 4 possible birth time ranges stand out: 6-7 AM, 1-2 AM; 6-7 PM and 12-1 PM. Notice the opposition relationship of the 6-7 AM and PM times and the 1 AM and PM times. And, the 6-7 AM/PM times are in a square relationship to the 1 AM/PM times. The time ranges reflect the tight squares and oppositions that are activated in the natal chart at key life events, however it is also possible that such polarized times may correspond to the Angles. Even though the MC and IC are opposite, and the ASC and DSC are opposite, one cannot assume that the Angle polarities are 90 degrees apart. Remember 6 hours of clock time equals 3 signs, or 90 degrees, and 12 hours of clock time equals 180 degrees.

Table 23 Finding the Most Likely Birth Times to Search in Detail

Hours	AM Possible Times	Total	PM Possible Times	Total
12-1	3	3	3,3,3	9
1-2	(Moon possible 6) 3,3,3	9 or 15		
2-3	3	3		
3-4				
4-5				
5-6				
6-7	3,3,3,3,3,3	18	3,3,3,3	12
7-8				
8-9			3	3
9-10				
10-11	3,3	6		
11-12	3,3	6	3	3

"For each of these two times, I'll next look at contacts to the Progressed Sun and Angles. It is clear that the Sun doesn't move enough between these two times to make a difference. The Progressed Angles by conjunction only are effective for 8 of the 12 events (6 clearly applicable to the event) for a birth of 0:53 AM and 12 of the events (9 clearly applicable to the event) for 1:45 AM. This suggests that the 1:45 AM time is best."

In one last search for confirmation of the 1:35 – 1:45 AM times derived and supported by most students, the Solar Eclipses may make close aspect to an Angle or the Moon at key life events. A range of 3 degrees is applied here, but one could as well use a 4 – 5-degree orb for Solar Eclipses – precisely why they are unreliable for the initial search. Now practice your skill at rectification by seeing how other prominent life events align with these important close hard aspect patterns at the appropriate age at the event. As you proceed, one birth time should gradually become a more consistent marker for the Angles to be declared the rectified birth time, though do not be tempted to interpret Midheaven or Ascendant signs or degrees without the confirmation of corresponding life events through testing. The student may stop here and proceed with his own searches to determine the correct Jimmy Swaggart birth time. The professional astrologer may prefer to continue reading to find a discussion of the important life events and graphics incorporating the answer – the recorded birth certificate and AA-rated time.

Figure 38 Swaggart Outer Planet Transits for Age 25 Using the Noon Time

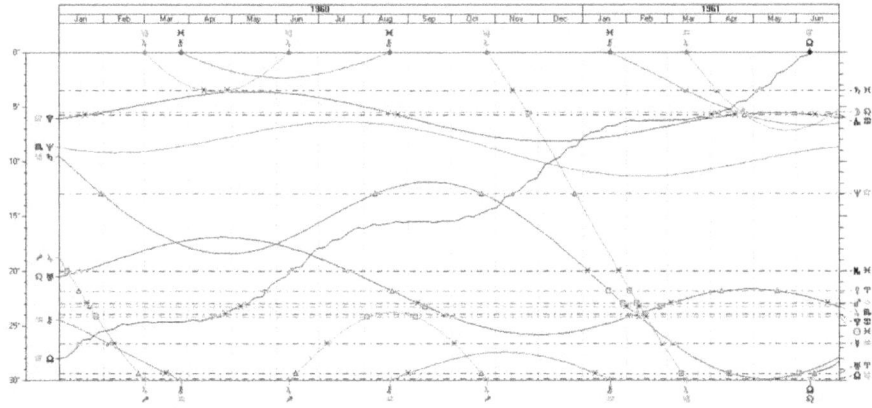

The rectification process of aligning the movement of the Angles to make 4th harmonic aspects to key challenging life events is a good first step to rectification. Moving planets to Angles and Angles to planets by the Solar Arc method is easiest to work with, but certainly the Secondary Progression gives important clues as well. Remember that planet-to-planet contacts, though important for defining some life events,[1] are virtually useless in determining an

---

1. All Jimmy Swaggart biographical data was taken from: Ann Rowe Seaman, Swaggart: The Unauthorized Biography of an American Evangelist, Continuum Publishing Company, New York, 1991, pp.432.

unknown birth time. Only experimentation with the Angles and the Moon can provide the necessary clues to crack the case.

The following graphics show Life Progressed Declinations, Secondary Progressions and Outer Transits for some key years in Jimmy Swaggart's life. Of course, you will no doubt run many additional charts and graphs of your own in the process of elimination of possible birth times and defend those that are astrologically most consistent with events.

Figure 39 Life Declination Graphic for Jimmy Swaggart Using the Noon Birth Time

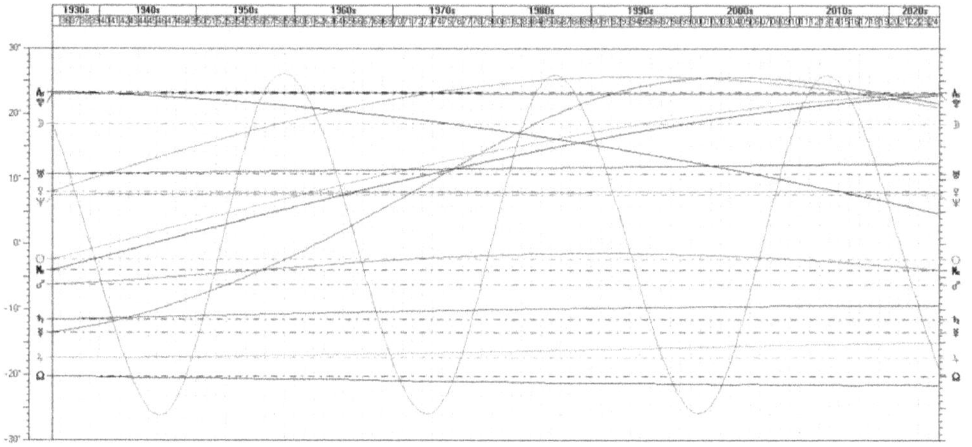

The Swaggart Marriage

Starting with the life overview seen in the Life Declination Graphic, the Progressed Moon Declination was at a critical crossover point that coincides with the marriage of Jimmy and Frances Swaggart on October 10, 1952. Seventeen-year-old Jimmy and fifteen-year-old Frances married against the wishes of their parents, which may explain why it appears to be such a stressful period for him astrologically. The Progressed (solar arc) Midheaven was at 2 Scorpio 49 making a trine to natal Saturn, appropriate for a commitment, and Progressed Venus was trine Neptune for idealistic love. It is interesting to note that Jimmy's early teen years were extremely troubled as he pulled away from the church and began stealing and associating with prostitutes at the same time the Progressed Midheaven opposed natal Uranus and squared the Nodal axis and natal Moon. The Midheaven moving to trine Saturn proved to be his salvation from heading even deeper into bad company. At his marriage, transiting Saturn moved across his Midheaven squaring his Progressed Ascendant, and replacing the transiting Neptune that had been there during his troubled teens. The hard reality of Saturn fell upon him, but it was a decided improvement from his "stealing and whoring" days when Neptune was there. Charts that follow use the actual birth time of 1:35 AM to show more specific details for key events in Jimmy Swaggart's life.

Figure 40 Swaggart Progression Age 13   Figure 41 Swaggart Progression Age 17

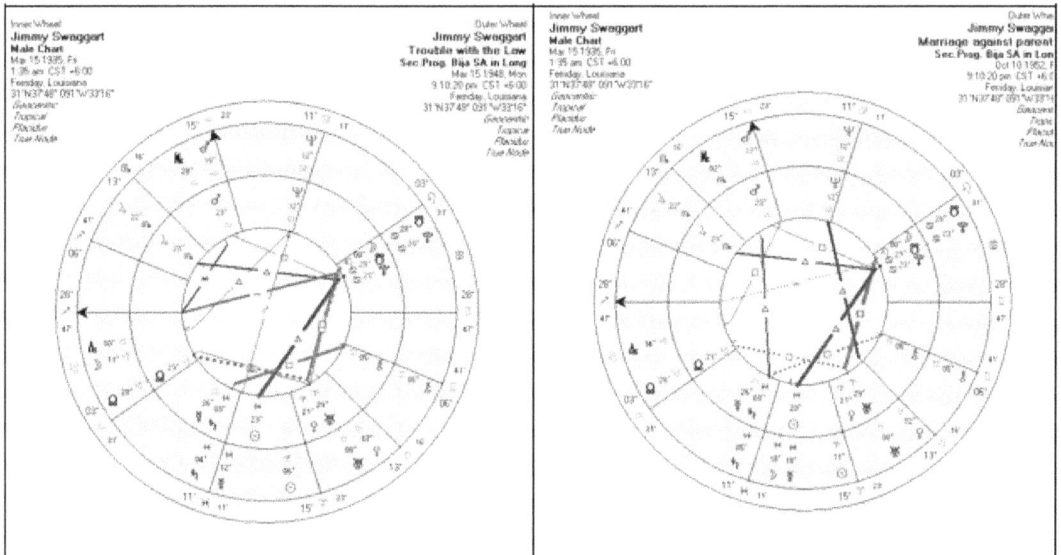

Death of two key women and mentors - mother and grandmother

At Jimmy's mother's death, July 9, 1960, his Progressed Moon Declination had just turned the corner from maximum North, as key time for transition from one phase of life to another. Notice that Jimmy's natal retrograde Mars doesn't turn direct until he is 65 years old in the year 2000, so we can assume that as it now moves direct that some of the same situations involving Mars will be revisited. Back to the death of his mother, Mars had progressed to his Midheaven, though a birth time of 5 to 8 minutes earlier than 1:35 AM would make the aspect exact for the event. The notable Progression in effect at this time was Progressed Ascendant forming a Grand Square to natal Venus, Mars and Pluto. Progressed Jupiter quincunx the natal Moon signaled the loss as well. In addition, transiting Saturn square the natal Midheaven, and transiting Jupiter conjunct the natal Ascendant in square to the Sun forms a "mid-point of aspect" that completes the appropriate "stacking up" of stress aspects to signify such a loss. Midpoint of aspect is exactly that – a midpoint that activates a wider-orb natal pattern.

Jimmy's grandmother died just a few months later on February 19, 1961, so nearly the same Secondary Progressions are in place, but now the Progressed Moon has moved to square his Midheaven. Since his grandmother was his childhood mentor in matters of Pentecostal faith, her death was definitely the greater loss. The Progressed Moon Declination in Figure 4 had now moved to parallel Uranus to mark the suddenness of the event but look for this same pattern to be repeated exactly when Jimmy was first arrested for consorting with a prostitute. At his grandmother's death, Neptune was transiting Jimmy's Progressed Midheaven, Uranus was transiting square his natal Jupiter, and the transiting Jupiter/Saturn conjunction were just

Figure 42 Swaggart Progression Age 25   **Figure 43 Swaggart Progression Age 25**

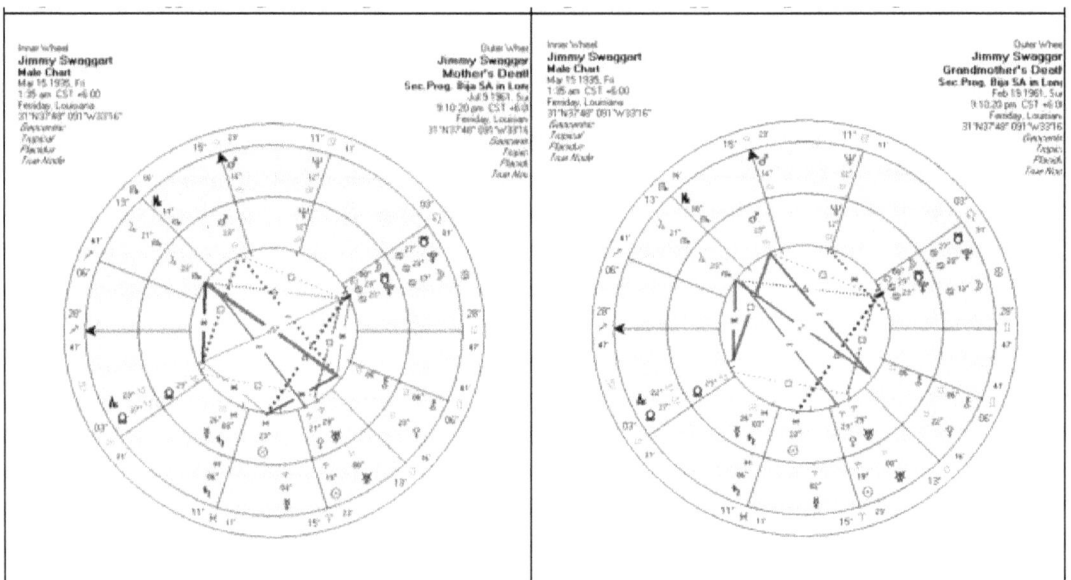

past the square to his natal Mars and opposition to Pluto. Again, we see appropriate planetary contacts to describe the loss of one so spiritually close.

Jimmy is Arrested with Prostitute

Even though other memorable events occurred in the ensuing years since his mother's and grandmother's deaths, the most notable event occurred on October 17, 1987 when Jimmy was arrested with a prostitute, and actually, it wasn't until February 21st of the next year before he had to face the consequences of his actions when a fellow televangelist made public the damning evidence of photos of Jimmy with the prostitute. Many of us can still remember Jimmy Swaggart's tearful confession televised around the world for all to see his shame. Interestingly, the Progressed Moon Declination was in the same position as at his grandmother's death, parallel to natal Uranus.

Several progressions had moved into place to form a "stacking up" of planetary contact that almost always signifies an important life event. Ironically, in this case all of the 23-degree planets were activated – Mars and the natal Grand Trine of the Sun, Jupiter and Pluto – rather than the expected natal angular Moon, Moon's Nodes and Uranus T-square. Several Progressions and Transits converged to bring hard aspects to this Grand configuration that had worked very easily in his life so far. First, by 1987 the progressed Midheaven, Chiron, Saturn, Pluto, and Lunar Nodes had all moved into 1-degree orb of long-term hard aspect, so any faster moving progression, outer transit or Progressed Moon contact to the configuration would tumble the row of dominoes. Notice also that the Progressed Midheaven forms a close double

Figure 44 Swaggart Progression Age 52   **Figure 45 Swaggart Progression Age 53**

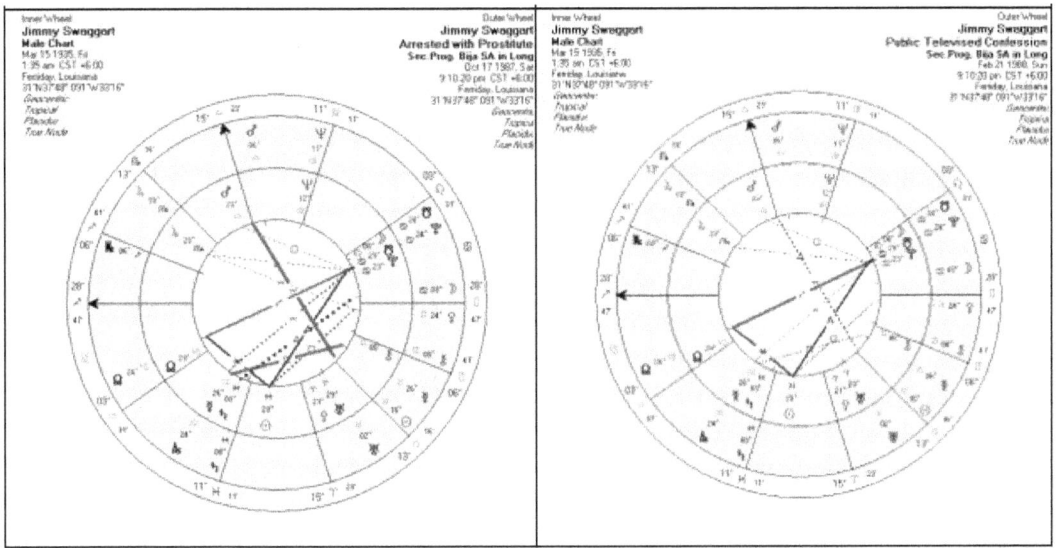

sesqui-square aspect to natal Venus and Pluto at the time of the first arrest – all very appropriate aspects and astrological symbolism to describe one facing problems (Pluto) of reputation (MC) being ruined (in this case the double sesqui-square) through sexual pleasure (Venus).

At the arrest Jimmy's Progressed Venus had moved to square his natal Sun and quincunx Jupiter, suggesting a major conflict between the pleasures of life and his faith.

Figure 46 Six Months of Transits from Swaggart's 1st Arrest to Public Confession

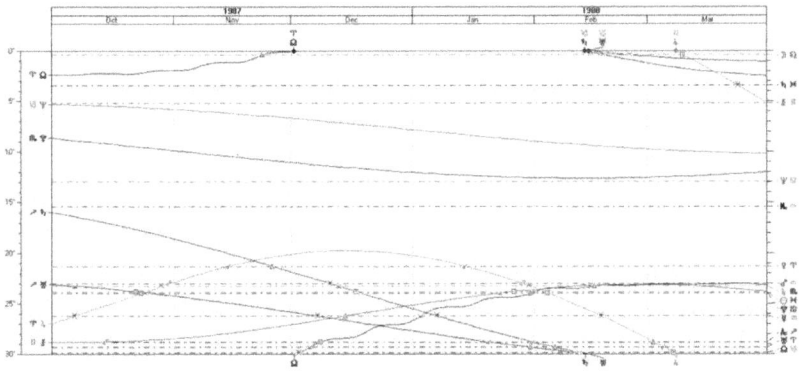

To compound the issue, his Solar Arc Progressed Midheaven had moved to sesqui-square natal Pluto and Progressed South Node, both suggesting that he may be forced to learn important lessons related to sexuality. At the same time, his Progressed Ascendant was inconjunct Pluto and square Venus – all indicators that his sexual dalliances would cause big problems. It comes as no surprise that transiting Uranus was also activating this same configuration to bring the sordid truth to public knowledge. Transiting Uranus squared Swaggart's natal Sun and opposed Progressed Venus. Transiting Pluto sesqui-squared both natal Sun and Progressed Venus, and transiting Jupiter (not Saturn!) squared natal Pluto and opposed Mars. At the same time, Jupiter squared Progressed Pluto and the Lunar Nodes. This case provides a sterling example of a very fortunate natal Grand Trine turning sour from the "stacking up" of hard aspects by progression and transit.

Even working from a known birth time and many life events, it is evident that there is always "background noise" from the many other facets of life we all deal with every day and which complicate the rectification search – even at times of major life events. It is for this reason that I recommend isolating the few natal planets in 1-degree aspect as the most reliable way into a rectification search. Of course, the astrologer only searching a span of a few minutes variance of the birth time is less challenged by such complexities.

Public Confession on Television/ Defrocked as Minister

Four months later, the public learned of Jimmy Swaggart's fall from grace and disbarment from the ministry when a fellow televangelist got his revenge by exposing actual photos of Jimmy and the prostitute together. He couldn't talk his way out of trouble any more. Interestingly, transiting Jupiter had retrograded away from the cluster of progressed planets in hard aspect at the arrest, only to go direct and hit the cluster again at the time of his public confession. The Secondary Progressions, and even the outer planets Saturn though Pluto had not moved much from their positions 4 months earlier so their effect was still present. Astrologically, I might

Figure 47 Swaggart Transits First Arrest   **Figure 48 Transits at Public Confession**

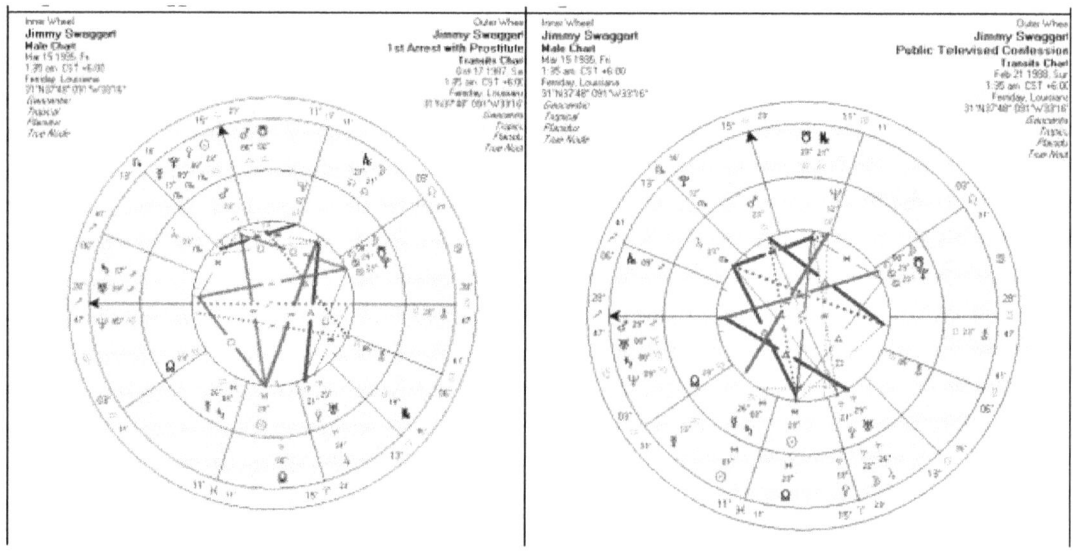

Table 24 Directed Midheaven Times Conjunct Aspect Networks at Age 52

Planet Contacted By Conjunction	First Arrest/Prostitute Oct 17, 1987	Public Confession Feb 21, 1988	Defrocked as Minister April 8, 1988
Grand Trine			
Jupiter 23:15 Scorpio	0:43 AM MC 1:04 Libra	0:41 AM MC 0:44 Libra	AM 0:40 AM MC 0:47 Libra
Pluto 23:57 Cancer	4:31 PM MC 0:56 Gemini	PM 4:30:20 PM MC 0:36 Gemini	PM 4:30 PM MC 0:01 Gemini
Sun 23:48 Pisces	9:40 AM MC 13:13 Aquarius	9:39:20 AM MC 12:35 Aquarius	9:39:13 AM MC 12:30 Aquarius
T-Square			
Venus 21:49 Aries	10:40 AM MC 28:40 Aquarius	10:38:45 AM MC 28:20 Aquarius	10:38:40 AM MC 28:15 Aquarius
Mars 23:01 Libra	10:45:30 PM MC 0:45 Virgo	10:43 PM MC 0:05 Virgo	10:42:55 PM MC 0:00 Virgo
Pluto 23:57 Cancer	4:31 PM MC 0:56 Gemini	PM 4:30:20 PM MC 0:36 Gemini	PM 4:30 PM MC 0:01 Gemini
T-Square			
NNode 29:53 Capricorn	4:54:30 AM MC 6:05 Sagittarius	4:53:50 AM MC 5:45 Sagittarius	4:53:55 AM MC 5:40 Sagittarius
SNode 29:53 Cancer	4:52:30 PM MC 6:05 Gemini	4:51:50 PM MC 5:45 Gemini	4:53:55 PM MC 5:40 Gemini
Moon 00:23 Leo	5:12:23 PM MC 10:45 Gemini	5:09:33 PM MC 10:05 Gemini	5:09:18 PM MC 10:00 Gemini
Uranus 29:20 Aries	11:10:30 AM MC 6:45 Pisces	11:08:15 AM MC 6:05 Pisces	11:08 AM MC 6:00 Pisces

have chosen Saturn as the master of consequences, but in this case a crisis of faith seemed to be the issue so the several connections to Jupiter by progression and transit are not surprising.

Table 25 Directed Ascendant Times Conjunct Aspect Networks at Age 52

Planet Contacted By Conjunction	First Arrest/Prostitute Oct 17, 1987	Public Confession Feb 21, 1988	Defrocked as Minister April 8, 1988
Grand Trine			
Jupiter 23:15 Scorpio	6:40: 30 PM ASC 1:04 Libra	6:37:45 PM ASC 0:30 Libra	6:37:30 PM ASC 00:25 Libra
Pluto 23:57 Cancer	9:39:20 AM ASC 0:56 Gemini	9:37:30 AM ASC 0:36 Gemini	9:36 AM ASC 0:01 Gemini
Sun 23:48 Pisces	9:40 AM ASC 1:13 Aquarius	9:39:20 AM ASC 1:35 Aquarius	9:39:13 AM ASC 1:30 Aquarius
T-Square			
Venus 21:18 Aries	5:11:39 AM ASC 28:55 Aquarius	5:10 AM ASC 28:35 Aquarius	5:09:45 AM ASC 28:30 Aquarius
Mars 23:01 Libra	4:14:45 PM ASC 00:20 Virgo	4:15:30 PM ASC 00:00 Virgo	4:15:15 PM ASC 29:59:45 Leo
Pluto 23:57 Cancer	11:30 AM ASC 1:25 Gemini	11:28:30 AM ASC 1:05 Gemini	11:26 AM ASC 1:00 Gemini
T-Square			
NNode 29:53 Capricorn	11:45:34 PM ASC 5:45 Sagittarius	11:44 PM ASC 5:25 Sagittariu	11:43:43 PM ASC 5:20 Sagittarius
SNode 29:53 Cancer	9:58 AM ASC 5:45 Gemini	9:55:54 AM ASC 5:25 Gemini	9:51 AM ASC 5:20 Gemini
Moon 00:23 Leo	10:04:36 AM ASC 7:50 Gemini	10:03 AM ASC 7:30 Gemini	10:02:45 AM ASC 7:25 Gemini
Uranus 29:20 Aries	5:34:48 AM ASC 7:00 Pisces	5:33:30 AM ASC 6:40 Pisces	5:30 AM ASC 6:35 Pisces

Table 26 Times Directed Opposite the T-Square Apex Planets at Age 52

T-Square Apex Planet Opposition	First Arrest/Prostitute 10/17/1987	Public Confession 2/21/1988	Defrocked as Minister 4/8/1988
Opposed Pluto 23:57 Capricorn	4:33 AM MC 0:50 Sagittarius	4:31:30 AM MC 0:35 Sagittarius	4:31 AM MC 0:30 Sagittarius
	11:22:15 PM ASC 0:50 Sagittarius	11:21 PM ASC 0:35 Sagittarius	11:20:45 PM ASC 0:30 Sagittarius
Opposed Uranus 29:20 Libra	11:10 PM MC 7:05 Virgo	11:07:45 PM MC 6:30 Virgo	11:07:15 PM MC 6:25 Virgo
	4:58:50 PM ASC 7:05 Virgo	4:56:30 PM ASC 6:30 Virgo	4:56 PM ASC 6:25 Virgo

- **Jimmy Is Arrested Again with Prostitute**

By the time of Jimmy's second arrest with a prostitute, October 11, 1991, his Progressed Moon Declination had moved to parallel Uranus. Though several notable connections stand out in the progressed-to-progressed contacts, the close one-degree natal configurations are at the forefront. Progressed Venus moved to the Descendant at the same time Jimmy's Progressed Ascendant moved to inconjunct his natal Moon and South Node, while transiting Saturn opposed them. So now the close natal T-square configuration is activated to bring hidden secrets

Figure 49 Swaggart Progressions Second Arrest   **Figure 50 Transits at Second Arrest**

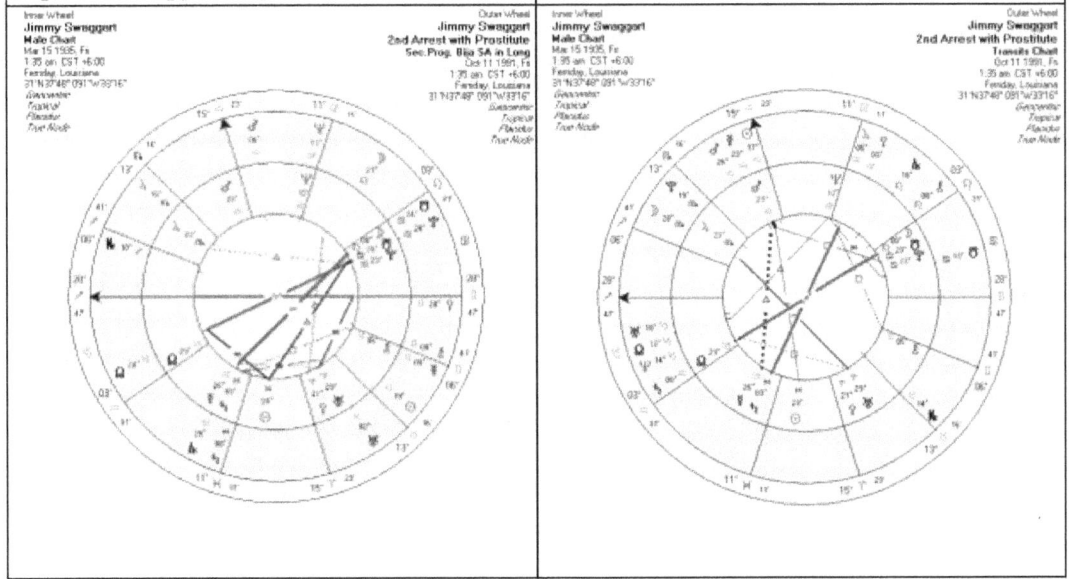

Table 27 Confirming the Birth Time from Several Important Events

Hours	Moon AM Time Estimate	AM Times Age 25		AM Times Age 52		PM Times Age 25		PM Times Age 52		Total
		MC	ASC	MC	ASC	MC	ASC	MC	ASC	
12-1		3		3		9		3		**18**
1-2	Moon	3	3							**Moon +6**
2-3		9								**9**
3-4										
4-5				6				9	6	**21**
5-6					6			3		**9**
6-7		12	3		3	12				**30**
7-8										
8-9										
9-10				3	9					**12**
10-11		6		3	3			3		**15**
11-12		6		3	3	3		3	6	**24**
Total		39	6	18	24	24	0	18	15	
Total		AM Times	= 87			PM Times	= 57			

from the past (Nodes) to light (Uranus). And sure enough, Jupiter and the natal Grand Trine were back in the game. Transiting Pluto moved to conjunct natal Jupiter at the same time the progressed Moon squared natal Jupiter and made an inconjunct to the Sun. Clearly, both closely aspected natal patterns, the T-Square and the Grand Trine, accurately describe the drama of Jimmy Swaggart's glory as a minister and his demons as a man.

Table 27 shows the possible birth times derived from 3 key life events at age 25 combined with 3 additional key events at age 52, and the same peaks persist from 11 to 2 AM/PM and 6-7 AM/PM clearly confirming our earlier suspicion that natal chart squares are activate at major life events.

From analyzing the Table 27, and using the major events clustered around ages 25 and 52, we again find an emphasis on the Midheaven involvement at these key events with 89 hits, and much less for the Ascendant with 45 hits. That is not to say that, when all major events are plotted, the balance may be altered. The total for 4-5 AM/PM is not highlighted because no positions at that hour were active at age 25, an extremely critical year in Swaggart's life. Also notice that even without the Moon included, a distinct peak is found in the AM times, which occur with 50% greater frequency than PM times. As you continue to search and refine techniques for establishing the "working Angles" and rectifying them with a birth time consistent to life events, it is apparent that good computer search software is a distinct advantage.

Below is an example of the quick search results obtained from the Jigsaw 2.2 software mentioned earlier. With input of only Swaggart's birth date and location (with no birth time at all) and the 19 bolded dates of his key life events, Jigsaw 2.2 narrowed the possible birth times using Outer Transits, Directions and Progressions to natal planets and possible Angles as shown in Table 28.

Table 28 Jigsaw 2.2 Swaggart Birth Time Rectification Search

Possible Birth Time	Corresponding Midheaven	Corresponding Ascendant	Transits	Progressions	Directions	Percentage Accuracy
12:39 AM	1-2 Libra	0:50-1:41 Capricorn	4/7	4/8	6/8	66%
6:39 AM	1-2 Capricorn	1:11-2:22 Aries	3/7	3/8	5/8	53%
12:37 PM	1-2 Aries	0:50-1:41 Cancer	4/8	3/7	5/8	56%
6:37 PM	1-2 Cancer	1:11-2:22 Libra	4/8	3/7	6/8	63%

Note that the same time ranges show peaks using all of our search methods: the Jigsaw 2 rectification software; our hand-calculations working from a Noon time; and our computer search with general astrology software to find the Angles appropriate for the major events at ages 25 and 52. Again, the spread of possible birth times reinforces the close square aspects of multiple planets as the correct starting point for checking the correspondence of other life events. If using the Jigsaw 2.2 software to search possible birth times, one would certainly test other life events for confirmation. Even though the Swaggart birth time is "AA" data supported with a birth certificate, one cannot assume that it is a precise as the atomic time used today. It is not unusual to find variances of as much as half-hour in recorded birth times and very common to find variance of only a few minutes. The correct birth time should show appropriate astrological symbolism at all life events.

The following is the thought process of recent OCA 202 student, Cheryl Manley, in solving the Jimmy Swaggart rectification problem using Jigsaw 2.2 and working from the same list of events to sort for Directions, Secondary Progressions and Transits that correlate. Working from her table of "Time Analysis", Cheryl concludes that, "…conjunctions are most important, then oppositions, then squares."

"Of the most promising set of contacts [from the Jigsaw search] 0:53 AM appears to be the strongest and 0:42 a close second. Of the longer-range aspects, 1:45 AM seems to be the strongest with 7:55 PM a close second and 4:34 PM third.

Because there are lots of transits ranging from 17-19 degrees with no planets at those degrees, I would assume that at least one of the angles has to be in that range (1 degree is reasonably close to the tight T-square at 29 degrees [of the Moon's Nodes, Uranus and possibly the Moon], and 4 degrees Saturn and 26 degrees Mercury to the Venus/Mars/Pluto T-square. This [evidence] rules out the 4:34 PM time, which has the angles at 1 and 4 degrees. I also rule out the 7:55 PM time, because the Secondary Progressed aspects do not line up…This leaves me with one time frame around 0:53 AM and another around 1:45 AM. (Quote continues after table)

Table 29 Transits to Angles and Planets for Two Possible Times

	0:53 AM			1:45 AM		
Event	Conjuncts	Squares	Opposite	Conjuncts	Squares	Opposite
Brother Died	tMars/Uran tNNode/Mars	tMars/Mars tSaturn/Moo tNNode/Plut		tMars/Uran tNNode/Mars	tMars/Mars tSaturn/Moo tNNode/Plut	
Marriage		tPluto/Jupit	tNept/Venus	tMars/Asc tSaturn/MC	tPluto/Jupit tUran/Asc	tNept/Venus
Mother Died			tMoon/Moon tPluto/Saturn	tJupiter/Asc	tSaturn/MC	tPluto/Saturn
Grandma Died	tMars/Desc	tMars/MC tUran/Jupiter	tMoon/Jupite		tMoon/MC tUran/Jupiter	tMoon/Jupiter
Record Success			tJupiter/Nept			tJupiter/Nept
1st Radio Show				tSaturn/IC		

Table continues

Event	0:53 AM Conjuncts	Squares	Opposite	1:45 AM Conjuncts	Squares	Opposite
1st TV Show	tUranus/Mars	tMars/Venus		tUranus/Mars	tMars/Venus	
1st Arrest	tNNode/IC	tNNode/Asc tMoon/Jupit tJupiter/Plu tUranus/Sun			tMoon/Jupit tJupiter/Plu tUranus/Sun	
2nd Arres		tMars/Moon tSaturn/Uran			tNNode/MC tSaturn/Uran tNept/MC	
Event	Conjuncts	Squares	Opposite	Conjuncts	Squares	Opposite
	0:53 AM			1:45 AM		

"For each of these two times, I'll next look at contacts to the Progressed Sun and Angles. It is clear that the Sun doesn't move enough between these two times to make a difference. The Progressed Angles by conjunction only are effective for 8 of the 12 events (6 clearly applicable to the event) for a birth of 0:53 AM and 12 of the events (9 clearly applicable to the event) for 1:45 AM. This suggests that the 1:45 AM time is best."

In one last search for confirmation of the 1:35 – 1:45 AM times derived and supported by most students, the Solar Eclipses may make close aspect to an Angle or the Moon at key life events. A range of 3 degrees is applied here, but one could as well use a 4 – 5-degree orb for Solar Eclipses – precisely why they are unreliable for the initial search.

Table 30 Solar Eclipses at Jimmy Swaggart Important Life Events

	Event	Eclipse	Date	Age	Aspect
1	Brother died of pneumonia/Jimmy ill	19 Libra	Feb, 1940	4+	Conjunct MC Oppos Venus
2	Preached of several bomb/flood prophecies	27 Cancer	July, 1944	9	Conjunct SNode/ Moon
3	Married suddenly against parents' wishes/ Never dated	28 Leo	Oct 10, 1952	17	Trine Uranus
4	Got fired for stealing	28 Leo	Winter, 1952	17	Inconj NNode
5	Ill with pneumonia/ Made the Ministry his career	30 Libra	Jan 1, 1958	22	Square Moon

Table continues

	Event	Eclipse	Date	Age	Aspect
6	Ordination as minister	28 Virgo	Jun 23, 1960	25	Trine NNode Sextile Moon Inconj Uranus
7	Mother, Minnie Bell, died in hospital	28 Virgo	July 9, 1960	25	Trine NNode Sextile Moon Inconj Uranus
8	Grandma Ada Died of stroke-Jim devastated	26 Aquarius	Feb 19, 1961	25	Conjunct Merc Square Jupiter Inconj SNode Inconj Moon
9	1st radio broadcast of "Camp Meeting Hour"	29 Virgo	Jan 1, 1969	33	Trine NNode Inconj Uranus
10	Began televising "Camp Meeting Hour"	14 Capricorn	Spring, 1973	38	Square MC
11	Found daughter-in-law in affair w/ guitarist	30 Gemini	June, 1982	47	Conjunct 7th Inconj NNode
12	"Frontline" aired documentary on Jimmy's ministry	23 Sagittarius	May 19, 1983	48	Square Sun Inconj Pluto Near ASC
13	Arrested with prostitute by cop, son of rival	30 Virgo	Oct 17, 1987	52	Trine NNode Inconj Uranus Inconj Mercury
14	Swaggart hedged on confession/ Gorman released photos to police /made tearful TV public confession	28 Pisces	Feb 21, 1988	52	Square ASC Trine Moon Trine SNode
15	Defrocked by Assemblies of God	28 Pisces	April 8, 1988	53	Square ASC Trine Moon Trine SNode
16	CNN Broadcast prostitute/Jimmy photos	26 Capricorn	Jun 25, 1991	56	Conj NNode Oppos Moon Square Uran
17	Second arrest with prostitute	19 Cancer	Oct 11, 1991	56	Square MC Square Venus
18	News of 2nd arrest hit the national news		Oct 12, 1991	56	Square MC Square Venus

For some interesting local color just a few miles from my home, Clark's Gas Station in Indio, California sports a large brass plaque announcing it as the place where the great televangelist, "Jimmy Swaggart, minister of God", was arrested in 1991 for soliciting a prostitute.

Jimmy Swaggart was born at 1:35 AM on March 15, 1935 in Ferriday, Louisiana 31N37'48", 91W33'16". Astro.com verifies the time from the donor with "birth certificate in hand", and classifies the data with the top AA rating. The Seaman biography states 1:30 AM, however, no verification of source is given for that time. In applying the various timing techniques for rectification to connect with key life events, there is better support for a birth time near 0:53 AM or one at 1:45 AM than the recorded 1:35 AM or the 1:30 AM noted in his biography. However, in activation of aspects, it is generally acknowledged that midpoints of aspect, and therefore time, can play a role. In this case, the difference between the speculative times of 0:53 and 1:45 AM is 52 minutes of clock time, or 9 degrees, which normally is too wide a range. But to be considered is the range of aspects connecting all of the planets of each tight aspect network in this chart from Venus at 21 degrees to the Moon at 0 degrees. It equals a range of 9 degrees. In such cases as this, a time set at a midpoint in range of activating the close aspects at major life events may be considered and tested. So, 27 minutes added to the speculative 0:53 AM birth gives a midpoint of 1:20 AM which may come close to events. But other students have supported 1:27, 1:35 and 1:40 AM birth times. All such possibilities and variations give just cause to the endless complexity of a rectification search. After all of the work to rectify a chart, at best, the astrologer can only claim that the rectified time is highly consistent with life events, which is good enough for most of the forecasting work we do for clients.

Chapter 5

What Movement Techniques Work Best?

Know What Moves How Fast to Activate a One-Degree Orb

In modern astrology, the techniques commonly used for the process of rectification provide varying degrees of success. Indeed, the process is so complex that few astrologers attempt the task because the time involved is extensive and few clients want to pay the fee for an extended search. As a practical result, little is written on the topic, and therefore, few astrologers feel schooled enough in the art to offer birth time rectification as a service.

Now that the groundwork of listing the dates of important life events is completed, the next step is to search the natal planetary placements for close aspect connections within one-degree. The premise is when planets or the Moon's nodes are in close natal aspect, when one of them is activated by movement so are the other planets or points in the configuration. Therefore, we should list all the one-degree close-aspect networks of the chart in order of orb closeness. Orbs beyond two-degrees are less helpful as the "Aspect Hook" upon which to begin the rectification search.

Of course, it is possible that the natal Moon or an Angle may also be involved in the close aspect network, but that cannot be determined with reasonable certainty until later in the rectification process. One might correctly argue that the moving planet or Angle can also activate a single planet or point, but close aspect configurations provide the easiest "Hook" to start the search to appropriately align appropriate astrological descriptors to actual life events. If there are no one-degree major aspects in the chart (even the trine or sextile), activation of a lone planet or Angle works.

As a reminder, the key to all rectification work is to know what moves how fast and how long it will activate a planet or point in the natal chart within one-degree in each movement technique. The following Tables may guide the choice of which movement systems best serve the search.

Table 31 Average Time Movement Methods Activate 1-degree Applying, 1/2-degree Separating

	S. Arc Direct.	Second Progres	Tertiary Progress	Minor Progress	Outer Transit	Inner Transit	Progress Declin.	Solar Eclipse	Lunar Eclipse
MC	1 ½ yrs	1 ½ yrs	3 days	1½ days		6 min	1 ½ yrs		
ASC	1 ½ yrs	1-2 yrs	2-3 days	1½ days		6 min	1 ½ yrs		
Sun	1 ½ yrs	1 ½ yrs	6 weeks	3 weeks		1 ½ dys	1 ½ yrs	6 mos	2 wks
Moon	1 ½ yrs	1 ½ mo	2 days	1 day		3 hrs	2 mos	6 mos	2 wks
Mercury	1 ½ yrs	1-1½ yr	5-6 wks	3 weeks		1-2 dys	1 ½ yrs		
Merc R	3-5 yrs		1-2 mos	2-4 wks		4 days	2-3 yrs		
Venus	1 ½ yrs	1-2 yrs	5-6 wks	3 weeks		1 ½ dy	1 ½ yrs		
Venus R		3-5 yrs	1-2½ mo	5-7 wks		1 wk	2-3 yrs		
Mars	1 ½ yrs	2 years	2 mos	1 month		2 days	2 yrs		
Mars R		9-10 yr	4 mos	2 mos		1 ½ wk	3-5 yrs		
Jupiter	1 ½ yrs	6-7 yrs	6 mos	3 mos	1 week		4 yrs		
Jupit R		12-13 y	1 year	6 mos	7 mos		8-16 yrs		
Saturn	1 ½ yrs	10-14 y	1 year	6 mos	2 wks		5 yrs		
Satur R		15-25 y	1 ½ yr	9 mos	9 mos		10-20 yr		
Uranus	1 ½ yrs	18-30 y	3 years	1 ½ yrs	1 year		14-24 yr		
Neptun	1 ½ yrs	22-35 y	4 years	2 years	1 ½ yrs		17-30 yr		
Pluto	1 ½ yrs	26-40 y	5 years	2 ½ yrs	2 years		20-35 yr		
NNode	1 ½ yrs	30 yrs	1 ½ yrs	9 mos	1 mo		2 yrs		

NNode and SNode are in Direct motion only in the Solar Arc Direction system. In all Progressions, Transits and Eclipses the Lunar Nodes move retrograde.

Table 32 Approximate Time for Moving Factors to Activate 1-Degree in the Natal Chart

1 year+	Secondary Progression of Sun, Mercury, Venus and angles Solar Arc Direction of all planets and angles Retrograde area between Pluto, Neptune, Uranus transit stations Out-of-bounds or maximum N or S of Moon's declination
11 months	Retrograde shadow area between stations of Saturn
9 ¾ months	Retrograde shadow area between stations of Jupiter Secondary Progression of Mars
6 ½ months	Retrograde shadow area between stations of Mars
6 months	Solar and Lunar Eclipses Transit stations of Pluto Transit stations of Neptune
3 ½ months	Retrograde shadow area between the stations of Venus
3 months	Transit stations of Uranus Parallel or contra-parallel of Moon Declination
1 ¾ months	Retrograde shadow area between the stations of Mercury
1 month	Transit of Saturn Transit of Moon's nodal axis Secondary Progression of the Moon Stationary Period of Jupiter through Pluto
2 weeks	Transit of Jupiter Stationary Period of Mars
1 week	Stationary Period of Venus Stationary Period of Mercury
2 days	Transit of Mars (not near station or in shadow)
1 day	Transit of Venus Transit of Mercury
2 hours	Transit of Moon
4 minutes	Diurnal transit of angles and house cusps

Table 33 Movement Technique Timing to Activate the Natal Chart and When to Use

Technique	Activates One-degree Applying/Separating	Function	Best Use
Solar Arc Direction	1-year / 6-months	Confirms birth time	First test
Secondary Progression	1-year / 6-months	Confirms birth time	Later test
Progressed Moon	1-month / 2-weeks	Narrows time range	Early test
Progressed New Moon	6-months / 3-months	Narrows time range	Early test
Progressed Full Moon	6-months / 3-months	Narrows time range	Early test
Tertiary Progression	1-month / 2-weeks	Confirms birth time	Later test
Minor Progression	2-weeks / 1-week	Confirms birth time	Later test
Progressed Declination	1-year / 1-year	Narrows time range	Later test
Transit Pluto	2-years	Narrows time range	Early test
Transit Neptune	1-year 9-months	Narrows time range	Early test
Transit Uranus	1-year	Narrows time range	Early test
Transit Saturn	2-weeks to 9-months	Narrows time range	Early test
Transit Jupiter	1-week to 5-months	Narrows time range	Early test
Transit Lunar Nodes	3-weeks / 2-weeks	Narrow time range	Early test
Solar Eclipse	6-months	Emphasizes event	Later test
Lunar Eclipse	2-weeks	Influences event	Later test
ASC Decan/Dwad	4-minutes clock time	Confirms birth time	Precise last test
MC Decan/Dwad	4-minutes clock time	Confirms birth time	Precise last test
Solar Return	1-year	Needs correct birth time	Last test

Software Settings Make a Difference

In a recent article circulated throughout the astrology community by one of our respected researchers, Ron Tiggle, PhD, made a convincing case for changing our astrology software settings for symbolic movement to the Bija method that corrects for the increasing inaccuracy of directions, progressions and their derivatives as we age. An excerpt from Dr. Tiggle's article, "Improve the Accuracy of Fractal Progressions…and Solar Arc Directions", clarifies the importance of correct software settings that relate to movement techniques.

"According to L. Edward Johndro[1][2] and Cyril Fagan[3], Astrologers have been calculating the Secondary Progressed Chart and Solar Arc Directions incorrectly. My own analysis agrees

---

1. Tiggle, Ron, Article, "Improve the Accuracy of Fractal Progressions and Solar Arc Directions", Mountain Astrologer, Seattle, WA Fall 2020

Table 34 Planetary Speed in Three Movement Systems: Transits, Progressions and Directions

CYCLE	TRANSIT	PROGRESSION	DIRECTION
Ascendant	361° daily	1° yearly-variable by sign ♍/♎-45°-♓/♈ 2°-♌	1° yearly
Midheaven	361° daily	1° yearly	1° yearly
Moon = 28 days	11-15° daily	1° monthly	1° yearly
Sun = 365 days	1° daily	1° yearly	1° yearly
Mercury 365 days	1+° daily + 3 ℞ cycles yearly	1° yr. variable due to ℞ cycle	1° yearly
Venus = 225 days	1+° daily + 1 ℞ cycle yearly	1° yr. variable due to ℞ cycle	1° yearly
Mars = 2½ years	45" daily + 1 ℞ cycle bi-yearly	45"yr. variable due to ℞ cycle	1° yearly
Jupiter = 12 yrs.	30° yearly or 1 sign	30"yr. variable due to ℞ cycle	1° yearly
Saturn = 29 yrs.	12° yearly or 1 sign / 2½ yrs.	15"yr. variable due to ℞ cycle	1° yearly
Chiron = 50 yrs.	8° yearly or 1 sign / 4 years	Very little in a lifetime	1° yearly
Uranus = 84 yrs.	4 1/2° yearly or 1 sign / 7 yrs.	Very little in a lifetime	1° yearly
Neptune = 164 yrs.	1-2° yearly or 1 sign / 14 yrs.	Very little in a lifetime	1° yearly
Pluto = 250 yrs.	1-3° yearly or 1 sign / 21 yrs.	Very little in a lifetime	1° yearly
Nodes = 19 yrs.	1° in 3 weeks clockwise	Very little in a lifetime - clockwise	1° yearly

with their conclusion. The difference between the two techniques though small, accumulates at the rate of 1 day per year of life. So, by the time you are 60 years old, progressed aspects (both secondary and tertiary) and solar arc directions which appear to be exact are actually coming due 60 days too early. Fagan notes, the correction should be used independently of which zodiac you prefer. Also, he notes, the progressed Moon aspects can be off by as much as 3 months and if mundane charts are done on countries several hundred years old, the progressed Moon may be off as much as 7 or more degrees. My own analyses confirmed these observations. For example, the USA was born in 1776, Secondary progressions and Solar Arc Directions computed for 2020 would be 244 days off and the secondary progressed Moon would be off by 9 degrees. Many years ago, the Church of Light conducted extensive statistical analyses of Secondary Progressions and accurately found that the Progressed Moon was not a reliable timer of events. They used the standard method of calculating secondary progressions (1 solar day = 365.24 days) which Johndro and Fagan have pointed out is incorrect. The reason why the standard method of equating a solar day = year is incorrect is that its diurnal rotation of 361 degrees cannot be accurately equated to 365.24 days. When the Bija method (1 solar day = 366.24 days) is used the Progressed Moon becomes a reliable timer of events. … The error that astrologers have been making is setting a solar day=365.24 days when it is really equal to 366.24 due to its longer diurnal rotation. Although these corrections are small for each day, they accumulate at the rate of 1 day per calendar year. Thus, by the time you are 30 years old, your progressions will be coming due @ 30 days too early."

The Bija setting is an option listed in most all astrology software of the twenty-first century, so if the default setting for movement systems is not Bija, it is in your list of options to select. Movement accuracy is critical to the rectification process of aligning a lifetime of events to a consistent chain of appropriate astrological descriptors.

Assessing the Year with Solar Arc Directions

The Solar Arc Direction system has one advantage over all other methods of moving the chart in that it is easy to estimate the approximate motion using mental math to target important years. Of course, we use the precise calculation of the Solar Arc to move each of the chart planets and Angles, but the ease of spotting past or forming patterns serves the astrologer well to get a handle on the important life events to open a dialogue with the client. To be clear, the Solar Arc system of Directions is a completely different method of forecasting that is totally symbolic, except for the Sun. None of the other planets will ever be at any of the event placements in real time, whereas the Progressed system is built upon actual planetary motion, and only the concept of synchronicity in "Day for Year", "Day for Month" and "Month for Year" is symbolic. Therefore, when using the Solar Arc Direction system, the planets and Angles for the target year will always be in the same relationship as they are in the Natal chart. All chart factors are moved at the Solar Arc rate according to the client's age for the target date. In the Directed system, the directed planets are interpreted only as they contact natal planets or points – not directed to directed positions as in the Progressed system. Transits are accepted universally as a timer for activation of the natal chart. With lesser emphasis, transits are also applied to the Directed or the Progressed chart by advocates of either system.

Solar Arc Directions do have some common links to Secondary Progressions because both systems move the Midheaven at the Solar Arc rate of one day for a year. As well, the Sun in both systems moves at the Solar Arc rate. Only the Ascendant, planets and sensitive points based on the Angles move at different rates in the two systems. In the Solar Arc system, the Ascendant and planets are all moved at the Solar Arc rate. In the Secondary Progressed system, the Ascendant is derived from the latitude of birth which varies greatly at higher latitudes and the planets move at their own rate of speed, including retrograde cycles.

The "one-degree orb" rule applies to Directions as well as Progressions. One degree marks an activated period of two years – one applying to the aspect, and one separating from the aspect, though many astrologers now use a half-degree separating. During the time that a Direction activates a planet or angle within the one-degree orb, additional faster moving planetary contacts such as Transits are necessary to trigger the action described by the planets, houses, and aspect. A Direction or even a Progression rarely works alone and, most often, is triggered by an important outer planet transit.

Some astrologers hold that the activating transit must be from one of the planets involved in the Direction aspect; however, experience shows that broader interpretation of potential triggering factors including all planets and Angles holds up. Another argument for allowing any transiting factor to serve as a trigger for the already aligned Direction is the importance attached to such distinctions as chart ruler, house ruler, mutual reception, or even the most elevated planet. The broader interpretation of what can be an activating planet allows the astrologer to use the wide range of his predictive tools. In short, once a Direction to a planet is in place, any transiting outer planet can activate the Direction to a planet, or combination of planets in close orb of natal aspect. The principle of "stacking up" of moving factors is very important to accurate forecasting and timing of events, situations or feelings. When several directed aspects and transit triggers "stack up", the time orbs may overlap and thereby extend their action to a somewhat longer period. Some astrologers focus only on the major and minor hard aspects formed by the 8th harmonic – conjunction, semi-square, square, sesqui-square and opposition – because this family of aspects indicates action of external notice, rather than the static and often internal nature of the sextiles and trines.

Another important advantage of the Solar Arc Direction method of chart movement is that it easily allows the astrologer to assess the accuracy of the birth time by a few well-placed questions to the client. For example, if the astrologer sees that the natal Midheaven is at 13 Cancer and the natal Moon is at 20 Cancer, he can reasonably assume that when the directed Midheaven conjuncted the natal Moon about age 7 an event involving a change in the home life with strong emotional overtones occurred. If that Moon is closely and heavily aspected with troublesome conjunctions, squares and other hard aspects, the impact of the directed Midheaven to the Moon can be greatly compounded. Conversely, if the natal Moon carries several close harmonious aspects, the contact can pass by almost unnoticed. If the client does not confirm such feelings and events at that time but suggests that those circumstances prevailed at a different age not too distant, the astrologer may question the accuracy of the birth time. It may be appropriate to confirm the source of the client's data since the general public is not so "precision timing" conscious as the astrologer. Only if many major life events do not seem to align with the Directed indicators should the astrologer consider rectifying the chart to a time when the events match the astrological indicators. Rectification is a complicated process even in the hands of a professional astrologer, but the Directed chart may provide the first clues to the need for that infrequently used process.

Other signals of important change are suggested by the Directed chart when a planet, angle or cusp changes sign or moves into a new natal house. Keep in mind that the whole Directed chart of planets and angles moves together in tandem at the same rate, so closely aspected planets or angles in the natal chart change signs or houses almost simultaneously. A planet or angle making a sign or house change is felt more subtly by the person; but the natal planet or angle contact is the most notable descriptor of important issues and the resulting changes. Any change of sign or house brings a new perspective on the issues described by the planet(s). For instance, when my directed Sun moved from Virgo to Libra, artistic capabilities came to the forefront of activity; about 30 years later when the directed Sun moved into Scorpio, I delved into learning astrology. Always remember that the moving planet or point brings the message, shaped by its key words, to the natal planet or point to take action on the message in its own character.

Of course, estimating the timing of directed aspects is valuable for gaining a broad sense of life development; however, it is important to remember that exact calculation is necessary at some early point. Even though we can say that the Sun averages 59' 08 minutes of motion each day, it moves from :57 minutes per day in the summer to 61 minutes (1:01) per day in the winter. If we direct the chart using only the Sun's average motion of 59' 08 and always apply that constant to move the whole chart to a target year, we are using the Naibod Method of Direction. The method is not commonly used by modern astrologers for two reasons: 1) computers have made calculation much faster and easier so the astrologer doesn't need such short-cuts, and 2) the system proves to be increasingly inaccurate in forecasting life events or situations as the Sun's arc lengthens or shortens according to the seasons. If one were born near either the summer or the winter solstice, then by the time he reached fifteen our forecast for him would already be off by 6 months by the Naibod average measure (2 minutes more or less than the average solar motion times 15 years equals 30 minutes or a directed 6 months). Clearly, such loose accuracy is inexcusable for the modern astrologer.

In the Directed system natal planets late in the mutable houses and early in the cardinal houses are the most important in the formative years because they will move to the natal angles during childhood. Any natal planets late in a mutable house will arc to an Angle in childhood. Similarly, planets early in the cardinal houses take added importance in childhood because the Angles will be directed to contact them sometime during the first Saturn cycle of life – indeed, the first Saturn half-cycle. It is no wonder that Michel and Francoise Gauquelin found the 10-degrees before each angle and the 5-degrees after to be so prominent in distinguishing the careers of thousands of famous and notable people. Yes, the Gauquelin's confirmed that the peaks of prominence occur about 5-degrees back into the mutable houses, most prominently the twelfth house, diurnally after the Ascendant, and the ninth house, diurnally after the Midheaven.

The Directed system has many plusses for ease of calculation and spotting the formation of planetary contacts; however, it includes confusing information during ages that replicate a major or minor aspect. At age 30 every planet and angle is semi-sextile to its natal position; at age 45 every planet and angle is semi-square to tis natal position; at age 60 all are sextile their natal position and at 90 they are all square their natal position. Certainly, everyone who reaches 90 does not have the extreme challenges of so many squares forming at once, nor is age 60 so full of unbridled opportunity for everyone. The Solar Arcs for these periods are more meaningful as marking life turning points that occur within a range of years for the effective solar arc depending upon whether the Sun is moving faster or slower. So, the semi-square will occur between 42 and 46 years; the sextile between 58 and 62 years, and the square between 88 and 92 years. It looks like we have described the very normal stages of life: "mid-life crisis", "retirement planning" and "transition planning". That argument made, it is also true and important to not overlook that the Directed planets and angles can activate natal planets or angles other than themselves at the same time. For instance, at age 30 Saturn will have arced to semi-sextile its natal position, but also at the same time arc to conjunct the Midheaven, which describes one moving into a responsible position as a leader in his field.

When interpreting Directions, the arcing planet (the one that is moving to contact a natal position) takes the message to the natal planet or point. The interpretation begins with the symbolism of the arcing planet, then that of the receiving natal planet. Next, consider the house positions of both the arcing and contacted natal planet or point in its condition, house placement and aspects to describe the situation and to what extent. Yes, we can interpret and forecast "to what extent" by assessing the list of modifying statements about the planets to determine the potential outcome. For example, if Mars arced to conjunct Venus in the 7th house at 15-Scorpio and opposite Saturn in the 1st, and both are at the "bendings" of the Lunar Nodes (square). The messenger, Mars, brings a fight to challenge a romantic situation that is already limited by the personal blocks from the opposing Taurus Saturn in Venus's sign, and also the Taurus Ascendant ruler. To add to the challenge of learning to give and receive love, both natal planets are also challenged by the painful life lessons needed for character growth, the Lunar Nodes in the 4th and 10th square Venus and Saturn in the 1st and 7th houses. Mars is strong in his Scorpio rulership, but he is just the messenger – it's not his fault. Mars simply activated a pattern of natal planets and points that needed to work through learning to give and get respect in love relationships, the life issues described by their natal condition. However, we can't totally let Mars off the hook – his condition in the natal chart may be very well-aspected and in good condition, which might mitigate his "do something about it" message. Of course, if the arcing Mars is debilitated in the natal chart, the outcome could be ugly and hurtful to both parties to the extent that the hurt feelings may over-ride any positive learning from the situation.

- When the arcing planet is the Sun, the individual brings focus and conviction to the picture; when the arcing planet is the Moon, emotions are deeply invested in the issue
- When Mercury is the arcing planet, intellect or communication is to the natal planet to take action (unless clouded by a Neptune contact)
- When Venus is the arcing planet, the natal planet is given the message attuned to creating beauty in the environment and harmony through the character of the natal planet or point
- When Mars is the arcing planet, the message to the natal planet or point is to stir things up with challenge and action, sometimes in over-drive
- The outer planets are more societal than interpersonal, but their contact by Solar Arc Direction lasts the same as the direction of an inner planet, unlike the Secondary Progressed system where planets move at their own speed that may include a retrograde period.
- When Jupiter is the arcing planet, enthusiasm, hopefulness and faith is brought to the

natal planet or point to carry out the message

- When Saturn is the arcing planet, the message is responsibility and caution brought to the natal planet or point and the area of the activated house
- When Uranus is the arcing planet, the message of individuality and freedom is brought to the natal planet or point to act out
- When Neptune is the arcing planet, the message of idealism, unrealistic hopes and confusion is brought to the natal planet or point to act out
- When Pluto is the arcing planet, the message of control and power is brought to the natal planet or point to act out – and with a Pluto contact to and Angle or Light, there will be issues!

Chelsea Clinton

As a clear demonstration of Solar Arc Direction, Chelsea Clinton's chart was dramatically activated in September of 1998 just as she started her freshman year in college and her father, President Bill Clinton, was publicly outed for his infidelity with a young White House intern – and in the Oval Office no less! First study the natal chart for planets and points in 1 to 2-degree major aspect, because in Solar Arc, they move in tandem for life at the rate of the Sun. For example, Chelsea's natal Venus is opposite Pluto, but Mercury and Neptune are also at 21-22-degrees. In Solar Arc Direction they all move together at the rate of the Sun, and as a team, they can dramatically activate the natal chart.

Chelsea's natal Venus/Pluto arced to square her natal Moon, at the same time her natal Moon arced to activate the lunar nodes, and if that weren't hard enough, her Ascendant arced square her natal Mars/Jupiter conjunction in the 10th house. As astrologers, we cannot be surprised at the emotional strain she was under from her father, she so adored, being vilified as a coward, a liar, and a cheater. The good news, astrologically, was the press left her alone. Amid all the chaos, Solar Arc Mercury trined her natal Moon.

Many modern astrologers use both the Solar Arc Directed system and the Secondary Progressed system either as a double confirmation for unfolding patterns, or to derive the benefits and strengths of each system. Some astrologers even use the faster Progressed Moon for timing in the Directed system, but most rely on outer transits to serve as the faster timing factor to set the life events more precisely in time.

Noted proponent of the Solar Arc Direction method, Noel Tyl, characterizes the difference between the two systems thus:

"... Secondary Progression measurements simply cannot match the vast spectrum of arcs and midpoint pictures possible in the Solar Arc system. It is interesting to note that the system of Secondary Progressions was introduced to the United States by British astrologers at the

Figure 51- Chelsea Clinton Natal Chart   Figure 52- Chelsea Clinton Directed to Natal

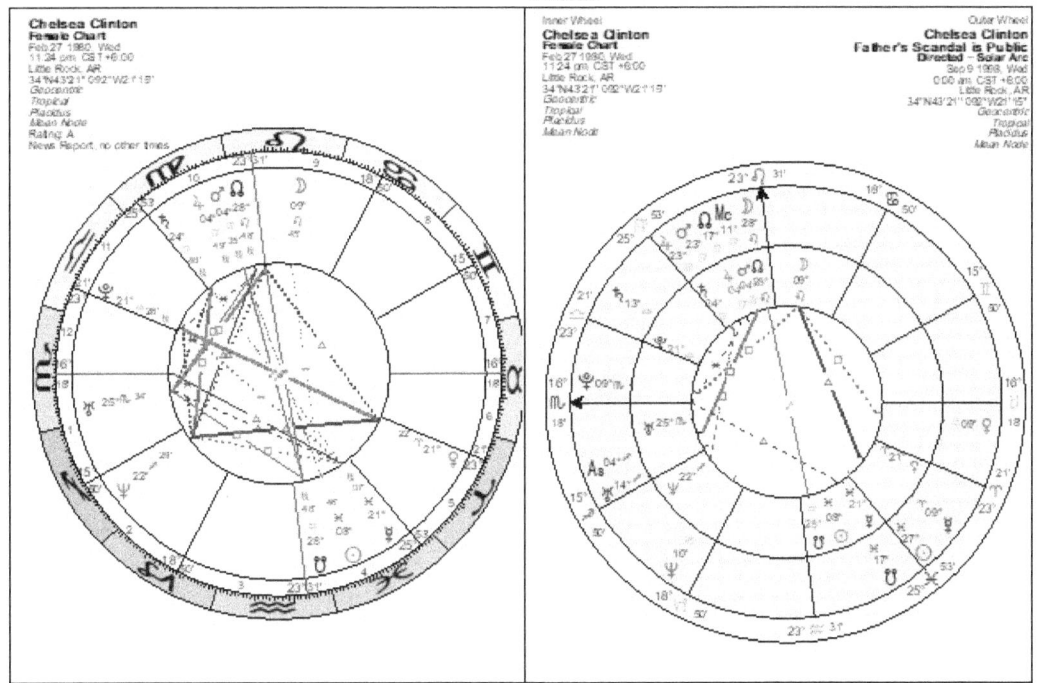

turn of the [20th] century. Meanwhile, Europe was building the system of Solar Arcs to eventually bloom with the Cosmobiological work formulated by Rheinhold Ebertin. Astrology on two continents developed in different directions to harness the cycles of time. It is our time now – for astrologers in the United States to work with Solar Arcs in tandem with transits, together the most powerful prediction system we have in astrology."[2]

Assessing the Year with Secondary Progressions

"The natal chart shows the basic character tendencies we have built into our nature. The secondary progressed chart shows the unfolding of those tendencies in action."[3]

Once the natal chart and its prominent patterns are well understood, we can look to the Secondary Progressed chart, one day in the ephemeris for a year, to get the broad view of the activated planets for the year in question. Since relatively few exact aspects are formed by Progressions to the natal chart in one year, issues are brought to the forefront as indicated by

---

2. Tyl, Noel, Prediction in Astrology: A Master Volume of Technique and Practice, Llewellyn Publishing Co, ST Paul, MN 1991
3. Dobyns, Zipporah, Progressions and Rectification, American Federation of Astrologers, Tempe, AZ 2010

the moving planets making contact and those natal planets receiving contact. In addition to activating the natal chart, newly formed aspects are created by Secondary Progressed planets and points, so it is interpreted as a "stand-alone-chart" for the year before being compared to the natal chart. According to Zip Dobyns, "Signs seem the least fruitful chart element to explore."[4] In Secondary Progressions, only the Angles, Sun, Mercury, Venus, and Mars move fast enough in ninety days (equal to ninety years of life) after the birth to form new aspects to the natal planets and sensitive points. Therefore, most astrologers combine Outer Planet Transits, with Secondary Progression of the Angles, Lights and Personal Planets to forecast for the year in question.

Many astrologers agree that the progressed chart reveals internal changes that are then triggered into action by the transits. If an appropriate activating transit does not occur within orb of the progressed planet, then the energy is not released and remains internal. The duration of active progressions varies greatly, depending upon which planet is making the contact according to its cycle. If the Moon progresses to activate another planet or sensitive point by aspect, the effect will only last about six-weeks to two-months because the progressed Moon, on average, moves just over one-degree per month, or thirteen-degrees per year in "day for a year" motion. If the acceptable orb of aspect in Progressions is one-degree, then it would take the Moon about six-weeks to two-months to activate a one-degree orb, one-degree applying and one-degree separating from the aspect.

On the other hand, Mars moves much more slowly averaging about forty-five minutes per day, so a Mars progression would be active close to three-years. Add into the assessment of the varying planetary speeds, the fact that Mercury, Venus, and Mars have significant retrograde periods, which if involved in the progression, could extend the active aspect for many years. For instance, if Mars progresses to make a one-degree aspect to a natal planet as it is slowing down to turn retrograde, it could be as much as 25 days, or 25 years, before Mars moves beyond that progressed aspect. In such cases, the results of such long-term activation will vary widely depending upon the planets involved and the nature of the aspect. Also keep in mind that when dealing with such long-term aspects, the period is better marked by other faster-moving methods to define the stages of the period.

Natal configurations, such as the T-square, Stellium, or Grand Cross, are often activated earlier in life by progression of the Moon and faster moving inner planets. Early challenges often add strength to the character and at least a little wiser.

Compare Bill Clinton's natal chart to his Secondary Progressed chart for September 9, 1998, when news of the scandal broke. Natal Mercury at 7 Leo and Jupiter at 23 Libra are not in aspect; however, by Progression, they are conjunct at 3-4 Scorpio.

---

4. Dobyns, Zipporah, Progressions and Rectification, American Federation of Astrologers, Tempe, AZ 2010

Figure 53- Bill Clinton Natal Chart   **Figure 54- Bill Clinton Directed to Natal**

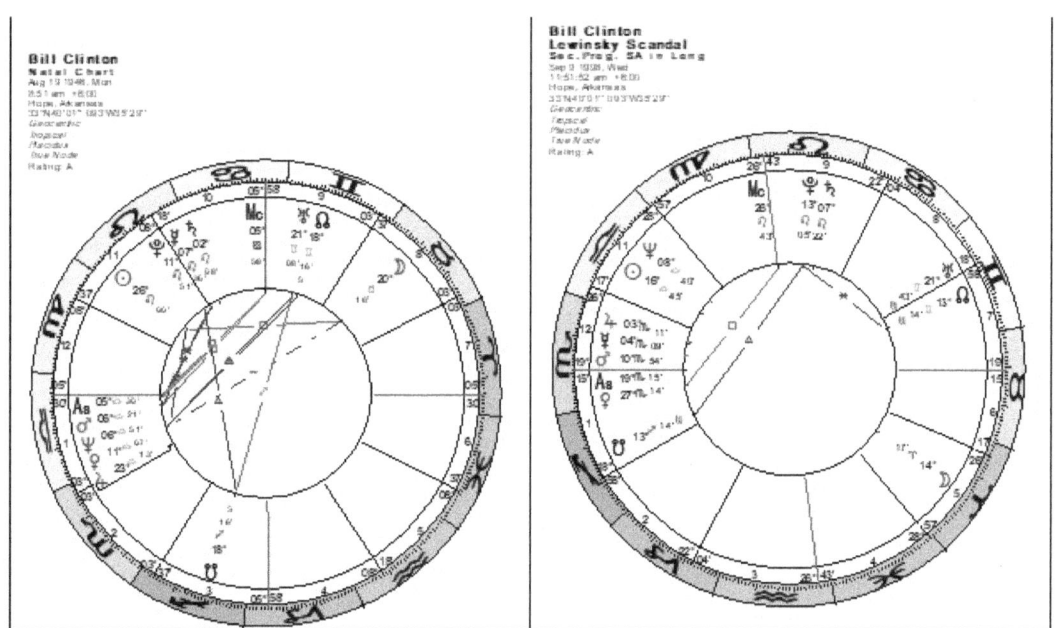

At the time of the 1998 event, Bill Clinton's Secondary Progressed Moon trines his Progressed Midheaven and he was getting away with denial. But put the Progressed chart around the natal chart in a bi-wheel format to see what is activated within one-degree orb. Clinton's chart still looks pretty good, but Saturn progressed to conjunct his Mercury will bring out the truth, progressed Midheaven conjunct his Leo Sun puts him in the news in a big way and progressed Mercury/Jupiter are conjunct square Saturn, all pointing to the challenge of responsibility and truth. The Ascendant progressed opposite natal Moon in the 8th house suggests the personal involvement and an emotional choice about possible sexual situation. As the Moon progresses about one-degree a month, now in the 7th house opposing natal Venus, but by another year it will begin to square all of his Leo planets. By that time, he is impeached the world knows he lied. We all know the infamous "blue dress" with DNA evidence is preserved in the Smithsonian.

Prioritize What's Important in the Progression

In calculating the Progressed chart, the location or relocation of the native adds information, but in my view, the natal chart is king. Most astrologers run the secondary progression for the birthplace, but if the person has moved a few hundred miles East or West of the birthplace, the relocated Angles can give added information about the activated issue. In relocation, the planets retain their natal degree and minute, but they may change houses and have new

Figure 55- Bill Clinton Progressed to Natal Chart

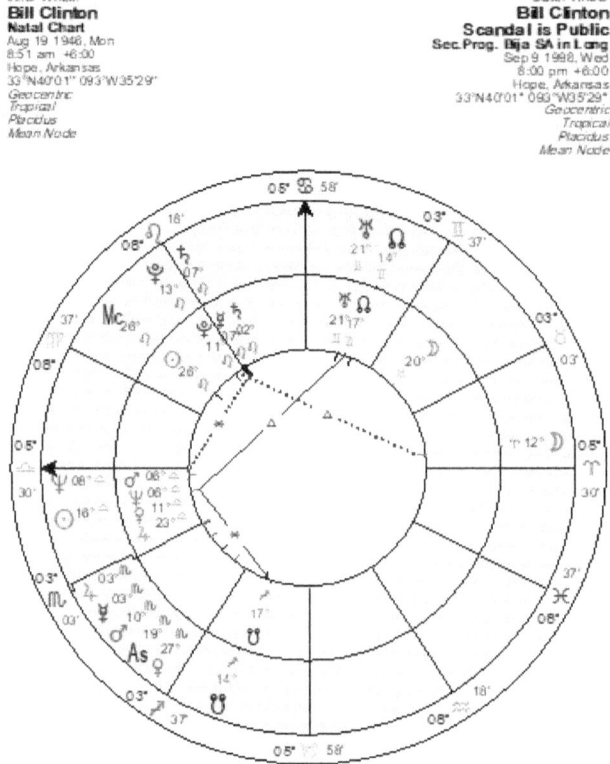

Angles, which modifies interpretation. Use the natal chart for all Progressions, but don't overlook the relocated coordinates for a supplemental view of the Progressed chart.

Outer planet transits also activate the natal chart and the progressed chart, though outer planet transits to the natal chart are most informative. In looking at the outer planet transits to the natal or the progressed chart, the difference from any location in the world is that planets move to different houses – actually, it is the diurnal motion of the Angles that move the wheel one-degree every four-minutes of clock time. If you are looking at an event that has already occurred, some astrologers use the relocated coordinates for the transits, but I give dominance to the natal chart.

The allowable orb for any progression is one degree applying and one degree separating; however, the aspect diminishes quickly after it has become exact. As a result, many astrologers discount the Progressed aspect once it has moved a half-degree past exact. In any event, the closer to exact the aspect, the more potent its effect on appropriate action.

One or two active aspects by Secondary Progression may be relatively mild, but if triggered by multiple transits or the progressions activate a natal planetary network, the effect can be greatly amplified to bring a significant event. The astrologer looks for a "stacking up" of planetary energy from the Natal, Progressed and Transit charts to signal important life situations, changes and events. Further, "midpoint of aspect" is another phenomenon that works when multiple planets, usually transits, surround an activated area by triggering when the average of their distances equals the exact aspect. Transiting planets within an orb of one to five-degrees can work together to activate another planet by aspect.

The more aspects involving the Angles, either natal or progressed, the more significant is the time period for important life changes and events. Next in importance are progressions and major transits involving the Sun or the Moon, though the Midheaven is solar in nature and the Ascendant somewhat lunar. Major transits and Progressions to any of the Angles bring a personal component to events and often mark major turning points in the life. Of the aspects, the conjunction, square and opposition are the most notable harbingers of change by taking action to modify a situation, expecting it to be better.

Following the Angles and the Lights, the Ascendant ruler should be noted for active aspects to signal important life issues. As mentioned before, any planets that are joined together by close aspect in a configuration gain special importance. Certainly, natal configurations are storehouses of information about important life issues, but such planetary networks can form in progressions and transits as well. Take note of any such configurations forming in the Progressed and Transit charts especially as they activate the Natal chart. Interpreting the chart in time is more difficult than natal interpretation. The task is akin to transforming the "still picture" of the Natal chart into the "moving picture" of the developing individual shown in the yearly movement of Directions, Progressions and Outer Transits.

Finally, planet to planet progressions reveal more subtle life changes. When planets that are in aspect in the natal chart are once again linked through progression, opportunity is ripe for the natal condition to operate. If the birth aspect is harmonious, and the progression or outer transit brings a hard aspect, then the condition of the natal aspect will prevail, though with greater difficulty. Strain or challenges to the aspected planet will be resolved once the contacting planet leaves active orb. The converse is true. A harmonious progression or outer transit to an afflicted natal planet will provide the opportunity to remedy or more objectively approach the difficult pattern and its representative situation.

Secondary Progressed Moon and Transiting Saturn Work as a Team

Two books by Celeste Teal published by Llewellyn, Predicting Events with Astrology and Identifying Planetary Triggers are excellent resources for elaboration on the intricacies of Secondary Progressions and Planetary Returns, but additionally, she notes the peculiarities of some planetary cycles. I have often observed what she dubs "Saturn chasing the Moon" as an important long-term trend especially in charts where the two are in orb of aspect at birth.

Transiting Saturn moves in its 29-year cycle at nearly the same rate as the progressed Moon in its 28.6-year cycle. Therefore, an aspect between them can be maintained for years. If the natal aspect is a conjunction, square or opposition, the long-term effect of Saturn and the Progressed Moon moving together in hard aspect can be difficult in childhood with shyness or lack of confidence. The good news is that the progressed Moon moves faster than transiting Saturn and moves out of the hard aspect by late childhood or early teens. In any event, it is good to note such planetary combinations and their moving rates of speed early on.

Realize that interpreting the current patterns for a client is more difficult than natal interpretation, because part of the natal pattern has unfolded, and the client can give some feedback. On the other hand, forecasting work starts with more unknowns, with only the backdrop of the natal chart as a guide. The process of forecasting is akin to transforming the "still" of the natal chart into the "moving picture" of the developing individual. Proceed with caution.

Assessing the Month with the Progressed Moon

The Moon is another matter; on average, it moves thirteen-degrees a day faster than the Sun and other personal planets, and it never goes retrograde. The Progressed Moon is the "fast

Figure 56- Donald Trump Progressed to Natal Chart

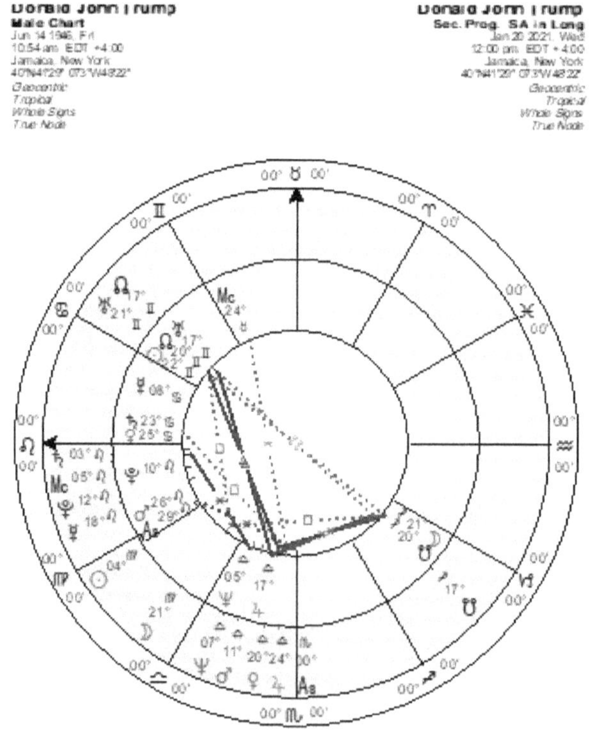

timer" universally used. We can even estimate the progressed Moon at about one-degree per month to activate the natal chart. For example, on Inauguration Day at Noon January 20, 2021, Donald Trump's progressed Venus made trine and sextile aspects involving his strong Sun/Moon/Uranus/Nodes configuration suggesting a good outcome. But at the same time, progressed Jupiter was squaring his natal Venus/Saturn in the 12th house and the progressed Moon moved to square the Sun/Moon configuration suggesting that Donald Trump would be exceedingly unhappy that his loss to Joe Biden was public and final.

Assessing Life Turning Points with Progressed New and Full Moons

First of all, the progressed New and Full Moon cycle is the secondary progressed relationship to the secondary progressed Sun – not the progressed Moon to the natal Sun. The Moon transits just over 13-degrees a day or progresses about 13-degrees a year. Once the progressed Moon conjuncts the natal Sun, it must catch up with the progressed Sun to create a progressed New Moon, or opposite the progressed Sun for a progressed Full Moon. Applying that concept to adjusting or establishing birth time, it would take 2-hours of birth time adjustment (plus or minus) to change the progressed New or Full Moon date by one month; 4-hours to change the New or Full Moon date by two months; 6-hours to change the New or Full Moon date by three months. Nonetheless, the periods of the life emphasized by a progressed New or Full Moon are notable and helpful to narrow the birthtime range for searches beyond six hours.

Within a month or so of the progressed New Moon relative to the house activated and planets therein or closely connected, one begins a new phase of life such as: single to married, a new career or creating something new. Of course, there are many variations of a new beginning in the story told by the activated natal chart. To continue, within a month or so of the progressed Full Moon relative to the house activated and planets therein or closely connected, one reaches a peak of achievement and realization of goals such as: honors and recognition, promotion or self-fulfillment.

Figure 57 Progressed New & Full Moon - Bill Gates. October 23, 1955, 10:00 pm PST, Seattle, WA

P1 (H)	Asp	P2 (H)	EXL	Type	Date	Time	Zone	Age	Pos1	Pos2
☽ (10)	☍	☉ (4)	(X)	Sp-Sp	Oct 31 1957	09:34:30 am	PST	2.008	07°♉02' D	07°♏02' D
☽ (5)	☌	☉ (5)	(X)	Sp-Sp	Feb 13 1972	11:07:18 pm	PST	16.296	21°♏20' D	21°♏20' D
☽ (11)	☍	☉ (5)	(X)	Sp-Sp	May 13 1987	04:23:59 am	PDT	31.539	06°♊41' D	06°♐41' D
☽ (5)	☌	☉ (5)	(X)	Sp-Sp	Dec 30 2001	06:20:40 pm	PST	46.174	21°♐30' D	21°♐30' D
☽ (12)	☍	☉ (6)	(X)	Sp-Sp	Nov 23 2016	10:42:56 pm	PST	61.075	06°♋38' D	06°♑38' D
☽ (6)	☌	☉ (6)	(X)	Sp-Sp	Nov 28 2031	09:10:57 pm	PST	76.086	21°♑54' D	21°♑54' D

The interesting thing about the progressed New and Full Moon cycle is that once the first progressed New or Full Moon is established, the next follows fifteen years later and the next another fifteen years later, and so on, moving clockwise through the houses in diurnal mo-

Figure 58 Progressed New Moon 1972 and Progressed Full Moon 1987

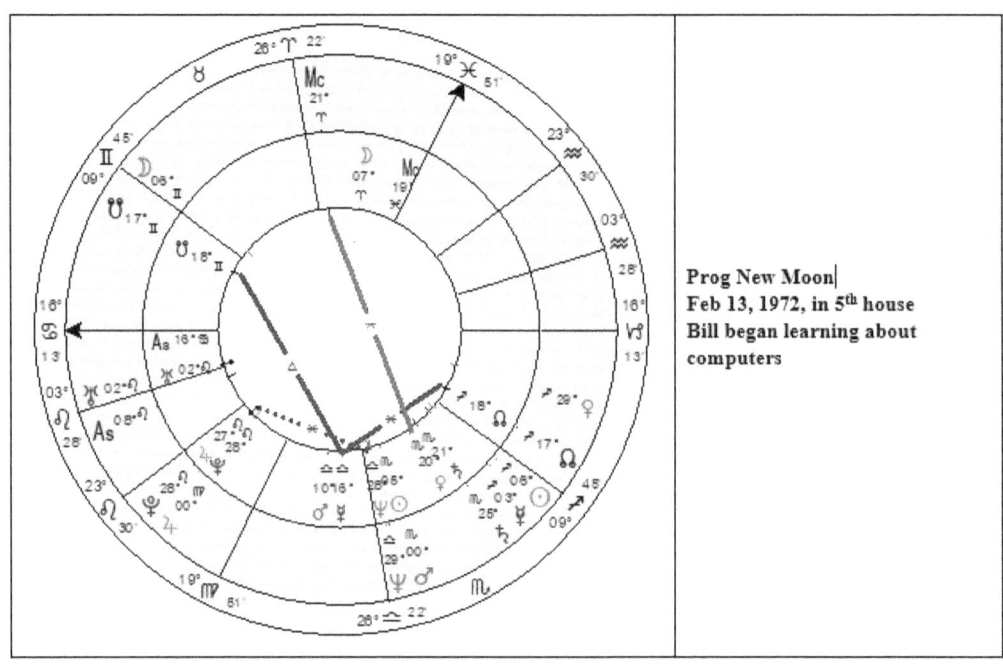

Prog New Moon
Feb 13, 1972, in 5th house
Bill began learning about computers

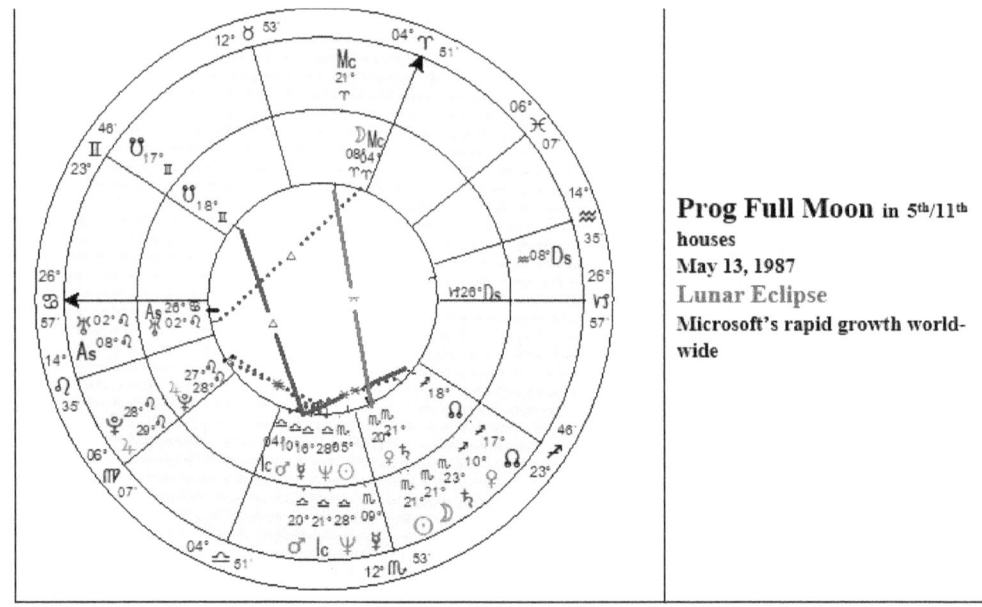

Prog Full Moon in 5th/11th houses
May 13, 1987
Lunar Eclipse
Microsoft's rapid growth worldwide

Figure 59 Bill Gates Progressed New Moon Solar Eclipse 2001 & Progressed Full Moon 2016

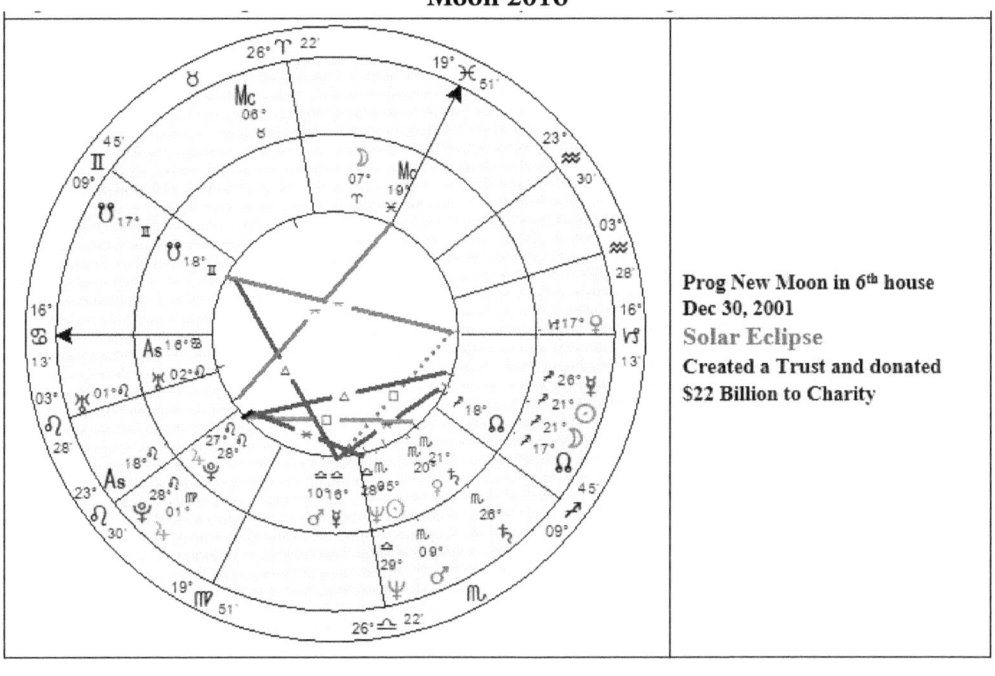

Prog New Moon in 6th house
Dec 30, 2001
Solar Eclipse
Created a Trust and donated
$22 Billion to Charity

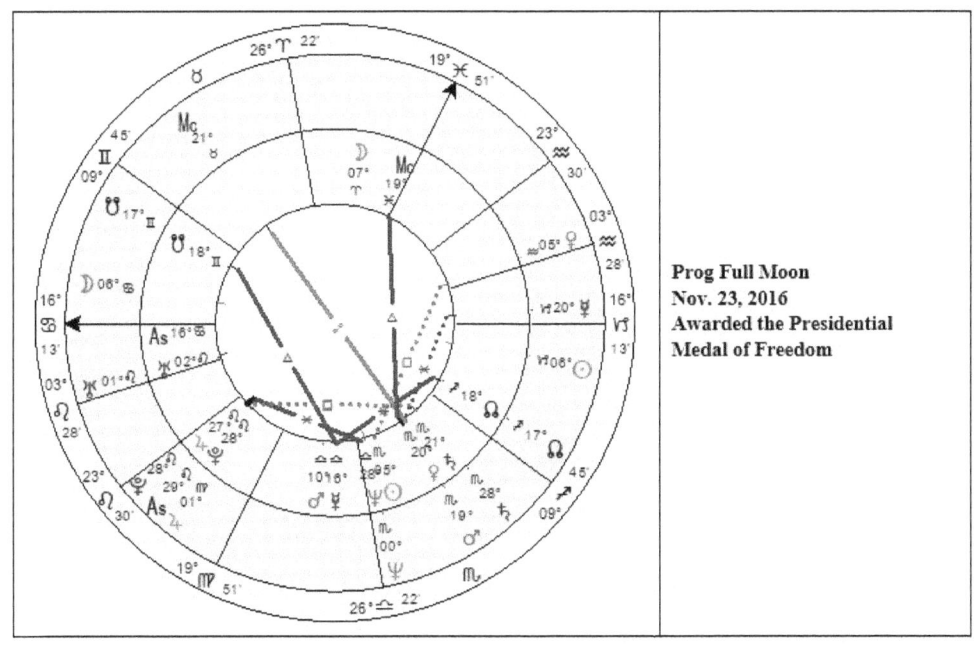

Prog Full Moon
Nov. 23, 2016
Awarded the Presidential Medal of Freedom

What Movement Techniques Work Best?

tion. Follow the pattern of progressed New and Full Moon for Bill Gates. It is easy enough to estimate that Mr. Gates will embark on a major new enterprise in late 2031 in the 7th house. Will he remarry? Will he become another billionaire sending rockets into space for interplanetary research? We don't exactly know from just the progressed New Moon, but we do know it relates to seventh house issue with this simple test.

In a one-hour birth time range, the Progressed New and Full Moons occur only nine days apart, hardly an effective tool to rectify the birth time, though the techniques can be very useful to verify a birth certificate or otherwise known time. To further emphasize the point that Progressed New and Full Moons are not helpful to rectify birth time, times within a three-hour range only change the occurrence by twenty-seven days. Again, the Progressed New and Full Moon occurrences are great indicators of new beginnings and fulfillment of goals that confirm a known birth time or suggest an approximate position of the Moon for someone with no birth time, but they are not the precision tools to rectify birth time to a specific hour and minute that is needed for accurate interpretation and forecasting.

Assessing the Year with Progressed Declination

Many astrologers have too long ignored the interpretive information provided by declination, which is a North/South measurement from the Celestial Equator. Our eyes are well trained to search the chart wheel for planets and points, their placement and condition, but those positions only represent their longitude, an East/West measurement from the Ecliptic. To give a brief declination background, the technique fostered by astrology software developer, Neil Michelsen, in the early 1970's. His research inspired other astrologers of the era to adopt the system and integrate the declination interpretation with the traditional longitude interpretation.

"From declination comes the contrasts and seasons of life related within the broader picture derived from celestial longitude."

Declination brings its own important key words and new aspects to properly use the system. The Parallel aspect is interpreted like a conjunction in longitude, defined as two or more planets sharing the same degree of Declination, both North or both South. The Contra-Parallel aspect is interpreted like an opposition in longitude, defined as two or more planets sharing the same degree of Declination, one North and one South. The Declination 1-degree orb for a parallel or contra-parallel aspect is important. With the Sun's travel from 23:27 North declination to 23:27 South declination the total range is just over 46-degrees, about one-eighth of the 360-degree wheel. Compared to the longitude aspect orbs used in the wheel, the 8-degree orb of a conjunction (equal to a parallel) and the 7-degree orb of an opposition (equal to a contra-parallel) is nearly eight times larger than the declination span. Therefore, a 1-degree orb for the two declination aspects is logical.

Declination: A Planet or Point at Crossover

The big dividing line of North from South declination is the Celestial Equator, which is the Earth's Equator projected into space. When a planet or point is at the North/South dividing line we say it is at Crossover, with interpretive meaning to fit which direction it is moving. In my experience, a planet moving North to South at Crossover faces sudden changes that suggest personal or first house issues; and a planet moving South to North at Crossover faces sudden changes that suggest relationship or seventh house issues. The movement is fast at Crossover, so the issues raised by the planet are activated suddenly. The person is caught off guard and is often off-balance for a time to adjust and take appropriate action.

Declination: A Planet or Point at Maximum North or South

Another important declination consideration is the Maximum North or Maximum South position of a planet or point. The Sun, Mercury or Venus at maximum N or S is not uncommon; they Crossover North to South and South to North twice a year at the Spring and Fall Equinoxes, 0-degrees Aries and 0-degrees Libra. The Sun, Mercury and Venus reach their Maximum North and Maximum South once a year at the Summer and Winter Solstices, 0-degrees Cancer and 0-degrees Capricorn. Mars at maximum North or South is even less unique because most people born during the year have it. They are go-getters and diligent workers, modified by the condition of Mars in the natal chart.

Jupiter and Saturn move so slowly that the maximum North or South position would be shared by everyone born within two or three years. The outer planets are generational at Maximum North or South just over ten years, but still modified by natal condition. If the Sun especially is at Maximum North or South, but also Angles or personal planets in that position, tend to identify as the "transformers of society" through the specialty described by the planet and its condition. "The Greatest Generation", born from 1915 to 1923, who experienced two World Wars and the Great Depression, had Jupiter, Neptune, and Pluto at Maximum North declination and those like President John F. Kennedy with Venus and Ascendant involved by parallel and contra-parallel were deeply involved in the serious issues of the time.

Declination: A Planet or Point Out-of-Bounds North or South

This is important especially if the planet is Out-of-Bounds, beyond the Sun's maximum path of 23:27 degrees. The Sun sets the maximum limits, but a planet at the North declination limit seems to relate tenth house issues or a career situation, often with some control in the matter. A planet at the South declination limit seems to relate to fourth house issues or a family situation, often with less control in the matter. The Out-of-Bounds position is exceptional in some way related to the planet and its natal condition. For instance, President Trump has Mercury out-of-bounds by several degrees, suggesting exceptional mental capacity; however, his Mercury is closely square Neptune, suggesting that he may have extreme issues with the truth or communicates a delusional sense of reality.

Not all planets go Out-of-Bounds. The Sun, the Angles and Saturn NEVER go beyond the Sun's path, but all of the other planets do. Asteroids regularly exceed the out-of-bounds limit by over 34-degrees north or south, so pending further research they are less interpretively useful in declination. The Moon's declination cycle is regular as clockwork completing one full transit cycle every 27.32 days, even when it goes out-of-bounds, though its OOB cycle only occurs in alternating decades. People with Moon OOB tend to be more independent and willing to express outside of the box of social convention. Having grown up in unconventional situations, they are often survivors, strengthened by their experience of being different in some way.

It is not uncommon for parents with an OOB Moon have children with an OOB Moon, since a generation averages about 20 years. To them, unconventional life situations are normal, and they adapt. People with in-bound Moons more willingly march in line with what is expected of them by others and societal norms. Though the natal Moon declination may be in-bounds, the progressed Moon may move OOB marking a more unconventional or freer period of life as the progressed Moon takes a few years to round the turn to change direction.

Declination: Personal Planets Out-of-Bounds North or South

People with personal natal planets out-of-bounds are distinctive by the nature of the planet, its natal condition and house placement. Mercury OOB suggests the mental ability may be exceptional in some way, or that one's ideas are unconventional. The person could also be a free thinker who communicates outside of traditional venues. Venus OOB suggests one experiences pleasure in unconventional ways or has unusual friends or romantic relationships. OOB Venus may also suggest less concern for physical appearance or possibly social graces. Mars OOB indicates one who is extremely work driven, or who is very active in physical pursuits. Distinctive qualities of leadership may be evident, though some possibility of being unseated from that authority by adversaries exists. OOB Moon, Mercury and Venus appear to be evident in roughly 15% of the few thousand charts in my files. OOB Mars is more common, with roughly 20% of the few thousand charts in my files. Jupiter and the other planets move OOB so narrowly and for so long that they describe generations and have little personal interpretive use, unless of course, the Moon, Mercury, Venus or Mars is involved by parallel or contra-parallel.

The progressed declination can narrow the wider birthtime range for rectification, especially as an early test to develop a case theory. For instance, the Jimmy Swaggart example in Chapter Four, I started with a 24-hour search set for Noon and the major life events placed in the declination graphic for 50-years. Consistently the appropriate astrological descriptors aligned much earlier than Noon, so the 24-hour search was quickly reduced to a 12-hour search. On the other hand, progressed declination is not as birthtime specific as other measures because one-hour of birthtime adjustment only changes the alignment of events by one month. However, once the chart is rectified and confirmed by several tests that point to a specific birthtime, progressed declination can provide amazing interpretive information. O.J. Simpson's secondary progressed declination clearly defines the dramatic and tragic event of the double murder on June 12, 1994.

Figure 60 O. J. Simpson Comparison of Natal Declination to Progressed Declination

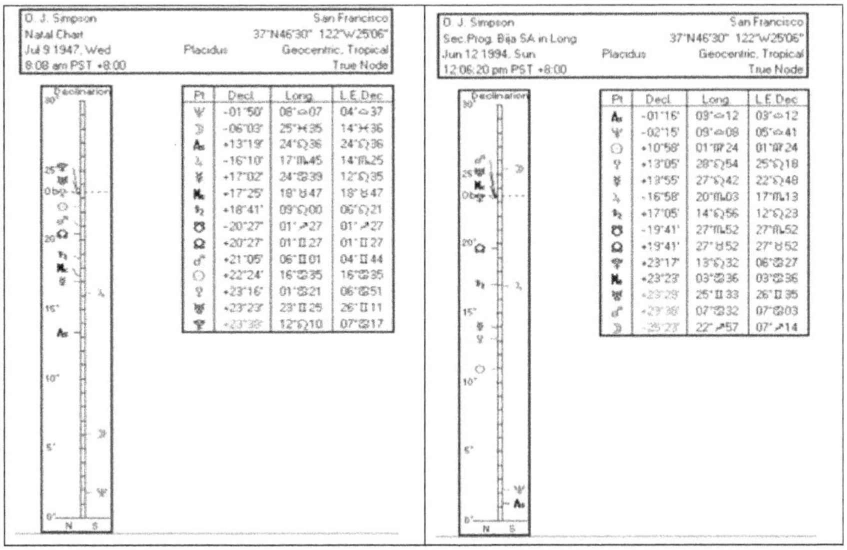

Not only has O.J.'s Midheaven and Mars moved by progressed declination to parallel his natal Pluto OB and Venus and Uranus maximum North, but now the progressed Moon, Mars and Uranus have moved Out-of-Bounds. With a correct birthtime and progressed declination alone, any astrologer could forecast trouble for O.J.'s ability to control his temper in 1994.

Assessing a Month with Tertiary and Two-Weeks with Minor Progressions

Tertiary and Minor Progressions, little used today in Modern astrology, are sub-sets of the Secondary Progressed system. Secondary Progression, an Earth/Sun relationship, is a symbolic measure where one day in the ephemeris equals one year (365.2 days) of life. The faster moving Tertiary Progression is a symbolic measure where one day in the ephemeris equals one lunar month (27.32 days) of life and 13.37 ephemeris days (lunar months) equal one year in an Earth/Moon relationship. To carry the method further, the even faster moving Minor Progression is a symbolic measure where one lunar month (27.32 days) in the ephemeris equals one year of life in a Moon/Sun relationship. Several authors have used the analogy of a clock to describe the relationship between the various methods of chart progression to a given date.

The Secondary progressed chart is the hour hand; Tertiary progressed chart the minute hand; Minor progressed chart the second hand. Interestingly enough, all of these timing methods work to mark important life developments, in the year, the month and a two-week period. The following graphics show two years of Secondary Progression for O. J. Simpson in Graph 1, two years of Tertiary Progression in Graph 2, and two years of Minor Progression in Graph 3. The Tertiary Moon moves 13.37 times faster than normal and the Minor Moon moves 27.32 faster than normal racing around the chart. The Tertiary Sun and inner planets also progress 13.37 times faster than normal and the Minor Moon progresses 27.32 faster than normal. Even the outer planets are interpretively useful by Tertiary and Minor Progression.

Secondary, Tertiary and Minor progressed movement is based on actual planetary motion.

- **Secondary Moon progresses about half a sign per ephemeris day,**

  13.11 degrees a day x 1 day = 13.11 degrees or one year.

- **Tertiary Moon progresses about six signs in 13.7 ephemeris days,**

  on average, 13.11 degrees a day x 13.37 ephemeris days = 180-degrees for a Tertiary year.

- **Minor Moon progresses about twelve signs in 27.32 ephemeris days,**

  13.11 degrees a day x   27.32 ephemeris days = 360-degrees for a Minor year.

- **Secondary Sun, Mercury and Venus progress 1-degree per ephemeris day,**

  1-degree a day x 1- ephemeris day = one year.

Figure 61- O. J. Simpson Secondary Progression Birth to 3 years- Compare to Minor and Tertiary

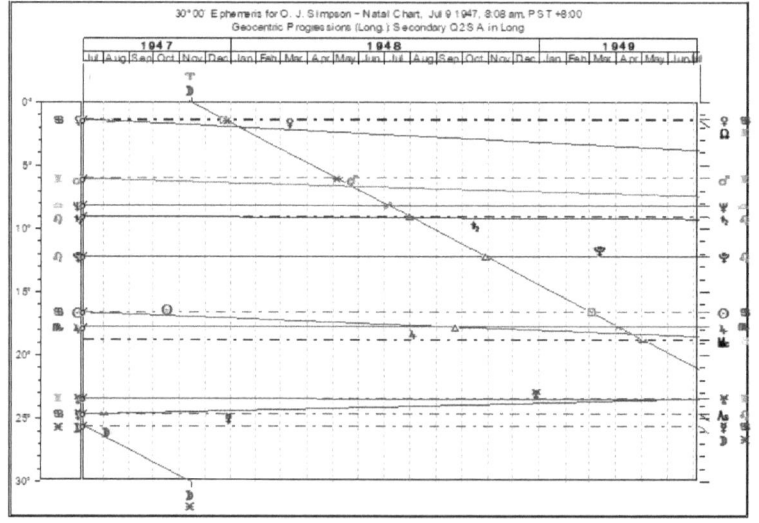

Figure 62 O. J. Simpson Tertiary Progression Birth to 3 Years - Compare to Secondary and Minor

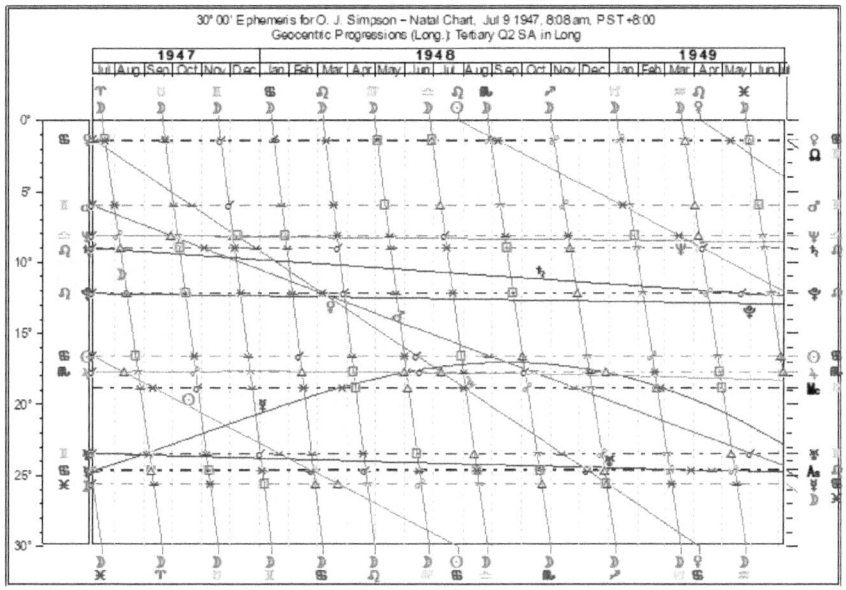

Figure 63 O. J. Minor Progression Birth to 3 years - Compare to Secondary and Tertiary

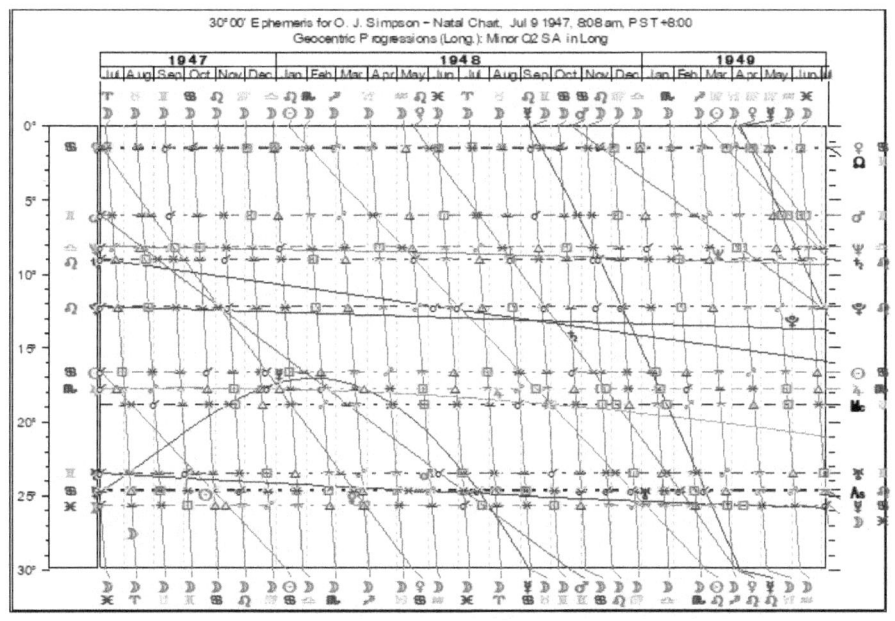

What Movement Techniques Work Best?

- **Tertiary Sun, Mercury and Venus progress about half a sign in 13.37 ephemeris days,**

    1-degree a day x 13.37 ephemeris days = 13.37-degrees or about half a sign per Tertiary year.

- **Minor Sun, Mercury and Venus progress about one sign in 27.32 ephemeris days,**

    1-degree a day x 27.32 ephemeris days = 27.32-degrees or one sign per Minor year.

- **Secondary Mars progresses about ¾ of a degree per ephemeris day,**

    45-minutes a day x 1 ephemeris day = 45-minutes per Secondary year. (45 minutes = 75% of 1-degree)

- **Tertiary Mars progresses about 10-degrees, one-third of a sign per 13.37 ephemeris days,**

    .75 degrees x 13.7 days = 10.27-degrees per Tertiary year.

- **Minor Mars progresses about 20-degrees, or two-thirds of a sign per 27.32 ephemeris days,**

    .75 x 27.32 = 20.5-degrees per Minor year.

Table 35 Movement Comparison of Secondary, Tertiary and Minor Progressions Over 51 Years

Eph	Sec	Ter	Min	Eph	Sec	Ter	Min	Eph	Sec	Ter	Min
1	1y	1m,	2w	18				35	35		
2	2y			19	19			36	36		
3	3y			20	20			37	37		
4	4y		1m	21	21	18m	9m	38	38		17m
5	5y			22	22			39	39		
6	6y			23	23			40	40		
7	7y	6m	3m	24	24		11m	41	41y	3yr	18m
8	8y			25	25			42	42y	3yr	18m
9	9y			26	26			43	43		
10	10y		5m	27	27y	2yr	1yr	44	44		19m
11	11y			28	28			45	45		
12	12y			29	29			46	46		
13	13y	1yr	6m	30	30		13m	47	47		42m	21m
14	14y			31	31			48	48		
15	15y			32	32			49	49		
16	16y			33	33			50	50		
17	17y		8m	34	34		30m	15m	51	51	

Minor progressions double the movement of the Tertiary progressions, which show progressed movement in the outer planets as well. Minor Progressions are a symbolic measure of time where one lunar month of 27.32 days equals one year of life, a 27:1 ratio. The Minor progression is good for observation of developing situations over two weeks or for assessing activation of a child's chart with not enough life span for slower movement techniques to activate the natal chart.

Minor Moon conjuncts all planets and points in one lunar month, 27.32 days, because it progresses through the entire 360-degree wheel. The Tertiary and Minor progressions are applied to O.J. Simpson's chart for June 12, 1994, the date of the double murder for which he was tried and acquitted.

Tertiary and Minor Progressions work well to align the client's major events in a consistent pattern with appropriate astrological descriptors to confirm and/or adjust birthtime, but they are best used in tandem with Secondary Progressions, parent of the progressed method. For instance, by Tertiary progression, one hour of birthtime gives fourteen months to align to an event date, a half-hour gives seven months to align to an event date and ten minutes of birthtime gives about two months to align to an event date. The Minor progression is even more precise where one-hour of birthtime shortens the range for alignment to events by half of the Tertiary progression. The Minor progression gives seven months to align with and event date, one half-hour of birthtime gives just over three months to align to an event date and ten minutes of birthtime give about six-weeks to align to and event date. Don't worry about fully understanding how Tertiary and Minor Progressions are created, just trust your computer software to provide the information to test the major life events to confirm birthtime.

Timing Months and Years with Outer Planet and Lunar Node Transits

Outer planet transits activate the natal chart as well as any directions or progressions in place that tend to wait to until activated by an outer transit, Jupiter through Pluto. Many astrologers add Mars as an outer planet, though its 2-year cycle is much faster than Jupiter's 12-year cycle, Saturn's 29.6-year cycle, Uranus's 84-year cycle and Neptune and Pluto with cycles far greater than a human lifetime. Transits to the natal chart are foremost, but they can also activate the directed and progressed charts.

The generic planetary cycles and synodic returns of planetary pairs set the backdrop for important life periods of growth and development, but what is activated in the natal chart at a given date and all that comes with it tells the story, either in the past, the present or the future. It is always important have a clear understanding of the natal chart before applying movement methods to activate it.

Transits are the actual planetary contact of one body, by aspect, with another. A transit making contact activates the energy described by the planets involved: the current aspect, and applicable orb both applying and separating; the natal condition of those planets, their transit and natal house positions; and to a lesser extent, their signs. To complicate the matter, we must deal with a complex web of transiting planets and lesser bodies all at the same time: most importantly, the outer planets Jupiter through Pluto; the faster moving bodies, the Sun through Mars; and to a lesser extent, the Moon, the Moon's nodes, Chiron and the Asteroids. The good news, however, is that both symbolic methods of moving the natal chart to a given time period – Secondary Progressions and Solar Arc Directions – use outer planet transits to provide the activating trigger for the natal planetary symbolism.

Figure 64- O.J. Simpson Secondary Progressed to Murder Event

Figure 65- O.J. Simpson Tertiary Progressed to Murder Event

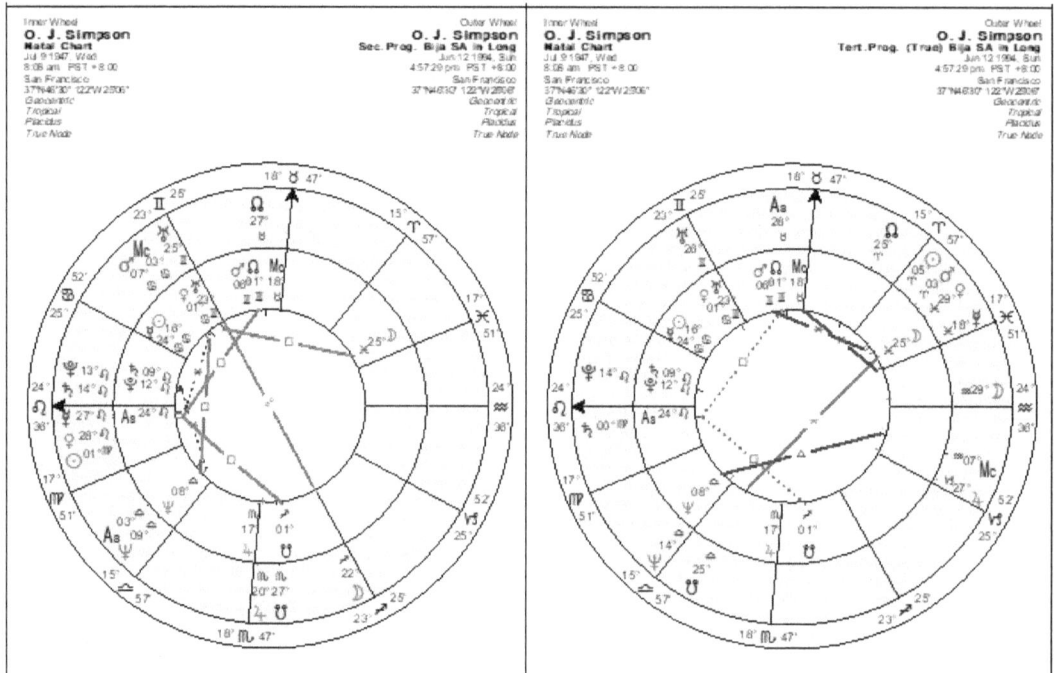

First it may help to know the generic transit cycles of the outer planets, because they correlate well with our human growth and development. The quarter cycles of each outer planet's transits in hard aspect to its natal position provides insight to the stages of growth, especially what is known as "midlife crisis". The following Table 36 provides a visual of outer planet quarter-cycles that converge at key ages of life.

At age 15 transiting Jupiter squares its natal position near when transiting Saturn opposes its natal position. With Jupiter activated, the teenager is sure he can handle any life situation and at the same time as he goes out in the world Saturn opposes itself and help from parents is needed. Somewhere in our mid-forties, transiting Jupiter and Saturn once again oppose their natal positions, and near the same time transiting Uranus opposes its natal position, and if that

Figure 66- O.J. Simpson Minor Progressed to Murder Event

Figure 67- O.J. Simpson Quad Wheel with Chart and Secondary, Tertiary and Minor Progressions to Murder Event

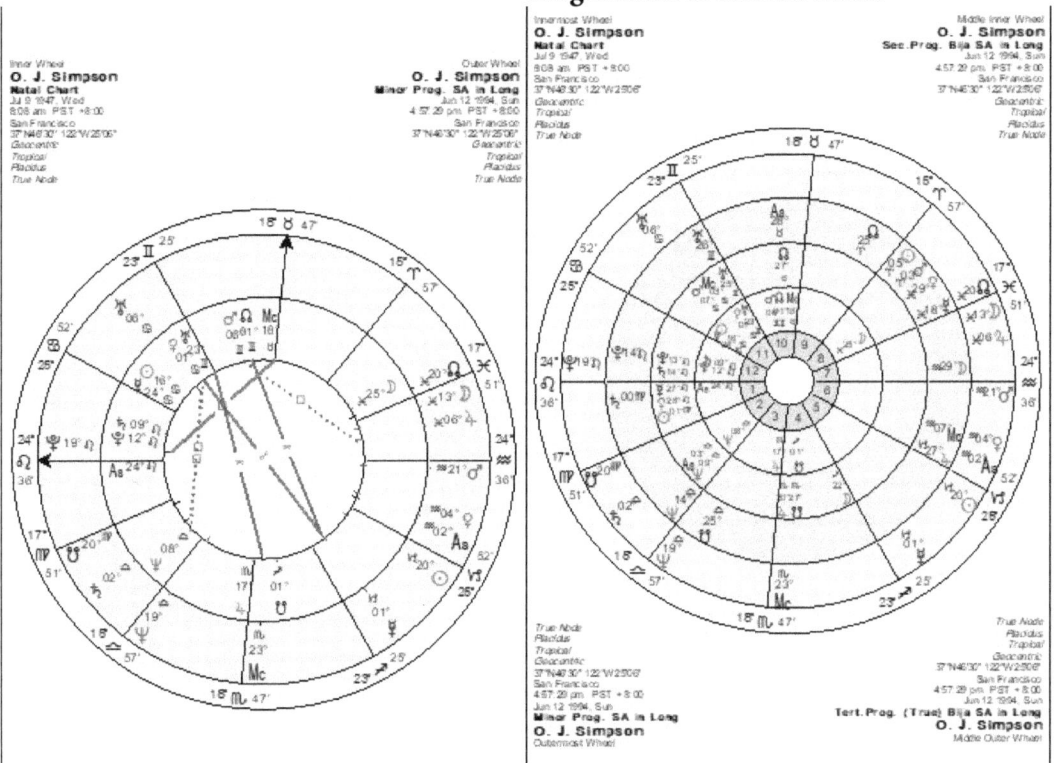

isn't enough, transiting Neptune and Pluto reach the square to their natal positions. If all of those outer planet convergences in our mid-forties activate an Angle, Light or personal planet in our chart the forces for challenge and growth touch us personally.

Just because we are now looking at actual planetary transits, don't forget that knowing the complete transit cycle of an outer planet, you can still estimate the year when that planet will make its generic quarter, half and return cycles to each of your natal planets and angles. The only notable variation comes from the planet Pluto. For those born in the early 19th century, Pluto took 30-years to transit one sign; whereas those born late in the 20th century, Pluto took only 12 ½ years to transit one sign. So, Pluto's average of 20-years to transit one sign varies greatly across generations. The following table shows Pluto's variance over two centuries.

A Transformative Two Years with Transiting Pluto

I would suggest the first task for any transit search is to find the "Sensitive Point Listing" available in most astrology programs. Be sure not to over-crowd the listing with asteroids,

Table 36 Outer Planet Generic Cycles Align at Critical Life Growth and Turning Points

Planet	First ¼	½ cycle	Last ¼	Return	# Cycles
Jupiter	3 years	6 years	9 years	12 years	1
Jupiter	15 years	18 years	21 years	24 years	2
Jupiter	27 years	30 years	33 years	36 years	3
Jupiter	39 years	42 years	45 years	48 years	4
Jupiter	51 years	54 years	57 years	60 years	5
Jupiter	63 years	66 years	69 years	72 years	6
Jupiter	75 years	78 years	81 years	84 years	7
Jupiter	87 years	90 years	93 years	96 years	8
Saturn	7+ years	15 years	22 years	29 ½ years	1
Saturn	37 years	44 years	51 years	58 years	2
Saturn	65+ years	73 years	80 years	87 ½ years	3
Uranus	21 years	42 years	63 years	84 years	1
Neptune	42 years	83 years	124 years	165 years	1
Pluto	38-93 years	90-150 y	140-190	248 yrs	1

stars and the like. Include all the planets known within one-degree orb, which may eliminate the Moon if the search range is more than 3-hours. The angles should not be listed unless the search range in less than fifteen minutes of clock time. The pared-down "Sensitive Point Listing" gives aspects to all planets and points through the signs beginning with Aries for the given chart. I would further recommend searching only the major Ptolemaic hard aspects: conjunction, opposition, square, and to a lesser extent, the quincunx, trine and sextile in one-degree orb applying or separating. Basically, streamline the list to the most dramatic or intense indicators.

Interpreting outer planet transits in a retrograde cycle, it is generally accepted that when the transiting planet first activates the natal planet or point by direct motion, the natal issue described by the activated planet or point, their house placement and condition comes to the forefront – the issue is awakened. When the transiting planet returns to the degree of the activated planet or point by retrograde motion, the person takes action to do something to mitigate the issue. Then at the final direct transit over the activated planet or point degree, the issue is resolved, and the consequences of the action are evident.

Begin the transit search with Pluto because it is the slowest in motion and activates any particular degree for more than a year. Even though astronomers pulled Pluto's from planet to dwarf planet, it is still a full force planet for astrologers known as "the transformer". We know that endings and beginnings are a natural part of life for us all, but often fear of the unknown grips us and those endings become very painful, even wrenching; however, with some life experience, most of us can acknowledge that the transition brought by transiting

Table 37 Pluto Transit Variation in 200 Years by Decade or One Sign a Year

Birth Date	Average age at Pluto square natal Pluto	Average age for Pluto transit of a sign
1800-1810	88-89	29 ½
1810-1820	89-91	30
1820-1830	90-90	30 ¼
1830-1840	89-91	30
1840-1850	86-89	29
1850-1860	83-86	28
1860-1870	80-83	27
1870-1880	75-80	26
1880-1890	71-75	24 ½
1890-1900	65-71	23
1900-1910	59-65	21
1910-1920	54-59	19
1920-1930	49-54	17
1930-1940	45-49	15 ½
1940-1950	40-45	14
1950-1960	38-40	13
1960-1970	37-38	12 ½
1970-1980	37-39	12 ½
1980-1990	40-43	14
1990-2000	43-48	15

Pluto could not have been reached unless the old life condition had dramatically changed. In astrology, words like "transition" are metaphorical descriptors of the transiting Pluto effect rather than literal. Pluto brings passionate, even compulsive feelings to the forefront and signals us to deal with issues that have been swept under the carpet for too long as too embarrassing or too painful to acknowledge. Often the skeletons in the closet relate to sexuality issues in some form, or control issues as the victim or the perpetrator since Pluto rules the sexual/reproductive organs of both sexes. The sexual energy associated with Pluto is metaphorically equated with the use and abuse of power, and the lesson to be learned is self-respect. A sense of self-worth and fair play heals many life problems.

In addition, review the close orb (1 to 2 degree) aspect networks between the natal planets and points because when one leg of the network is activated by transit, the other planets or points in the network will also be activated for a more dramatic effect. For example, in my chart developed in Chapter Two, the 5-degree orb of the Moon/Saturn/Mars T-square is not as important or dominant when activated by progression, direction or outer transit because it takes five to ten years for the outer planet transit to activate the wide degree range of those planets. Even a Saturn transit would take about 10 months, the better part of a year, to activate the wide span of planets thereby allowing more time to address and deal with the issues brought to the forefront by the transiting messenger. However, the 1-degree network of Sun/Venus conjunct the 12th house cusp, sesqui-square/semi-square Saturn/Pluto and Lunar Nodes in a T-square is activated all at once when any leg of the configuration is activated and interpretively much more powerful. To repeat the mantra, pay major attention to natal planets and points close by degree in aspect or configuration because, when activated, they all pile up near the same time for a major event.

Figure 68 Tebbs Chart in 8th Harmonic to Show Semi-squares and Sesqui-squares

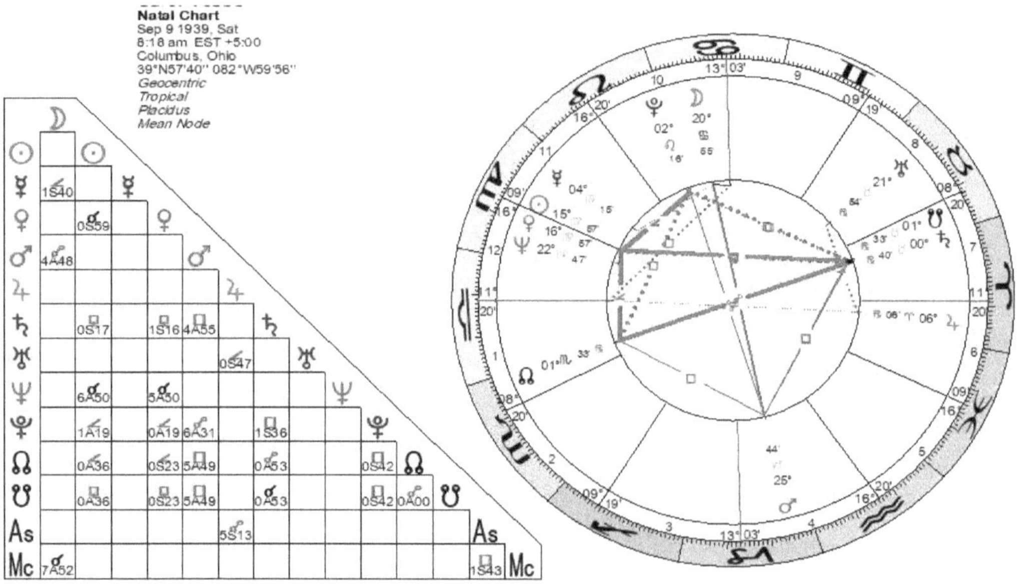

A Pluto Transit

In conjunction by transit, the power/sexuality issues of Pluto will be dealt with in a more open manner through the areas described by the contacted planet and house. In hard aspect by transit, the Pluto energy is in active conflict with the status quo. The square, semi-quadrate and sesqui-square activate the power/sexuality issues in such a way that one will take action to remedy an uncomfortable situation. The opposition brings an ultimatum or a choice to be made whereas the quincunx forces a crisis with few to no good choices. It is as if one is pulled between two equally stressful, demanding situations neither of which one is in a position to control. The soft or easy aspects, the trine and the sextile, seem to slide by without notice because the control of life is somehow one's own. Reward, either metaphorical or literal, for what one does well is possible with some recognition from a boss or the public.

Pluto Retrograde Period: No one escapes a Pluto transit without facing the impact of at least three hits, and sometimes 5 hits, to any planets or points activated within a one-degree orb of aspect. Of the average 20 years for Pluto to fully transit a sign, every single degree is retraced by Pluto's retrograde cycle. From the mid-20th century to mid-21st century, Pluto is fast in its orbit. For that time span Pluto moves 5 degrees direct, 3 degrees retrograde, 5 degrees direct, 3 retrograde for 12 to 14 years in that part of its 248-year cycle. When Pluto moves into its slower rate of motion, late in the 21st century, the degrees direct will lessen to about 4 and stretching that part of its cycle to notably more than 20 years.

Figure 69 Sample of a Pluto Transit with Its Shadow Range

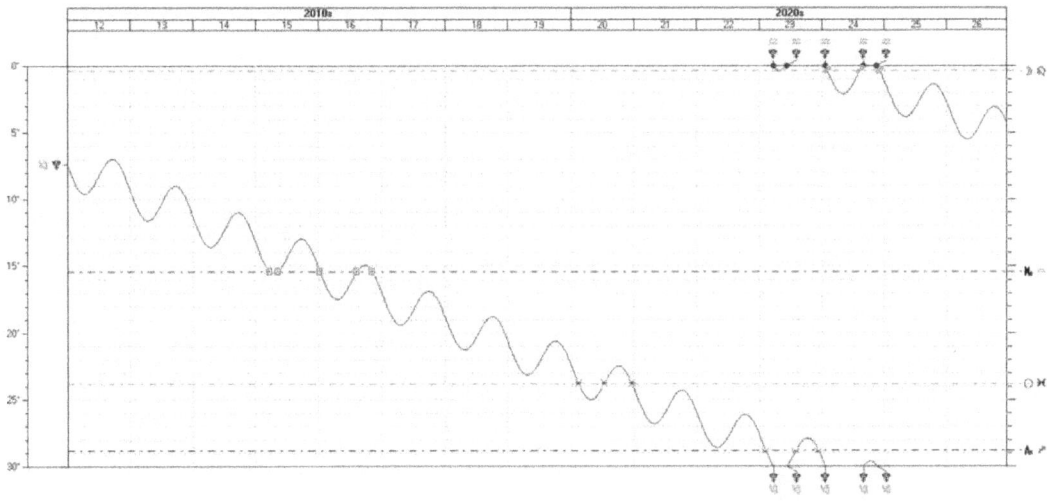

In every Pluto retrograde cycle of 5 degrees, one degree is hit 5 times and the other within a few minutes of 5 times, because of the double retracing that occurs at the degree of the retrograde stations. Therefore, a Pluto transit to a personal planet or Angle most certainly ushers in a period of intensity and focus for nearly 2 years, depending on the aspect and the planet(s) contacted. The duration of the Pluto transit to move through the sensitized retrograde and "shadow" degree area is currently about 18 – 22 months and will increase when Pluto is much slower in its cycle in several generations to come. Basically, every degree is in a "shadow" sensitized area when Pluto is within 3-4 degrees.

A Confusing Year and a Half with Transiting Neptune

Neptune in conjunction brings emphasis to our dreams and ideals. What we hope for, and the goals we set to get there, are ruled by Neptune. I am reminded of Carl Sandburg's poem, "Nocturne In A Deserted Brickyard", which describes a dirty old trash heap of bricks and building materials as seen by moonlight after a rain. The images by moonlight are absolutely beautiful whereas those same images by day they are quite ugly. So with Neptune when harsh reality is made beautiful with hope and trust that things will turn out well. The hard aspects of Neptune bring tears and disillusionment. The square, semi-quadrate and sesqui-square forces one the face reality and deal with a situation as it is, not as it might be. These hard aspects do bring positive action for change once the individual stops clinging to false hopes. The opposition transit often brings the urge to follow the dreams even at the expense of practical realities. The quincunx aspect, however, is often the most difficult to integrate because all of the dreams seem hopelessly out of reach at the moment.

A Neptune transit is generally in effect about two plus months prior and to the date of exact and at least a month or more after, because Neptune contacts every degree of the zodiac 5 times in its 168-year orbit around the earth. As a result, the effect of a Neptune transit may color one's life for the better part of 1 ½- years. Neptune slows in its apparent motion as seen from earth from time to time, and then its effect could extend to as much another 3-months during the retrograde and shadow period. It is important to remember that, like Uranus, Neptune activates every degree along its path three times and sometimes five. Most astrologers who have worked with clients have observed the effect of outer transits. The first transit hit raises the issue described by the activated natal planet, its location, aspects and condition. If the outer planet later retrogrades over the same natal planet, the client often makes a decision or takes action to address the issue, and when the outer planet makes its last pass across the activated natal planet, the issue is resolved. That doesn't necessarily mean the issue will work in the client's favor; that depends upon the planet's natal condition and aspect connection to other planets, angles or lunar nodes.

Neptune Retrograde Period: Like the Uranus transit, no one escapes a Neptune transit without facing the impact of at least 3 to 5 hits to every planet or chart point. Of the average 14 years for Neptune to fully transit a sign, every single degree is retraced by the retrograde cycle. The better part of 2 years is colored by Neptune's influence as it moves 5 degrees direct, 3 degrees retrograde, 5 degrees direct, 3 retrograde, and so on as it works its way through the zodiac.

In every Neptune retrograde cycle of 5 degrees, one degree is hit five times because of the double retracing that occurs at the degree of the retrograde stations. Therefore, a Neptune transit to a personal planet or Angle at such a point most certainly ushers in a notable period of confusion, delusion or illusion for the better part of 2 years, depending upon the aspect and the planets contacted.

Figure 70 Sample of a Neptune Transit with Its Shadow Range

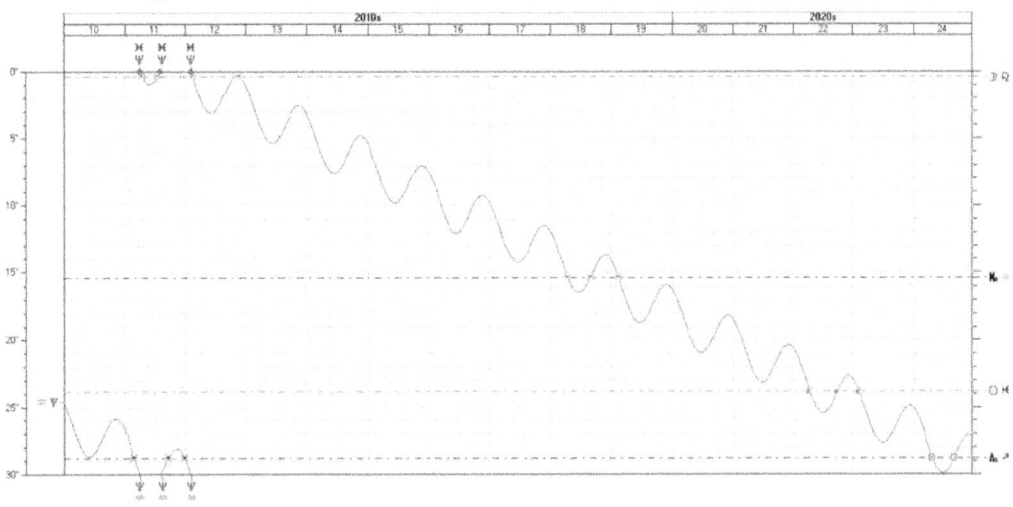

The duration of the Neptune transit to move through the sensitized retrograde and "shadow" degree area is actually about 18 – 20 months depending upon whether Neptune is slow or fast in its cycle over several generations. And like the Uranus transit, no matter where one starts counting the cycle, Neptune still takes at least 18 months to complete. Basically, every degree is in a "shadow" sensitized area when Neptune is within 3-4 degrees.

Figure 71 Sample of a Neptune Transit Making 5 Hits to a Point in Its Shadow Range

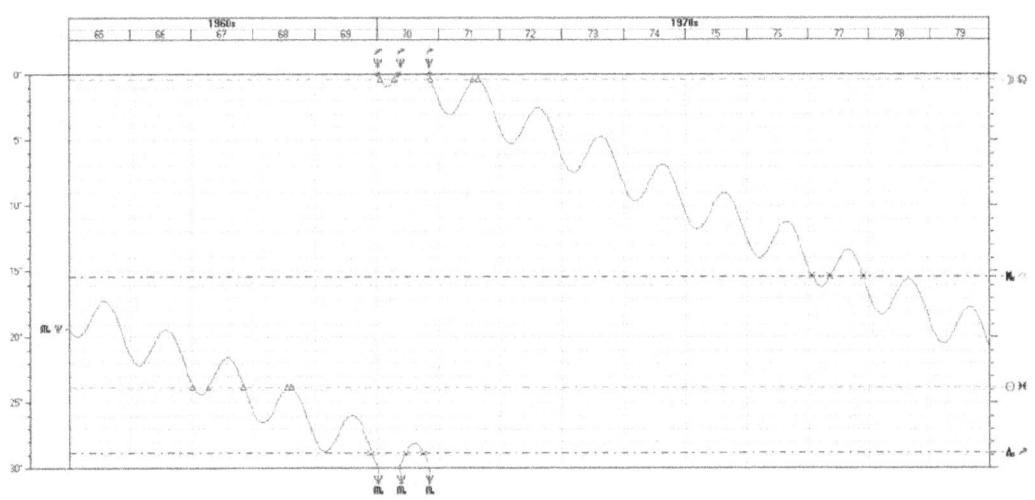

A Surprising Year with Transiting Uranus

Unlike other planetary cycles, the transit of Uranus contacts each degree of the zodiac three times in its direct, retrograde and direct motion. When the last forward aspect contact occurs, approximately seventeen months after the first contact, "awakening" is signaled in the area of life described by the house position and the planet activated, and at the final pass, the issues are usually resolved. The conjunction brings the urge to take action before considering all of the possibilities and consequences. Often sadder but wiser, we often reflect that "it seemed like a good idea at the time" – and it was a "helluva lot of fun". Where the Sun, Ascendant or chart ruler is involved, the individual is often the initiator of action, but other contacts seem to signal that the change is initiated by others leaving one with little choice. Interestingly, in the 17-month Uranus transit cycle, Uranus moves forward 8 degrees, retrogrades 4 degrees, again moves forward 8, retrogrades 4, and so on to hit every degree of the zodiac three times as the planet makes its 84-year cycle.

The hard aspects of Uranus bring break-ups of the status quo often with painful readjustment unless other factors such as Saturn bring the thought and preparation for big life changes. The ease aspects, sextile and trine bring life's happy surprises and opportunities we never thought we would have. For example, when Uranus transited conjunct the Chapter Three client's Sun/Venus/12th cusp natal conjunction, she fell into an absolute dream job of teaching art at the school next door that put her nearby home and her pre-school age children. She almost didn't even apply for a job after college graduation because of the child-care issue. However, on a slim chance that a job that met all of her requirements might be open so close to the start of fall term, she applied on Friday and began teaching on Monday. An astrologer might have forecast the sudden good fortune just by seeing the multiple transiting Uranus aspects.

A Uranus transit is generally in effect about one month prior to the date of exact and at least a couple of weeks after. Uranus slows in its apparent motion as seen from earth from time to time, and then its effect extends to as much as three months during the retrograde and shadow period. Remember that transiting Uranus contacts every degree of the zodiac 3 times over 12 months in its orbit around the earth.

Uranus Retrograde Period: Now beginning with the Uranus transit, and Neptune and Pluto to follow, no one escapes without facing the impact of 3 hits to every planet or chart point contacted, with Uranus key words of "sudden change" for interpretation. Of the average 7 years for Uranus to fully transit a sign, every single degree is retraced by its cycle of 8 degrees direct, 4 degrees retrograde, then another 8 degrees direct. The duration of the Uranus transit cycle to activate any 4 degree area is always 9 months no matter where one starts counting. If one is so fortune to live 84 years, the whole chart will have been activated by Uranus that will, no doubt, describe many of life's most memorable events or situations.

Figure 72 Sample of the Uranus Transit Movement with Its Shadow Range

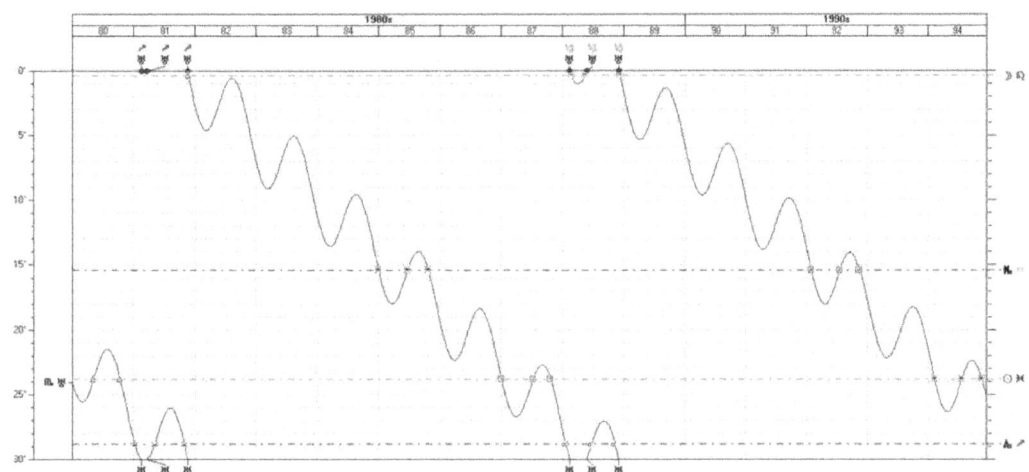

A Healing Half-Year with Transiting Chiron

Because Chiron's orbit is highly elliptical like Pluto's, it moves quickly through some signs and slower through others. While the entire cycle takes 50 years to complete, the 1st quarter square can occur anywhere between the ages of 5 and 23. Melanie Reinhart has found that when the 1st quarter Chiron square is experienced before the 1st Saturn square the experience is often more traumatic.

The Chiron cycle represents the process of individualization and integration. It represents the phases experienced as we receive or become aware of wounds and deal with our woundedness to find a safe space to seek balance in life. The phases of the 4th harmonic, the conjunction, separating square, opposition, applying square and conjunction, mark major turning points in life that often accompany a change of course. The phases tend to be deeply marked in the psyche as times of wounding, be they the initial wound or where old wounds were opened up for healing, to signal the need to complete unfinished business. Physical illness can mark these times as well. Rebalancing and realigning with one's center, as well as an awakening of the quest for self-discovery and meaning, is what this cycle is all about.

A Chiron transit is generally in effect about three weeks prior to the date of exact and a week or more after. Chiron slows in its apparent motion as seen from earth from time to time, and then its effect extends to as much as two and one-half months during the retrograde and shadow period. Notation in the ephemeris indicates any noticeable effective time variance.

Figure 73 Sample of the Chiron Transit Movement with Its Shadow Range

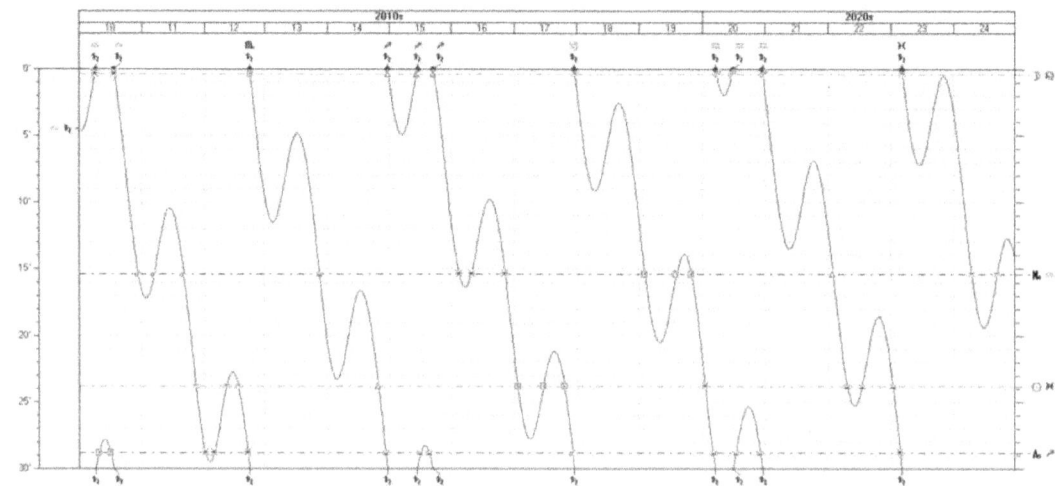

A Responsible Season with Transiting Saturn

Saturn transits the zodiac in 29+ years and is memorable because after the first cycle, all the issues expressed by the planetary contacts and placements in our natal chart have been activated. Every Saturn transit thereafter is an echo of the first. It is important to make a connection to what happened the last time Saturn made the contact and make a correlation between the two events – there is one. Further, any planets or points activated by Saturn when it moves in its retrograde and shadow period are especially felt because the aspect duration is prolonged by the three hits of forward, retrograde and forward motion.

The hard aspects of Saturn bring the lessons we need, but don't want. It is a rare person who looks forward to the discipline of putting responsibilities ahead of personal wishes. The one good thing to remember about Saturn, even if the lessons are painful, is the responsibilities with which we are saddled are and should be the consequences of our own choices. If one gets the sense of being a victim, then it is important to ask, "What role did I play in allowing this to happen"? – and then deal with it, rather than rail against others. The soft aspects of Saturn bring the rewards and happiness we have earned – no more, no less.

A Saturn transit is generally in effect about two weeks prior to the date of exact and at least a week after. Saturn slows in its apparent motion as seen from earth from time to time, and then its effect extends to as much as two months during the retrograde and shadow period. Notation in the ephemeris indicates any noticeable effective time variance.

Saturn Retrograde Period: In the average Saturn transit more than half of each sign, 16 degrees in all, is hit three times by the retrograde and direct motion taking nearly 11 months to complete the extended stay in the sensitized "shadow" degree range. No wonder we tend to take notice when an extended Saturn transit activates key areas of the chart. On the other hand, the other 14 degrees of each sign that only receive one Saturn pass during the cycle are each activated for about 7 to 14 days, obviously much easier by comparison. Allowing for a 1-degree orb, the activating potential of the Saturn pass could extend from 2 weeks to just short of a month, depending upon the planet's speed. Certainly, it is easy to understand why the retrograde cycle of any planet is so important in good astrological forecasting.

So, from our earth point of view, Saturn moves 21- 22 degrees direct, 7 degrees retrograde, 21+ degrees direct, 7 retrograde, and so on as it moves through the zodiac. Add the degrees of direct and retrograde motion together and 29 years is the time Saturn takes to move through the zodiac.

Figure 74 Sample of the Saturn Transit Movement with Its Shadow Range

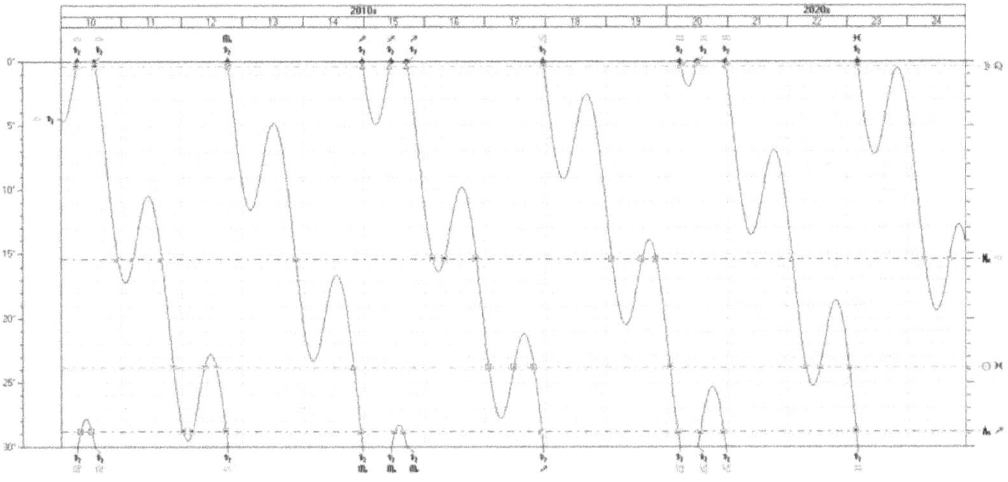

A Fruitful Period with Transiting Jupiter

Jupiter transits the zodiac in 12 years moving through 1 sign per year. Note that the retrograde periods do extend the effect of a Jupiter transit over a particular degree area. The expansion of the Jupiter influence brings excess in the nature of whatever it aspects. A Jupiter transit to a well-aspected natal planet such as Venus can signal plenty good things like social gatherings, gifts, even romance – sometimes too much, if the Jupiter influence is not balanced by other transits. The Jupiter transit can be a lesson in, "Be careful what you ask for – you may get it!" A Jupiter transit to a natal planet, such as a Moon that has several hard aspects, might trigger the excess of emotion. Jupiter seems rather neutral, bringing only excess and good or bad experiences only when hard aspects are involved by the Jupiter transit aspect itself or to a natal planet or point that is heavily besieged with hard aspects.

You may refer to any "Transit" text for specific transit to planet interpretations, but simply armed with a good basic understanding of planets, aspects, houses, and to a lesser extent, signs, one has the tools to synthesize the ingredients into a valid interpretation. It is only by studying the charts we know well that comparing outer transits to actual life events confirms our "book-learning" and develops the astrologer's art of interpretation.

A Jupiter transit is generally in effect about one week prior to the date of exact and several days after. Jupiter slows in its apparent motion as seen from earth from time to time and then its effect extends to as much as one month to account for the retrograde and shadow period. Notation in the ephemeris indicates any noticeable effective time variance.

Jupiter Retrograde Period: During the average Jupiter transit of one sign per year only one-third of the sign, 10 degrees, is sensitized by the Jupiter's retrograde motion over degrees it had already crossed. The whole sensitized area is called the "shadow" because those degrees receive three hits from the planet's transit really emphasizing what might otherwise pass unnoticed. So, not only does the "shadow" include the retrograde itself, but also the same degrees retraced in forward motion both approaching and returning. In the case of Jupiter, the effect of the "shadow" lasts approximately 10 months; whereas a single pass Jupiter transit across the other 20 degrees of the sign lasts about 5 to 10 days. Allowing for a one-degree orb of influence, one could easily extend the activating potential of the planet to about 2 weeks, depending upon Jupiter's speed.

Figure 75 Sample of the Jupiter Transit Movement with Its Shadow Range

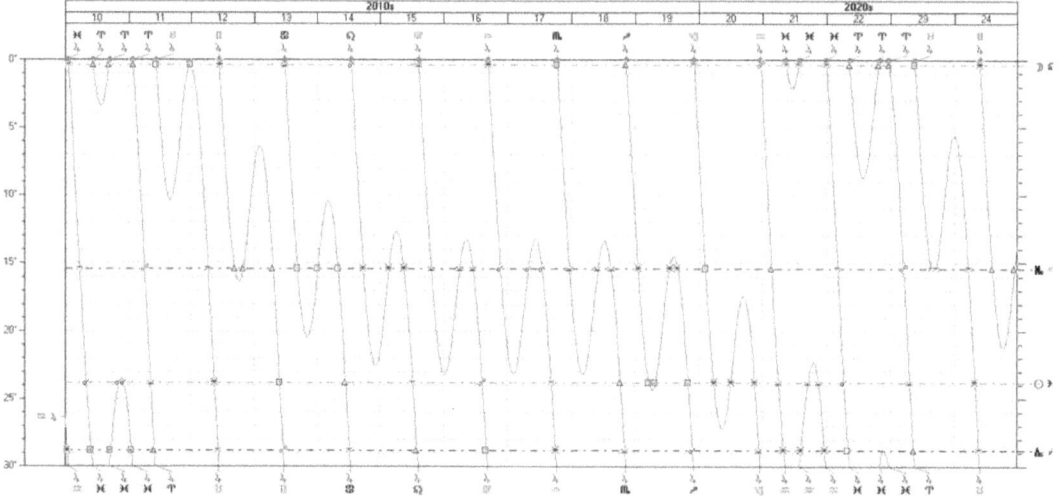

From our earth point of view, Jupiter moves 40 - 42 degrees direct, 10 degrees retrograde, 40+ degrees direct, 10 retrograde, and so on, as it moves through the zodiac. Add the degrees of direct and retrograde motion together and 52 weeks, or one year, is Jupiter's time to move around the zodiac.

Retrograde Periods Extend the Effect of Any Transit

The retrograde, station and complete shadow area of each planet's motion are of paramount importance in guiding the astrologer to emphasize the importance of a transit or not. There is a very great difference in the astrologer's interpretation of a 10-month visit of a Saturn transit in its retrograde cycle over a personal planet or Angle, as opposed to only a couple of weeks when it skates right through. Keep in mind that two-thirds of Jupiter's transit cycle does not retrograde to re-activate a degree area, so his influence is at best a week or two. And one-third of Saturn's cycle does not retrograde to re-activate a degree area, so his influence is at best two or three weeks. Especially for Jupiter and Saturn transits, this is an important interpretive distinction. Transits of Uranus, Neptune and Pluto are not tricky at all, because they are ALWAYS in some part of a retrograde cycle and activate a degree area multiple times that extend from one year for transiting Uranus and nearly two years for transiting Neptune and Pluto.

Retrograde periods, including the direct motion returning to the initial retrograde point, sensitize the whole span of degrees in between. As evident from the outer planet transit graphs included for each outer planet, each moves at a different rate, and sensitizes a varying number of degrees during its direct/retrograde/direct cycle. Obviously, when two or more of these outer transits activate the natal chart in a narrow time span, the effect is greatly compounded with more intense life experience.

Transiting Lunar Nodes are the Royalty of Retrograde

Of course, we know the Lunar Nodes are not planets, but their transit cycle is 18.6 years spanning each sign in one and a half years, steadily moving retrograde or clockwise. The Lunar Nodes bring their message of important life lessons and personal growth into most astrological traditions where there is a variation of interpretation. In Vedic astrology the Lunar Nodes are depicted as two halves of a depraved and hedonistic beast. The North Node is the top half of the beast known as "Rahu" taking in excessively, suggesting difficulty through "insatiable worldly desire and materialistic compulsion" and the South Node is the bottom half of the beast known as "Ketu" eliminating excessively, suggesting difficulty through making trouble, sowing confusion and stress, even privation. In modern astrology the North Node is described as the life experience leading toward one's life purpose. The South Node is described as the life experience that set one's foundation of family values and habits to learn, modify and grow toward a life of purpose and fulfillment. I include the Lunar Nodes with the transits, to emphasize how different their transit movement is to their Solar Arc Directed movement, which is counterclockwise at the same pace as the Sun. Otherwise the Lunar Nodes travel clockwise by transit about 3-minutes of longitude a day, 1 ½ degrees a month, and 18 degrees a year to complete the 18.6-year cycle. By Secondary Progression, the Lunar Nodes don't move enough in a lifetime to be interpretively useful; however, if we test with Tertiary or Minor Progression, still moving clockwise, they again can be very interpretively useful. For rectification, we must have a good understanding of what moves how fast, in what direction, in each technique and how long it activates one-degree of the natal chart.

Figure 76 Mean Lunar Node Movement Varies from True Node Movement

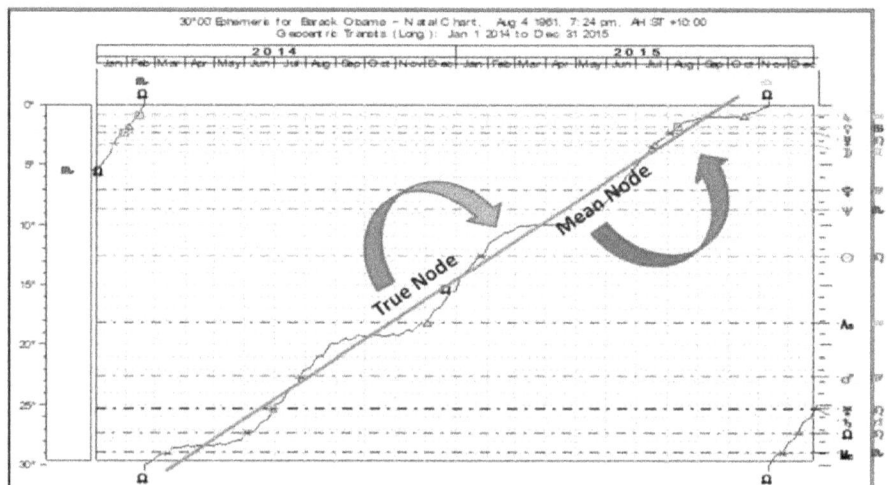

Timing a Half Year with Solar and Lunar Eclipses

"One of the difficulties when reckoning with eclipses is that they appear to be very inconsistent in their expression. We know the timing of the eclipse, and we also know that they tend to be stressful…What we are not sure of, however, is the nature of the stress. …"[5] Bernadette Brady

"If there is one common factor which unites predictions using eclipses, it would surely be 'expect the unexpected".[6] Rob Hand

"Solar Eclipses tend to relate to sudden events that disrupt our normal conscious functioning; … external as it may appear, it is actually our own unconscious and subconscious at work.[7] Kevin Burk

Astrologers and authors agree that Eclipses activating our natal planet(s) in the opposing pair of houses in the course of a year send the message to pay attention to the issues described by the planets. Of course, we know that Solar and Lunar Eclipses are connected; a Lunar Eclipse cannot occur alone, but only two weeks before a Solar Eclipse, or two weeks after – and sometimes, a Lunar Eclipse may occur before AND after the Solar Eclipse. We also know that the Solar Eclipse must have the Sun and Moon conjunct and parallel AND parallel to one of the Lunar Nodes within 17-degrees. The Lunar Eclipse must have the Sun and Moon opposite and parallel AND contra-parallel to one of the Lunar Nodes within 23-degrees.

Figure 77 A Retrograde (Diurnal Motion) Seesaw Pattern of Solar Eclipses

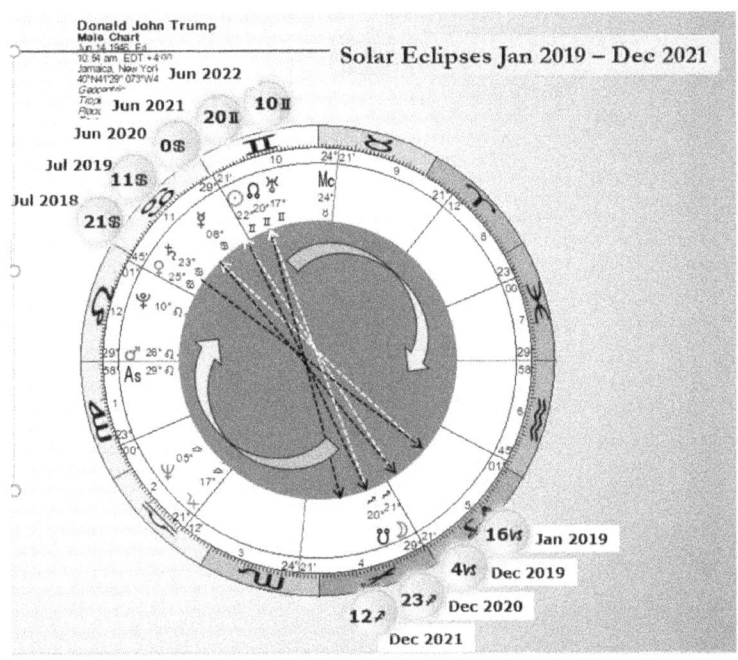

"An Eclipse is interpretively important when conjunct or opposite a planet or important point within 5-degrees."[8] [particularly the Lights and Angles] Bernadette Brady

"A number of authorities suggest that you look at all major aspects to the eclipse position. My personal observation is that most will only be able to relate to situations represented by conjunctions or oppositions – After all, eclipses deal exclusively with conjunctions and oppositions."[9] Robert Carl Jansky

"The house activated by the eclipse and the overall theme of its Saros Series emphasizes, 'Deal with this area of life now', even if there is no planetary contact."[10] Rob Hand

A Solar Eclipse sheds light on issues of the house and any planets therein for about 5 ½ months:

Well-aspected, it is a time to reap benefits; poorly aspected, it speaks of a challenge or dilemma involving vitality or conscious, outward expression.

Table 38 Solar Eclipses Help Choose the Best Birth Time in Hilary Clinton's 24-hour Search

Age	Date of Event	Degree Sign	1:55A	2:45A	6:06A	7:00A	8:15A	10:08A	1:55P	2:45P	6:10P	7:10P	8:15P	10:00P
21	10-Jun-69 Graduated Wellesley	27 Pisces	7th △♃ 3rd	7th □♅ 10th △♃ 3rd	5th ☌☽ 5th □♅ 8th △♃ 2nd	5th □♅ 8th △♃ 1st	4th □♅ 8th △♃ 1st	4th □♅ 7th △♃ 1st	☌IC □♅ 7th △♃ 12th	1st ☌☽ 1st □♅ 4th	☌☽ 11th □♅ 8th △♃ 8th	10th ☌☽ 11th □♅ 1st	☌☽ 10th □As □♅ 1st △♃ 6th	9th □♅ 12th △♃ 5th
27	11-Oct-75 Marriage	19 Taurus	9th □♄ 12th ☍☿ 3rd	3rd ☌♀ 3rd □♂ 11th □♅ 11th	7th ☍☿ 1st ☍♀ 1st □♄ 10th	7th □♄ 10th □Mc 10th ☍☿ 1st	6th ☍☿ 12th ☍♀ 1st □♄ 9th	6th ☍☿ 12th ☍♀ 12th □♄ 9th	5th ☍☿ 12th ☍♀ 12th □♄ 9th	2nd ☍☿ 9th □♄ 6th	12th ☍♀ 6th ☍☿ 6th □♄ 3rd	12th ☍☿ 6th □♄ 3rd	12th ☍☿ 6th ☍♀ 5th □♄ 3rd	11th □♄ 2nd ☍☿ 5th
31	10-Jan-79 Arkansas First Lady	9 Libra	2nd ☌♆ 2nd	1st ☌♆ 1st	12th ☌♆ 12th	11th ☌♆ 12th	☌♆ 11th	☌♆ 10th	☌♆ 10th	7th ☌♆ 7th	☌♆ 5th	5th ☌♆ 5th	4th ☌♆ 4 th ⚻Mc	4th ☌♆ 4 th ☌IC
32	27-Feb-80 Chelsea born	27 Aquarius	6th △♅ 10th	6th △☉ 2nd	4th △♅ 8th	4th △♅ 8th	3rd △♅ 8th	3rd △♅ 7th	3rd △♅ 7th	12th △♅ 4th	2nd ☌♅ 2nd	10th ☌Mc △♅ 1st	9th △As △♅ 1st	8th △♅ 12th
45	January 20 1993 USA First Lady	2 Capricorn	4th ⚹☉ 2nd	4th ⚹☉ 2nd	3rd	2nd ⚹☉ 12th	2nd △Mc	1st	1st	10th ⚹☉ 9th	8th	7th ⚹☉ 5 th	☌Ds □☽ 10th	6th □☽ 9th
50	9-Sep-98 Husband's scandal	29 Leo	12th □♃ 3rd	12th □♃ 3rd	10th □♃ 2nd	10th □♃ 1st	9th □♃ 1st	9th □♃ 12th	9th □♃ 12th ⚻☽ 1st	6th □♃ 9th	4th □♃ 7th □As	4th ⚻☽ 11th	3rd ☌IC □♃ 6th	2nd □♃ 5 th ⚻☽ 9 th
53	7-Nov-00 US Senator	4 Capricorn	4th ⚹☉ 2nd	4th	3rd	2nd ⚹☉ 12th	2nd	3rd	2nd	10th	8th	7th ⚹☉ 5 th	☌Ds □☽ 10th	6th □☽ 9 th
61	1-Dec-08 US Secretary of State	9 Leo	11th ⚹♆ 2nd	11th	10th ☌Mc	7th ☍As	9th	8th	8th	6th ⚻As 1st	4th	3rd	3rd	1st △Mc
63	31-Jul-10 Chelsea's wedding	19 Cancer	11th △☿ 6th △☽ 7th	10th △☽ 7th △☿ 3rd	9th △♀ 1st △☿ 1st	9th △☿ 1st △☽ 5 th	8th △☽ 4th △♀ 12th △As △☿	8th △IC △☿ 12th △♀ 12th	8th △☿ 12th △♀ 12th	5th △♀ 8th ⚻Mc 10th	3rd △♀ 6th △☿ 6th	2nd △☿ 6th	2nd △♀ 5th △☿ 6th	12th △☿ 5 th
64	1-Nov-11 Mother's death	2 Sagittarius	3rd ☌♃ 3rd	3rd ☌♃ 3rd	2nd ☌♃ 2nd	1st ☌♃ 1st	☌♃ 1st □Mc	☌As ☌♃ 1st	12th ☌♃ 12th	9th ☌♃ 9th	☌Ds ☌♃ 7th	6th ☌♃ 6th	☌♃ 6th □Mc	5th ☌♃ 5 th
69	8-Nov-16 Lost Pres Election	9 Virgo	1st ☌As	12th	11th	10th ⚹As	☌Mc	3rd	7th □Mc	7th ☌Ds	3rd	4th	☍Mc	3rd

Solar Eclipses 2 ° orb Clearly Activate Angles Best for 8:15 PM Birth Time

A Lunar Eclipse involves emotions, inner, irrational forces, issues of family, security and sense of belonging. It is internal and unconscious for 2 - 3 months.

A Solar or Lunar Eclipse occurring within 3-degrees of a personal planet or angle, or on a leg of a closely aspected configuration, is interpretively more prominent. Eclipses seesaw back and forth clockwise moving about 10-degrees from the previous eclipse of its kind to light up opposing houses. With this seesaw pattern, a "polarity of houses" can be activated for about 2 years. Figure 75 illustrates the movement that we call the "Eclipse Season". In 2022 the Eclipse Seasons occurs in January and June.

Eclipses are not helpful in the wide time range rectification search for birthtime however,

5. Brady, Bernadette, Predictive Astrology - The Eagle and the Lark, Samuel Weiser, Inc. York Beach, ME, 1999
6. Hand, Robert, Horoscope Symbols, Whitford Press, Atglen, PA, 1981
7. Burk, Kevin, Understanding the Birth Chart, Llewellyn Publications, St Paul, MN 2001

once the birth time is narrowed to just a few times to test, Solar and Lunar Eclipses can clarify and confirm the best birthtime. For instance, Hillary Clinton is listed in Astro.com as DD-data. Several birthtimes are put forward but none are confirmed. However, it was in the news that someone in a crowd asked for her birthtime, and she replied 8:00 o'clock, without saying AM or PM. In testing several of the controversial times, including the 8 AM and 8 PM times, I found that both 8:00 o'clock times work, but the Solar Eclipses clearly favor the PM time for Hilary Clinton. Table 38 shows the results.

Assessing the Degrees of Angles with Decans and Dwads

Signs are the least informative part of the chart. Everyone knows his own Sun sign, but with only twelve signs of the zodiac and many billions of people in the world, the Sun sign provides even less information than saying I live in New York. With decans and dwads, we can know more specifically what kind of a Gemini, for instance.

If we think of the chart wheel as a clock, it is easier to visualize the information given by the Decans and Dwads that give specific information about specific degree areas within each sign. We know that the chart angles change 1-degree every 4-minutes of clock time, so the angles span an entire sign of 30-degree in 2-hours, and in 24-hours the angles move through all twelve signs. If we delve deeper into each sign, the decans represent one-third of a sign, 40-minutes of clock time in three 10-degree sub-divisions of the sign. The Triplicity method designates the first decan to rename the sign itself, giving the strongest emphasis of the sign to planets or angles in the first 10-degrees. It is important to know the element of the sign: fire (Aries, Leo, Sagittarius), earth (Taurus, Virgo, Capricorn), air (Gemini, Libra, Aquarius) or water (Cancer, Scorpio, Pisces) to determine the emphasis for the second and third 10-degree segments of the sign. For example, the Sun at 8-degrees of Gemini is described by the sign as, "one with many interests and a focus on communication". But being in the first 10-degrees of Gemini, the Sun receives additional emphasis of those qualities, because the Gemini decan also describes the first 10-degrees of Gemini. Of course, Gemini is an air sign, so the middle 10-degree segment of the sign Gemini would be described by the next air sign in sequence which is Libra. And it follows that the last 10-degree segment of the sign Gemini is the next air sign after Libra which is Aquarius.

Dwads follow the same logic, but they represent 10-minutes of clock time and 2 ½ -degrees of a sign. Envision a sub-set of all twelve signs describing each small part of the sign and renaming the sign as the first piece with the other sign in order describing each dwad segment. As you may guess, the first 2 ½-degree dwad renames the sign, again giving the strongest ex-

---

8. Brady, Bernadette, Predictive Astrology - The Eagle and the Lark, Samuel Weiser, Inc. York Beach, ME, 1999
9. Jansky, Robert, Carl, Interpreting Eclipses, Astrology Classics, 2013
10. 6. Hand, Robert, Horoscope Symbols, Whitford Press, Atglen, PA, 1981

pression of the sign to the first dwad. So, the sequence is 0-2 ½ Gemini dwad, 2 ½ -5 Cancer dwad, 5-7 ½Leo dwad, 7 ½-10 Virgo dwad, and so on, so the Sun in 8-degrees of Gemini is in the Gemini decan and the Virgo dwad. Interpretively, we now know the person is seriously involved in communication through writing or other media, analytical and focused on detail. The grid of signs, decans and dwads in the Triplicity method is a helpful took, but your astrology software also provides that information.

Table 39 Triplicity Method of Decanantes and Dwads

MOST USED MODERN TRIPLICITY DWAD SYSTEM

	0°–2°29	2°30–4°59	5°–7°29	7°30–9°59	10°–12°29	12°30–14°59	15°–17°29	17°30–19°59	20°–22°29	22°30–24°59	25°–27°29	27°30–29°59
AR	♈	♉	♊	♋	♌	♍	♎	♏	♐	♑	♒	♓
TA	♉	♊	♋	♌	♍	♎	♏	♐	♑	♒	♓	♈
GE	♊	♋	♌	♍	♎	♏	♐	♑	♒	♓	♈	♉
CN	♋	♌	♍	♎	♏	♐	♑	♒	♓	♈	♉	♊
LE	♌	♍	♎	♏	♐	♑	♒	♓	♈	♉	♊	♋
VI	♍	♎	♏	♐	♑	♒	♓	♈	♉	♊	♋	♌
LI	♎	♏	♐	♑	♒	♓	♈	♉	♊	♋	♌	♍
SC	♏	♐	♑	♒	♓	♈	♉	♊	♋	♌	♍	♎
SG	♐	♑	♒	♓	♈	♉	♊	♋	♌	♍	♎	♏
CP	♑	♒	♓	♈	♉	♊	♋	♌	♍	♎	♏	♐
AQ	♒	♓	♈	♉	♊	♋	♌	♍	♎	♏	♐	♑
PI	♓	♈	♉	♊	♋	♌	♍	♎	♏	♐	♑	♒

Decan | Decan | Decan

The Triplicity sub-sets of the signs, decans and dwads, are excellent tools to test the chart Angles, once other tests have narrowed the birth time to within fifteen minutes or so. In the late 1970's Geoffrey Dean of Australia challenged astrologers worldwide to distinguish between thirty sets of twins, identical and fraternal, all born within 23-minutes of each other. We were given a biographical paragraph of each twin that included their work and their personality description. Our Los Angeles group led by Dr. Zip Dobyns got 29 of the 30 pairs correct.

All the twins had the same planets at the same sign and degree and in the same house, including the Moon. The only chart element that could change in a 23-minute range is the degree of the Angles. And if the Angle degree is near the end of a sign, the Angle could possibly change sign as well. Within the range of 23-degrees, we had 3 possible decans and 10 possible dwads as sub-descriptors of the sign on the Angles to fit the description of the twin. Recently, as I searched www.astro.com for twin examples, I came across a quote that intrigued me, "Considering a biography" by Paul Cantin, "There is some confusion whether Alanis Morrissette was first (born 9:39) or second (born 9:51)." Alanis Morrissette is a well-known folk singer and song writer of the late 20th century and her twin brother, Wade Morrissette, is a well-known Reiki master and Yoga teacher. Using the decan and dwad descriptors for the Ascendant and Midheaven degrees for Alanis and Wade clearly confirms that the charts that Astro.com has for them are reversed and Paul Cantin's reference to confusion about which twin was born first is well-founded.

The chart labeled "Wade" has a Leo Ascendant and at 6-degrees is in the Leo decan, and the Libra dwad. This better describes the artistic performer, not the Yoga teacher and Reiki master. The chart labeled "Alanis" also has a Leo Ascendant and at 8-degrees is also in the Leo decan, but the dwad is Scorpio. This better describes the Reiki master and Yoga teacher, not the Folk singer and song writer.

If you're not convinced, test the Midheaven degrees. Both Alanis and Wade have Aries on the Midheaven and both in the last 10-degree triplicity of the Aries, the Sagittarius decan. But the chart labeled "Wade" with the 20-degree Aries Midheaven lands in the Sagittarius dwad very descriptive of the performer, Alanis, not the Yoga teacher Wade.

On the other hand, the chart labeled "Alanis" with the 23-degree Aries Midheaven, still in the Sagittarius decan, but that degree lands in the Capricorn dwad, much more descriptive of the Reiki master and Yoga teacher. Clearly, Alanis was born first at 9:39 am and her brother, Wade, was born at 9:51 am. Once the birth time is narrowed to within 15-minutes, or so, this Triplicity decan and dwad system can clarify and confirm birth time, best used as a final test.

Assessing the Year with a Solar Return and a Correct Birth time

The basic premise of the Solar Return is to calculate exactly when the Sun returns to its birth position; but it was difficult to calculate because accurate ephemerides did not exist in ancient times. This problem was not completely resolved until the late 18th early 19th centuries. During the 200 years when astrology was in decline (1700-1900) and no longer in the university, much knowledge was lost but the Solar Return stayed in use by astrologers. Astrologers up to the mid-19th century used only the planets Sun through Saturn for the Solar Return since Uranus, Neptune and Pluto had not yet been discovered. Now in the 21st century Solar Return, even traditional astrologers include the outer three planets.

With Whole Sign Houses, traditional astrologers relied on "profections" of the natal chart house ruler as "Lord of the Year" plus a Solar Return to forecast the client's year with the transiting Sun. Modern astrologers also use "profections" to the natal chart determine the "Lord of the Year", or instead, the Solar Return Ascendant ruler as the dominant planet for the year. The following Table 39 may be helpful to determine the Hellenistic "Lord of the Year".

Table 40 Find the Hellenistic Profected Year for a Person's Age

HOUSES	Age	Age	Age	Age	Age	Age	Age	Age
First	0	12	24	36	48	60	72	84
Second	1	13	25	37	49	61	73	85
Third	2	14	26	38	50	62	74	86
Fourth	3	15	27	39	51	63	75	87
Fifth	4	16	28	40	52	64	76	88
Sixth	5	17	29	41	53	65	77	89
Seventh	6	18	30	42	54	66	78	90
Eighth	7	19	31	43	55	67	79	91
Ninth	8	20	32	44	56	68	80	92
Tenth	9	21	33	45	57	69	81	93
Eleventh	10	22	34	46	58	70	82	94
Twelfth	11	23	35	47	59	71	83	95

A Return chart can be created for any of the planets and its duration is based on the time needed for the planet to return by sign, degree, and minute to its natal position. That is to say that the Lunar Return only takes 28-days to return to its natal sign, degree and minute that describes less than one calendar month. The Moon's condition and location in the Lunar Return is key to interpretation by using the transiting Moon as the timer to activate the planets and points therein. The same logic is applied to other planet Returns. Our software provides options for choosing a Return of any planet and for any time period. I have saved discussion of the Returns for last because, though they do provide interpretive information about what is activated by the transiting planet of the Return's name, they do not confirm birth time precisely enough for rectification. For example, a Mars Return would be correct for at least a half-hour, because Mars doesn't move fast enough to exceed the exact sign, degree, and minute of the natal Mars. Even Mercury and Venus move at varying speeds and direction, so in a retrograde cycle, which return to the natal position counts, the first direct hit, the retrograde hit, or the final direct hit? The Moon doesn't go retrograde, but the Lunar Return is problematic in that without a correct birth time, we are not sure of the Moon's natal position. The Moon transits, on average, 13.11 degrees daily, or about six-degree minutes per hour, so unless the birth time is correct within fifteen minutes of clock time, the Lunar Return would also be incorrect. My advice is to hold off on testing with any of the Return charts until you have the birthtime rectified to within ten minutes of clock time.

A Final Birth Time Test: Relocation

Once the rectification process has narrowed the birth time to one or two possibilities, relocating the natal chart to test the handful of major life events may clarify the final choice. In relocation, the natal chart planets remain at the natal sign, degree, and minute, but the angles and houses change according to the time zone and latitudes changes. Most astrologers use the relocated chart as supplemental to the natal chart and interpret it as: a place where planets respond in their new houses and, importantly, if planets make a close aspect to an Angle appropriate to experiences there. The birth date is the same as the natal chart unless the time zone variance pushes it into the next day, or back to the prior day. For instance, Elizabeth Taylor was born just past midnight at 2:00 am. If she moved even several time zones East from London, the angles and houses would change but the birth date would remain the same. However, by moving West even two time zones, the birth date would change to a day earlier.

Figure 80 Relocation Can Change Time Zones and Dates for the Chart to Keep Natal Positions

Ms. Taylor's 8-hour time zone change to the West moved February 27th back to February 26th. Again, the planets retain their natal sign, degree and minute, only the Angles and houses change.

Compare the natal and relocated charts for Mark Zuckerberg *(following page)* to see if the relocated chart is descriptive for his focus and situation. Do important descriptors of that focus come to and Angle in that location? Are we surprised that this tech genius who created the worldwide social media platform, Facebook, has Mercury on the Midheaven and Pluto on the Imum Coeli in San Jose, California? Even the descriptors of the relocated Angles by signs and rulers emphasize the promise of the natal chart – and it confirms that the natal chart is correct. Mr. Zuckerberg's natal promise of an innovative Aries Mercury in close trine to Neptune is brought to the forefront in the new location to fulfill its visionary natal promise. And the natal promise of Pluto to control is brought to the Imum Coeli, connected to Mercury and Neptune, awakens that natal promise to great influence in homes around the world. The natal Virgo Ascendant with Mercury as ruler is on the Midheaven in San Jose, California. And the relocated Leo Ascendant appropriately describes his personal pride and pleasure in public attention.

The relocated chart responds to movement in the same way as the natal chart. Current patterns modify even the best relocated chart. Standard movement techniques, such as transits, progressions, and directions, tell the current benefit in the new location. Remember, relocation is not part of the rectification process. However, it a useful tool to confirm the rectified birth time chosen.

Those also wanting to search Local House Cusps may find Davison's comments helpful: "If the person has moved from the birth location at the time of the event, it may be helpful to also search contacts to the local angles and house cusps once the search is narrowed to only a very few "working Angle" placements." Davison also suggests "... in progressing or directing the chart, the new locality should only be used beginning with the year equivalent to the person's age when the move was made.

Figure 81- Mark Zuckerberg Natal Chart   **Figure 82- Mark Zuckerberg RelocatedChart**

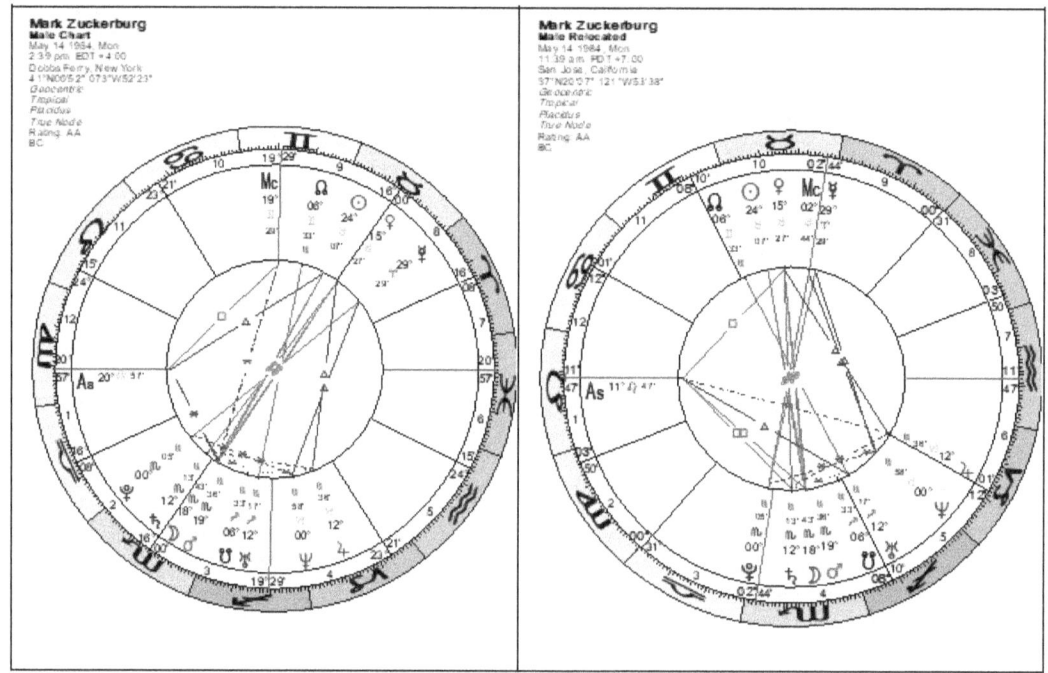

Chapter 6

How Do I Deal with Dirty Data?

Study the Resources for the Various Birth Time Claims

Many years ago, Lois M. Rodden's dream, and then a grand mission, was to gather birth data from celebrities and notable people around the world and share the information freely with the astrology community. She had ready access to celebrities because she lived in Hollywood, California, the movie and television capital of the world. Also, she was well-known in the astrology community and traveled across the world speaking at conferences and with local groups. Early in the 1980's, before the collection was digitized, Lois began publishing her collection of charts in volumes related to a common theme such as, "Profiles of Women", "The American Book of Charts", "The Occult Collection", "The Culture Collection" and "The Crime Collection". The books included only a small part of her data collection, so Lois worked with ISAR (International Society for Astrological Research) to transfer her more than twenty thousand data from 3" x 5" cards to a digital format. Several of us were part of that team, but programmer, Mark Pottenger, began the initial digitizing of the data in his spare time. A few years later, technology had advanced, and another programmer dedicated full time to complete the digital files for Lois's massive data collection. Remember all of this was developed at the dawn of the personal computer late in 1970's, when astrologers had few paths to get reliable birth data for the celebrities and prominent people featured in their books and other publications.

Each file in the then named "AstroDataBank", currently known as "Astro.com", contained a birth chart, a page of biography, a list of life events with dates, and details of the data source or sources, and its accuracy by the "Rodden Rating" scale of "AA" for most reliable with birth certificate in hand, "A" for reliable from mother's memory, "B" for less reliable from biography, "C" for caution or rectified, and "DD" for dirty data or multiple birth times, bringing all into dispute. A chart rated as" Dirty Data" is about as difficult to confirm or rectify as a twenty-four-hour search, because various astrologers have reported times from diverse second-hand sources, or they tried to rectify it and each astrologer has derived a different birth time. The more popular the newsworthy person, the more attempts astrologers made to rectify the birth time. By the 1970's there was an avalanche of "Dirty Data" in the astrology community, and most published without any references for the data source. An aside, other than helping Lois with the data project, I always roomed with her at conferences. She was in the process of creating the "Rodden Rating" scale and had decided on the AA, A, B and C key words, but was stumped by what to call the D category. In a wise-crack response, I suggested "Dirty Data". Lois quickly agreed and we toasted our dry martinis to the completion of the "Rodden Ratings". The astrology community quickly adopted "The Rodden Rating System" with references that raised the quality of astrological publications to academic standards.

Establish a "Working Chart" for the Midpoint of Known Time Range

The process of rectifying any birth time must begin by establishing a "working chart" set for the midpoint of the time search range for the date and location of the birth. Only then can the real work begin to align appropriate astrological descriptors with key life events near the correct date. Since the Angles are very time sensitive, transiting about 1-degree every 4 minutes of clock time, they are the key to any rectification search. The testing process is basically the same, but the wider the time range to test, the more testing that is needed. Don't forget to develop a case theory that is founded on the biography and personal characteristics of the client before any testing. Also, be clear to focus on involvement of the Angles at major events, planets moving to activate the "working angles" and "working angles" moving to activate planets within one-degree orb – and using at least three to four movement methods for the task.

When working with "Dirty Data", multiple undocumented birth times for the same person, the time range will likely exceed two-hours so the Moon degree, or even sign, needs to be tested first. Since the Moon transits an average of 1-degree every 2-hours, the Moon's position might range from a small fraction of 1-degree for time search ranges less than 1 hour, to as many as 3-degrees for time searches within a quarter of a day (morning, afternoon, evening, or night); and 6 to 7-degrees for a half-day (day or night). We need not allow a greater range for the Moon position in "Dirty Data" because setting the chart for midpoint of the time search range limits the Moon to, at most, within 6 to 7-degrees of exact by testing the angles in both directions from the time range midpoint. Starting the search at midnight for a 24-hour search doubles the possibilities for the Moon, and it is much easier for the "astrologer's eye" to spot a close aspect with the Moon from the search time range midpoint.

Testing various birth times is most easily begun with Solar Arc Direction, because the system eliminates the retrograde complication to planetary movement. One may safely assume that at least one pair of the Angles (MC/IC or ASC/DES), in the working chart for the movement technique, will be involved at major events. Personal issues such as health, and relationship most often show involvement of the Ascendant and Descendant axis (1st and 7th houses); and status, career and home issues show involvement of the Midheaven and Imum Coeli axis (10th and 4th houses). Remember, until a birth time is established, Angles and houses are not reliable. Indeed, until the birth time can be narrowed to within a one-hour range, the Angles and houses can be extremely misleading, regardless of the house system choice. And don't forget that the Angles are NOT the beginning of the signs marking the chart quadrants in the Whole Sign house system.

Michael Jackson, the King of Dirty Data, Must Start with a Case Theory

For years, astrologers have sought reliable birth time for "The King of Pop", Michael Jackson to no avail. For astrologers Michael was, "The King of Dirty Data", because he frequently went to a variety of astrologers practicing in a wide range of traditions and he never gave the same birth time. Even to colleagues, he gave vague and inaccurate birth time when asked. It is understandable that a man whose life was so public would want to protect his only privacy, with birth time that could be translated into a biographical narrative by an astrologer that could be newsworthy for the public, and profitable for the marketers.

Figure 83 The Range of Dirty Birth Data for Michael Jackson

- On p.6 the year and place are given, no date or time. Nelson George "The Michael Jackson Story," a Dell book, 1984, p.24, gives the date and place, no time.
- Richard Gehman called 9/l993 with a time of 7:54 AM CDT "from someone close to Michael."
- Grazia Bordoni writes 10/93 that Mercurio-3 gave 3:00 AM "from him."
- Zip Dobyns has 1:30 AM "from a close friend of Michael's to a fellow astrologer."
- Dobyns speculates late Aquarius rising.
- **Kim Baker speculates 12:09 PM** in NCGR Newsletter.
- **Lois Rodden spec-rectifies   8:47 AM CDT.**
- emailed the statement that "I had occasion, while playing in the opening act for the very last Jackson tour to ask Michael his birth time. **He said, "I will tell you as I told Jackie Onassis, all I know is that it was late in the evening, definitely after 10:30 PM."** As "Astrology of the Famed" was published in 1996 and Jackson's last tour was in 1984, Fearrington leaves himself open to some question of credibility.
- **Chakrapani Ullal gives 7:33 PM, "directly from Michael himself in 1998."**

Figure 84 Noon Chart Time Range Midpoint – Test Chart for Michael Jackson with Declination

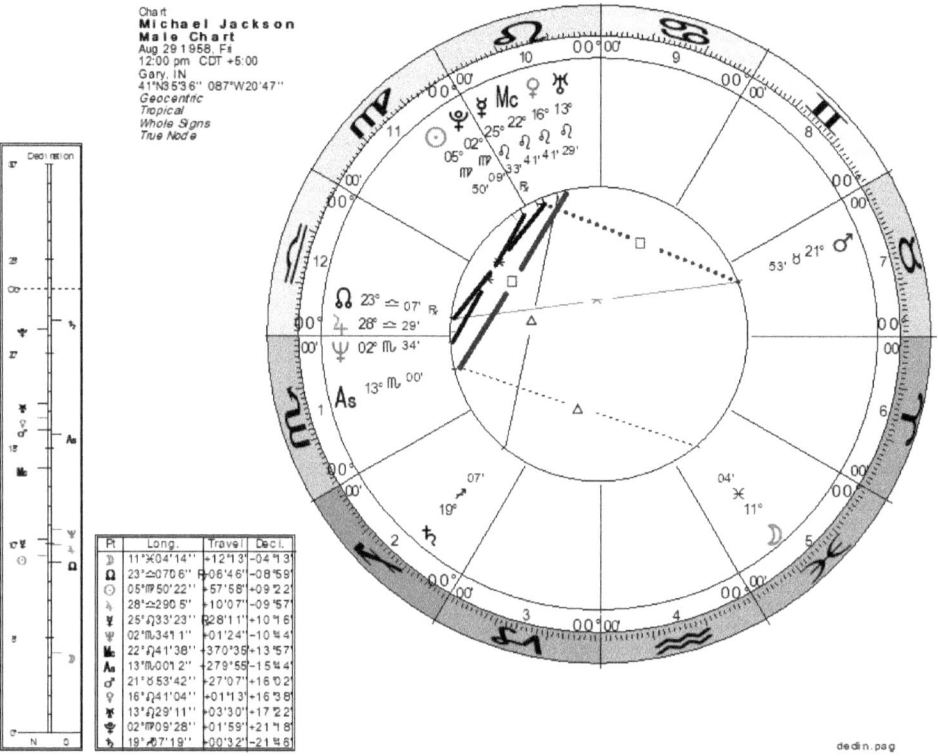

Venus/Uranus and Jupiter/Neptune are conjunct and parallel for all times on August 29, 1958 in Gary, Indiana, which compounds the interpretive importance of those planets. I would look for times that connect one, or both of those pairs to Michael's Ascendant or Midheaven. Further, I am inclined to start the search very early in the day for the Moon opposite Sun; or later in the evening for the Moon to square Saturn and quincunx Venus for emotional conflicts described in Jackson's biography. I also tested 7:45 pm that put his Leo/Virgo stellium in the 6th house for his lifelong emphasis on hard work. Years before Michael's death, I tested five charts based on birth times appropriate to my case theory, but because of the Moon's wider orb to square Saturn, I did not test 7:33 pm. However, I did test 7:45 pm that placed the Moon conjunct his Ascendant and the Leo/Virgo stellium in the 6th house to describe his intense work ethic. Each of the birth times that fit my case theory, 3:26 am, 1:34 pm, 7:45 pm, 9:40 pm and 11:01 pm fit some part of Michael's biography and I knew I was on the right track. Astrologers around the world were jubilant when Michel's cousin emailed confirmation of the 7:33 pm birth time for "The King of Pop".

Figure 85 Michael Jackson's Birth Certificate Confirmation Emailed from Jackson's Cousin

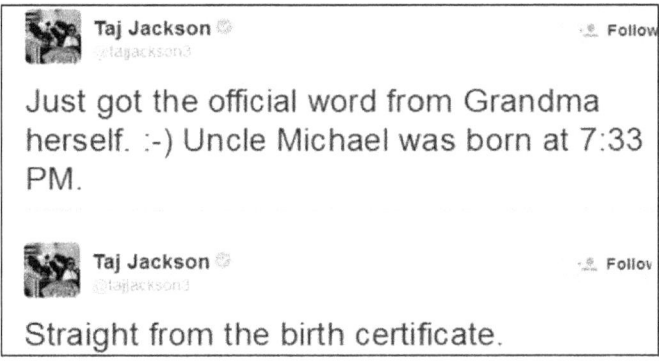

Figure 86 7:33 pm Chart for Michael Jackson's Birth Certificate Time

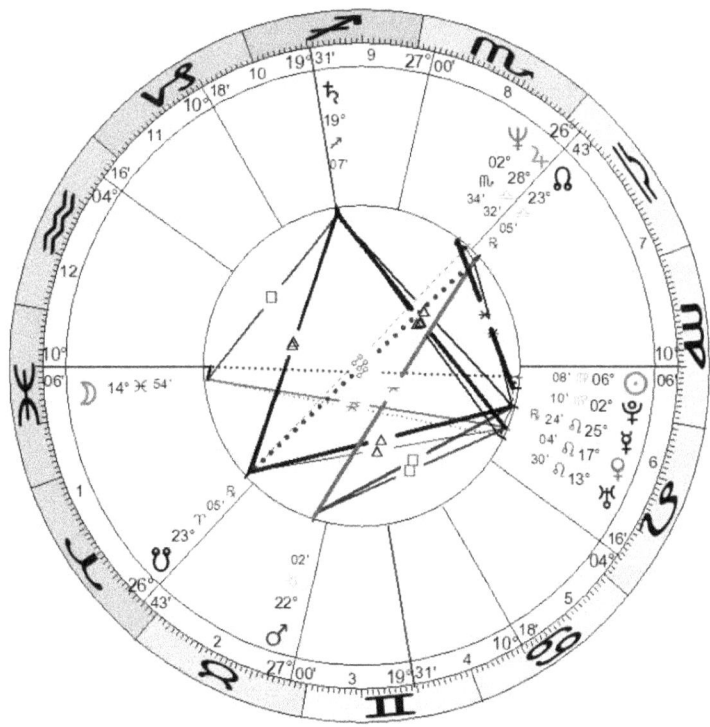

Figure 87 Michael Jackson's Life Event List from www.Astro.com

Date	Age	
1965	7	Began touring with family band, The Jackson Five
1969	11	Major acclaim
2/1984	25	Achieved six gold albums Won 8th Grammy
10/1984	26	Became "superstar" with release of "Thriller" album
8/17/1993	34	Child molestation charges Financial loss, settled $10 million
1/26/1994	35	Marriage to Lisa Marie Presley, Elvis' daughter
5/26/1994	35	
11/14/1996	37	Second marriage, to Deborah Rowe
2/13/1997	38	Daughter, Paris, born
4/3/1998	39	Son, Prince, born,
10/8/1999	41	Divorce
2/21/2002	43	Another son named Prince born (Blanket) Indicted
4/21/2004	45	by grand jury on child sex abuse charges Death,
6/25/2009	50	cardiac arrest from anesthesia overdose

To be sure that I missed something in my case theory for choosing three birth times that would align with Michael's biography and personal traits, I first ran the life events through the rectification search available in Jigsaw 2.2 and Sirius 4.1. I did get near confirmation of the early and late times that fit my case theory, but neither program produced strength for the 7:45 pm birth time, so I set it aside. Now that Michael Jackson's birth certificate time is now confirmed, I learned that I should have had more confidence in my case theory. Twelve minutes off with just case theory is not bad for a 23-hour birth time search!

Figure 88 Jigsaw 2.2 24-Hour Birth Time Search for Michael Jackson

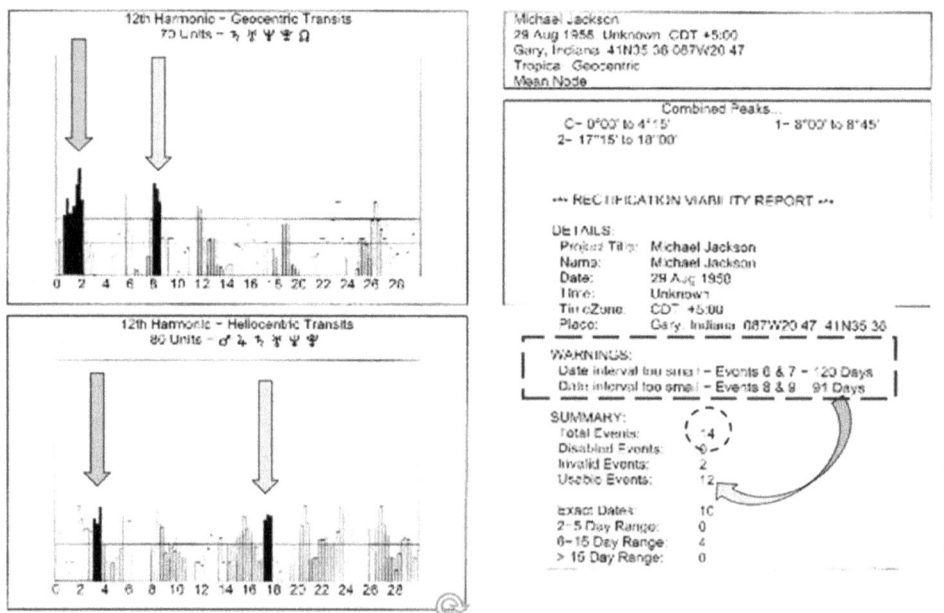

Figure 89 Jigsaw 2.2 Derives chart Angles 1-2-degrees, 8-9-degrees or 17-18-degrees of any Sign

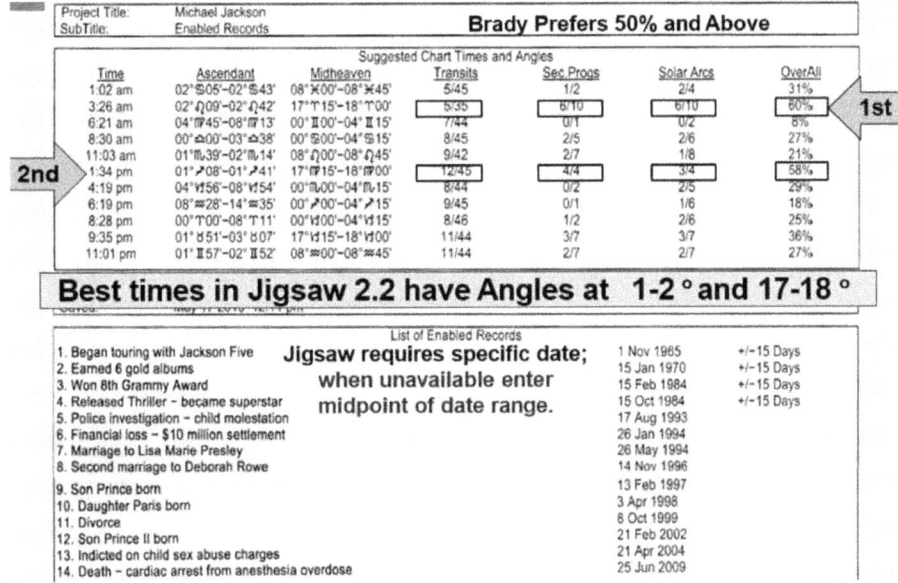

Figure 90 Sirius 4.1 Derives Possible Birth Times for Michael Jackson's Chart Angles to Fit Life Events

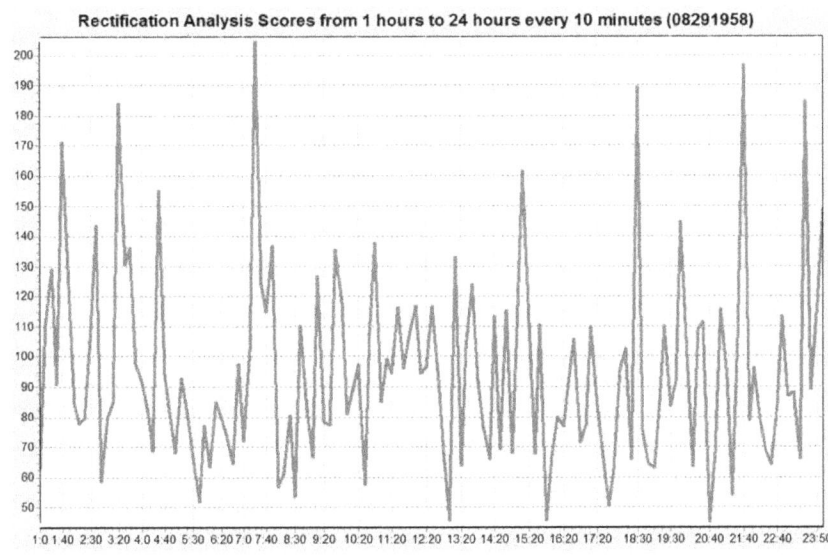

How Do I Deal with Dirty Data? 155

Software is Great, but A Trained Astrologer's Judgement is Better

Common Birth Times Shared by Jigsaw 2.2 and Sirius 4.1:
3:26-3:40 am = ASC 2-5 Leo, MC 17-20 Aries
1:34-1:40 pm = ASC 1-2 Sagittarius, MC 17-18 Virgo
9:35-9:40 pm = ASC 2-3 Taurus, MC 17-18 Capricorn
11:01-11:20 pm = ASC 1-5 Gemini, MC 8-12 Aquarius

Here I want to emphasize that software is a wonderful tool, but it does not match a well-trained astrologer's judgement. With the recent birth time confirmation by Michael Jackson's family from his birth certificate, 7:33 pm is confirmed. The 7:33 pm time is not listed at all in Jigsaw, and the closest time in Sirius is 7:20 am which does match a pair of Angles that mirrors 12-hours of time. The closest Jigsaw comes to the 7:33 pm birth certificate time is 6:30 pm – in the ballpark, but so far down the list we are unlikely to test it. This does bring up the point that testing a time that is appropriately descriptive of the person's life is worthy of testing its opposite twelve hours away. There is always a resonance between birth times 12-hours apart because 12-hours describes a pair of Angles. From there, it is fairly easy to test which birth time fits which angle. Software is a great tool, but a trained astrologer's judgement is better.

In a 24-hour search, multiples of approximately 6-hours represent Angles that are ninety-degrees apart at the Equator, but increasingly skewed as the latitude increases either North or South. The Progressed New Moons and Progressed Full Moons are broad enough in time to be good candidates for the First birth time test.

Figure 91 Jackson's Progressed New and Full Moons 7:33 pm for New Starts, New Fulfillment

Michael Jackson - Male Chart
Aug 29 1958, 7:33 pm, CDT +5:00
Gary IN, 41°N35'36", 087°W20'47"
Geocentric Tropical Zodiac
Placidus Houses, True Node

P1 (H)	Asp	P2 (H)	EXL	Type	Date	Time	Zone	Age	Pos1	Pos2
☽ (7)	☌	☉ (7)	(X)	Sp-Sp	Mar 6 1973	03:07:09 pm	CST	14.519	20°♍11' D	20°♍11' D
☽ (1)	☍	☉ (7)	(X)	Sp-Sp	Aug 16 1987	04:40:31 am	CDT	28.963	04°♈16' D	04°♎16' D
☽ (7)	☌	☉ (7)	(X)	Sp-Sp	Aug 17 2002	08:45:48 pm	CDT	43.968	19°♎01' D	19°♎01' D

Figure 92 Compare Jackson's Progressed New and Full Moons 7:33 pm for New Starts, New Fulfillment

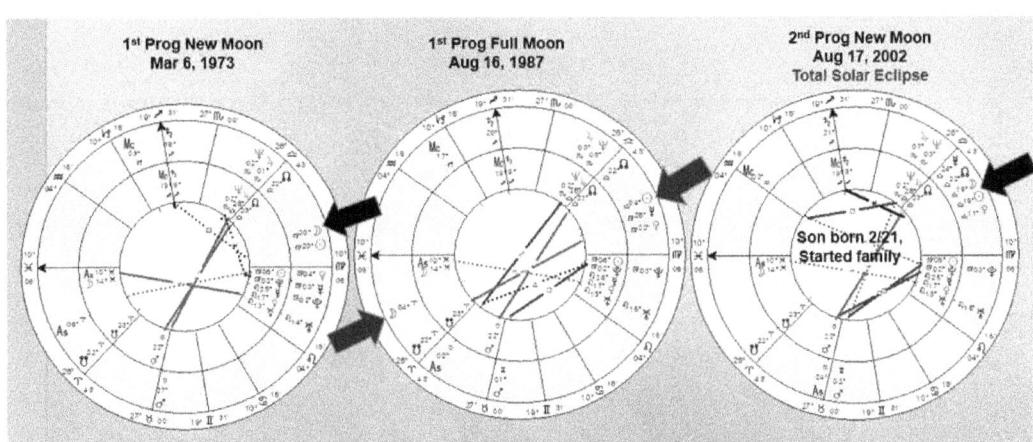

We have now faced the perennial problem with celebrity or historic charts – not enough important life events to confirm the birth time, even when we have found a legitimate birth certificate. The only major events that align with Michael's Progressed Full Moon in late 1987 is his eight awards into 1988 for his "Bad" album. Michael's second Progressed New Moon in 2002, also a Total Solar Eclipse, is very appropriately descriptive of his first son's birth on February 21, 2002. Astro.com does not provide any biography for Michael that is even close to the first Progressed New Moon in early 1973. However, Michael's first solo album came out late in 1971 which was the precursor of Michael's break from the Jackson Five that was solidified by 1973. To fill the biography gaps, more background information of Michael's early life is needed. Astro.com only gives us major events for his last 25-years. The events of his formative years are vague or missing. Since Michael did consult several astrologers, giving each a different birth time, it is doubtful that he gave a biographer straight and truthful information. In this case, with Michael a star from such an early age, the best bet for specific events of his early life is the news media – most of which is now available on the Internet.

Filling the Blanks of Michael Jackson's Childhood That Built the Man

In searching the Internet, several sources for Michael Jackson's childhood became available: www.Biography.com, a biography by Colin Bertram titled, Michael Jackson: His Early Years in Gary, Indiana with His Musical Family was a very good source among many.

"A strict taskmaster, Joe enforced long and grueling rehearsals for his sons in order for them to have their songs and routines polished. It is this coopting of a childhood Michael would come to lament the rest of his life. Michael often said he grew up in an adult world. 'I grew up onstage. I grew up in nightclubs. When I was seven, eight years old I was in nightclubs,' he revealed in a 2002

Gold magazine interview. 'I saw striptease girls take off all their clothes. I saw fights break out. I saw people throw up on each other. I saw adults act like pigs.' " [1]

When Jackson spoke of his childhood, it was often regarding the extreme loneliness he felt due to having no companions his own age other than his brothers. Jackson worked nonstop from before he turned five and wasn't able to enjoy any of the ordinary experiences typical of American childhood. This lack led Jackson to have a fixation on youth and happy children, which drove him to build Neverland ranch and start his "Heal the World" foundation.

Accepting the Grammy Legend Award in 1993, pop superstar, Michael Jackson, said, *"My childhood was taken away from me. There was no Christmas, there were no birthdays, it was not a normal childhood, nor the normal pleasures of childhood. Those were exchanged for hard work, struggle and pain and eventually material and professional success. But as an awful price I cannot recreate that part of my life. Nor would I change any part of my life."* [2]

Strong words from a performer whose early life – alongside eight siblings in a simple, two-bedroom house in Gary, Indiana – has been much discussed and analyzed for insights into the family that spawned some of the greatest entertainers of the last century. While many of the Jackson children, including Michael, have spoken fondly of their years in Gary, what has received most media coverage is the alleged physical and mental abuse and constant work doled out by patriarch Joseph Jackson. *"I never had the chance to do the fun things kids do," Jackson once said of his early life.* As an adult, Jackson created a haven in Neverland Ranch, an amusement park-like California home named after a location from the tales of the fictional character Peter Pan. Pan was a boy who could fly and never grows up. *"I totally identify with Peter Pan, the lost boy from Never Neverland,"* Jackson said.

Michael was afraid of his verbally, and sometimes physically, abusive father. If one of his children stepped out of line, Joe was quick to discipline them. Michael once revealed to Oprah Winfrey that he was so afraid of his father that it would cause him to vomit when he saw him. Physical beatings were not uncommon. *"I just remember hearing my mother scream, 'Joe, you're gonna kill him, you're gonna kill him, stop it,'"* Michael said during a 2003 TV interview. *"I was so fast he couldn't catch me half the time, but when he would catch me, oh my God, it was bad. It was really bad."*

All of Michael's narrative about his childhood and home life is clearly described through his 7:33 pm birth chart. The sixth house Virgo/Leo stellium of five planets, including the Sun, Mercury, Venus, Uranus, and Pluto, supports the narrative of Michael's artistic and creative talent. Mercury, Venus and Uranus closely conjunct, built his identity (Sun) around intensive work (6th house stellium) at the power of a demanding father (Pluto) adds his voice to the

---

1. www.Biography.com, a Biography by Colin Bertram titled, Michael Jackson: His Early Years in Gary, Indiana with His Musical Family

2. Michael Jackson, Grammy Awards, 1993

configuration. Besides the sixth house Leo/ Virgo stellium, Michael's emotional trauma is well supported by his natal Pisces Moon conjunct the Ascendant and quincunx his sixth house Venus Uranus conjunction in Leo. Michael's Moon, with only hard aspects, has little emotional joy, even in Pisces, a Jupiter ruled sign.

DD Birth Time Results with Appropriate Movement To and From Angles

As astrologers, we have more than a dozen movement techniques to test birth time Angles to appropriately align with life events. Before Michael Jackson's was revealed, I tested five possible times that fit my case theory and the software 23-hour search: 3:26 am, 1:34 pm, 7:45 pm, 9:35 pm and 11:01 pm. The testing techniques I chose were: Solar Arc Direction, Secondary Progression, Outer Planet Transits, Solar Eclipses, and Progressed Declination.

Figure 93 Test of 3:26 am Birth Time for Michael Jackson

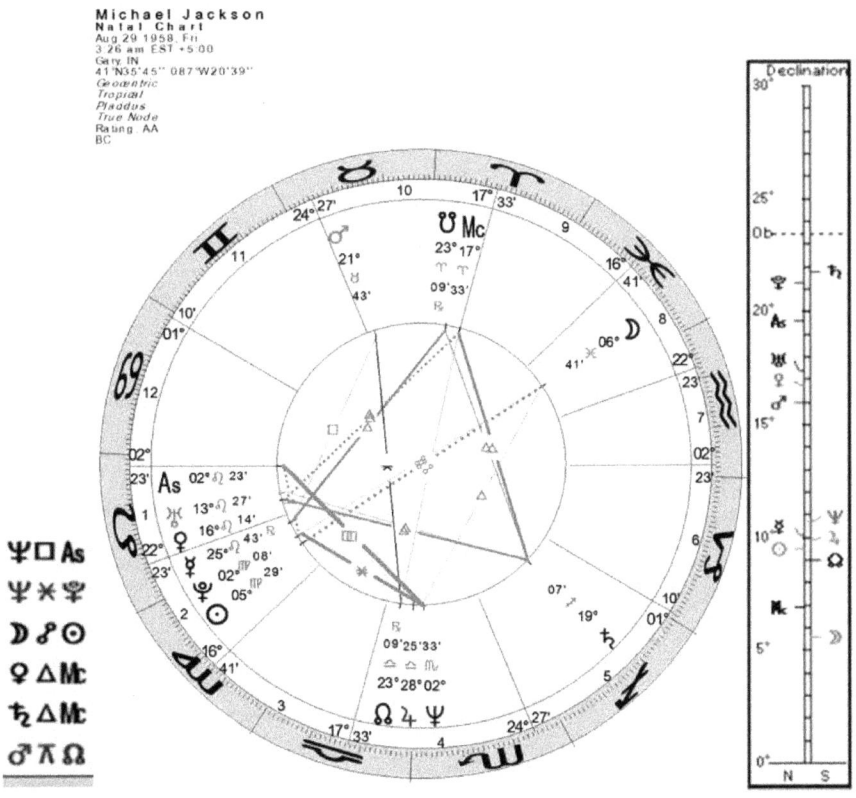

In the 3:26 am chart, there are only two reliable "Aspect Hooks", neither very good: Neptune sextile Pluto are two outer planets that are generational (everyone born that year has it), and Mars quincunx the North Node that can be a helpful hook. All of the other aspects are connected to the Moon, that may move 6 to 7-degrees in the search range, OR to an Angle that moves about 345-degrees in the search range.

This 3:26 am chart fits many characteristics of Michael's life:

1. The Fire Grand Trine to the Midheaven from 1st house Leo Venus/Uranus and from 5th house Saturn describes his creative genius on a public stage in a grand way.

2. The Moon in the 8th house is opposite his 2nd house Sun/Pluto, descriptive of his harsh and demanding father that had a lifelong emotional toll on Michael.

3. 4th house Neptune is partile square Michael's Leo Ascendant, descriptive of his love of performing, but with a confusing home life – a child thrown into an adult world too soon.

This 3:26 am birth time stood out by fitting so well with my case theory, but in testing it with the five techniques the life events only partially aligned with the appropriate astrological descriptors: Solar Arc directions 43%, Outer planet transits 33%, Secondary progressions 86%, Solar eclipses 36% and Progressed lifetime declination 100%. In each time tested, I was also looking for some connection by declination with the Angles and/or the Moon to possibly describe the extremes of Michael's life.

In testing the 1:34 pm birth time for Michael Jackson, I used the same five movement techniques to align his life events with appropriate astrological descriptors: Solar Arc Direction, Secondary Progression, Outer Planet Transits, Solar Eclipses, and Progressed Declination.

In the 1:34 pm chart, there are only two reliable "Aspect Hooks", neither very good: Neptune sextile Pluto are two outer planets that are generational (everyone born that year has it), and Mars quincunx the North Node that can possibly be a helpful hook. All of the other aspects are connected to the to an Angle that moves about 345-degrees in the 24-hour search range.

This 1:34 pm chart fits many characteristics of Michael's life:

1. The Virgo Midheaven trine a 6th house Mars describes an athletic focus on hard work to enhance his public profile. Even the Sagittarius ascendant confirms his personality we see as he performs.

2. The Pisces Moon in the 3rd house quincunx Uranus in the 9th house is descriptive of the close connection with his siblings, but with the problems of "too much" that separated them.

3. Michael's Sagittarius Ascendant is partile square his 10th house Pluto, descriptive of his father's abusive and controlling hand – and 1st house Saturn is square the Midheaven to emphasize his work ethic.

Figure 94 Test of 1:34 pm Birth Time for Michael Jackson

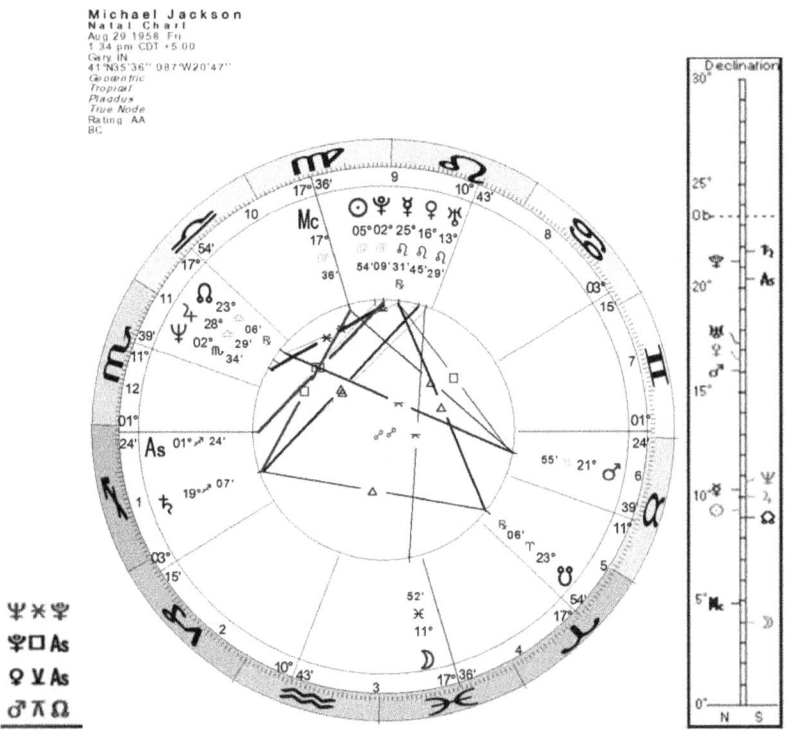

This 1:34 pm birth time did not fit as well with my case theory, but in testing it with the five techniques Michael's life events only partially aligned with the appropriate astrological descriptors: Solar Arc directions 21%, Outer planet transits 50%, Secondary progressions 14%, Solar eclipses 43% and Progressed lifetime declination 50%. In each time tested, I was also looking for some connection by declination with the Angles and/or the Moon to possibly describe the extremes of Michael's life. Here, Michael's Ascendant is parallel Saturn and contra-parallel Pluto, to confirm the restrictions and abuse and the Moon is contra-parallel the Midheaven and widely opposite by longitude, another tell.

In testing the 7:45 pm birth time for Michael Jackson, I used the same five movement techniques to align his life events with appropriate astrological descriptors: Solar Arc Direction, Secondary Progression, Outer Planet Transits, Solar Eclipses, and Progressed Declination.

How Do I Deal with Dirty Data?

Figure 95 Test of 7:45 pm Birth Time for Michael Jackson

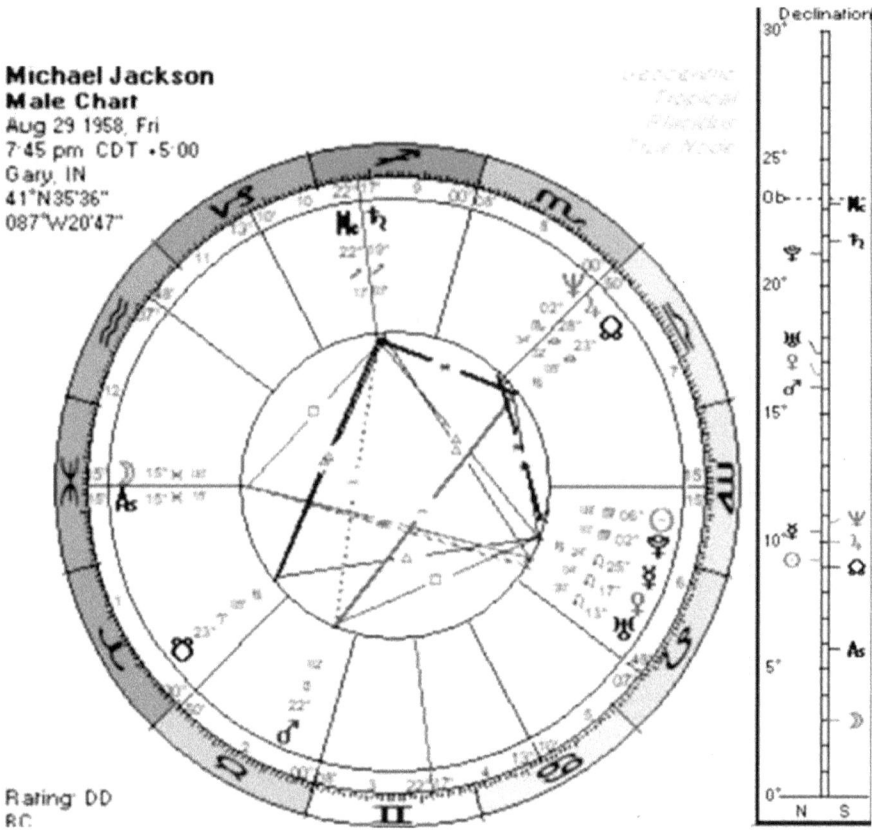

In the 7:45 pm chart, there are only two reliable "Aspect Hooks", neither very good: Neptune sextile Pluto are two outer planets that are generational (everyone born that year has it), and Mars square Mercury that can be a helpful aspect hook. All of the other aspects are connected to the Moon which may move 7 to 8-degrees, and an Angle that moves about 345-degrees in the 23-hour search range.

This 7:45 pm chart fits many characteristics of Michael's life:

1. The 6th house stellium with Leo Uranus, Venus, Mercury and Virgo Pluto, Sun confirms Michael's determined focus on hard work. The close Virgo Pluto/Sun conjunction in the 6th house clarifies the role of his controlling and abusive father in his work ethic.

2. The Pisces Moon conjunct the Ascendant confirms Michael's ethereal personality and

his strong fantasy life as well as his enchanting tenor voice.

3. Michael's Moon/Asc square 9th house Saturn and quincunx 6th house Leo Venus/Uranus confirms the emotional dissonance expressed in his real life.

This 7:45 pm birth time fit very well with my case theory, and in testing it with the five techniques, Michael's life events were the best fit, of the five times tested, to align with the appropriate astrological descriptors: Solar Arc direction 73%, Outer planet transits 68%, Secondary progressions 71%, Solar eclipses 83% and Progressed lifetime declination 94%. In each time tested, I was also looking for some connection by declination with the Angles and/or the Moon to possibly describe the extremes of Michael's life. Here, Michael's Midheaven is parallel Saturn to confirm the restrictions or responsibility he felt from his public life.

In testing the 9:35 pm birth time for Michael Jackson, I used the same five movement techniques to align his life events with appropriate astrological descriptors: Solar Arc Direction,

Figure 96 Test of 9:35 pm Birth Time for Michael Jackson

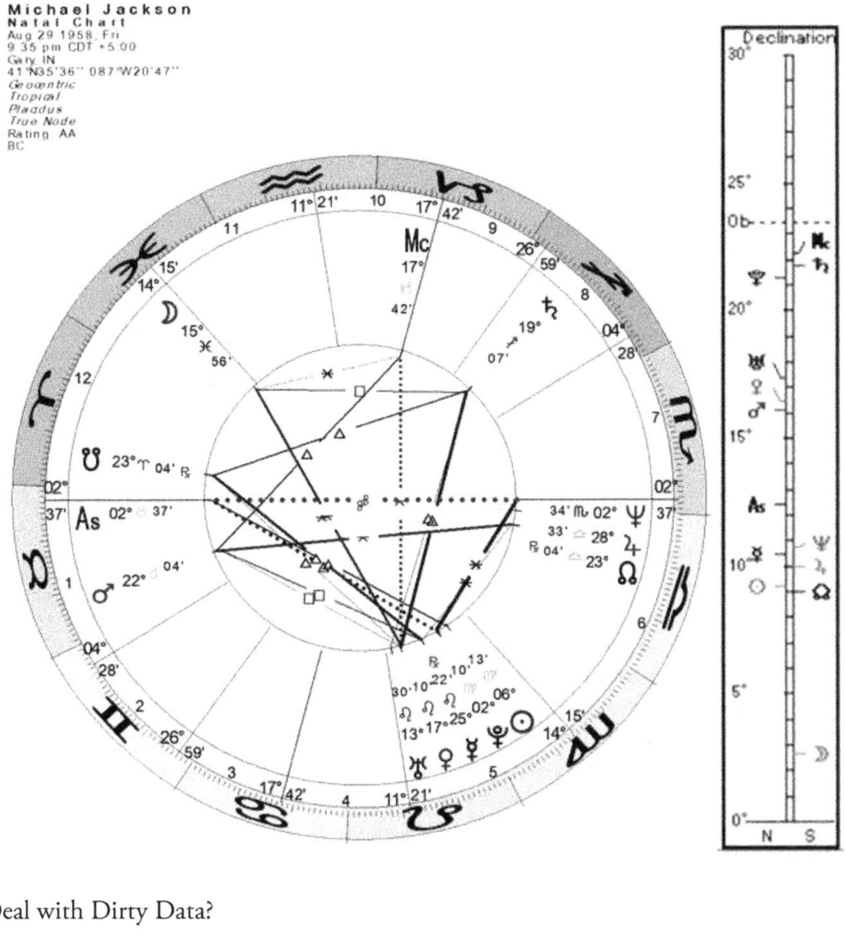

Secondary Progression, Outer Planet Transits, Solar Eclipses, and Progressed Declination.

In the 9:35 pm chart, there are only two reliable "Aspect Hooks", neither very good: Neptune sextile Pluto are two outer planets that are generational (everyone born that year has it), and Mars quincunx the North Node that may possibly be a helpful aspect hook. All of the other aspects are connected to the to the Moon which may move 7 to 8-degrees and an Angle that moves about 345-degrees in the 23-hour search range.

This 9:35 pm chart fits some characteristics of Michael's life but not convincingly:

1. The 5th house stellium with Leo Uranus, Venus, Mercury and Virgo Pluto, Sun confirms Michael's creative genius. The close Virgo Pluto/Sun conjunction in the 5th house clarifies his passion for children and reliving the childhood he missed, identifying with the fictional Peter Pan.

2. Michael's mid-Pisces Moon conjuncts the 12th house cusp, square 8th house Saturn and quincunx 5th house Venus/Uranus describes his emotional challenges and disappointments and with no ease aspects, his emotional life is under even more stress.

3. Michael's Moon widely square Saturn and Sun closely conjunct Pluto describe the controlling and abusive father, though not as convincingly as other birth times.

This 9:35 pm birth time did not fit as well with my case theory, and in testing it with the five techniques, Michael's life events, of the five times tested, weakly aligned with the appropriate astrological descriptors: Solar Arc direction 36%, Outer planet transits 42%, Secondary progressions 50%, Solar eclipses 0% and Progressed lifetime declination 71%. In each time tested, I was also looking for some connection by declination with the Angles and/or the Moon to possibly describe the extremes of Michael's life. Here, Michael's Midheaven is parallel Saturn and contra-parallel to confirm the pressure and restrictions or responsibility he felt from his public life.

In testing the 11:01 pm birth time for Michael Jackson, I used the same five movement techniques to align his life events with appropriate astrological descriptors: Solar Arc Direction, Secondary Progression, Outer Planet Transits, Solar Eclipses, and Progressed Declination.

Figure 97 Test of 11:01 pm Birth Time for Michael Jackson

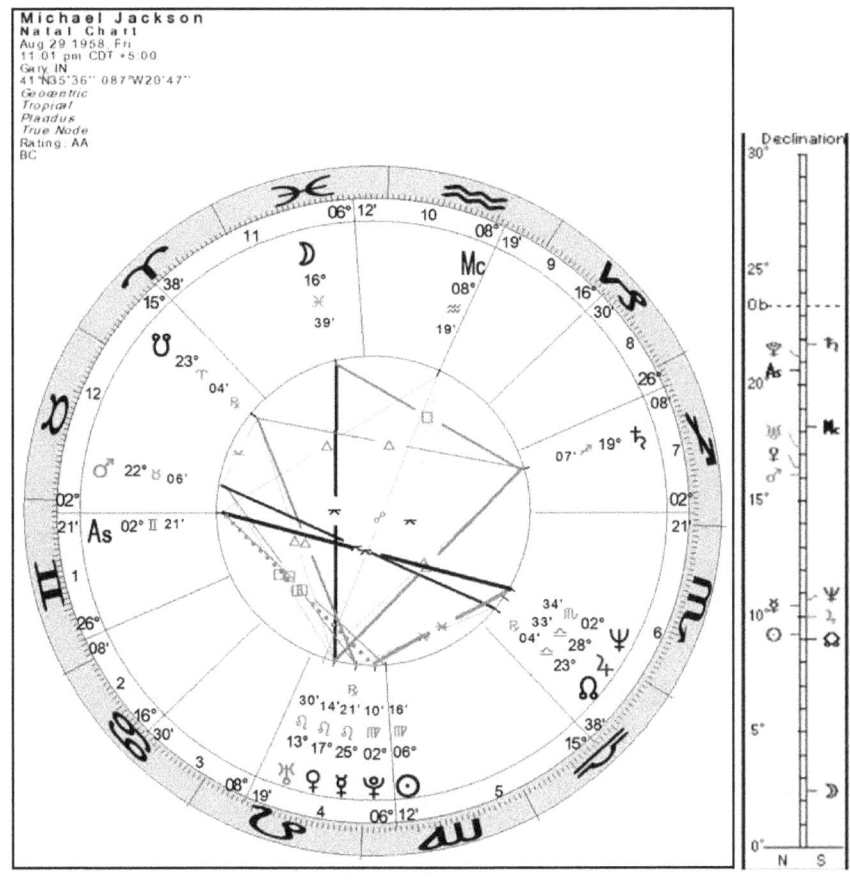

In the 11:01 pm chart, there are only two reliable "Aspect Hooks", neither very good: Neptune sextile Pluto are two outer planets that are generational (everyone born that year has it), and Mars quincunx the North Node that may possibly be a helpful aspect hook. All of the other aspects are connected to the to the Moon which may move 7 to 8-degrees and an Angle that moves about 345-degrees in the 23-hour search range.

This 11:01 pm chart fits some characteristics of Michael's life but not convincingly:

1. The 4th house stellium with Leo Uranus, Venus, Mercury and Virgo Pluto with the Sun moved to the 5th house confirms Michael's creative genius that is closely involved with the family.

2. Michael's mid-Pisces Moon in the 11th house squares 7th house Saturn and quincunx 4th house Venus/Uranus that describes his emotional challenges and relationship dis-

appointments and strong friction with his family. With no ease aspects to the Moon, his emotional life is stressed.

3. Michael's 6th house Jupiter/Neptune conjunction is closely quincunx the Ascendant, descriptive of the stress of his creative work. His Gemini Ascendant describes his ability to dance as part of his mercurial personality with the ruler, a Leo Mercury in the 4th house trine/sextile the South Node/North Node.

This 11:01 pm birth time fit quite well with my case theory, and in testing it with the five techniques, Michael's life events, of the five times tested, aligned with the appropriate astrological descriptors: Solar Arc direction 36%, Outer planet transits 50%, Secondary progressions 57%, Solar eclipses 43% and Progressed lifetime declination 100%. In each time tested, I was also looking for some connection by declination with the Angles and/or the Moon to possibly describe the extremes of Michael's life. Here, Michael's Ascendant is parallel Pluto and contra-parallel Saturn to confirm the pressure and restrictions or responsibility he felt from his personal life; and his Midheaven contra-parallel Uranus is descriptive of his eccentric public persona, ridiculed as, "Whacko Jacko".

Table 41 Comparison of Birth Times Tested for Michael Jackson

	Direction	Transit	Progressed	Eclipse	Declination	Total
3:26 am	43%	33%	86%	36%	100%	60%
1:34 pm	21%	50%	14%	43%	50%	36%
7:45 pm	73%	68%	71%	83%	94%	78%
9:35 pm	36%	42%	50%	0%	71%	41%
11:01 pm	36%	50%	57%	43%	100%	57%

The final tally of the five birth times I tested for Michael Jackson clearly favors the 7:45 pm birth time, which I used until recently when his birth information was made public. Most often, we never get birth time confirmation from our rectification clients, so it is up to us to derive a birth time very close to what a birth certificate would likely confirm.

Taylor Swift has 3 Unverified Birth Times, so a 24-Hour Search is Needed

The multiple Grammy winner and international musical icon of the 21st century, Astro.com confirms that Taylor Swift, was born on December 5. 1989 in Reading, Pennsylvania and at age 3 moved to Wysomming, Pennsylvania. However, Astro.com posts three birth times 5:17 am, 8:36 am and 8:46 pm spanning nearly 16 hours, none of which is verified. That problem leads us to a 24-hour search.

Without Birth Time, Set the Wheel with a Noon Sun as the Ascendant

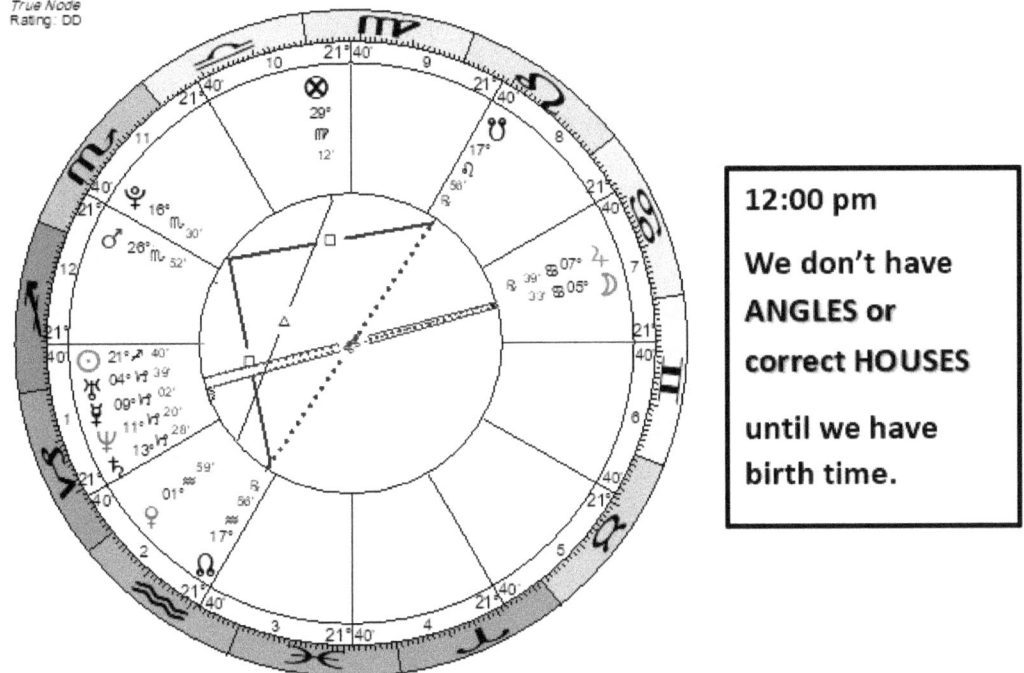

12:00 pm

We don't have ANGLES or correct HOUSES until we have birth time.

The location and the day, month, and year only gives us an approximate sign and degrees of the planets, but without birth time we have no angles or correct houses for the planets which makes natal delineation or forecasting impossible. The process of birth time rectification is a must to derive the actual birth time.

Begin any wide time range search by setting the Sun at the midpoint of the range; for a 24-hour search set the Sun for Noon and set is as the Ascendant for the working chart.

Gather the Person's Comprehensive Biography and Major Life Events

To briefly repeat, a comprehensive biography starts in childhood to the current time. It should include family dynamics and issues as well as personal interests, career and relationships. In addition, a list of at least 12 to 20 major life events with specific dates. Often, I am left with the month and year only because the client doesn't remember the day, but month and year is workable. It is also difficult to test events that are ongoing, such as cancer, other long term conditions.

Even with a comprehensive biography and adequate events, the 24-hour search gives 4 or 5 birth times that possibly fit. It is the astrologer's training and judgement to test each and narrow to 1 certain birth time. Sometimes, two rectified times work for the events that the client provided, so client feedback can easily say that one of the Ascendants fit, and the other not.

Start With the Moon to Narrow the Search Time Range

Taylor's Moon range in 24-hours is from 28:17 Gemini to 12:42 Cancer. Her fast Moon moving over 15-degrees allows us to use her biographical information to know her emotional temperament. There is a big difference between a Mercury ruled Gemini that is interested in everything and often not focusing on one, or a dignified Moon ruling Cancer that is sensitive, caring and family oriented. The public would likely choose Gemini rising for Taylor because she is prolific in creating new songs and meeting people around the world, however, even at age 35 in all of her travel and work, she talks to her mother every day. Her family is her foundation, though she does feel for and care about her public. Taylor's Moon is Cancer for sure, and now we can eliminate the 2 ½ hours of Gemini from 24 to search from 12:00 am to 9:30 pm. Still, that is now enough to determine the Ascendant sign because we have only eliminated 1 of 12 possible signs.

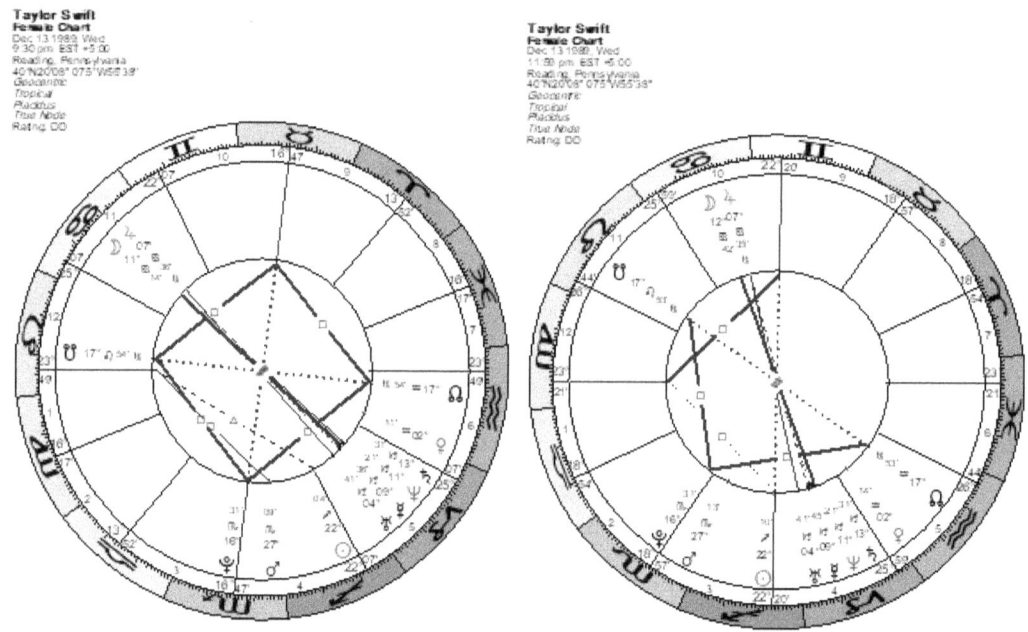

Narrowing the search range by 2 ½ hours only eliminated Virgo as a possible Ascendant. Now that we have exhausted the easy way to narrow the time range, it is now time for bringing good software to test the important life events. Don't forget, software is only a tool. You are the astrologer choosing which events and methods to make a learned judgement of the correct birth time. That said, for basics, I use Solar Fire software, and for rectification I use two very different software programs, each with a rectification module, Sirius 4.1 and Jigsaw 2.2. Sirius tests events with appropriate descriptors that match events, such as romance connected to the Moon in aspect to Venus. On the other hand, Jigsaw tests events by the number of hits to a specific degree of 360 degrees possible. In using both software, Sirius and Jigsaw, I look for the same birth times that are the top, or very near the top after testing every 4-minutes of clock time in the time range.

Again, I remind you that public figures do not confirm our rectification work, and indeed, they do not share non-public information about their lives.

The other reason for starting the birth time search at the midpoint of the search range, in Taylor's case noon, is because the Moon position is then plus or minus 5 ½ to 7 ½ degrees, rather than 11 to 15 degrees if starting at midnight. The range of Taylor's Moon movement in 24-hours is from 28:17 Gemini to 12:42 Cancer. To narrow the search time range, start with the Moon that will either be in the same sign all 24-hours, or part of two signs, one of which will definitely describe the emotional traits of the person — that is if you have a basis from the detailed personal biography. Since Taylor has not asked for a consultation, she has not provided the needed biographic detail, so I chose Cancer as the best fit for her Moon. Even at age 35, Taylor talks to her mother every day and wherever she is in the world performing her songs. It is also commonly known that Taylor has close family roots with a very supportive team behind her dreams and now her achievements. Now that Cancer is chosen for her Moon, the 2 ½ hours of Gemini, can be deleted bringing the search range to 21 ½ hours. This is only the beginning. That leaves a possible 11 signs for the Ascendant and the other 3 Angles, but before I begin testing major life events, I consider possibilities of the Ascendant.

Taylor's notable traits, talents and position:

Personality: friendly and articulate

Personality: creative and a hard worker

Childhood: very close family and sibling that is very supportive

Instrumentalist: guitar, banjo, ukulele, piano

Song writer: vocalist, country, pop, rock

Awards: Emmy, 14 Grammies, Top in her field

Wealth: Billionaire

Consider the qualities of each possible sign for the Ascendant:

Cardinal: Aries = fire, Cancer = water, Libra = air, and Capricorn = earth

Fixed: Taurus = earth, Leo = fire, Scorpio = water, Aquarius = air

Mutable: Gemini = air, Virgo = earth, Sagittarius = fire, Pisces = water

At this point I lean toward a mutable Ascendant sign and especially Pisces that fits her soulful and deep feeling songs based on actual life experiences.

This is as far as I can go to narrow the search time range, so it is time to start testing Taylors known major life events, one of which most of saw live when Taylor won her first Grammy award on her 20th birthday on December 13, 2009. That's the good news! As Taylor was giving her acceptance speech, Kanye West blurted loudly that Beyonce should have won and she was robbed by this young upstart. Taylor's mother put Kanye in his place with a curt but kindly response.

"After Kanye West's infamous VMA interruption, the MTV program quickly cut to a pre-recorded segment. Even so, several sources have given their perspective on the immediate fallout that followed the Swift-centered outburst. Amber Rose, who dated West from 2008 to 2010, recounted how contrite the 'Stronger' artist appeared when confronted by Swift's parents, Scott and Andrea. 'He was so remorseful. I mean he really felt so bad,' she told the Independent. The model's recollection of the events corresponds with the blog post that West shared the night of the VMAs, in which he both apologizes and mentions speaking to Andrea Swift. 'I'm sooooo sorry to Taylor Swift and her fans and her mom,' he wrote. 'I spoke to her mother right after, and she said the same thing my mother would've said' (per Rolling Stones). While the rap icon didn't specify what this was exactly, we wouldn't be surprised if he's referring to Andrea's words about West's future daughters. The moment was just another example of how much of a champion Mama Swift is for her daughter."

When we see an actual client for birth time rectification the client is asked not only for a list of major life events, but also the impact that the event created and then rate each from 1 to-5 from most impact to least. Since Taylor is not providing any such information, move on to testing for possible birth times with good astrology software. Solar Fire 9, Astro Gold, Time Passages, and several others available online like Astrodienst, Astroseek, Cafe Astrology and many others. All astrology software provided tools to test movement to activate the natal chart in several formats from transits, secondary progressions, solar arc directions and many more. Beyond basic astrology software, there are some that provide tools specifically for research and/or birth time rectification. Jigsaw 2.2 by Bernadette Brady.

"JigSaw version.[2] is a powerful astrological research tool designed to reveal the "big picture" in any group of charts. Authored by Bernadette Brady and Esoteric Technologies, JigSaw version.2 is divided into three sections of Rectification, Patterns (for examining the emergent patterns with a group of charts and a general astrological research set of tools. Jigsaw is a tool for the professional astrologer."[3]

Again, to remind readers of the differences between advanced rectification software, Jig-

---

2. Footnote: By Madison Emily Whisenand, March 4, 2024
3. Jigsaw 2.2 by Bernadette Brady

saw 2.2 is programmed to count the planetary hits for each event from 0 to 360 degrees in the chosen movement technique to derive birth time. Sirius 4.1 is very different in that it is programmed to count the appropriate astrological descriptors for each event, such as rom ance would have an ease aspect for the Moon and Venus. Remember, astrology software is your tool, and often the software results do not agree. The trained astrologer is far better to make the final birth time judgement.

For testing major life events to derive birth time, I prefer to use: Solar Arc Directions, Secondary Progressions, Tertiary Progressions and Outer Planet Transits as the checked boxes under the heading, Select Forecast Methods.

The Sirius 6:56 am time is interesting, but Sagittarius rising doesn't fit Taylor very well, and by Solar Arc Direction, her 1st Grammy Award is described by the Ascendant arcing to natal Mercury and Sun arcing to natal Neptune. Those are good astrological descriptors for her wonderful and happy event, but the difficult Mars has already arced one degree past the 6:56 am Ascendant, so 6:56 am is not confirmed by Solar Arc Direction for that event. However in the listing, three other methods may work for the high score.

Since there are two excellent advanced software programs that do rectification, I also test events with both Sirius 4.1 and Jigsaw 2.2 to compare results, and giving preference for times that both software programs agree.

Jigsaw tested the same 43 life events for Taylor Swift using the same four movement techniques, Solar Arc Direction, Secondary Progression, Tertiary Progression, and Outer Planet Transits and the advanced software programs do not agree. However, Jigsaw gives 11:55 Pisces as the Ascendant and 20:15 Sagittarius as the Midheaven for the best birth time of 12:03 pm for Taylor and is very close to the 11:52 am birth time that I rectified. Even the 11-minute difference between Jigsaw results and my birth time choice is only 3-minutes later with the Ascendant at 11:58 Pisces. In this case, the Jigsaw times are a better fit for Taylor Swift than the top times given by Sirius 4.1 software. However, that is not always the case, sometimes both software programs agree on the best time and sometimes I prefer the top time from Sirius 4.1. Again, good software is a good tool, but the astrologer's educated judgement makes the final best choice for the rectified birth time.

The Astro.com "Dirty data" times are very weak and movement to the natal chart in four methods give weak to middling results.

With Birth Time, We Now Have Angles and Appropriate Houses for Planets

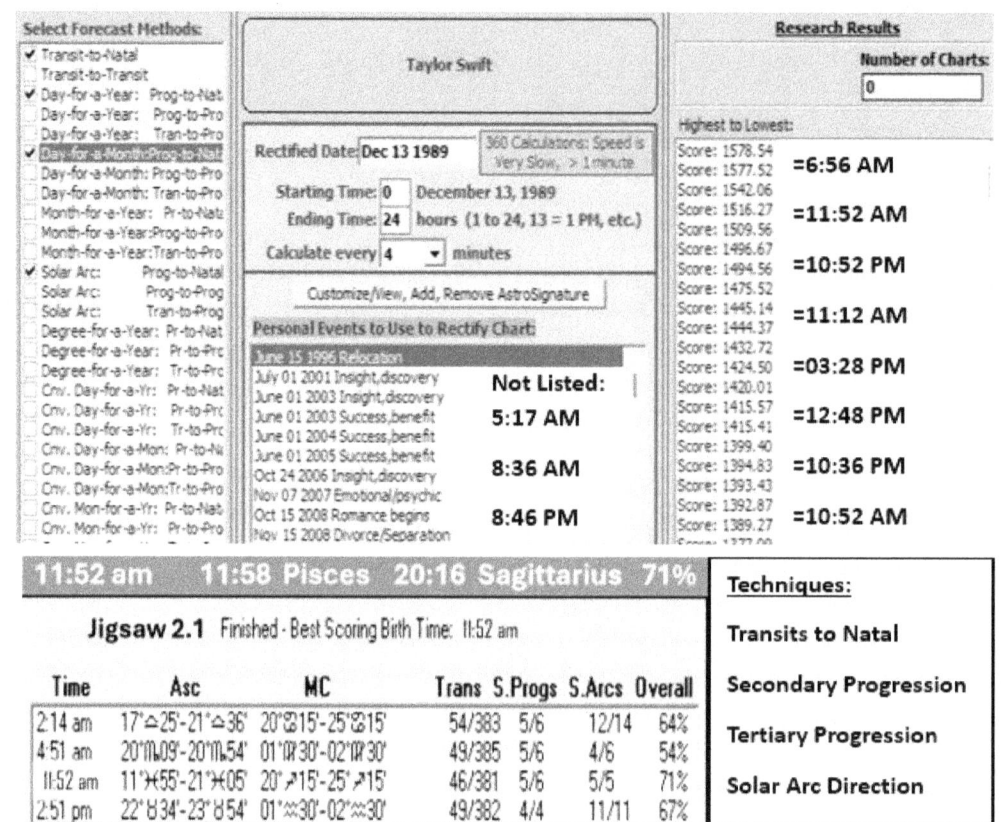

172   The New Complete Book of Chart Rectification

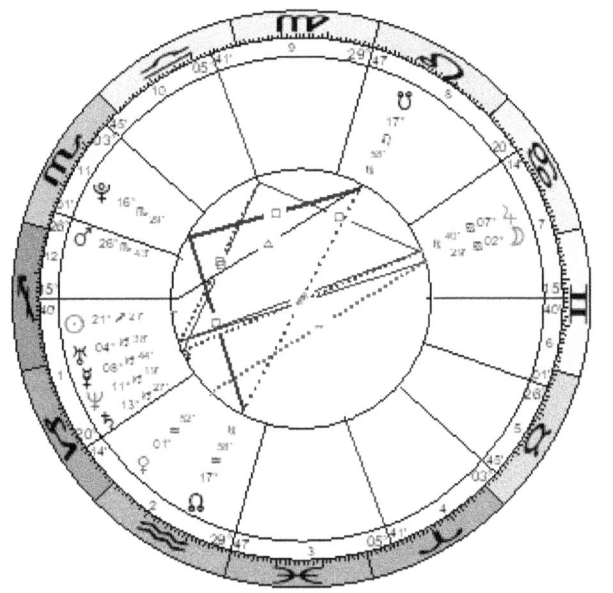

6:56 AM Sirius 4.1
Top birth time from testing Taylor's 43 events

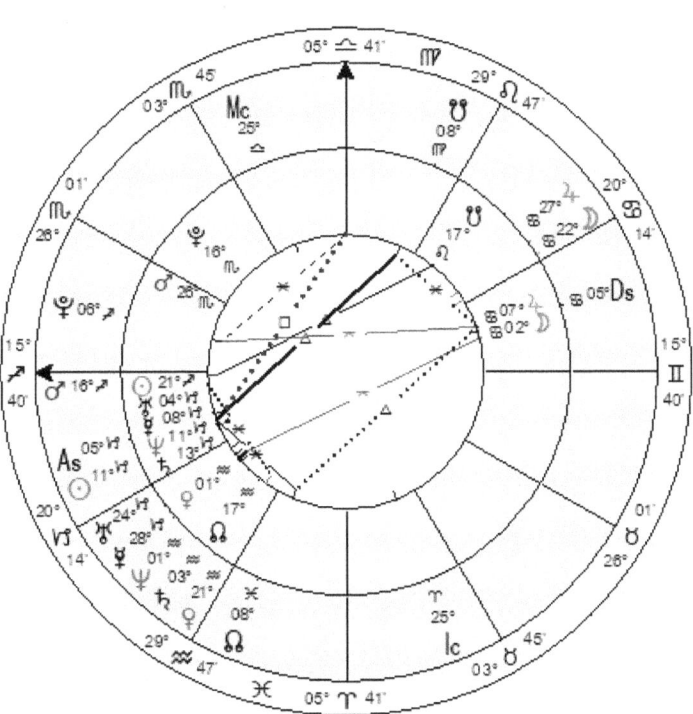

Solar Arc Direction to Dec 13, 2009

Kanye West's disruption of Taylor's first Emmy Award

How Do I Deal with Dirty Data? 173

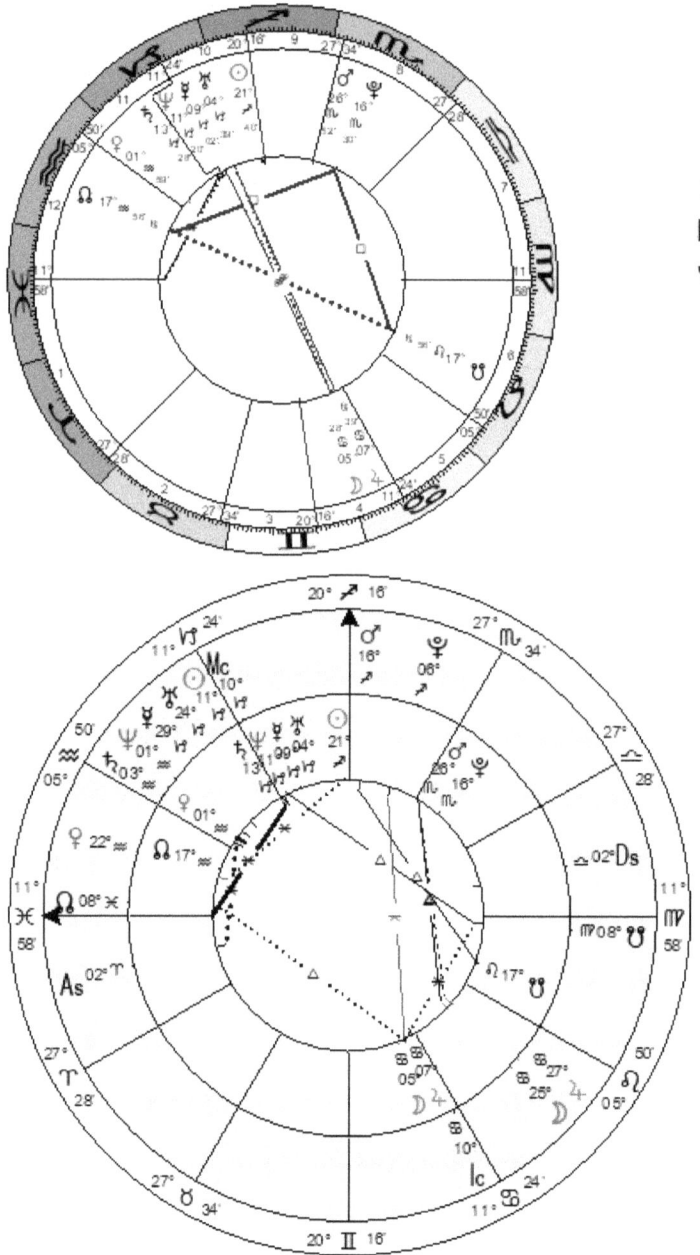

11:52 AM Tebbs rectified birth time for Taylor Swift with help from Jigsaw 2.2 and Sirius 4.1

Inner wheel is natal chart,

Outer wheel is Solar Arc Directions for the December 13, 2009 Kanye West outburst that made Taylor cry as she gave her acceptance speech for her first Grammy – and on her birthday, no less.

The New Complete Book of Chart Rectification

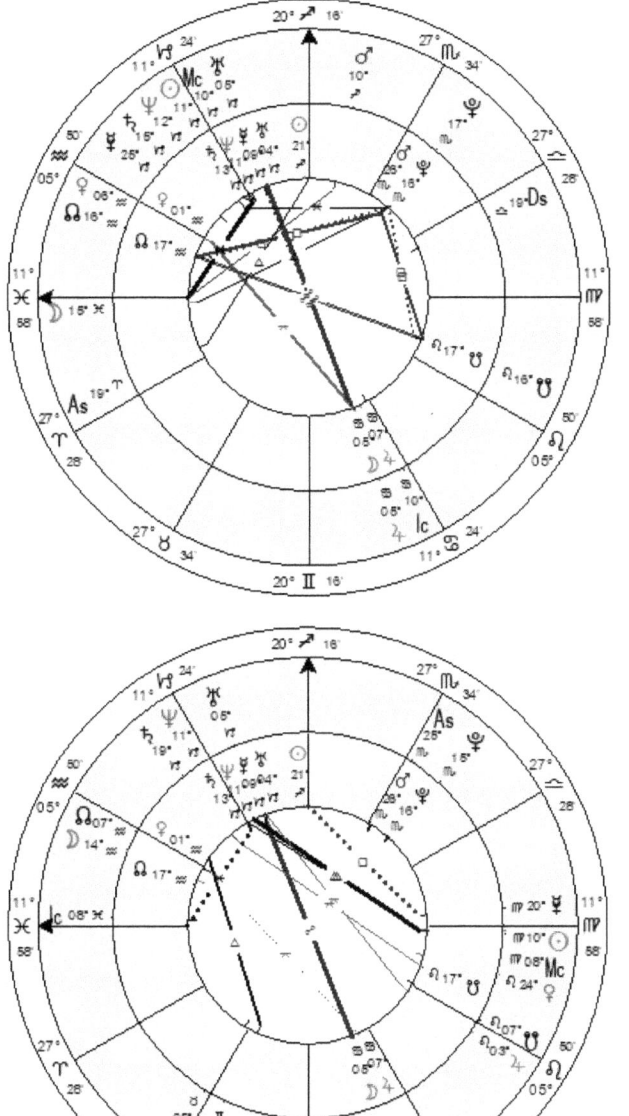

Inner wheel is natal chart,

Outer wheel is Secondary Progressions for the December 13, 2009 Kanye West outburst that made Taylor cry as she gave her acceptance speech for her first Grammy – and on her birthday, no less.

Inner wheel is natal chart,

Outer wheel is Tertiary Progressions for the December 13, 2009 Kanye West outburst that made Taylor cry as she gave her acceptance speech for her first Grammy – and on her birthday, no less.

How Do I Deal with Dirty Data?

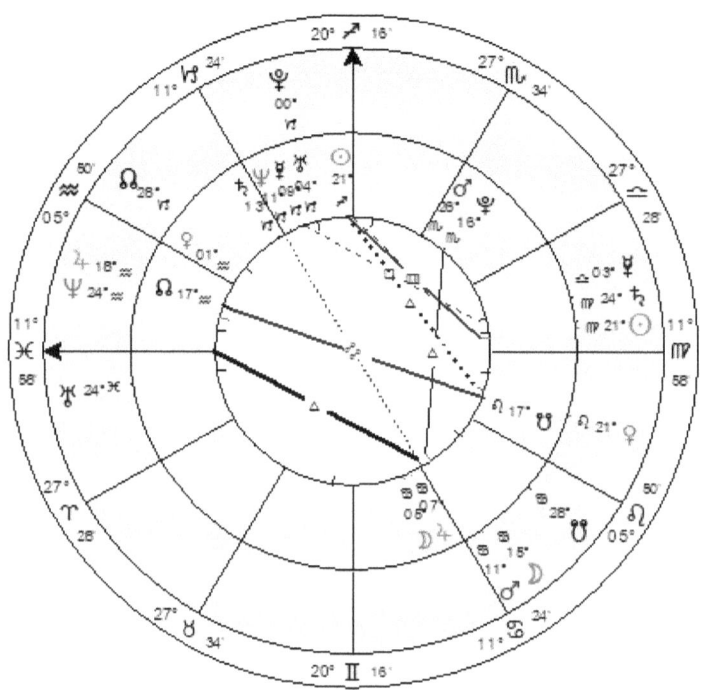

Inner wheel is natal chart,

Outer wheel is Outer Planet Transits for the December 13, 2009 Kanye West outburst that made Taylor cry as she gave her acceptance speech for her first Grammy – and on her birthday, no less.

Astro.com	Dirty Data is weak	for Taylor's First	Grammy Award	& Kanye West Outburst
5:17 am	No activation	MC squar Moon	ASC opp. Sun	Saturn squares Sun
8:36 am	MC square Nodes	ASC conj. Venus	MC opp Mercu	all 24-hours
8:48 pm	MC opp. Mars	MC opp. Mars	MC conj Venus	
	Solar Arc Directions	Secondary Progs	Tertiary Progs.	Outer Plant Transits

176   The New Complete Book of Chart Rectification

Even Taylor is ecstatic about having a birth time that fits what we know about her public life and a bit of her personal life to derive a birth time that fits the Taylor we know and love.

    I cannot emphasize enough the importance of first developing a well thought out case theory based on sound astrological principles before delving into extensive testing with a variety of movement techniques. If testing is started before narrowing the time range with a solid case theory and possibly a search with advanced astrology software, such as Jigsaw 2.2 or Sirius 4.1, the 24-hour search can be overwhelming. As for movement methods, Chapter Five has provided a full list of movement possibilities for testing. But of course, it is the astrologer's choice of which four or five techniques to test the 24-hours to derive the correct birth time with rectification.

Chapter 7

How Do I Deal with No Birth Time?

Deriving Birth Time with Rectification Is Not Universally Accepted

The human is a complex being with dozens of roles and life issues evolving concurrently to grow and to fulfill the chosen goals and aspirations. We are all children, siblings, parents, workers, leaders, friends, helpers, and a host of other roles, so trying to derive a birth time from a dozen life events is, indeed, a gargantuan job with too little substantive or confusing information. And, of course, the wider the search time range, the more complex and difficult the search. For instance, we may see prominent success aspects activating the natal chart, and at the same time prominent challenge aspects that are hard to sort out. Sometimes the issue is internal and other times the issue comes out as an external event. It is for that reason the best rectification is developed when the client is open and involved in the process to clarify the internal issues from the event issues. That said, external events may seem as "Easy Hooks" but if they occur close in time, the sorting out is much more difficult. For instance, Payne Stewart won the US Open Championship June 20, 1999, but just four months later he died in a tragic plane crash October 25, 1999. As spotty and complicated the rectification process, as astrologers, we have many potential clients who do not have a reliable birth time and plead for a chart reading. A respected voice in the astrology community, Demetra George, shares her concerns:

"Personally, I question the validity of the doctrine of astrological rectification, which proceeds on the assumption that transiting, progressed, or solar arc planets crossing the angles manifest as dramatic outer events. I have repeatedly seen in charts with very reliable data that there are many times when planets cross angles and no outer event occurs." [1]

I agree with Ms. George's observation that not every angle crossing by a planet brings an external event. But to serve our clients in their quest for birth time, we must be clear with them about the challenges and imperfections of the process that may provide several times that appear promising. Finally, involve the client in choosing the final birth time by delineating the

---

1. George, Demetra, Astrology and the Authentic Self, Ibis Press. Lake Worth. Fl, 2008, pg. 72

Ascendant sign, degree, condition, and aspects, along with its Ruler, sign, degree, condition, and aspects. The client usually knows what fits.

Search the Recording Practice of Birth Country or State for Given Year

Fortunately, we have reliable Internet to search birth recording and time variations around the world, though for births prior to the twentieth century the information becomes sparse from records lost in war or never recorded at all. Several years ago my Kepler College student, Alexandra Khoo, revealed the "tip of the iceberg" of the birthtime recording problem.

- For Chinese births it is necessary to check if the person is stating his birth date in the Solar or Lunar calendar.
- It is very common for the older generations to remember their birth dates in the Chinese Lunar Calendar system.
- Although it is easy to find ways to convert the time, the Lunar Calendar is usually one month later than the Western solar dates.
- For example, my birth date in the solar calendar is in August, but in the Chinese calendar it occurs in the seventh month, September.
- I thought this happens only with the older generation until I spoke to a young Chinese chap, about 20, and he too quoted me his birth date in the Chinese Lunar Calendar.
- **For Singapore and Malaysia, the birth times are recorded on the birth certificate, but Japan does not record birth time at all.**

Example 1: Client

This woman was born on November 4, 1959 in Tachikawa, Japan and did not have a recorded birth time. She was also given for adoption at age three and had no family to ask about her birth. A rectification based on her biography and life events did derive a birth time that fit her biography and events with appropriate astrological descriptors. Nearly always, the rectified birth time is exact or very close if a situation arises where a birth certificate or some sort of birth record is found.

It is important to get a solid biography from my client with comments about her feelings, personality, work, interests, family background and relationships. For the list of important life events, a rating of each event's personal impact is equally important as the day, month and year.

- She is very intelligent, but a rebellious child and teenager who dropped high school, pregnant, and married at 15. Until age 43 she was a housewife with no work experience. As a widow, she was top of the class in nurse training.
- She is excellent at managing money and very lucky at the casinos. Her husband claims, "When she says we are broke, she has $20,000 in her bra."

- Since 2005 she works as the financial manager for her husband's company of 25 employees. She's tough on laggers
- She is very private and can be controlling, though generous with family.
- She is strongly attached to her son and granddaughter; being adopted, they are her only natural family.
- Her current husband's 4 adult children are from 2 prior marriages and are distant from her. She has no close friends but is polite and social at gatherings.
- She loves to fish, cook, garden, play with children, read avidly, and is very particular about having everything organized.

Study the working chart, first in whole sign, set for noon or midpoint of search range and find any planets that are in a 1-degree orb of a major Ptolemaic aspect. Since her Moon is fast, moving 14-degrees in 24-hours, we cannot include Moon aspects until the time range is significantly narrowed to within 2-hours.

<u>TEAM 1</u>: Mercury, Jupiter, Pluto conjunct and square

<u>TEAM 2</u>: Saturn square Nodes at the "bendings" and may include the Moon

<u>TEAM 3</u>: Sun, Mars, Neptune conjunct, 2-degree orb extends activation period

By movement techniques, such as Solar Arc Directions, Secondary Progression and Transits, any of these "teams" are activated at or very near the same time which impacts the natal chart dramatically!

Natal planets and points receiving a message from the moving planets react in their own nature that bring good news, interesting, evocative, inspiring or possibly bad news. The combination of planets, when activated, react according to their own nature.

Be aware that when several events occur in a close range of time, days or months, a close configuration may be activated to describe the events. This chart is set for Noon on November 4, 1959 in Tachikawa, Japan for the 24-hour search for birth time.

Next, narrow the search time range by choosing the appropriate Moon sign that fits the person's emotional foundation. Ask the client what fits or rely upon the detailed biography that was provided. It is not hard to do because there is a significant difference between any two adjacent signs. A mutable fire very open and interactive Sagittarius Moon ruled by Jupiter is a very different emotional foundation than a practical and cautious cardinal earth Capricorn Moon ruled by Saturn. From this person's biography, she clearly fits with the Capricorn Moon. The Moon's Sagittarius hours range from 12:00 am to 7:04 PM, on November 4, 1959 in Tachikawa, Japan, so by confirming the Moon's sign, only 4-hours and 55- minutes are left to test.

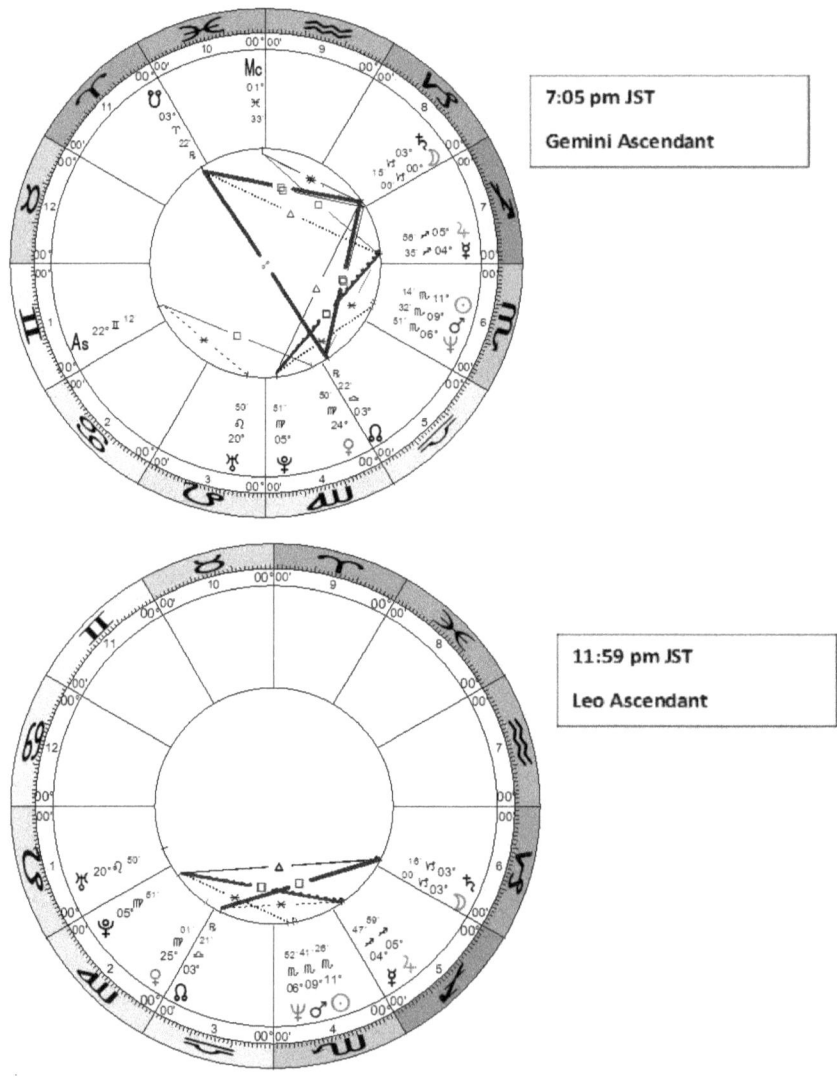

Possible Ascendants are Gemini, Cancer or Leo.

Gemini or Leo don't fit the person; Cancer Ascendant fits and narrows the search to 2-hours.

In the Cancer Ascendant range from 7:38 pm to 9:57 pm, set the working chart to the midpoint of the time range, 8:48 pm.

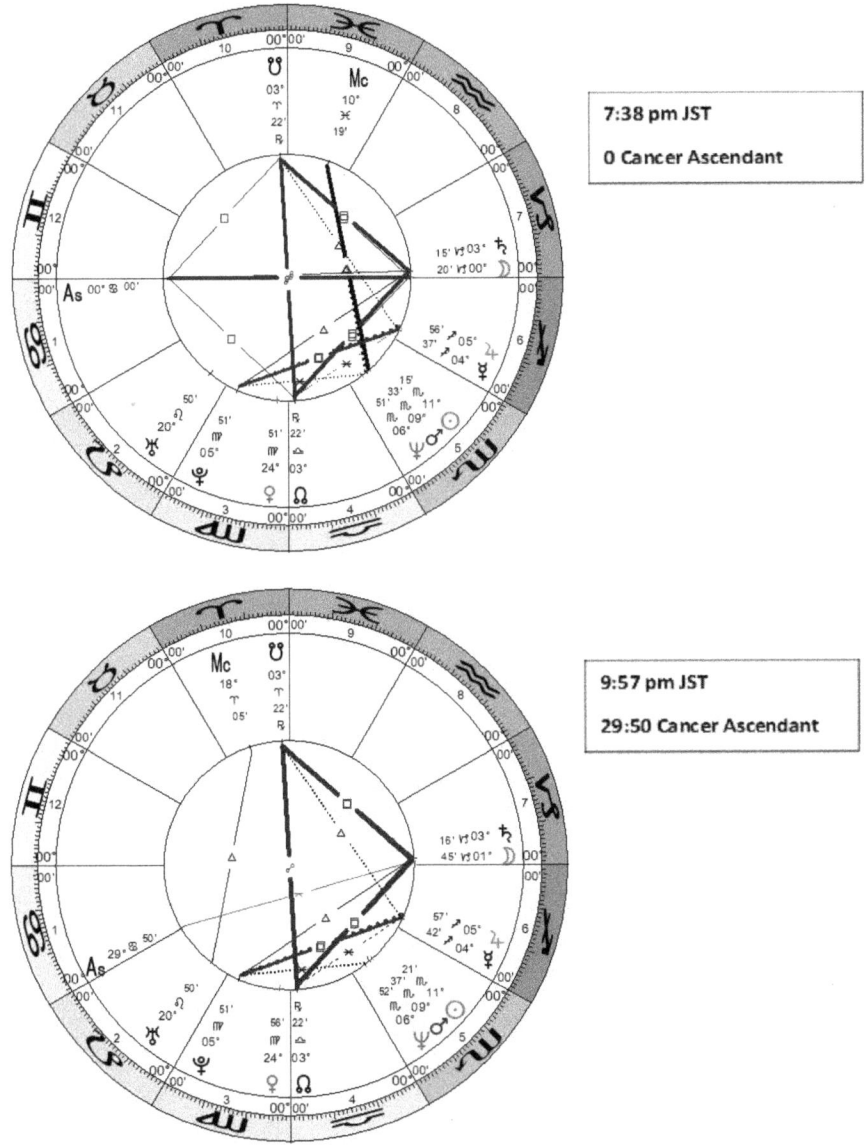

7:38 pm JST

0 Cancer Ascendant

9:57 pm JST

29:50 Cancer Ascendant

Now see what Midheaven sign and ruler fits the biography and how the person is known publicly. In this case, the Aries midheaven ruled by Mars does not fit the person at all. However, Pisces, ruled by Jupiter (Neptune by modern interpretation) fits the biography very well and now the search time range can again be narrowed to 7:38 pm to 8:48 pm.

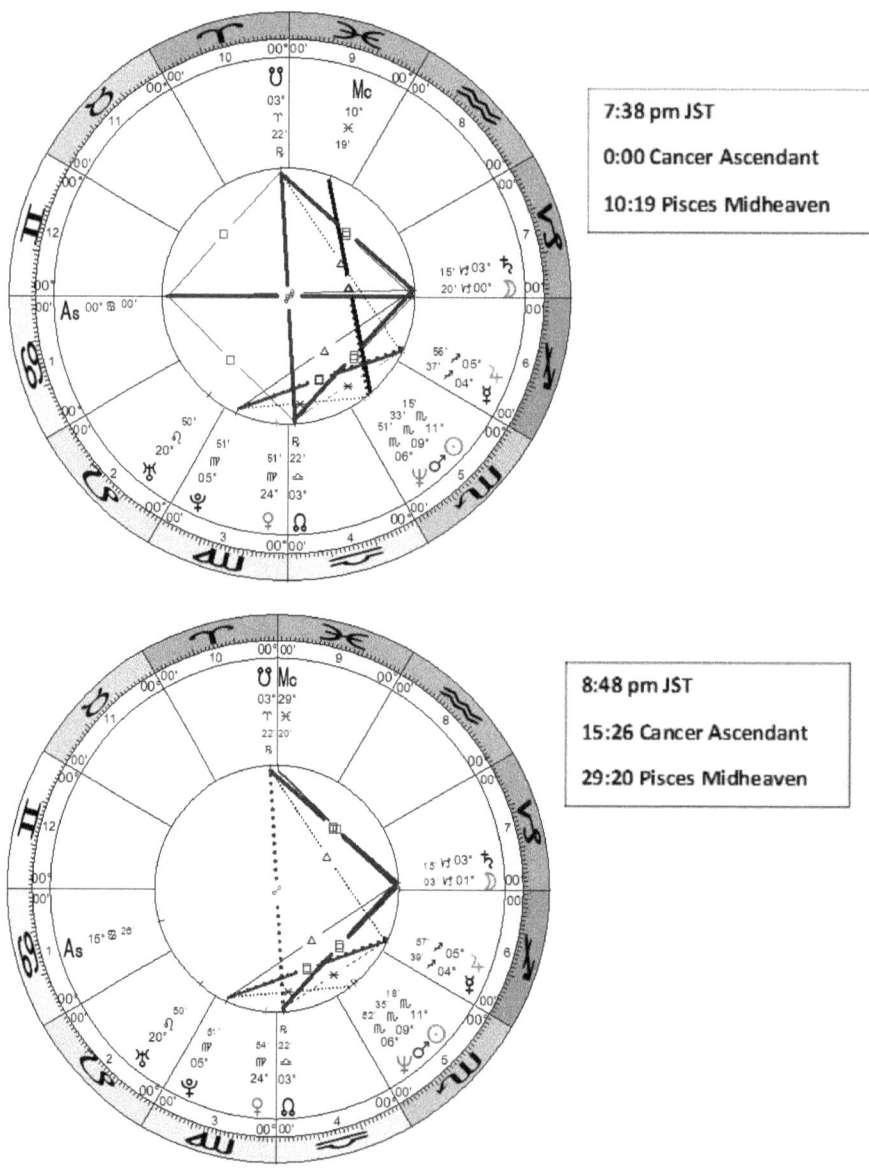

184   The New Complete Book of Chart Rectification

- Time has again been narrowed from 7:38 PM to 8:48 PM that leaves only 1 hour and 10 minutes to test for the rectified birth time.
- With Pisces MC / Cancer ASC and Capricorn Moon in place,

NOW FIND

- An appropriate Planet or Configuration arcing to an Angle at age 3 for adoption

OR

- An Angle arcing to an appropriate Planet or Configuration at age 3 for adoption.

Three times fit planet to angle or angle to planet for adoption: 7:38 pm, 8:06 pm and 8:48 pm.

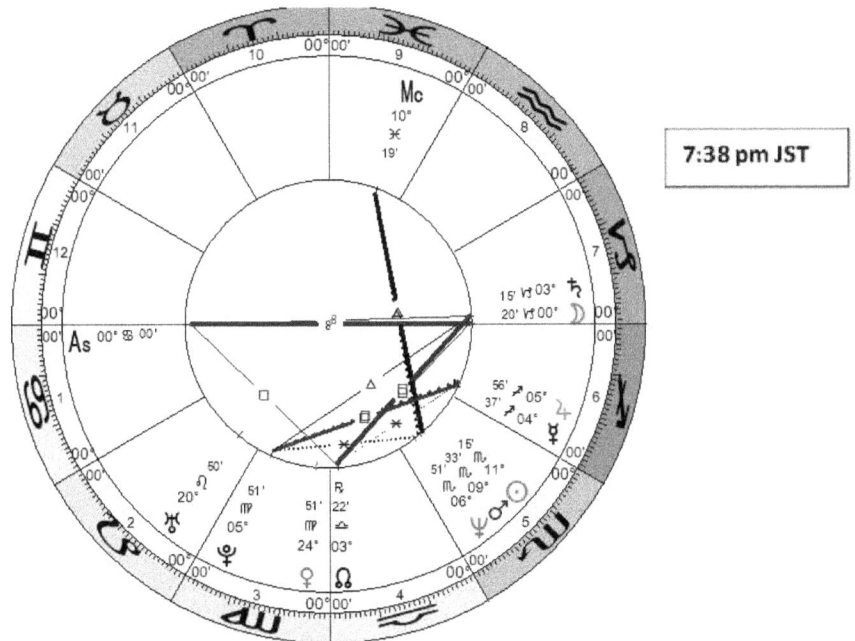

How Do I Deal with No Birth Time?

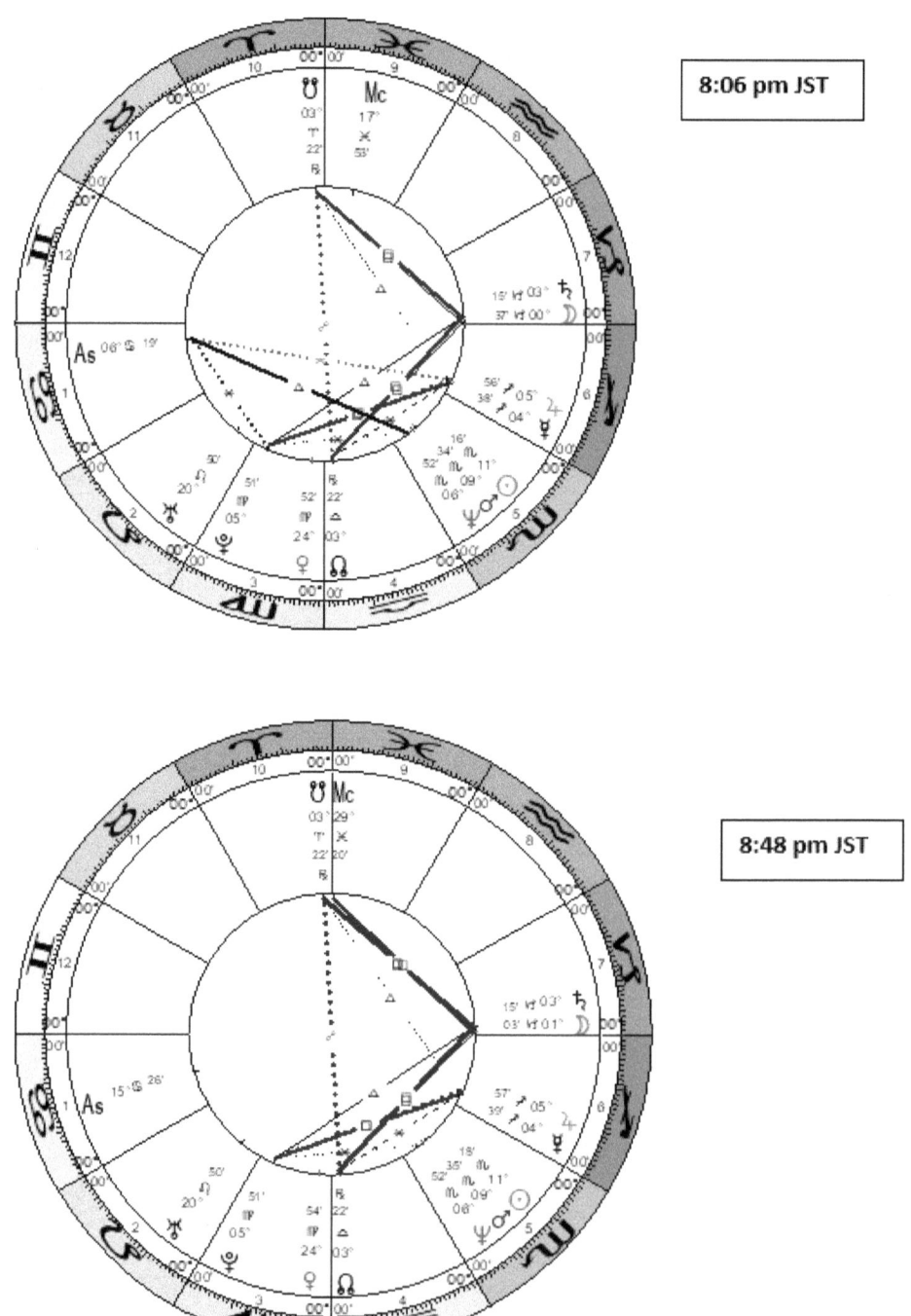

186   The New Complete Book of Chart Rectification

Test the Narrowed List of Birth Times with Several Movement Methods

Born: November 4, 1959 in Tachikawa, Japan

At Age:

  3 Mother gave her to adoptive parents: January 1, 1963

  3 New parents also adopted a boy: February 1963

  6 Came to USA: June 1, 1966

14 Was left in Guam in CPS custody, unruly teen: June 1, 1974

15 Married: February 1, 1975

15 Daughter born: April 7, 1975

16 Brought daughter to USA: March 1976

21 Son born: January 12, 1981

21 Husband's father died: April 5, 1981

28 Husband's mother died: March 21, 1988

35 Daughter died, motorcycle accident: February 13, 1995

41 Adoptive mother died: October 16, 2001 (client near 42)

43 Husband hospitalized: May 2003 / Died: July 16, 2003

44 Met future husband: August 7, 2004

47 Granddaughter born: January 8, 2007

52 Bankruptcy: July 2010

53 Moved to central US: February 13, 2011

54 Granddaughter in CPS custody: February 9, 2012

55 Son hospitalized, child still in custody: February 13, 2013

56 Married: July 5, 2014

Once the major life events are tested with several predictive techniques such as Solar Arc Direction, Secondary Progression, Outer Transits and other methods, tally the results for the few birth times that are the best choices.

TRUST YOUR ASTROLOGICAL JUDGEMENT --- SOFTWARE IS ONLY A TOOL

Decanates and Dwads are Another Tool to Test Birth Time

Decanates (Decans) for each sign of 30-degrees describes three 10-degree segments (a triplicity) with the first decan starting with the sign itself. Every sign is either fire, air, earth or water and each sign has a triplicity within its 30 degrees. Cancer is a water sign, protective, private and compassionate, so each of the triplicity decans is the next water sign in succession. If the Ascendant sign is Cancer, as in this case, the first decan starts from 0-Cancer to 9:59 degrees. The second decan starts at 10:00 Cancer to 19:59 degrees with Scorpio, and the third decan starts at 20:00 Cancer to 29:59 degrees with Pisces.

This client's derived Ascendant starts at 0:00 Cancer at 7:38 pm JST, so this time is in the first decan of Cancer. Indeed, the 8:06 pm JST time is also in the Cancer decan, but by 8:48 pm JST the decan moves to Scorpio, the next triplicity of water.

Working in tandem with the decans, dwads are smaller and divide each 10-degree decan into four 2 ½ degree segments that fill in the signs past over by the decan triplicities. In this case, Cancer, Scorpio and Pisces decans have three signs between each which includes all 12 signs. However, the dwads break down every 30-degree sign into 12 dwad segments of 2 ½ degrees, again representing all 12 signs. Decans and dwads are excellent tools to align appropriate astrological descriptors that fit the client's angle, in this case the Ascendant. Since this woman is very detail oriented with everything in its exact place, the Virgo dwad is the best descriptor within her Cancer Ascendant that fits the 7:36 pm and 8:06 pm JST times. The 8:48 pm time

MOST USED MODERN TRIPLICITY DWAD SYSTEM

	0°-2°29	2°30-4°59	5°-7°29	7°30-9°59	10°-12°29	12°30-14°59	15°-17°29	17°30-19°59	20°-22°29	22°30-24°59	25°-27°29	27°30-29°59
AR	♈	♉	♊	♋	♌	♍	♎	♏	♐	♑	♒	♓
TA	♉	♊	♋	♌	♍	♎	♏	♐	♑	♒	♓	♈
GE	♊	♋	♌	♍	♎	♏	♐	♑	♒	♓	♈	♉
CN	♋	♌	♍	♎	♏	♐	♑	♒	♓	♈	♉	♊
LE	♌	♍	♎	♏	♐	♑	♒	♓	♈	♉	♊	♋
VI	♍	♎	♏	♐	♑	♒	♓	♈	♉	♊	♋	♌
LI	♎	♏	♐	♑	♒	♓	♈	♉	♊	♋	♌	♍
SC	♏	♐	♑	♒	♓	♈	♉	♊	♋	♌	♍	♎
SG	♐	♑	♒	♓	♈	♉	♊	♋	♌	♍	♎	♏
CP	♑	♒	♓	♈	♉	♊	♋	♌	♍	♎	♏	♐
AQ	♒	♓	♈	♉	♊	♋	♌	♍	♎	♏	♐	♑
PI	♓	♈	♉	♊	♋	♌	♍	♎	♏	♐	♑	♒

Decan — Decan — Decan

is still in Cancer decan, but moves to the Libra dwad, which does not fit her biography and habits.

Once the major life events are tested with several predictive techniques such as Solar Arc Direction, Secondary Progression, Outer Transits and other methods, tally the results for the few birth times that are the best choices.

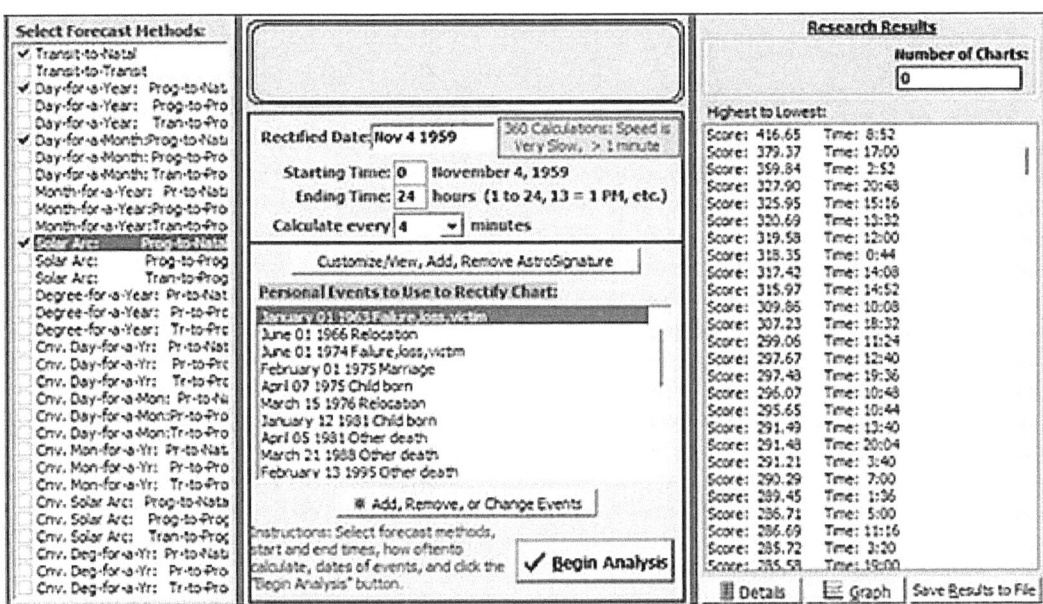

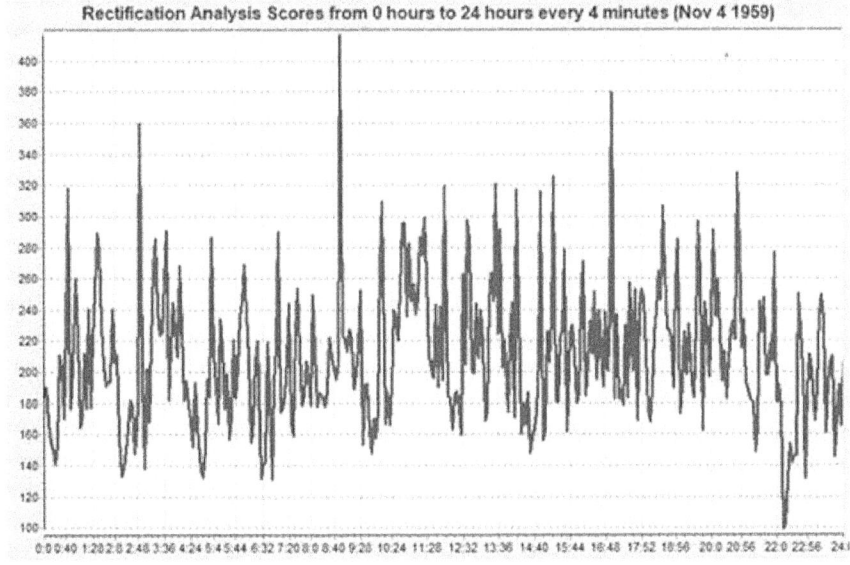

How Do I Deal with No Birth Time?   189

	8:38 PM			7:38 PM			8:06 PM		
Event	Direc	Trans	P-Mo	Direc	Trans	P-Mo	Direc	Trans	P-Mo
Mom gave her for adopt	MC Sq Saturn	Sat Sq Sun/Mar Ur Sq Mer	Opp Uran	ASC Op Sat...ASC Sq Nodes	Pluto Op MC	Sq Uranus	ASC Op Sat...ASC Sq Nodes		Sq Uranus
In CPS custody	Moon Op ASC	Sat Op Mo/Sat Sq Nodes Co ASC	Opp Sat Sq Nodes	Venus Op MC	Sat Con ASC	Sq Nodes Opp Satu	MC sq Sat MC Op Nodes	Sat Co ASC Plu Sq ASC	Opp Sat sq Nodes Conj MC
Daughter died	Ur Op MC ASC Co Ur	Jup Sq Pluto	Sq ASC		Sat Con MC			Sat Co MC	
Mom died	MC Con Sun	Jup Co ASC	Opp Moo Opp Satu Opp Nod	ASC Sq Sun	Sat Sq MC	Sq Nodes Opp Satu			Conj ASC
Husband died		Sat Op Moo/Sat/ Nodes	Jup Sq MC		Sat Con ASC		ASC Op Uranus	Plu Co ASC Sat SQ MC	
Bankrupt filing	ASC Sq Jup MC Sq Ur	Pluto Sq Sat/Node Ju Co No	Sat Opp MC	ASC Co Uran	Uran Sq ASC/Sat Sq ASC		MC Op Mars	Sat Sq ASC	
Grandda CPS cust	Neptune Sq MC	Ur Sq Mo /Sat/Nod	Sq Uran	Nep Op ASC		Sq Uranus	MC OP Sun	Uran Sq ASC	Sq Uranus
Son ill in hospital	Uranus Sq ASC	Sat Co Sun/Mars	Co Merc Sq Pluto Con Jup			Conj Mer Conj Jup Sq Pluto		Uran Sq ASC	Conj Mer Conj Jup Sq Pluto
ANGLES Top 8:06	9	2	3 = 14	6	7	0 = 13	7	8	2 = 17

Directions, Transits, Progressed Moon Activation

Example 2: Hillary Clinton

The Secretary of State and the potential President of the United States in 2016 did not reach her goal. Astrologers did not have birth time information to not only delineate the natal chart but could not accurately forecast such a devasting blow as losing the 2016 presidency. At a 2016 international astrology conference two separate panels of five astrologers gave their forecast for the presidential election results, though all agreed it would be close, all but one said Hillary would win the presidency.

Without birth time it is impossible for an astrologer to forecast any event. Indeed, the best information we have had until recently for Hillary Clinton is her birth on October 26, 1947 in Chicago, Illinois.

Footnote: www.Astro.com: "Birth certificate in hand from Viktor E. The hour digit of the handwritten time is not too clearly read. It could look like a 6 but may possibly be a sloppily written 10. See the B.C. on the right. (The birth certificate with the time of 6:45 am is not given here since it is marked as 'for genealogy only'.)

Alois Treindl: The reading of the birth hour as 6 or 10 is not 100% clear. ...After careful deliberation with some data researchers, we hold the reading as 6 for the most likely.

I have removed earlier rectifications from the source notes, as a birth certificate makes these no longer meaningful. Previously this entry was shown with charts for the times 8:02am and 8:00pm, rated DD (Conflicting/unverified) ..."

From other sources, I have even more times for Hillary that span 19-hours: 1:30 am, 2:18 am, 8:02 am, 9:36 am, 8:02 pm and 9:36 pm. Hillary even answered to an astrologer in the crowd responding 8:00 o'clock, but didn't clarify whether it was AM or PM.

As you can see, astrologers did not have a confirmed birth time for Hillary Clinton until 2022, so the 2016 panel astrologers did not have accurate birth time information. No wonder that 9 out of the 10 well trained astrologers made incorrect 2016 election forecasts.

Another problem of rectifying birth time for public figures who are not the astrologer's personal client is that the early growing up years are not included. It is important to have all major life events from early childhood to the current date. It is rare that we know the early personal challenges, hopes or dreams. Only a handful of these life events had major personal impact for Hillary. Most of the events were public, so we don't know very much about Hillary the person.

Age 4:   Spring 1952 Victim, bullied by kids, learned to fight back

Age: 10 June 1969 Graduated Wellesley summa cum laude

Age 21: 10 June 1969 Graduated Wellesley summa cum laude

Age 25: 10 June 1973 Graduated Yale Law School

Age 26: 15 June 1974 Law professor University of Arkansas

Age 27: 11 October 1975 Marriage to Clinton

Age 31: 10 January 1979 Became Arkansas First lady

Age 33: 20 January 1981 Husband re-elected Governor of Arkansas

Age 45: 20 January 1993 Husband elected as USA President

Age 45: 27 April 1993 Father died

Age 47: Book released 1995, It Takes a Village

Age 50: Book released 1998

Age 50: 2 August 1998 Husband's affair became news

Age 52: 16 May 2000 Nominated as Senator for New York

Age 53: 7 November 2000 won Senate seat

Age 55: 9 June 2003 Book release of her biography

Age 59: 6 June 2006 Re-elected Senator

Age 59: 20 January 2007 Presidential Exploratory Committee

Age 60: 4 June 2008 Withdrew from race for President

Age 61: 1 December 2008 Nominated as Secretary of State

Age 61: 21 January 2009 Inaugurated Secretary of State

Age 61: 18 June 2009 Surgery, broken elbow

Age 63: 31 June 2010 Daughter's wedding

Age 64: 1 November 2011 Mother's death

Age 69: 8 November 2016 Lost run for USA President

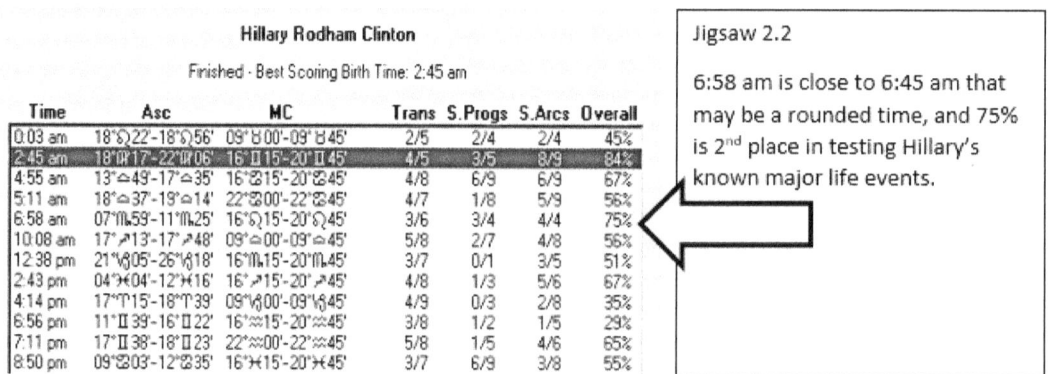

Jigsaw 2.2

6:58 am is close to 6:45 am that may be a rounded time, and 75% is 2nd place in testing Hillary's known major life events.

Once again, I emphasize that astrology software is an astrologer's tool. As amazing as it is, the astrologer's training and judgement makes the best decision for what astrological components fit the real person, not just what is available in their public biography. Rectifying birth time for public figures who do not personally give the astrologer a detailed personal biography and major personal life events to test is a fool's errand. T

Example 3: Mike Tyson

Mike Tyson Biography, astro.com

Get a List of Major Life Events, Childhood to Now, with

1. 1966 He and his 2 siblings were abandoned by their father before he was born, his mother died before he had achieved his success.

2. A mugger and thief by 1976, he was sent to school for juvenile delinquents. 1979, a counselor changed his life, taking him into his home, teaching him sports.

3. Reigned as Undisputed World Heavyweight Champion 1987 to 1990.

4. 10 February 1992, convicted of raping a Miss Black America contestant, 19 July 1991 to March 1995 prison.

5. 8 November 1996, he fought like an enraged animal, biting off a piece of Holyfield's ear, sentenced to 1-year in jail.

6. 5 February 1999 in jail for assaulting two motorists.

7. 22 Jan 2002, Tyson turned a Vegas press conference into a melee with Lennox Lewis, biting him on the leg.

8. 29 January 2002, denied license to fight in highly anticipated bout on 6 April 6.

9. Tyson, once $300 million filed bankruptcy 1 August 2003.

10. His 4-year-old daughter died on 25 May 2009.

Start With the Moon to Narrow Time Range

Start With Whole Sign

We Don't Have Houses or Angles Yet

Childhood Trauma = Moon

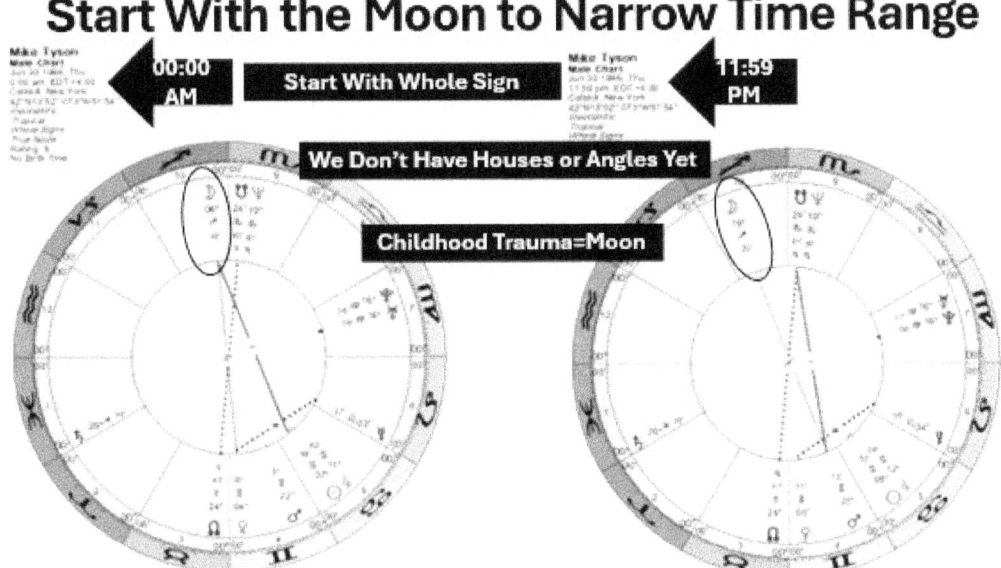

How Do I Deal with No Birth Time?

With Biography, Fit Moon to 1-Degree Aspects

- Mike Tyson was known as "Iron Mike", Kid Dynamite" and "the Baddest Man on the Planet".

- He and his two older siblings were abandoned by their father before he was born and his mother died of stomach cancer before he achieved his success.

- A mugger and thief by ten, he was sent to school for juvenile delinquents the following year.

Close Hard Aspects to Mike Tyson's Moon Reliably Fits His Early-life Trauma

- As a young teen, a counselor changed his life, taking him into his home and teaching him sports.

- He married actress Robin Givens in February 1988; they later divorced.

- February 10, 1992, convicted of raping a Miss Black America and served 3 years in prison.

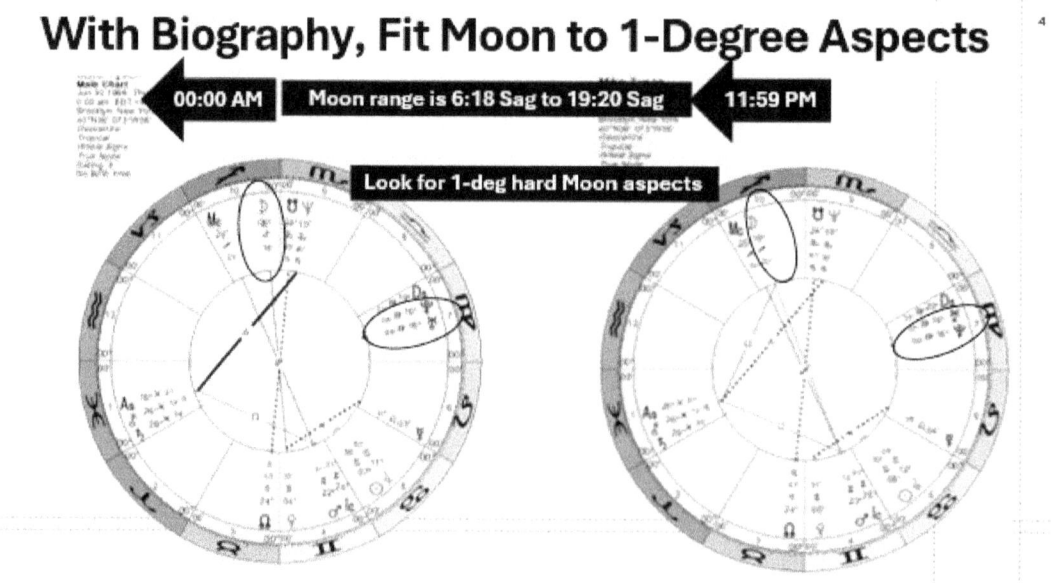

Moon Fits the Biography

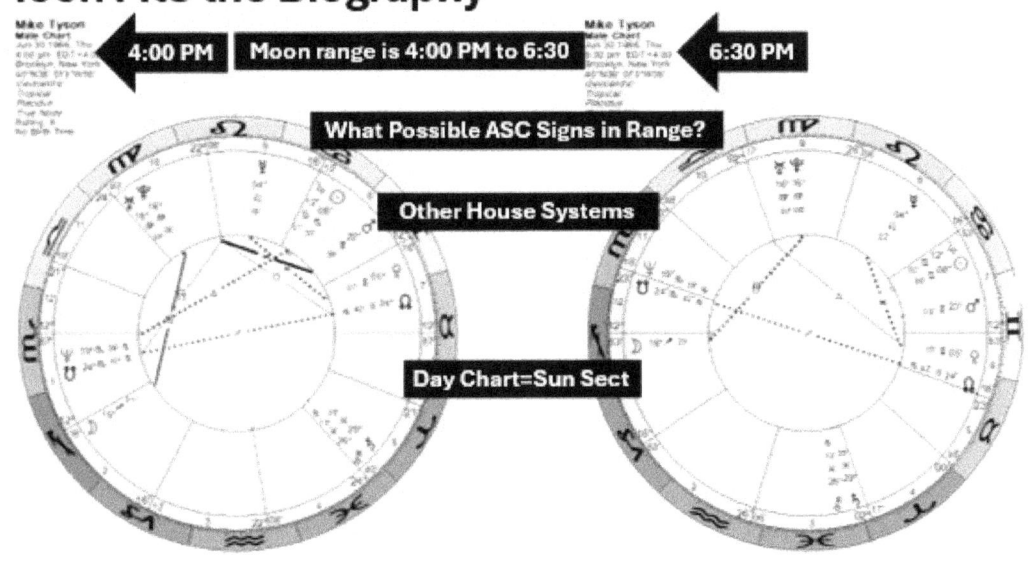

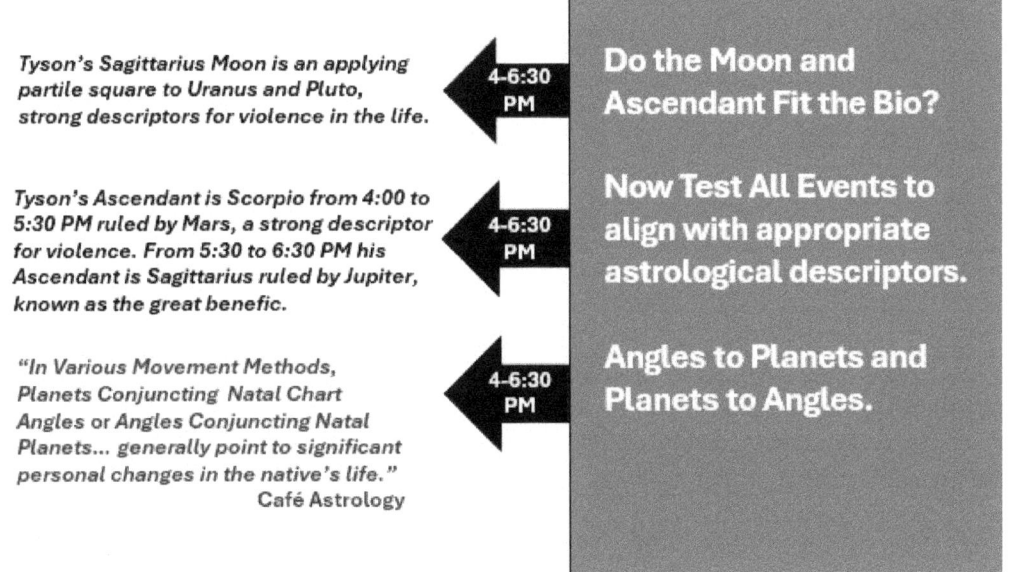

How Do I Deal with No Birth Time?   195

Software is Useful, But a Well-trained Astrologer is Better

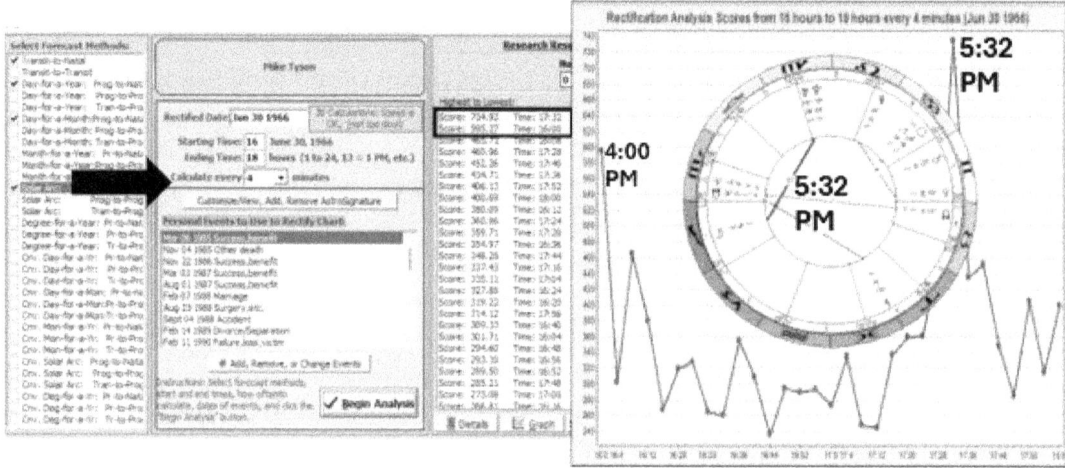

Software is Useful, But a Well-trained Astrologer is Better

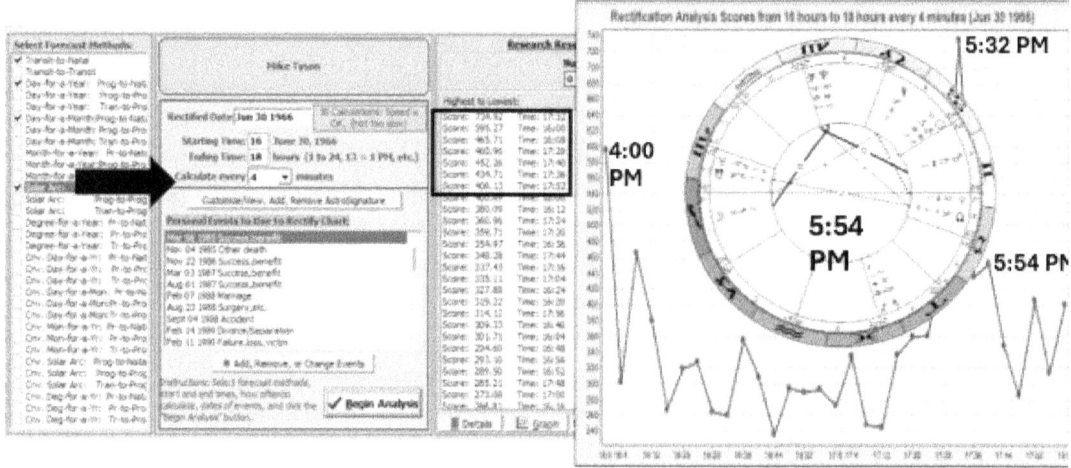

Years ago, I tested 100 family, friends, and clients with birth certificate times and for more than half, the software did not have the birth certificate time rated first, but within the top 10 and in reasonable range. Often, I override the software top times because it only tests events. It doesn't know the biography, the story of the person.

Chapter 8

Why are Time Twins so Different??

There is a big difference between fraternal or identical twins born of the same mother at the same location on the same date just a few minutes apart and "Time twins" born of different mothers on the same date at locations around the world and various times of day. In the case of natural twins, all of their planets are the same by house, sign, and degree with only the Angles 2 to 4-degrees difference that represent 8 to 16-minutes of clock time. Time and location difference creates notable chart differences. Even though all of the planets, except the Moon, may be at the same degree for both people, their birth time and location difference would greatly change the signs on the Angles and houses and their rulers to greatly alter the planetary expression. On average, the Angles move through a sign every 2-hours and the Moon moves 1-degree in 2-hours. It is clear that the Moon will not change for "Natural twins", whereas "Time twins" may have as much as a 13-degree Moon difference – and possibly a change of sign and its ruler. "Natural twins" most often share the same signs and rulers on the Angles, with just a couple of degrees difference. Therefore, the rectification tools must be more specific for the "Natural twins" and in Chapter 5 the discussion of "Decans and Dwads" are a helpful tool to solve the rectification puzzle where the only difference is the Angles. Remember, birth time is not recorded in many countries of the world, and natural twins interested in astrology may want a birth time for chart interpretation and forecasting of current chart activation.

Rectification Example One - Actress Elizabeth Taylor

- Search the Natal Chart for "One-Degree Aspect Hooks"
- Time to List the Important Life Events for Elizabeth Taylor
- Once Background Work is Complete, Begin the Rectification Search
- Search the Possible Dwad Positions of the Moon
- Select the Most Dramatic Events in Close Time Proximity for Initial Search

- Search the Progressed Sun Positions at Major Life Events
- Run Secondary Progressions in Smaller Increments of Narrow Time Range
- Now Use Outer Transits to Narrow to One or Two Promising Times
- Retrograde and Station Periods Greatly Extend the Effect of Any Transit
- Extenuating Circumstances Extend the Impact of Outer Transits
- Retrograde and Station Periods Mark Outer Transit Emphasis for Elizabeth
- If You are Still Undecided, Run Solar Eclipses for the Events

Elizabeth Taylor and Johnny Cash are what astrologers call "Time twins" born within 18-hours and 45-minutes of each other on February 26-27 in the year 1932. Even though Elizabeth was born in London, England and Johnny was born in Kingsland, Arkansas, all the planets and the Moon's Nodes are within one-degree of being the same in both charts. Certainly, the lives of these celebrities have taken very different courses, but the distinguishing differences in their charts may be found in 1) the position of the Angles – and subsequently the houses, and 2) the position of the Moon – both of which are the "heart of the matter" for rectification work. Of course, with different Angles and Moon degrees, and possibly signs, the aspects formed to or by them greatly distinguish the details of one life from the other and one chart from the other. Nonetheless, they do have similarities; both have struggled with alcohol and drug abuse most of their lives, and both are noted for multiple affairs, marriages, and unstable relationships.

In the case of Elizabeth, we face reported birth times from 1:30 AM to 9:00 PM on February 27, 1932 – a range of 19 ½ hours, though some birthtimes are more reliable than others, such as the 2:00 AM time given by her mother from memory. Astro.com lists a time of 2:15 AM GMT but it is a time not supported by any of the references, indicating that the 2:15 AM time may itself be rectified. Source Notes from the Astro.com "Full Dossier" for Elizabeth Taylor are:

"Bob Prince quotes Good Housekeeping magazine 3/1989, p.197, that has an excerpt from My Daughter Elizabeth, written by Mrs. Taylor, saying that, 'She was born around 2:00 AM.' Prince also has a signed photo from Taylor with 2:00 AM written on the back of the picture by Liz herself. The biography by Alexander Walker gives 2:30 AM. (Formerly, Church of Light gave 7:56 PM from Adrienne Ziegler, 1958. The same data was given in AQ Winter/1966 and by Pryor in AFA 10/1971, and in Fowler's, 'allegedly to a Lodge member from Taylor's mom.' Marion March had 6:56 PM from a British Astrology magazine 7/1970. Wilhelm Konig gave 1:30 AM, and Lucy Bonnet gave 9:00 PM.)"

It is clear that, even with such widely reported birth data, controversy over birth time is a persistent problem. To shed an interesting light on the alternative birth times, I entered the list of major life events for Elizabeth Taylor into the Brady/Dawson Jigsaw 2.0 program for

Research and Rectification and searched the time range from 1:30 AM to 9:00 PM on February 27, 1932 using the 4th harmonic (conjunction, square and opposition) and applied Outer Planet Transits; Solar Arc Directions; and Secondary Progressions with the following results:

Table 47 Jigsaw 2.0 Suggested Chart Birth Times and Angles for Elizabeth Taylor

Time	Midheaven	Ascendant	Solar Arc	Sec Prog	Outer Transits	Overall
2:07 AM	7:00 -8:45 Lib	8:11 - 9:24 Sag	3/5	1/5	4/10	50%
6:02 AM	7:00-8:45 Sag	8:21-11:25 Aqu	3/8	1/2	5/9	47%
9:26 AM	24:30-26:30 Cp	24:09-27:21 Tau	7/8	6/8	3/11	81%
7:15 PM	24:30-26:30 Ge	25:46-27:18 Virg	2/5	2/5	6/10	43%

My experience in testing the program with timed birth data, while still searching a full 24 hours, is that the actual or near actual birth time is regularly listed in the mix but often not with the highest percentage. In this case, the "mother's memory" time of 2:00 AM rates the second highest in planetary "hits" at appropriate life events, so it is confirmed as a viable starting point. The 9:26 AM time, rated the highest, corresponds closely with the speculated 9:00 PM time, if one flips the chart by 12 hours. And the 7:15 PM time is reasonably close to the speculated times of 6:56 PM and 7:56 PM. Since none of those speculative times are remotely close to the birth time of the "mother's memory", they are less reliable as a starting point for the rectification search.

Figure 158 Elizabeth Taylor's birth set for Mother's Memory of 2:00 AM

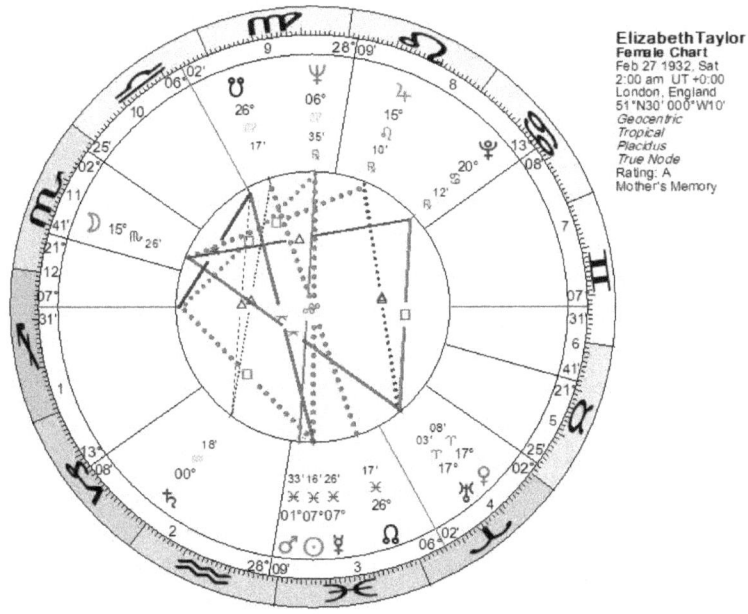

Why Are Time Twins So Different?

Next, Search the Natal Chart for "One-Degree Hard Aspect Hooks

The next strategy in a rectification search is to sort for the close (1-2 degree) hard aspect networks found in the natal chart. Three factors prevail in determining what to include in the aspect search:

1. The closeness of aspect orb, 1-degree or less greatly preferred
2. Major hard aspect patterns, and
3. Involvement of the Lights or personal planets.

Of course, the Angles are of primary importance, but since we are unsure of the birth time, they are not available for the search – Indeed, the Angles are exactly what we are looking for! Working from the 2:00 AM time of the "mother's memory", the qualifying aspect networks in Elizabeth Taylor's chart involve:

1. Sun conjunct Mercury – 10" orb

    Sun opposite Neptune – 40" orb

    Mercury opposite Neptune – 50" orb

    Sun square Ascendant – (possibly within 1 degree range)

    Mercury square Ascendant – (possibly within 1 degree range)

    Neptune square Ascendant – (possibly within 1 degree range)

2. Venus conjunct Uranus – 6" orb

    Venus semi-square Mars – 34" orb

    Venus trine Jupiter – 1'57" orb

    Uranus semi-square Mars – 29" orb

    Jupiter trine Uranus – 1'52" orb

    Moon inconjunct Venus/Uranus – (possibly within 1'28" orb)

Remember, the Moon is still suspect, and the Angles are yet untested. Until such time as we can determine if the Moon or Ascendant are involved in either of the two close aspect patterns, these two multiple-planet configurations do provide us with very good "hard aspect hooks" to move into the chart and link them with important life events.

Time to List the Important Life Events for Elizabeth Taylor

The list of Elizabeth Taylor's important life events was culled from the Alexander Walker biography, Elizabeth: The Life of Elizabeth Taylor, published in 1997. The most prominent events are bolded, but other life events are included to provide proper background and context.

Table 48 Notable Life Events for Elizabeth Taylor – Bolded Events More Prominent

	Event	Place	Age	Date
1	Family moved to America	Pasadena, CA	7	4-15-1939
2	Debuted in movies	Los Angeles, CA	10	4-21-1942
3	Signs 7-year contract MGM	Los Angeles, CA	10 ¾	1-5-1943
4	Writes children's book	Los Angeles, CA	13	6-1-1946
5	On cover of Time magazine	Los Angeles, CA	16 ½	8-22-1949
6	Marries Nicky Hilton (1)	Beverly Hills, CA	18	5-6-1950
7	Divorced/hospital-virus/breakdown	Los Angeles, CA	19	1-29-1951
8	Marries Michael Wilding (2)	London, England	20	2-21-1952
9	Birth of son, Michael	Beverly Hills, CA	20 ¾	1-6-1953
10	Birth of son, Christopher	Beverly Hills, CA	23	2-27-1955
11	Divorced/Severe fall/ spinal surgery	Beverly Hills, CA	23 ¾	11-4-1955
12	Marries Michael Todd (3)	Acapulco, Mexico	25	2-2-1957
13	Birth of daughter, Elizabeth	Beverly Hills, CA	25 ½	8-6-1957
14	Husband killed in plane crash	Beverly Hills, CA	26	3-23-1958
15	Marries Eddie Fisher (4)	Las Vegas, NV	27	5-12-1959
16	Tracheotomy/near death	London, England	29	3-4-1961
17	1st Oscar "Butterfield 8"	Hollywood, CA	29	4-17-1961
18	Year of scandal/ love affair w/Burton	London, England	30	All 1962-63
19	Married Richard Burton (5)	Montreal, Canada	32	3-15-1964
20	2nd Oscar "Who's Afraid of Virginia Woolfe?"	Hollywood, CA	35	4-10-1967
21	Receives Krupp diamond/ largest	London, England	36	5-17-1968
22	Surgery/ hysterectomy	London, England	36 ½	7-21-1968
23	Death of father	London, England	36 ¾	11-22-1968
24	Death of 1st husband, Hilton	London, England	37	2-5-1969
25	Receives Cartier diamond/ huge	London, England	37 ¾	10-25-1969
26	Extravagant birthday party/ diamond	Budapest, Hungary	40	2-27-1972
27	Divorced Burton	Saarinen, Switzerla	42	6-26-1974
28	Remarries Burton (6)	Botswana, Africa	43 ½	10-10-1975
29	Divorced Burton again	Haiti	44 ½	8-1-1976
30	Marries John Warner (7)	Middleburg, VA	44 ¾	12-4-1976
31	Death of 2nd husband Wilding	London, England	47 ½	7-16-1979

Table 48 continues

	Event	Place	Age	Date
32	Divorced from Warner	Washington DC	50 ¾	11-1982
33	Rehab/ alcohol/pills at Betty Ford	Rancho Mirage, CA	51 ¾	12-5-1983
34	Collapses /news of Burton's death	Bel Air, CA	52 ½	8-5-1984
35	Begins AIDS crusade/ fundraising	Hollywood, CA	53 ½	8-6-1985
36	AIDS Research national chairwoman	Hollywood, CA	55	3-3-1987
37	Receives Legion of Honor award	Paris, France	55	5-14-1987
38	Returns to rehab alcohol/pill abuse	Rancho Mirage, CA	56 ½	10-1988
39	Collapse/pneumonia/near death	Hollywood, CA	58	4 - 5-1990
40	Marries Larry Fortensky (8)	Santa Maria, CA	59 ½	10-6-1991
41	Life Achievement Award/ film	Hollywood, CA	61	3-11-1993
42	Hip replacement surgery	Hollywood, CA	62	3-24-1994
43	Death of Mother	Rancho Mirage, CA	62 ½	9-11-1994
44	Divorced Fortensky	Hollywood, CA	64	6-1996

Once Background Work is Complete, Begin the Rectification Search

Now that the background work is in place, let's take a look at Elizabeth's natal chart for the time that her mother remembered as a base point for the rectification search. Indeed, one might proceed by running all of the variables to the several charts for the birth times reported by www.Astro.com, but there are so many that, instead, it may be easier to search the complete time range in dispute from 1:30 AM to 9:00 PM GMT.

Let's begin with a Moon search to determine the most likely dwad position of the Moon that describes Liz's passion for expensive and beautiful things, such as three of the most magnificent and expensive diamonds in the world. For those unfamiliar, knowing the dwad, or 2½ degree sub-section of each sign, may be helpful if one knows enough of the character and personality of the individual to use this handy fine-tuning device. Each 30-degree sign contains 3 decans of 10 degrees each that emphasize the triplicity of the sign, and 12 dwads that emphasize the sign divided into 2 ½ degree segments. Table 3 may serve as a handy, but optional, reference for determining the dwad position of the Moon, or indeed, any of the planets or Angles once determined.

Table 49 A Moon Search - Signs, Decanates and Dwadasamsas – Fine-tuning of Degrees

0 – 2 ½	Aries	Taur	Gem	Canc	Leo	Virgo	Libra	Scor	Sagit	Capr	Aqua	Pisc
2 ½ - 5	Taur	Gem	Canc	Leo	Virgo	Libra	Scor	Sagit	Capr	Aqua	Pisc	Aries
5-7 ½	Gem	Canc	Leo	Virgo	Libra	Scor	Sagit	Capr	Aqua	Pisc	Aries	Taur
7 ½-10	Canc	Leo	Virgo	Libra	Scor	Sagit	Capr	Aqua	Pisc	Aries	Taur	Gem
10-12½	Leo	Virgo	Libra	Scor	Sagit	Capr	Aqua	Pisc	Aries	Taur	Gem	Canc
12½-15	Virgo	Libra	Scor	Sagit	Capr	Aqua	Pisc	Aries	Taur	Gem	Canc	Leo
15-17½	Libra	Scor	Sagit	Capr	Aqua	Pisc	Aries	Taur	Gem	Canc	Leo	Virgo
17½-20	Scor	Sagit	Capr	Aqua	Pisc	Aries	Taur	Gem	Canc	Leo	Virgo	Libra
20-22½	Sagit	Capr	Aqua	Pisc	Aries	Taur	Gem	Canc	Leo	Virgo	Libra	Scor
22½-25	Capr	Aqua	Pisc	Aries	Taur	Gem	Canc	Leo	Virgo	Libra	Scor	Sagit
25-27½	Aqua	Pisc	Aries	Taur	Gem	Canc	Leo	Virgo	Libra	Scor	Sagit	Capr
27½-30	Pisc	Aries	Taur	Gem	Canc	Leo	Virgo	Libra	Scor	Sagit	Capr	Aqua

If Elizabeth were indeed born about 2:00 AM as the mother remembers, the Taurus dwad of her Scorpio Moon describes exactly that trait of loving the pleasures of life and beautiful things. The Moon in Scorpio, itself, can be descriptive of covetousness and a passionate intensity to delve into the extremes of both life and death that may be supported by Elizabeth's dedication to AIDS research, but in combination with the Taurus dwad, the approximate 2:00 AM birth time is supported. More dramatic evidence in support of the time range of 2:00 – 3:00 AM is in the "stacking-up" of multiple close hard aspects of the natal Moon to the Ascendant, Venus, Jupiter and Uranus, very descriptive of the multiple volatile and unstable relationships that has led to 8 marriages and 8 divorces – and still counting.

Table 50 Possible Natal Moon 1-Degree Aspects for 24 Hours, AM and PM

Aspects	AM Moon	Dwad	Time	Dwad	PM Moon	Aspects
Square Jupiter Conjunct Asc	14:15 Scorp	Aries	12:00	Cancer	21:23 Scorp	
Square Jupiter	14:50 Scorp	Aries	1:00	Cancer	21:58 Scorp	
Square Jupiter Inconjunct Venus Inconjunct Uranus	15:26 Scorp	Taur	2:00	Leo	22:34 Scorp	Sesqui-square MC
Square Jupiter Inconjunct Venus Inconjunct Uranus Semi-square Asc	16:02 Scorp	Taur	3:00	Leo	23:09 Scorp	Inconjunct MC
Inconjunct Venus Inconjunct Uranus Semi-square Asc	16:38 Scorp	Taur	4:00	Leo	23:44 Scorp	
Inconjunct Venus Inconjunct Uranus Sextile Asc	17:13 Scorp	Taur	5:00	Leo	24:20 Scorp	Opposite MC
Inconjunct Venus Inconjunct Uranus	17:49 Scorp	Gemi	6:00	Leo	24:55 Scorp	
	18:25 Scorp	Gemi	7:00	Virgo	25:31 Scorp	
Opposite Chiron	19:00 Scorp	Gemi	8:00	Virgo	26:06 Scorp	Trine NNode Sextile SNode
Trine Pluto Opposite Chiron Sextile MC	19:36 Scorp	Gemi	9:00	Virgo	26:41 Scorp	Trine NNode Sextile SNode
Trine Pluto Opposite Chiron	20:12 Scorp	Canc	10:00	Virgo	27:16 Scorp	Trine NNode Sextile SNode
Trine Pluto	20:47 Scorp	Canc	11:00	Libra	28:27 Scorp	Trine NNode Sextile SNode

Now Select the Most Dramatic Events in Close Time Proximity for the Initial Search

Of the seventeen most dramatic (painful) events appearing in bold type in the list of important life events in Table 30, note that events 22 and 23, Liz's hysterectomy surgery and the death of her father, occurred with just 4 months apart, greatly compounding the importance of the July 21 through November 22 period of 1968. These events related to the self and to the father occurring in such close time proximity suggest that both the Ascendant and the Midheaven might be activated at the time by one or more of the moving time markers. Indeed, the close sextile of the Midheaven and Ascendant in the 2:00 – 3:00 AM time range may be a relevant connection. Other pairs of events show a similar pattern of first a physical illness or surgery, and a few months later, the death of a close loved one, which makes them prime choices for the initial search.

Table 51 Four Important Events or Event Clusters for Liz's Rectification Search are:

14	Husband, Todd, killed in plane crash	Beverly Hills, CA	26	3-23-1958
22	Surgery/ hysterectomy	London, England	36 ½	7-21-1968
23	Death of father	London, England	36 ¾	11-22-1968
33	Rehab/ alcohol/pills at Betty Ford	Rancho Mirage, CA	51 ¾	12-5-1983
34	Collapses /news of Burton's death	Bel Air, CA	52 ½	8-5-1984
42	Hip replacement surgery	Hollywood, CA	62	3-24-1994
43	Death of Mother	Rancho Mirage, CA	62 ½	9-11-1994

One or more of the close "natal aspect hooks" should show activation at most of the critical life events. Starting with the most dramatic "event hooks" above, we begin the initial search by moving the "derived Angles" from Elizabeth's age at the event to conjunct the "close aspect hooks" of the natal patterns. By counting backward from each planet within these patterns by the number of degrees equal to her age at the selected major life events, we hope to establish a very narrow the list of possible birth times that suggest a Midheaven and Ascendant consistent with the timing of major life events, and which can be tested by additional measures.

Using the Solar Arc to move the possible Midheaven and Ascendant backward from each leg of the close aspect patterns in the natal chart, we will work from dates of the four devastating losses of Liz's loved ones: 1) husband Mike Todd's tragic death; 2) her father's death; 3) husband Richard Burton's death; and 4) her mother's death. Remember that events 2, 3 and 4 are combined with one of Liz's life-threatening surgeries just prior, so they are doubly important. Any major events may be chosen, but the more painful the event, the more prominent the astrological indicators for rectification. Elizabeth's age is noted at each of the chosen events, so we count backward in the zodiac that same number of degrees to derive a "working Midheaven" that would conjunct the planet at the time of the event. For quick mental math using the average Solar Arc of 1-degree and knowing that Elizabeth was 26 at Michael Todd's death, we count 26 degrees back from (or before) her 7:16 Pisces Sun to 11:16 Aquarius. She was age 36 ¾ at her father's death, so 36 ¾ degrees back from her 7:16 Pisces Sun is 0:31 Aquarius. She was age 52 ½ at Richard Burton's death, so 52 ½ degrees back from her 7:16 Pisces Sun is 17:46 Capricorn. And, she was 61 ½ at her mother's death, so 62 ½ degrees back from her 7:16

Pisces Sun is 7:46 Capricorn. The process is repeated for each planet in the natal close aspect network – including the major hard aspect "apex" points of the planets in the close aspect networks. Use the computer software "rectify" function to determine the appropriate birth time for each of the possible "working angles". Of course, we will tally the results at the end of the initial Midheaven, Ascendant and Apex Point searches to narrow to the few birth times best supported by appropriate aspects to describe the event at the correct timing.

Table 52 Directed Midheaven Times Conjunct Aspect Network at Four Losses

Planet Contacted by	Todd's Death	Father's Death	Burton's Death	Mother's Death
Conjunction	3-23-1958	11-22-1968	8-5-1984	9-11-1994
Elizabeth's Age at Event	26	36 ¾	52 ½	62 ½
Grand Opposition:				
Sun 7:16 Pisces	10:31 AM MC 11:16 Aqu	9:47 AM MC 0:32 Aqu	8:46 AM MC 17:46 Cp	8:10 AM MC 7:46 Cp
Mercury 7:26 Pisces	10:32 AM MC 11:26 Aqu	9:48 AM MC 0:42 Aqu	8:47 AM MC 17:56 Cp	8:11 AM MC 7:56 Cp
Neptune 6:35 Virgo	10:27 PM MC 10:35 Leo	9:44 PM MC 0:05 Leo	8:36 PM MC 14:05 Cn	7:53 PM MC 4:05 Cn
Planetary Network:				
Venus 17:08 Aries	1:03 PM MC 21:08 Pisc	12:07 PM MC 6:23 Pisc	11:28 AM MC 25:38 Aq	10:49 AM MC 15:38 Aq
Uranus 17:03 Aries	1:03 PM MC 21:03 Pisc	12:07 PM MC 6:18 Pisc	11:28 AM MC 25:32 Aq	10:49 AM MC 15:33 Aq
Jupiter 15:10 Leo	8:58 PM MC 19:10 Can	8:12 PM MC 8:25 Can	7:03 PM MC 22:40 Ge	6:20 PM MC 12:40 Ge
Moon 15:26 Scorpio (est)	2:49 AM MC 19:26 Lib	2:09 AM MC 8:41 Lib	1:12 AM MC 22:56 Vir	0:35 AM MC 12:56 Vir
Mars 1:33 Pisces	10:08 AM MC 5:33 Aqu	11:24 AM MC 24:48 Aq	8:16 AM MC 9:03 Cap	7:32 AM MC 29:03 Sag

Table 53 Directed Ascendant Times Conjunct Aspect Network at Four Losses

Planet Contacted By Conjunction	Todd's Death	Father's Death	Burton's Death	Mother's Death
	3-23-1958	11-22-1968	8-5-1984	9-11-1994
Elizabeth's Age at Event	26	36 ¾	52 ½	62 ½
Grand Opposition:				
Sun 7:16 Pisces	10:31 AM AS 16:45 Gem	9:47 AM AS 3:20 Gem	8:46 AM AS 12:01 Tau	8:10 AM AS 19:51 Ari
Mercury 7:26 Pisces	10:32 AM AS 16:56 Gem	9:48 AM AS 3:35 Gem	8:47 AM AS 12:12 Tau	8:11 AM AS 20:03 Ari
Neptune 6:35 Virgo	10:27 PM AS 0:14 Scorp	9:44 PM AS 23:42 Lib	8:36 PM AS 10:46 Lib	7:53 PM AS 3:08 Lib
Planetary Network:				
Venus 17:08 Aries	1:03 PM AS 20:30 Can	12:07 PM AS 9:26 Can	11:28 AM AS 0:51 Cn	10:49 AM AS 21:24 Gem
Uranus 17:03 Aries	1:03 PM AS 20:25 Can	12:07 PM AS 9:21 Can	11:28 AM AS 0:46 Cn	10:49 AM AS 21:24 Gem
Jupiter 15:10 Leo	8:58 PM AS 14:37 Lib	8:12 PM AS 6:26 Lib	7:03 PM AS 24:22 Vir	6:20 PM AS 16:45 Virg
Moon 15:26 Scorpio	2:49 AM AS 17:06 Sag	2:09 AM AS 9:21 Sag	1:12 AM AS 23:42 Sco	0:35 AM AS 22:06 Sco
Mars 1:33 Pisces	10:08 AM AS 10:00 Gem	11:24 AM AS 00:07 Cn	8:16 AM AS 22:57 Ari	7:32 AM AS 27:31 Pisc

Table 54 Times Directed Opposite the Apex Planets at Four Losses

Angles to Apex Point of Aspect Network at Event	Todd's Death 3-23-1958	Father's Death 11-22-1968	Burton's Death 8-5-1984	Mother's Death 9-11-1994
Elizabeth's Age at Event	26	36 ¾	52 ½	62 ½
Square Sun, Mercury, Neptune Opposition				
7:21 Gemini	8:24 PM MC 11:21 Can AS 8:42 Lib	7:37 PM MC 0:36 Canc AS 0:27 Libra	2:30 PM MC 14:51 Aries AS 6:26 Leo	1:53 PM MC 4:51 Aries AS 29:49 Can
7:21 Gemini	12:16 PM AS 11:21 Can MC 8:31 Pisc	11:26 AM AS 0:36 Canc MC 26:20 Aqua	8:02 AM AS 14:51 Aries MC 5:45 Capr	7:45 AM AS 4:51 Aries MC 1:51 Cap
7:21 Sagittarius	8:26 AM MC 11:21 Cap AS 28:21 Aries	7:39 AM MC 0:36 Capr AS 1:33 Aries	2:32 AM MC 14:51 Libra AS 13:44 Sag	1:55 AM MC 4:51 Libra AS 6:42 Sag
7:21 Sagittarius	4:35 AM AS 11:21 Cap MC 16:59 Scor	3:52 AM AS 0:36 Capr MC 6:00 Scor	8:59 PM AS 14:51 Libra MC 19:28 Can	8:02 PM AS 4:51 Libra MC 6:18 Can
Opposite Venus, Uranus				
17:03 Libra 17:08 Libra (combined)	1:05 AM MC 21:05 Virg AS 27:29 Scor	0:25 AM MC 10:20 Virg AS 20:24 Scor	11:21 PM MC 24:33 Leo AS 9:52 Scor	10:42 PM MC 14:33 Leo AS 3:01 Scor
17:03 Libra 17:08 Libra (combined)	6:44 PM AS 21:05 Virgo MC 18:22 Gem	5:43 PM AS 10:20 Virgo MC 4:03 Gem	4:13 PM AS 24:33 Leo MC 11:56 Taur	3:16 PM AS 14:33 Leo MC 27:08 Ari
Opposite Moon				
15:26 Taurus	2:47 PM MC 19:26 Aries AS 9:26 Leo	2:07 PM MC 8:41 Aries AS 2:21 Leo	1:10 PM MC 22:56 Pisc AS 21:45 Can	12:33 PM MC 12:56 Pis AS 14:38 Can
15:26 Taurus	8:09 AM AS 19:26 Aries MC 7:35 Cap	7:51 AM AS 8:41 Aries MC 3:20 Cap	7:25 AM AS 22:56 Pisc MC 27:17 Sag	7:08 AM AS 12:56 Pisc MC 23:21 Sag
Opposite Jupiter				
15:10 Aquarius	8:59 AM MC 19:10 Cap AS 14:43 Taur	8:13 AM MC 8:25 Cap AS 21:26 Aries	6:30 AM MC 14:40 Sag AS 22:54 Aqua	5:48 AM MC 4:40 Sag AS 4:29 Aqua
15:10 Aquarius	5:02 AM AS 19:10 Cap MC 23:47 Scor	4:24 AM AS 8:25 Cap MC 14:11 Scor	2:37 AM AS 14:40 Sag MC 16:07 Libr	1:44 AM AS 4:40 Sag MC 1:50 Libra

By examining the "derived birth times" from the Midheaven and Ascendant searches at key life events, only conjunctions with the natal Moon, likely involved in one of the "aspect network hooks", confirms the 2:00 AM approximate birth time. As for the Directed Angles making a conjunction to the "apex point" of planets in close hard aspect, it seems that only the Directed Midheaven conjunctions correspond to the selected life events in support of the approximate 2:00 AM birth time. The tally (below) of the times from Tables 7, 8 and 9 does, however, reveal a pattern that helps narrow to four time ranges, which interestingly confirm the results of the Jigsaw 2.0 search presented earlier in Table 3. The tally gives a single count for event 1 hits and a double count for events 2-4, since they are compounded by another major event close in time.

Table 55 Tally of the Results of MC, AS and Apex Searches From Several Important Events

Total	AM Event 1	AM Event 2	AM Event 3	AM Event 4	Hours	PM Event 1	PM Event 2	PM Event 3	PM Event 4	Total
6		2		4	12-1	1	8		2	11
9	1		4	4	1-2	4		2	2	8
10	2	4	4		2-3	1	2	2		5
2		2			3-4			2		2
3	1	2			4-5			2		2
3	1			2	5-6		2			2
2			2		6-7					0
16		4	2	10	7-8		2	4	4	10
22	2		14	6	8-9	2	4	2		8
11	1	10			9-10	2	4	2		8
8	6	0			10-11	2			2	4
14		6	8		11-12			2		2
106	14	32	34	26	Total	11	22	18	14	65

At this point, we have a preponderance of data supporting an AM birth time, over a PM time with 106 AM hits compared to only 65 for the PM times. In studying the results of the of "derived times", it is clear that we may reasonably narrow the rectification search to the few highlighted time ranges of:

1. 2-3 AM   **2.** 7-9:30 AM   **3.** 11 AM-1 PM   **4.** 7-9 PM

Keep in mind that we are accumulating evidence with several different methods of birth time confirmation. So far, the natal Moon search supports the 2:00-3:00 AM time, and after the Directed Midheaven, Ascendant and Apex Point searches, the early AM time range is still in the running. Refer to the Jigsaw 2.0 search using the same criteria at the beginning of the chapter (repeated below) and note the similarities.

Table 56 Jigsaw 2.2 Rectification Search (Repeated)

Time	Midheaven	Ascendant	Solar Arc	Sec Prog	Outer Transits	Overall
2:07 AM	7:00 -8:45 Lib	8:11 - 9:24 Sag	3/5	1/5	4/10	50%
6:02 AM	7:00-8:45 Sag	8:21-11:25 Aqu	3/8	1/2	5/9	47%
9:26 AM	24:30-26:30 Cp	24:09-27:21 Tau	7/8	6/8	3/11	81%
7:15 PM	24:30-26:30 Ge	25:46-27:18 Virg	2/5	2/5	6/10	43%

The results of our initial search echo the time ranges given by the Jigsaw 2.0 search and echo the range of conflicting reported birth times for Elizabeth. As we proceed from this narrowed time range, none of the reported birth times are remotely close to the 11 AM – 1 PM time range, or the 7 – 9:30 AM range, therefore it is safe to eliminate them from further searches. An even better reason to eliminate them from further searches comes in the understanding of cycles and aspect resonances. Note that the 7-9 AM times are in opposition to the 7-9 PM times, so one must be the resonance of the other, or the flip of the chart. On the other hand, the 2-3 AM time range is approximately in opposition to the 11 AM-1 PM range, showing another resonance or flip of the chart. Since only the 2-3 AM and 7-9 PM ranges span the reported birth times for Elizabeth, it follows that the others may safely be eliminated. If you remember the discussion of time principles presented earlier in this text, observe that approximately 6 hours separates each grouping of times, confirming that each grouping should resonate with the actual birth time by square or opposition aspect. We may now proceed with confidence in using additional techniques to choose a birth time from the 2-3 AM range or the 7-9 PM range for Elizabeth Taylor. Since the natal Sun differs ¾ of a degree, or 43 minutes, from the 2:00 AM position at 7:16 Pisces and the 7:00 PM position at 7:59 Pisces, we must search both of the approximate times to see which most closely describes the event at the right time. As well, it is important to determine which approximate time could be moved slightly ahead or back to best fit the life events and to derive the correct birth time.

Table 57 Progressed Sun Positions at Life Events for Elizabeth Taylor

Progr Sun 2 AM	Progr Sun 7 PM	Aspect Contacts of Prog Sun	Age at event	Corresponding Life Events	Date of Event
1-14-40 4-20-40	4-1-39	Inconj Jupiter Trine Moon	7	Family moved to America	4-15-39
			10	Debuted in movies	4-21-42
			10 ¾	Signs 7 year contract MGM	1-5-43
1-24-45	5-8-44	Trine Pluto	13	Writes children's book	6-1-46
	9-7-49	Trine Moon	16 ½	On cover of Time magazine	8-22-49
			18	Marries Nicky Hilton (1)	5-6-50
	5-27-51	Conjunct NN	19	Divorced/hospital-virus/breakdown	1-29-51
2-23-52		Conjunct NN	20	Marries Michael Wilding (2)	2-21-52
			20 ¾	Birth of son, Michael	1-6-53
1-31-55 3-19-55	4-18-54 7-31-54	Sesqui-sq Jupit Sextile Saturn	23	Birth of son, Christopher	2-27-55
5-8-55		Sesqui-sq Moon	23 ¾	Divorced/ Severe fall/ spinal surgery	11-4-55
			25	Marries Michael Todd (3)	2-2-57
			25 ½	Birth of daughter, Elizabeth	8-6-57
			26	Husband Todd dies in plane crash	3-23-58
			27	Marries Eddie Fisher (4)	5-12-59
7-23-61	10-1-60	Inconj Neptune	29	Emergency tracheotomy-near death	3-4-61
			29	1st Oscar "Butterfield 8"	4-17-61
			30	Year of scandal/ love affair w/Burton	All 62-63
		Sesqui-sq Moon	32	Married Richard Burton (5)	3-15-64
			35	2nd Oscar "Who's Afraid of Virginia Woolfe?"	4-10-67
			36	Receives Krupp diamond/ largest	5-17-68
			36 ½	Surgery/ hysterectomy	7-21-68
			36 ¾	Death of father	11-22-68
			37	Death of 1st husband, Hilton	2-5-69
4-5-70 7-12-70	6-21-69	Trine Jupiter Inconjunc Moon	37 ¾	Receives Cartier diamond/ huge	10-25-69

Table 57 continues

Progr Sun 2 AM	Progr Sun 7 PM	Aspect Contacts of Prog Sun	Age at event	Corresponding Life Events	Date of Event
3-2-72 4-2-72	6-30-71 5-24-72	Conj Uranus Conj Venus	40	Extravagant birthday party/diamond	2-27-72
5-18-75	8-29-74	Square Pluto	42	Divorced Burton	6-26-74
10-15-6	1-23-76	Sesqui-sq Neptu	43 ½	Remarries Burton (6)	10-10-75
			44 ½	Divorced Burton again	8-1-76
			44 ¾	Marries John Warner (7)	12-4-76
	2-1-80	Inconjun Moon	47 ½	Death of 2nd husband Wilding	7-16-79
7-30-82	10-31-81	Inconj SNode	50 ¾	Divorced from Warner	11-82
			51 ¾	Rehab/ alcohol/pills at Betty Ford	12-5-83
			52 ½	Collapses /news of Burton's death	8-5-84
9-12-85	1-24-85	Square Saturn	53 ½	Begins AIDS crusade/ fundraising	8-6-85
12-25-6	11-7-86	Sextile Mars	55	AIDS Research nat'l chairwoman	3-3-87
			55	Receives Legion of Honor award	5-14-87
			56 ½	Returns to rehab for alcohol/pill abuse	10-88
			58	Collapse/viralpneumonia/Neardeath	4 & 5-90
6-6-91	2-27-92	Trine Neptune	59 ½	Marries Larry Fortensky (8)	10-6-91
11-8-92 1-9-93	11-17-92 9-6-93	Sextile Sun Sextile Mercury	61	Life Achievement Award/ film	3-11-93
			62	Hip replacement surgery	3-24-94
			62 ½	Death of Mother	9-11-94
			64	Divorced Fortensky	6-96

* Mean Nodes were used   **Only near time hits are highlighted

Note that the 2:00 PM contacts to the close Venus/ Uranus conjunction occur in close order because only 5 minutes separate their conjunction; whereas the 7:00 PM contacts take several months to span the distance between Uranus and Venus because, at 17 hours later, Venus has moved 50 minutes further away. As a result, any progressing planet will take much longer to make contact with Uranus and then Venus in the 7:00 PM chart. The same is true for the Sun/ Mercury conjunction. At 2:00 PM, only 10 minutes of arc separate them, while at 7:00 PM, 46 minutes is the difference the progressing planet must travel. It is clear from the

Progressed Sun search that 10 events line up with appropriate aspects and planetary indicators at the time of events for the 2:00 AM approximate time, and only 3 events line up for the 7:00 PM time range, so from this point the focus is on refining the 2:00 AM time to within a minute of accuracy. The Sun is quite useful in this intermediate search because the reported birth times span nearly three-quarters of a day. At the Sun's progressed movement of 1 degree a year, equivalent to 1 day in the ephemeris, the 19 ½ hour span between the two speculative birth times for Elizabeth translates to about 46 minutes of arc, or about 9+ months of calendar time difference in the activation of inner planets. The difference is great enough to allow one time to stand out over the other when measured by events.

Now, Run Secondary Progressions for Smaller Increments of the Narrowed Time Range

For the next search, run a Secondary Progression Graphic for Elizabeth Taylor for 1958 – 1968 and 1983 – 1994 for each of the two best birth times supported by events, 2:00 AM and 2:50 AM.

Figure 159 Secondary Progression Graphic for Elizabeth Taylor 1958-1968

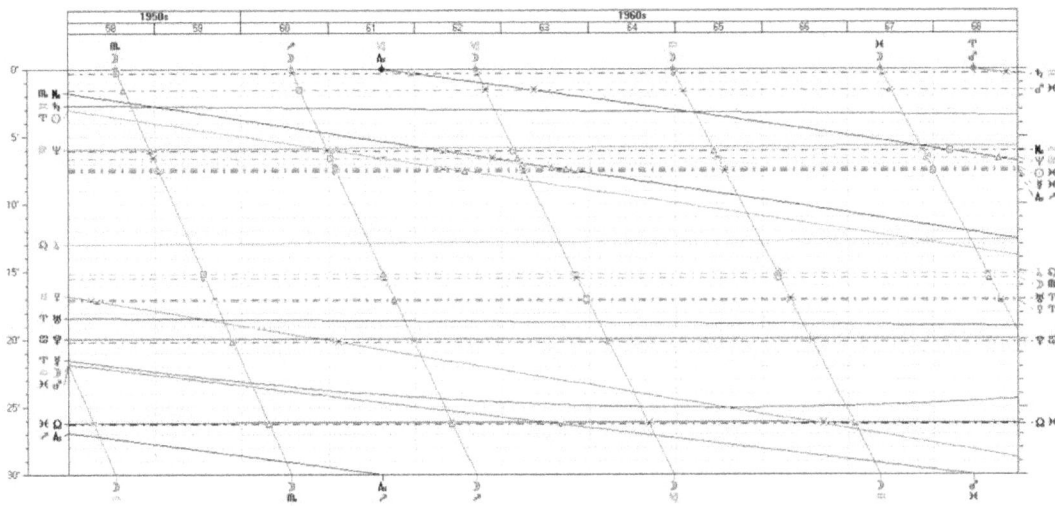

With a ruler, highlight (vertically) the month of the events of Mike Todd's death on 3-23-1958, Liz's hysterectomy surgery on 7-21-1968 and the death of her father on 11-22-1968 as closely as possible with the width of the pen accounting for a reasonable orb of a month either way. Do the same highlighting for the important events in the Figure 159 Secondary Progression Graphic for the dates of her drug rehab on 12-5-1983, the news of Burton's death on 8-5-1984, her near death bout with viral pneumonia during April and May of 1990, her hip replacement surgery on 3-24-1994, and the death of her mother on 9-11-1994.

Figure 160 Secondary Progression Graphic for Elizabeth Taylor 1983-1994

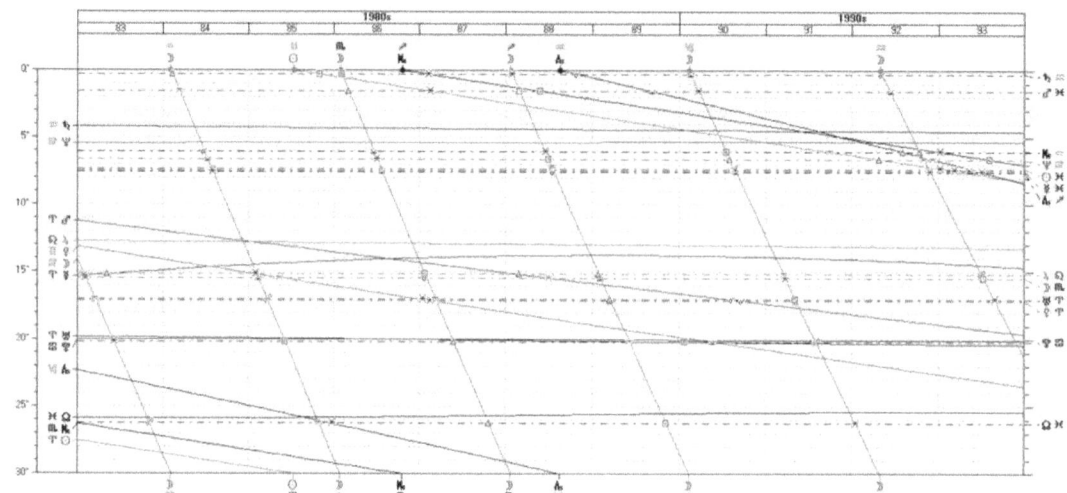

Record the active Secondary Progressions in major hard aspect to natal planets, Angles and the Moon's nodes in a table that includes each probable time set for the 4 key event years we earlier selected to search. More ambitious souls may elect to include progressed to progressed planets and points in the search as well with the goal of finding which time reveals more appropriate hard aspect contacts involving the Angles at the most painful life events.

Table 58 Secondary Progression of Angles, Planets and Nodes for Two Birth Times

	2:00 AM				2:50 AM			
Event	Conjun	Square	Oppos	Inconj	Conjun	Square	Oppos	Inconj
Todd died in plane crash 3-23-58		pMoon/ Saturn pASC/ nNNod		pMoon/ nNNod		pMoon/ nSaturn		pMoon/ nNNod pVen/ nASC
Hysterectomy 7-21-68				pMoon/ nJupit				pMoon/ nJupit
Father's death 11-22-1968						pMoon/ nASC		pMoon/ nMC
Drug Rehab 12-5-1983			pMC/ nNNod	pMoon/ nMars		pASC/ nJupit		pMoon/ nMars
Burton's death 8-5-1984	pMoon/ nMC			pMoon/ nSun nMerc				pMoon/ nSun nMerc

214   The New Complete Book of Chart Rectification

Table 58 continues

Event	2:00 AM Conjun	Square	Oppos	Inconj	2:50 AM Conjun	Square	Oppos	Inconj
Hip surgery 3-24-1994	pMC/ nASC	pMC/ nSun					pASC/ nNept	
		nMerc						
Mother's death 9-11-1994	pMoon/ nMars	pMars/ nPluto			pMoon/ nMars pASC/ nSun nMerc	pMars/ Pluto		

Without providing the same graphics for the 2:50 AM time in this text, the results of that search is compared with the 2:00 AM search. A study of Table 57 reveals only slightly more Secondary Progression hits in hard aspect to the Angles for the 2:00 AM time, though aspects to the planets and Nodes are the same for either time. Nonetheless, several "stand-outs" set the 2:00 AM time ahead of the 2:50 AM time. At Mike Todd's death, the progressed Ascendant square the Moon's Nodes of the 2:00 AM time is much more telling of the tragedy and its effects on Elizabeth than the progressed Venus inconjunct the Ascendant of the 2:50 AM time. At her father's death, the 2:50 AM time does show the progressed Moon square the Ascendant and inconjunct the Midheaven, whereas the 2:00 AM time shows no progressions for the event. However, the Outer Transits shown later in Table 58 quite adequately describe the event in support of the 2:00 AM birth time.

The progressed Moon conjunct Liz's 2:00 AM Midheaven at Richard Burton's death is much more telling than no progressed aspects for the 2:50 AM time. And certainly, the progressed Midheaven conjunct Liz's natal Ascendant at the same time it squared her progressed Midheaven, progressed Sun and progressed Mercury for the 2:00 AM time far outweigh the progressed Ascendant opposite Neptune at her hip replacement surgery for the 2:50 AM time. At her mother's death, the Secondary Progressions of the Moon to conjunct Mars, and Mars to square Pluto alone adequately describe the loss. The additional progressed Ascendant conjunct natal Sun and Mercury for the 2:50 time better describe her professional success in the AIDS crusade than the surgery and tragic loss. Thus, the 2:00 AM birth time is again confirmed, though the 2:50 AM time provided a tempting alternate choice. Most astrology software includes such advanced features as Graphics, which greatly aid any birth time rectification search.

Now, Use Outer Transits to Narrow to One or Two Promising Times

From all of the searches run thus far for Elizabeth Taylor, only the 2:00 – 3:00 AM time range is consistently synchronous with life events. One may go directly to running Outer transits to the 2:00 AM chart for Elizabeth or search further. If the latter is chosen, run natal charts set for 10-minute intervals within the range, for: 2:00; 2:10; 2:20; 2:30; 2:40; 2:50 and 3:00 AM, then create a table for the Angles at each of those times, noting Outer Transits in major hard aspect to each set of Angles for the chosen major event years:

1958 – Mike Todd's sudden death

1968 – Drug and alcohol rehab and Richard Burton's death

1984 – (Gift of the Krupp diamond), hysterectomy and death of father 1994 – Hip surgery, death of mom

Table 59 provides an example set according to the noted criteria, though certainly one might choose to set up the table in a different format or even as a "spreadsheet". The main point is to easily compare the Outer Transits in hard aspect to natal or progressed planets, Angles, or the Moon's Nodes at the major life events with particular attention to hard aspect contact to the Angles that makes one time stand out over another. It is clear that the 2:00 AM "mother's memory" birth time for Elizabeth holds up rather well; however, the transits overwhelmingly are more appropriate and prominent for the 1:57 AM birth time and even a 2:07 AM birth time, because of the prominence of natal Angle involvement at the important life events.

Table 59 Outer Transits at Selected Events Narrow the Possible Birth Time Range

	Transits	All Times	1:57	2:00	2:10	2:20	2:30	2:40	2:50	3:05
Todd died in plane crash 3-23-58	Jup 0 Scorp Sat 25 Sag Uran 7 Leo Nept 4 Scorp Pluto 0 Virgo	Sq Sat Sq pNN Inc Sun Inc Merc Op Mars	Conj pMC							
Hyster-ectomy 7-21-68	Jup 6 Virgo Sat 25 Aries Uran 26 Virgo	Op Sun Op Merc Inc pSN Con pSN	Squ ASC							Sq ASC
	Nept 23 Scor Pluto 21 Virg									
Father's death 11-22-1968	Jup 1 Libra Sat 19 Aries Uran 3 Libra Nept 26 Scor Pluto 25 Virg	Con MC Inc Mars Sq Pluto Con Ven Con Ura Con pSN	Squ pAS Con MC Con pMC							

216 The New Complete Book of Chart Rectification

Event	Transits	Aspects							
Drug Rehab 12-5-1983	Jup 4 Sagitt Sat 11 Scorp Uran 9 Sagitt Nept 28 Sagit Pluto 1 Scorp	Inc Pluto Inc pMar Sq Nep Sq Sun Sq Merc Sq pMoo Sq NN Sq Satur			Con ASC				Con
Burton's death 8-5-1984	Jup 4 Capric Sat 10 Scorp Uran 9 Sagitt Nept 29 Sagit Pluto 29 Libr	Sq Nept Sq Sun Sq Merc Sq pMoo Sq Satur	Sq MC		Con ASC				
Hip surgery 3-24-1994	Jup 13 Scorp Sat 6 Pisces	Con Moo Sq pJup Con Nep Opp Sun Op Merc	Sq ASC						
	Uran 25 Cap Nept 23 Cap Pluto 28 Scor								
Mother's death 9-11-1994	Jup 11 Scorp Sat 8 Pisces Uran 22 Cap Nep 20 Cap Pluto 25 Scor	Op pSun Con Sun Con Mer Op Pluto Sq pMars Sq pUran Op Pluto Sq pMars Sq pUran	Sq ASC Sq pMC						

Why Are Time Twins So Different?

Figure 161 Transit Graphic Ephemeris for 3-23-1968 Surgery and 11-22-1968 Dad's Death

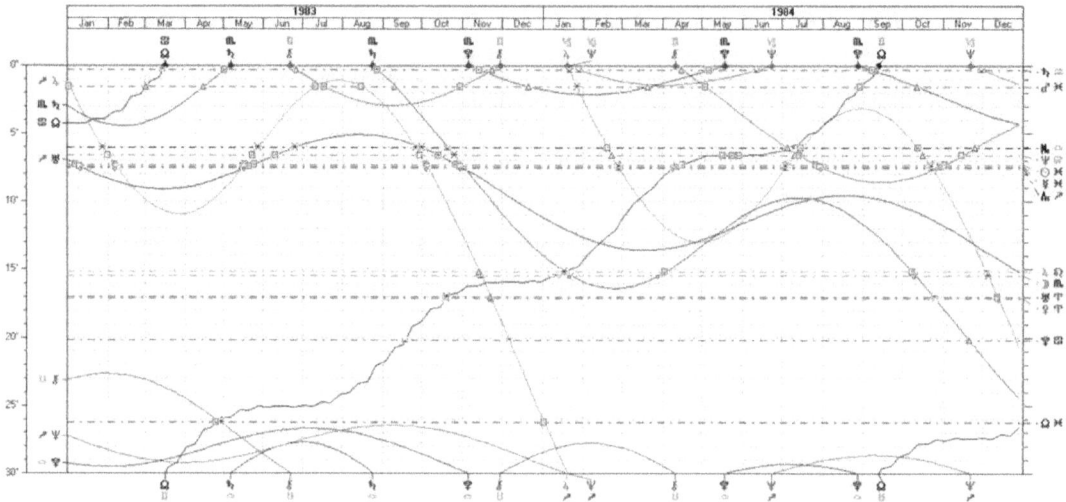

Figure 162 Transit Graphic Ephemeris for Events: 12-5-83 Rehab and 8-5 84 Burton Death

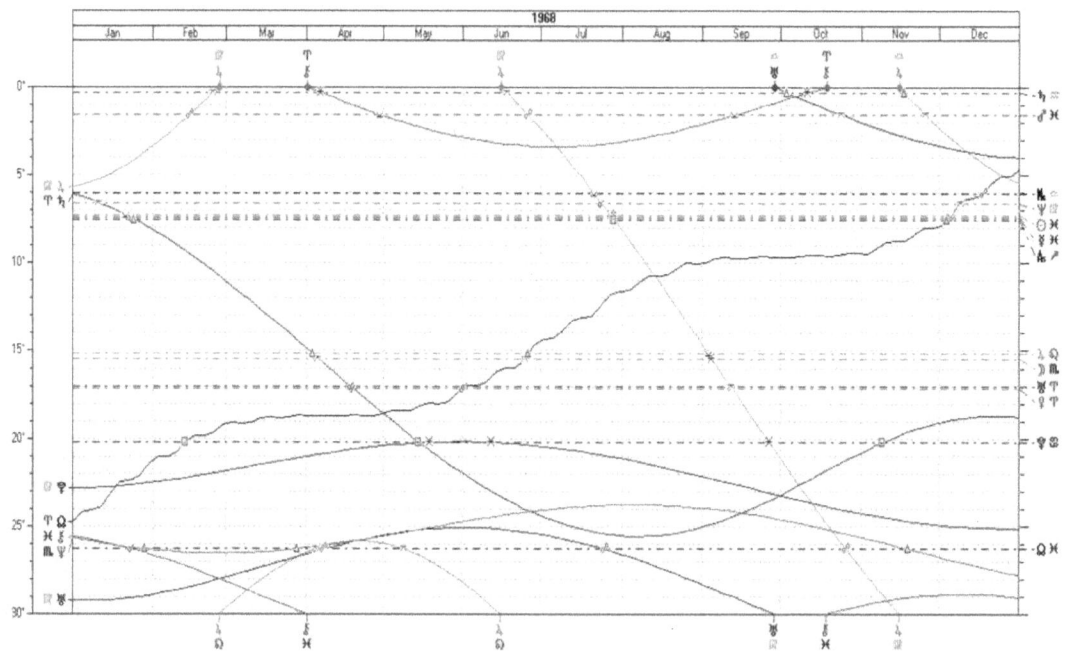

Figure 163 Transit Graphic Ephemeris for 3-24-1994 Surgery and 9-11-1994 Mom's Death

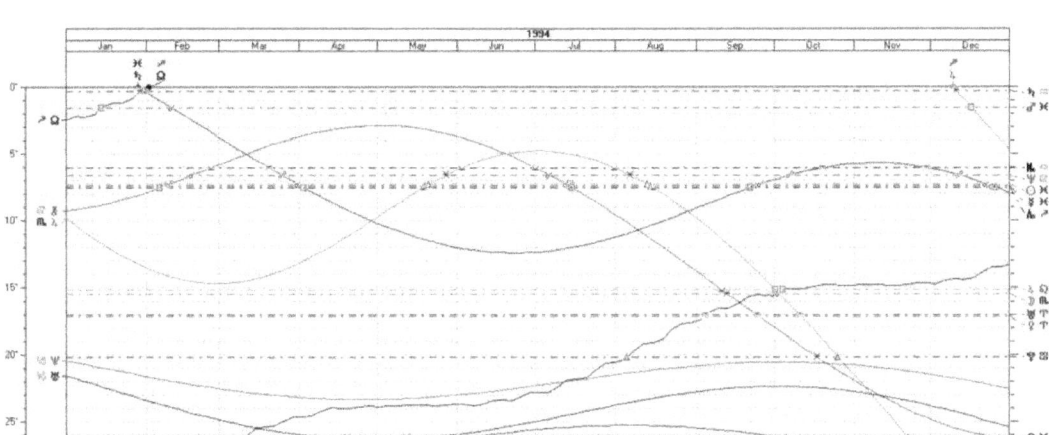

Back to Basics, Retrograde and Station Periods Greatly Extend the Effect of Any Transit

The shadow period is defined as the sensitized degree area marked by a planet transiting, then returning by retrograde motion and then again by direct movement. The degrees that mark the retrograde station and the direct station points define the whole sensitized degree range, including the whole span of degrees in between. Therefore, the effect of an outer planet transit may be felt even though the transiting planet is not yet, or past exact in its aspect, orb notwithstanding. Each of the Outer Planets moves at a different rate and sensitizes a varying number of degrees during its direct-retrograde-direct period according to its own cycle. Obviously, when two or more planets cast their "shadow" on planets or personal points in the natal chart and these patterns occur within a narrow time span, the effect is greatly compounded with much more prominent life experiences in focus. A brief synopsis of the distinctive characteristics of the Jupiter through Pluto planetary cycles follows, with a more detailed discussion found in Appendix D.

The Jupiter Retrograde Period: During the average Jupiter transit of one sign per year only one-third of the sign, 10 degrees, is sensitized by the Jupiter's retrograde motion. The whole sensitized area is called the "shadow" because those degrees receive three hits from the planetary transit emphasizing what might otherwise pass unnoticed. In the case of Jupiter, the effect of the "shadow" lasts approximately 10 months; whereas the other 20 degrees of each sign that receive a single pass of Jupiter lasts about 5 to 10 days. Allowing for a one-degree orb of influence, one could easily extend the activating potential of the planet to about 2 weeks, depending upon Jupiter's speed. From our earth point of view, Jupiter moves 40 - 42 degrees direct, 10 degrees retrograde, 40+ degrees direct, 10 retrograde, and so on, as it moves through the zodiac. One year in each sign, Jupiter moves around the zodiac in 12 years.

Saturn Retrograde Period: In the average Saturn transit more than half of each sign, 16 degrees in all, is hit three times by the retrograde and direct motion taking nearly 11 months to complete the extended stay in the sensitized "shadow" degree range. No wonder we tend to take notice when an extended Saturn transit activates key areas of the chart. On the other hand, the other 14 degrees of each sign that only receive one Saturn pass during the cycle are each activated for about 7 to 14 days, obviously much easier by comparison. From our earth point of view, Saturn moves 21- 22 degrees direct, 7 degrees retrograde, 21+ degrees direct, 7 retrograde, and so on, as it moves through the zodiac in about 29 years.

Uranus Retrograde Period: Beginning with the Uranus transit, no one escapes without facing the impact of 3 hits to every planet or chart point. Of the average 7 years for Uranus to fully transit a sign, every single degree is retraced by the direct-retrograde-direct cycle. The duration of the Uranus transit to move through the sensitized retrograde and "shadow" degree area is always 17 months. Basically, every planet or personal point in the chart is in a "shadow" or "sensitized area" when Uranus is within 4 degrees. From our earth point of view, Uranus moves 8 degrees direct, 4 degrees retrograde, 8 degrees direct, 4 degrees retrograde, and so on, as it moves through the zodiac.

Neptune Retrograde Period: Like the Uranus transit, no one escapes a Neptune transit without facing the impact of at least 3 to 5 hits during its stay in aspect to a natal planet or chart point. Of the average 14 years for Neptune to fully transit a sign, every single degree is retraced by the direct-retrograde-direct cycle. As a result, the better part of 2 years is colored by Neptune's influence as it moves 5 degrees direct, 3 retrograde, 5 direct, 3 retrograde, and so on, as it works its way through the zodiac. In every Neptune retrograde cycle of 5 degrees, one degree in the span is hit 5 times because of the double retracing that occurs at the retrograde stations. Consequently, a Neptune transit to a personal planet or Angle near the Neptune's station points most certainly ushers in a doubly heightened period of confusion, delusion or illusion for the better part of 2 years, depending upon the aspect and the planets contacted.

The duration of the Neptune transit to move through the sensitized retrograde and "shadow" degree area is actually about 18 – 20 months depending upon whether Neptune is slow or fast in its cycle over several generations. And like the Uranus transit, no matter where one starts counting the cycle, Neptune still takes at least 18 months to complete. Basically, every degree is in a "shadow" sensitized area when Neptune is within 3-4 degrees.

Pluto Retrograde Period: Like the Uranus and Neptune transits, no one escapes a Pluto transit without facing the impact of at least three hits to any activated planets or points. Of the average 20 years for Pluto to fully transit a sign, every single degree is retraced by the retrograde cycle. From the mid-20th century to mid-21st century, Pluto is fast in its orbit, so for that time span Pluto moves 5 degrees direct, 3 retrograde, 5 direct, 3 retrograde for 14 years in that part of its 248-year cycle through the zodiac. When Pluto moves into the slower phase of its cycle, the number of direct degree motion will lessen to about 4 and stretch that part of Pluto's cycle to a bit more than 20 years.

Like Neptune, in every Pluto retrograde cycle of 5 degrees one degree is hit 5 times and the other within a few minutes of 5 times, because of the double retracing that occurs at the degree of the retrograde stations. Therefore, a Pluto transit to a personal planet or Angle most certainly ushers in a period of intensity and focus for 2 years or more, depending upon the aspect and the planets contacted. The duration of the Pluto transit to move through the sensitized retrograde and "shadow" degree area is currently about 18 – 20 months and will increase when Pluto slows in its cycle. Basically, every degree is in a "shadow" sensitized area when Pluto is within 3-4 degrees.

Conclusions On Extenuating Circumstances on the Impact of Outer Transits

There are transits, and then there are transits! The retrograde, station and shadow periods of each planet's motion are of paramount importance in guiding the astrologer to emphasize the importance of a transit or not. Planets and personal points in the natal chart that are aspected by degree at the Stationary Retrograde or Stationary Direct points of an outer planet transit are dramatically activated. And more than one such transiting outer planet activation of the natal chart in a close range of time signals an even more extreme situation, depending upon the aspect and the involved planet and its natal aspect network. There is a very great difference in the astrologer's interpretation of an 11-month visit of a Saturn transit over a personal planet or Angle as opposed to only a few weeks of a single pass; or a simultaneous "stacking up" of a Neptune station on the same or another personal planet or Angle at the same time to amplify stress and extend the challenge over a couple of years. It is just such nuanced judgment by the astrologer that distinguishes a computer chart interpretation from the expert direct consultation.

Retrograde and Station Periods Mark Outer Transit "Shadows" for Elizabeth Taylor

The following two 5-Year Transit Graphs of Figures, 164 and 165, reveal a distinct difference in Outer Transits to the Angles for Elizabeth's 2:00 AM "mother's memory" birth time and the 2:07 AM rectified time reported in Astro.com for events of the early 1990's. Even though the transits are well within the "shadow" range at the 2:00 AM time, note that the Ascendant and Midheaven for the 2:07 AM time is just enough different to provide direct transit hits for the key events of that 5-year period.

Figure 164 5-Year Outer Transit Graphic for Elizabeth Taylor – 2:00 AM Birth Time

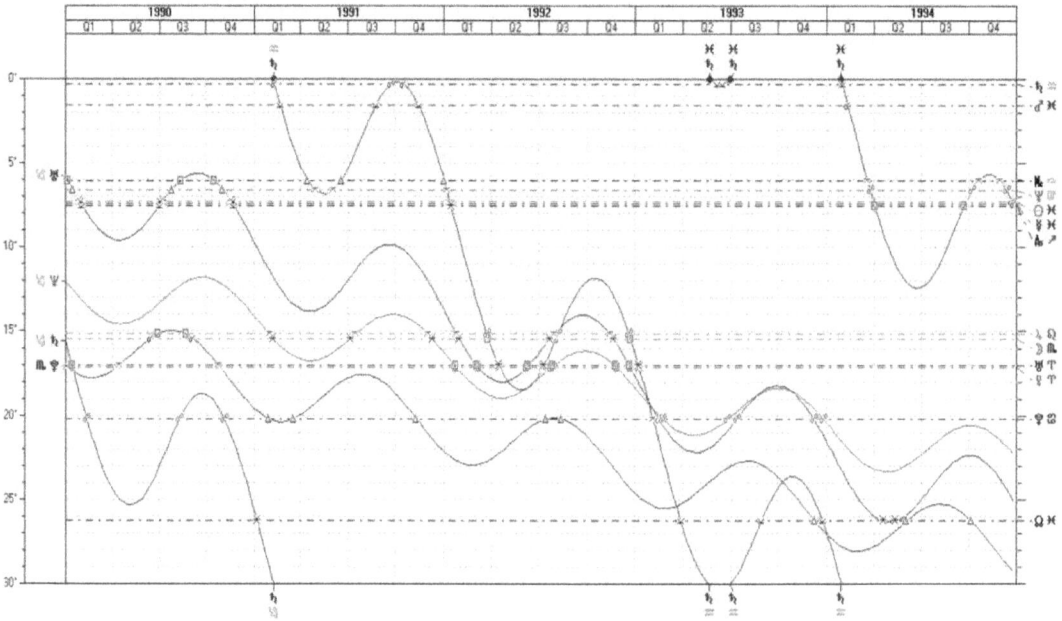

Figure 165 5-Year Outer Transit Graphic for Elizabeth Taylor – 2:07 AM Birth Time

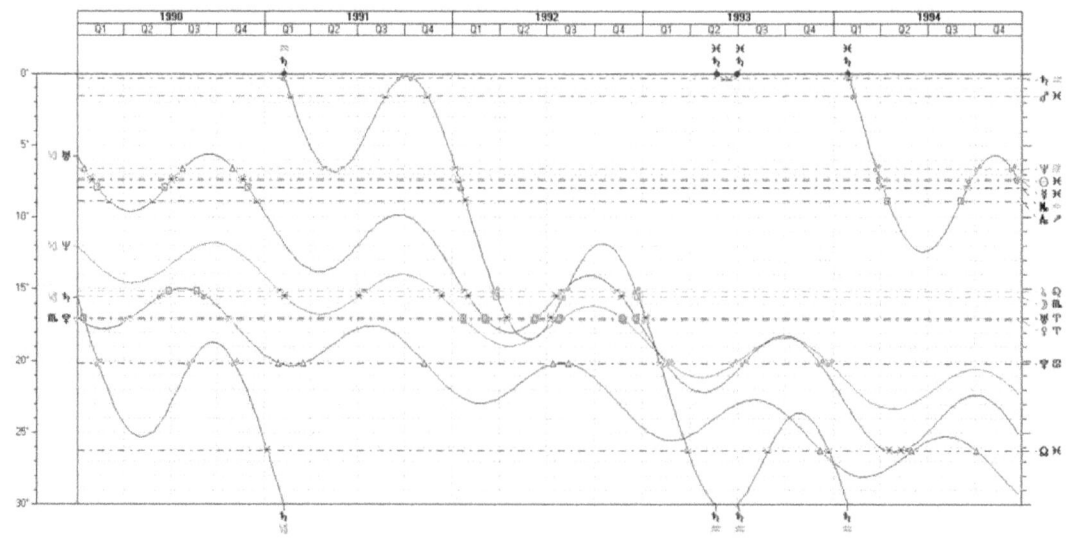

Table 60 Four Important Events for Elizabeth Taylor

39	Collapse/viralpneumonia/Neardeath	Hollywood, CA	58	4 & 5-1990
40	Marries Larry Fortensky (8)	Santa Maria, CA	59 ½	10-6-1991
41	Life Achievement Award/ film	Hollywood, CA	61	3-11-1993
42	Hip replacement surgery	Hollywood, CA	62	3-24-1994
43	Death of Mother	Rancho Mirage, CA	62 ½	9-11-1994

In Figure 164, the graphic of outer transits for a 2:00 AM birth time shows Uranus transiting square to Elizabeth's natal Midheaven hitting in early January and early fall of 1990 at her collapse and near scrape with death of viral pneumonia, which did not actually occur until April and May of 1990. However, in Figure 8 the graphic of outer transits for a 2:07 AM birth time shows Uranus transiting square to Elizabeth's natal Midheaven exactly at the time of the near=death event in April and May. Further, the outer transits for the 2:07 AM birth time bring transiting Saturn inconjunct the Midheaven and square the Ascendant nearer to the time of Liz's hip replacement surgery and her mother's death; whereas the 2:00 AM time sets those transits as exact a bit earlier in March and a bit later in mid-September, not aligned to the actual event. Besides, the 2:07 AM birth time is a double hit with both the Ascendant and Midheaven being appropriately activated at the time of the actual events. Thus, the 2:07 AM birth time looks to be the most promising for consistent results in forecasting for Ms. Taylor.

If You are Still Undecided on the Best Birth Time, Run Solar Eclipses for the Events

Back to the rectification for Elizabeth Taylor, by now you have a pretty good idea of the best time that corresponds with her life events, but one last search may help confirm the results. The Solar Eclipses serve as general activation triggers to emphasize the affairs described by a house, or more personally when a planet, Angle or Moon's Nodes are contacted by hard aspect. Since the Eclipses occur two or three times per year and influence a 3 to 5-degree orb (6-10 degree range) for about 6 months, the eclipse effect is greatly compounded if it also activates an Angle, planet or point by major hard aspect, particularly in the 4th harmonic (conjunction, square and opposition).

Table 61 Solar Eclipse Contacts at Key Life Events for Elizabeth Taylor 2:00 AM Birth

	Event	Event Date	Age	Eclipse	Aspect/Planet/Angle
1	Family moved to America	4-15-1939	7	29 Aries	Inconjunct SNode
2	On cover of Time magazine	8-22-1949	16 ½	8 Taurus	Sextile Sun Sextile Mercury Trine Neptune
3	Marries Nicky Hilton (1)	5-6-1950	18	27 Pisces	Conjunct NNode
4	Divorced/hospital-virus/breakdown	1-29-1951	19	19 Virgo	Inconjunct Venus Inconjunct Uranus
5	Divorced/Severe fall/ spinal surgery	11-4-1955	23 ¾	28 Gemin	Square NNode Square SNode
6	Husband, Todd dies in plane crash	3-23-1958	26	0 Scorpio	
7	Emergency tracheotomy/near death	3-4-1961	29	26 Aquar	Inconjunct SNode
8	1st Oscar "Butterfield 8"	4-17-1961	29	26 Aquar	Inconjunct SNode
9	2nd Oscar "Who's Afraid of Virginia Woolfe?"	4-10-1967	35	20 Scorp	Trine Pluto
10	Surgery/ hysterectomy	7-21-1968	36 ½	8 Aries	Inconjunct Neptune
11	Death of father	11-22-1968	36 ¾	29 Virgo	Conjunct SNode
12	Rehab/ alcohol/pills at Betty Ford	12-5-1983	51 ¾	12 Sagitt	Conjunct Ascendant Square Sun Square Mercury Square Neptune
13	Collapses at news of Burton's death	8-5-1984	52 ½	9 Gemini	Conjunct Descendant Square Sun Square Mercury Square Neptune
14	Collapse/ viral pneumonia/ near death	4 & 5 1990	58	7 Aquar	Inconjunct Neptune
15	Life Achievement Award/ film	3-11-1993	61	2 Capric	Sextile Mars
16	Hip replacement surgery	3-24-1994	62	22 Scorp	Trine Pluto
17	Death of Mother	9-11-1994	62 ½	20 Taurus	Conjunct Chiron Sextile Pluto
18	Divorce of Fortensky	6-1996	64	28 Aries	Inconjunct S Node

Note that the Eclipses in effect at the time of the Liz's most difficult life events are most consistent with the 2:00 AM "mother's memory" birth time even, though the time range from 1:57 AM and 2:07 AM is still viable. If we choose to rectify the birth time to 1:57 AM, more consistent with the Outer Transit hits, the 6 Sagittarius Ascendant is still in range for the Eclipse conjunction to an Angle, though the Eclipses are closer to exact in aspect at a 2:00 AM or even a 2:07 AM birth time with a 9 Sagittarius Ascendant shown in Table 60, events 12 and 13. My preference is for accepting the birth time with the most confirmation to important life events from Directions, Secondary Progressions, Outer Transits and Eclipses. In this rectification study for Elizabeth Taylor, the evidence best supports the 1:57 AM, 2:00 AM and 2:07 AM birth time range, but all factors weighed, I believe I will use the 2:07 AM as the best, knowing that the other items searched are still in close "orb of aspect" range as well as in the "shadow" range of the relevant Outer Transits. Nonetheless, one can easily justify support for using the "mother's memory" 2:00 AM time as the midpoint within the range that brings the exact aspect hits within the effective 1-degree orb limit.

Rectification Example Two – Singer Johnny Cash Time Twin

- Set the Working Birth Time for Johnny and Find the Hard Aspect Hooks
- Create the list of Notable Life Events
- Find the Dwad Placement of Johnny's Natal Moon
- Begin the Search to Derive the Birth chart Angles from Life Events
- Tally Preliminary Search Results to Narrow the Possible Birth Time Range
- Search the Secondary Progressions to Confirm Early Results
- Search the Outer Planet Transits to Confirm Early Results
- Search Solar Eclipses for Key Events for Final Birth Time Confirmation

Singer Johnny Cash provides a similar example as Elizabeth Taylor's where the mother gives an approximate birth time for him of 7:30 AM "from memory". The birth certificate, according to Astro.com, is in hand and the date and place is confirmed by Bob Garner, his biographer. Since other conflicting birth times have not appeared, we may safely assume that the mother's memory is not too far off the mark. The recent Michael Streissguth biography of Cash does not give a birth time for him at all. However, any time a birth that is given as even number may be a rounded-off time to the hour, half-hour or quarter-hour. In such instances, the astrologer and client should seriously consider rectifying the time to accurately correspond with life events. In the instance of Johnny Cash, where there are no reported conflicting times, the search may reveal only a small birth time variation from the "mother's memory" which makes the rectification search very much easier than the 19 ½ hour search conducted for Elizabeth Taylor or the 24-hour searches for Jimmy Swaggart and the female client studied in earlier chapters.

To get a second opinion from Jigsaw 2.2 up front, as in the case of Elizabeth Taylor, I entered the list of major life events for Johnny Cash into the Brady/Dawson Jigsaw 2.2 program for "Research and Rectification" and searched the time range from 7:00 AM to 8:00 AM on February 26, 1932 using the 4th harmonic (conjunction, square and opposition) and applied Outer Planet Transits; Solar Arc Directions; and Secondary Progressions with the following results:

Table 62 Jigsaw 2.2 Suggested Chart Birth Times and Angles for Johnny Cash

Time	Midheaven	Ascendant	Solar Arc	Sec Prog	Outer Transits	Overall
7:31 AM	25:00 -27:15 Sag	21:38 – 25:23 Pi	7/11	2/4	3/10	57%

Already it is clear that our rectification search will be easy and only a small modification, if any, will adjust the birth time to accurately correspond to life events. Nonetheless, it is always safest to begin the search by setting a chart for the most reliably reported birth time, or in the mid-range of all of the possible times. Since no competing birth times are offered for Cash, the search should begin with the birth time of the "mother's memory", 7:30 AM, to confirm that the Moon is part of the Sun/Mercury/Neptune natal 1-degree close aspect opposition pattern.

Set the Working Birth Time for Johnny and Find the Hard Aspect Hooks

From the 7:30 AM time of his "mother's memory", the qualifying aspect networks in John Cash's chart of Figure 9 involve:

1. Sun/Mercury conjunction – approximately 17' orb
   Sun/Mercury opposite Neptune – 8' to 10' minutes orb with the
   Moon very likely in 1-degree trine to Sun/Mercury and sextile Neptune

2. Venus conjunct Uranus – 6' minutes orb
   Venus/Uranus semi-square Mars – 35' to 41' minutes orb
   Venus/Uranus trine Jupiter – 1:52 to 1:58 orb

3. MC may possibly be within 1 degree of square the
   Moon's Nodes, but it is a less reliable "hook" for the early searches

With the Moon suspect of being within 1-degree orb, and the Angles yet untested, the first two multiple-planet configurations do provide us with very good "aspect hooks" into the chart to begin the rectification search.

Figure 166 Johnny Cash Natal Chart Set for 7:30 AM

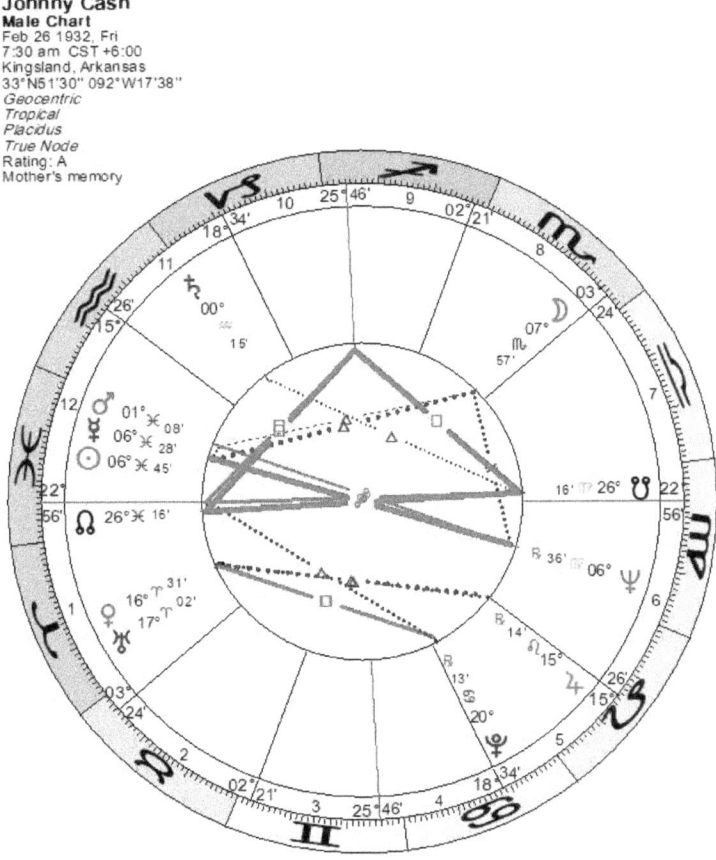

Once the "working chart" is set, again, we begin the process of rectification by creating a list of important life events with dates for John R. Cash, named for his father, J. R. Cash. The information for the list of life events was culled from the 2006 biography released by Michael Streissguth entitled, *Johnny Cash, the Biography*. Rather than pose the events in narrative form, the table format allows the astrologer to research the events in chronological order to more easily spot patterns of events that may be correlated with patterns of planetary aspects in the natal chart as they are activated and unfold in time.

Table 63 Notable Life Events for Johnny Cash

	Event	Place	Age	Date	Time
1	Family Moved	Dyess, Arkansas	3	3-15-1935	
2	**House Flooded/ Lost/ Forced Move**	**Dyess, Arkansas**	**5**	**4-10-1937**	
3	Older brother hurt/ skill saw through abdomen/ John witnessed/ felt guilty/ brother didn't speak to him on death bed/ father said to John, "Too bad it wasn't you."	Dyess, Arkansas	12	5-15-1944	
4	**Jack died**	**Dyess, Arkansas**	**12**	**5-20-1944**	
5	Performed songs at high school graduation	Dyess, Arkansas	18	5-19-1950	
6	Enlisted in Air Force	Dyess, Arkansas	18	7-7-1950	
7	Assigned to top secret decoding work	Germany	19	4-1-1951	
8	**Marriage to pre-war sweetheart, Vivian Liberto**	**San Antonio, Texas**	**22½**	**8-7-1954**	
9	**His band, Johnny Cash and the Tennessee Two, appeared on radio and recorded first record**	**Dyess, Arkansas**	**22½**	**10-1954**	
10	Daughter, Roseanne, born	Dyess, Arkansas	23	5-1955	
11	First record released, Cry, Cry, Cry	Dyess, Arkansas	23	6-21-1955	
12	**On top of country music charts**	**Dyess, Arkansas**	**23½**	**12-1-1955**	
13	First appeared on TV/ Louisiana Hayride – a big success	Dyess, Arkansas	23¾	11-13-1955	
14	Folsom Prison Blues/ top of country charts	Memphis, TN	24	2-10-1956	
15	**Arrested for spousal abuse (contrary to myth, he never served prison time)**	**Memphis, TN**	**24**	**3-1956**	
16	Daughter, Kathy, born	Memphis, TN	24	3-1956	
17	Opened at Grand Ole' Opry	Nashville, TN	24	7-14-1956	
18	**Appeared on Jackie Gleason Show/ launched national career**	**New York, NY**	**25**	**6-1957**	
19	Left Sun Records and went to Columbia Records	Nashville, TN	26½	7-1958	
20	Daughter, Cindy, born	Memphis, TN	26	3-1958	

21	Began heavy drug use-amphetamines (1958-1967 worst time)	Nashville, TN	26	5-1958	
22	**Moved to California**	Memphis, TN	26 ½	7-1958	
23	Released 3 hit albums	Los Angeles, CA	27	6-1959	
24	Guest on The Ed Sullivan Show	New York, NY	27 ¾	11-1959	
25	Best recording sessions of his career- most creative	Los Angeles, CA Los Angeles, CA	29 29	2-24-1961 2-27-1961	
26	Daughter Tara, born	Los Angeles, CA	33	8-24-1961	
27	**Appeared at Carnegie Hall/ totally drugged out/ was a flop!**	**New York, NY**	34	**5-10-1962**	
28	**Full-blown affair with June Carter/ both married to others/ scandal**	**Los Angeles, CA**	30 ½	**10-1962**	
29	Friends with Bob Dylan/ wrote protest song, Ballad of Ira Hayes	New York, NY	32	3-1964	
30	Appeared at Newport Folk Festival/ very successful crossover	New York, NY	32 ½	7-25-1964	
31	**Accidentally starts forest fire/ loses lawsuit/ fined $82,000**	**Los Angeles, CA**	33 ½	**6-1965**	
32	**Arrested on federal drug charges/ in the news/ drug use now public**	**El Paso, Texas**	33 ¾	**10-4-1965**	
33	Racists boycotted his music/thought his wife Vivian was black	Mobile, Alabama	34	1-10/1966	
34	Vivian files for divorce	Los Angeles, CA	34 ½	9-1966	
35	**June Carter gives ultimatum about NO drugs, move closer to his children/ Johnny drug-free 'til 1976**	**Los Angeles, CA**	35 ½	**10-21-1967**	
36	**Performed live from Folsom Prison/ a huge hit/ Live album recorded also hit/ recorded prisoner's song**	**Los Angeles, CA**	36	**1-13-1968**	
37	Married June Carter, his soul mate	Hendersonville, AK	36	3-1-1968	
38	**Friend, Luther Perkins, died in house fire while drunk, Johnny had ignored his call/felt guilty for death**	**Los Angeles, CA**	36 ½	**8-3-1968**	

Table 63 continues

	Event	Place	Age	Date	Time
39	Live at San Quentin Concert/ very successful	Los Angeles, CA	37	2-24-1969	
40	**Gets his own TV show, The Johnny Cash Show**	Los Angeles, CA	**37 ¼**	**6-7-1969**	
41	Son, John, born	Los Angeles, CA	38	3-1970	
42	The Johnny cash Show is cancelled	Los Angeles, CA	39	3-1971	
43	Canadian National Expo/ sold out/ added extra show that also sold out/ extreme success/ biggest payday ever	Montreal, Canada	39½	8-1971	
44	Release of film, The Gospel Road/ a total flop, but a work dear to his heart	Arkansas/South	41	2-1973	
45	Long time manager, Holiff, quit/Career at a low point	Los Angeles, CA	41	3-1973	
46	Minister, Shaw, attempted suicide	Los Angeles, CA	42 ¾	12-24-1974	
47	Career revived/hosted NBC special/got new, Johnny Cash Show	Los Angeles, CA	44 ½	7-1976	
48	**Prisoner who wrote Greystone/ suicide/ influenced John's activism for prison reform/again, John felt guilty for firing him from band**	**Los Angeles, CA**	**46**	**4-1978**	
49	**Entered drug and alcohol rehab/ and had stomach, intestine and spleen surgery to save his life**	**Palm Springs, CA**	**51 ¾**	**12-1983**	
50	**Father died of Parkinson's disease**	**Memphis, TN**	**53 ¾**	**12-23-1985**	
51	Signed with Mercury Records/ more creative license	Los Angeles, CA	54 ½	8-21-1986	
52	**Double bypass heart surgery**	**Los Angeles, CA**	**56 ¾**	**12-1988**	
53	Again in drug and alcohol rehab	Palm Springs, CA	57 ¾	11-23-1989	
54	**Abscessed tooth removed/ jaw cyst scraped off/ left disfigured/ in pain**	**Los Angeles, CA**	**58 ¾**	**1-1990**	

55	Moved to Branson to semi-retire and perform at his own theater complex/ builder went broke/project fizzled	Branson, MO	60	3-1991	
56	**Mother, Carrie, died – she was his greatest encouragement and fan**	**Memphis, TN**	**60**	**3-1991**	
57	John won $1.6 million suit against builder	Branson, MO	62	3-1993	
58	**Brother, Roy, died/another big fan**	**Memphis, TN**	**62 ¾**	**11-1993**	
59	Overdose of pain pills/ cancelled tour	Los Angeles, CA	64	4-1995	
60	Grammy Award for Best Contemporary Folk Album	Los Angeles, CA	66	4-1997	
61	**Hallucinations begin/ diagnosed w/ Shy-Drager Syndrome/ hospitalized for pneumonia and blood poisoning**	**Los Angeles, CA**	**66 ½**	**10-11/1997**	
62	Hospitalized for pneumonia	Los Angeles, CA	67 ¾	10-1998	
63	Pneumonia again/ another album out	Los Angeles, CA	70	3-2002	
64	**June brain dead after heart surgery in May 2003/ she died 3 days later on 5-15-2003 just before sundown**	**Los Angeles, CA**	**71**	**5-12 thru 5-15-2003**	
65	**John hospitalized w/peritonitis**	**Los Angeles, CA**	**71**	**4-24 thru 9-9-2003**	
66	**Rushed to hospital/ died 9-12-2003 at 2:00 AM**	**Los Angeles, CA**	**71 ½**	**9-11 thru 9-12-2003**	**2:00 AM**

Find the Dwad Placement of Johnny's Natal Moon

Next, the dwad placement of Johnny's natal Scorpio Moon may give some insight into the sort of sub-influence he expressed. From the "working chart" we see that his natal Moon is 7:57 Scorpio and, according to the dwad listings in Table 5 in Chapter Three, it is in the Aquarius dwad in square aspect to its sign, Scorpio. Any planet or personal point in the 7 ½ -10-degree range or the 22 ½ to 25-degree range of any sign is in a dwad that squares its own sign placement. Planets or personal points in those degree ranges are challenged throughout life (by the nature of the square) to integrate the conflicting dwad/ sign influences through the planet and its house placement. Just a glance at the list of Johnny Cash's life events indicates a life-long struggle with emotional (Moon) issues from parental conflict to serious womanizing, to serious drug and alcohol abuse and self-destruction. Of course, the Moon in a dwad square to its sign is not always so dramatic, but Cash's internal conflicts were played out on a very public stage with little tolerance for his foibles.

Table 64 Johnny Cash Natal Moon Dwad and 1-Degree Aspects for 7:00-8:00 AM

Aspects	AM Moon	Dwad	Time	Dwad	PM Moon	Aspects
Trine Sun Trine Mercury Sextile Neptune	7:39 Scorpio	Aquarius	7:00			
Trine Sun Trine Mercury Sextile Neptune Sesq-sq Ascendant	7:57 Scorpio	Aquarius	7:30			
Trine Sun	8:15 Scorpio	Aquarius	8:00			

Already Table 64 shows that the 7:30 time is close to accurate with the added aspect of the Moon sesqui-square to the Ascendant that further describes John's life-long problem with substance abuse. Now search the list of life events for the few most dramatic life-defining events to begin testing some of the major life events.

Table 65 Johnny Cash First Test of Major Life Events

2	House Flooded/ Lost/ Forced Move	Dyess, Arkansas	5	4-10-1937
32	Arrested on federal drug charges	El Paso, Texas	33 ¾	10-4-1965
50	Father died of Parkinson's disease	Memphis, TN	53 ½	12-23-1985
66	Rushed to hospital/ died 9-12-2003 at 2:00 AM	Los Angeles, CA	71 ½	9-11 thru 9-12-2003

Begin the Search to Derive the Birth Chart Angles from Life Events

We begin the search for the best placement of the Angles by directing the Midheaven and then the Ascendant to conjunct each leg of the selected 1-degree hard aspects natal patterns and their "Apex points" to align the Angles appropriately with actual life events. Remember that we are only looking at the conjunctions to the selected points, and so it follows that we will find a resonance of that contact in approximate 6-hour intervals for the applying square, opposition and separating square. Of course, the inconjunct (150 degree) aspect is now regarded by many astrologers as a major hard aspect, but it might best be left for later searches if there is still doubt. Likewise wait until another time to search the semi-square of Mars to natal

Venus and Uranus, and its sesqui-square to Jupiter for such an uncontested birth time.

Remember that to arrive at the Directed position of the Midheaven, Ascendant or Apex point, the client's age at the event must be subtracted from the "Planet Contacted by Conjunction" listed position for each event to derive the birth time that would correspond with that planet being contacted by conjunction at the time of the event. In John's case, subtract 5-degrees (equal to his age at the flood event) from each planetary position in the far left column. Then use your astrology software search function to find a birth time that corresponds to the Midheaven at that derived degree, in this case 1:45 Pisces. Continue searching for derived birth times that correspond to a Directed Midheaven conjunction to each of the other planets, (Mercury, Neptune, Venus, Uranus, and Jupiter) for the flood event. For the drug arrest event, subtract 33 ½ degrees (his age at the arrest) from each of the planet positions in the far left column and derive a birth time that would be consistent with the Directed Midheaven conjunct each of the planets at the time of the event. Continue the process for the father's death and John's own death.

Table 66 Directed Midheaven Times Conjunct Aspect Network at Four Major Events

Planet Contacted By Conjunction	House Flood 4-10-1937	Drug Arrest 10-4-1965	Father's Death 12-23-1985	Own Death 9-12-2003
John's Age at Event	5	33 ½	53 ½	71 ½
Grand Opposition:				
Sun 6:45 Pisces	12:02 PM MC 1:45 Pisces	10:10 AM MC 3:15 Aquar	8:44 AM MC 13:00 Capr	7:31 AM MC 26:00 Sg
Mercury 6:28 Pisces	12:01 PM MC 1:30 Pisces	10:09 AM MC 3:00 Aquar	8:43 AM MC 12:45 Capr	7:30 AM MC 25:45 Sg
Neptune 6:36 Virgo	0:04 AM MC 1:36 Virgo	10:07 PM MC 3:06 Leo	8:43 PM MC 12:51 Can	7:30 PM MC 25:51 Ge
Conjunct, Trine:				
Venus 16:31 Aries	2:29 PM MC 11:31 Aries	12:45 PM MC 13:00 Pisc	11:30 AM MC 23:16 Aqu	10:21 AM MC 6:01 Aqu
Uranus 17:02 Aries	12:31 PM MC 12:02 Aries	12:47 PM MC 13:32 Pisc	11:31 AM MC 23:47 Aqu	10:22 AM MC 6:33 Aqu
Jupiter 15:14 Leo	10:36 AM MC 10:14 Leo	8:37 PM MC 11:45 Canc	7:09 PM MC 21:29 Gem	5:58 PM MC 4:45 Ge

The search process is exactly the same for the Ascendant search of finding a derived birth time for when the Ascendant would conjunct each listed planet by conjunction at the time of the event.

Table 67 Directed Ascendant Times Conjunct Aspect Network at Four Major Events

Planet Contacted By Conjunction	House Flood 4-10-1937	Drug Arrest 10-4-1965	Father's Death 12-23-1985	Own Death 9-12-2003
John's Age at Event	5	33 ½	53 ½	71 ½
Grand Opposition:				
Sun 6:45 Pisces	6:33 AM AS 1:45 Pisces	5:05 AM AS 3:15 Aquar	3:51 AM AS 13:00 Capr	2:39 AM AS 26:00 Sg
Mercury 6:28 Pisces	6:32 AM AS 1:30 Pisces	5:04 AM AS 3:00 Aquar	3:50 AM AS 12:45 Capr	2:38 AM AS 25:45 Sg
Neptune 6:36 Virgo	5:31 PM AS 1:36 Virgo	3:13 PM AS 3:06 Leo	1:38 PM AS 12:51 Can	12:22 PM AS 25:51 Ge
Conjunct, Trine:				
Venus 16:31 Aries	8:18 AM AS 11:31 Aries	7:03 AM AS 13:00 Pisc	6:08 AM AS 23:16 Aqu	5:15 AM AS 6:01 Aqu
Uranus 17:02 Aries	8:20 AM AS 12:02 Aries	7:05 AM AS 13:32 Pisc	6:10 AM AS 23:47 Aqu	5:17 AM AS 6:33 Aqu
Jupiter 15:14 Leo	3:48 PM AS 10:14 Leo	1:33 PM AS 11:45 Canc	12:03 PM AS 21:29 Gem	11:00 AM AS 4:45 Ge

Continue the same process of searching for derived birth times that correspond to the Apex points of the planets involved in the close hard aspect natal pattern that conjunct each planet at the time of the event. This process may be too tedious for so small a search as Johnny Cash's rectification, but it provides an invaluable confirmation for searches that span several hours or even a whole day.

Table 68 Times Directed Opposite the Apex Planets at Four Major Events

T-Square Apex Planet Opposition	House Flood 4-10-1937	Drug Arrest 10-4-1965	Father's Death 12-23-1985	Own Death 9-12-2003
John's Age at Event	5	33 ½	53 ¾	71 ½
Square Sun, Mercury, Neptune Opposition				

6:36 Gemini	5:44 PM MC 1:36 Gem AS 4:21 Virgo	3:52 PM MC 3:06 Taurus AS 11:05 Leo	2:32 PM MC 12:15 Aries AS 24:27 Canc	1:35 PM MC 26:06 Pisc AS 11:51 Can
6:36 Gemini	10:47 AM AS 1:36 Gem MC 12:29 Aqua	11:26 AM AS 3:06 Taurus MC	8:20 AM AS 12:15 Aries MC 7:21 Capr	7:38 AM AS 26:06 Pisc MC 27:40 Sag
6:36 Sagittarius	5:46 AM MC 1:36 Sag AS 15:52 Aqua	3:52 AM MC 3:06 Scorp AS 13:21 Cap	2:34 AM MC 12:15 Libra AS 24:53 Sag	1:35 AM MC 26:06 Virg AS 12:00 Sag
6:36 Sagittarius	0:45 AM AS 1:36 Sag MC 12:38 Virg	10:23 PM AS 3:06 Scorpio MC 7:04 Leo	8:44 PM AS 12:15 Libra MC 13:22 Canc	7:28 PM AS 26:06 Virgo MC 25:45 Ge
Opposite Venus, Uranus				
16:45 Libra 16:45 Libra (combined)	1:55 AM MC 1:45 Libra AS 16:25 Sag	0:25 AM MC 10:20 Virgo AS 20:24 Scorp	11:21 PM MC 24:33 Leo AS 9:52 Scorp	10:42 PM MC 14:33 Leo AS 3:01 Scorp
16:45 Libra 16:45 Libra (combined)	7:54 PM AS 1:45 Libra MC 1:54 Canc	5:43 PM AS 10:20 Virgo MC 4:03 Gem	4:13 PM AS 24:33 Leo MC 11:56 Taur	3:16 PM AS 14:33 Leo MC 27:08 Arie
Opposite Jupiter				
15:10 Aquarius	1:53 PM MC 1:45 Aries AS 16:19 Canc	8:39 AM MC 11:40 Capr AS 19:16 Aries	7:11 AM MC 21:25 Sag AS 15:43 Pisc	6:00 AM MC 4:40 Sag AS 20:50 Aqua
15:10 Aquarius	7:52 AM AS 1:45 Aries MC 1:02 Capr	3:45 AM AS 11:40 Capr MC 1:19 Scorpio	2:18 AM AS 21:25 Sag MC 8:00 Libra	1:00 AM AS 4:40 Sag MC 6:37 Virgo

Tally the Preliminary Results to Narrow the Possible Birth Time Range

As before, the results must be tallied to narrow the search to no more than 4 possible birth times. Remember that they are likely to fall into a range of approximately 6 hours between each time, which represents the squares and the opposition to the actual birth time. The highlighted times above represent variations of 21-26 Sagittarius suggested by the earlier Jigsaw 2.2 search and 7:28-7:38 AM range still is prominently in the mix.

Table 69 Tally of the Results of MC, AS and Apex Searches from Four John Cash Events

Total	AM Event 1	AM Event 2	AM Event 3	AM Event 4	Hours	PM Event 1	PM Event 2	PM Event 3	PM Event 4	Total
3	2	1			12-1	3	2	1		7
3	1			2	1-2	1	1	1	1	4
4			2	2	2-3	1		1		2
4		2		2	3-4	1	2		1	4
0					4-5			1		1
5	1	2		2	5-6	2	1		1	4
5	2		2	1	6-7					0
8	1	2	1	3	7-8	1		1	2	4
6	2	1	3		8-9		1	2		3
0					9-10					0
6	2	2		2	10-11		2		1	3
4		1	2	1	11-12			1		1
47	11	11	12	13	Total	9	9	8	1	33

At this point, we have a preponderance of data supporting an AM birth time, over a PM time with 47 AM hits compared to only 33 for the PM times. In studying the results of the tally of "derived birth times", it is clear that we may reasonably narrow the rectification search to the few highlighted time ranges of:

1. 7-8 AM **2.** 8-9 AM **3.** 10-11 AM **4.** 12-1 PM

Keep in mind that we are accumulating evidence with several different methods of birth time confirmation. So far, the natal Moon search supports the 7:30 AM time, and after the Directed Midheaven, Ascendant and Apex Point searches, the early AM time range is still in the running. In fact, the 7-8 AM time range has the highest number of hits, confirming that the "mother's memory" is very close to correct. At this point, we may safely eliminate the 8-9 AM, 10-11 AM and 12-1 PM time ranges, since they do not span the reported and undisputed birth time. Refer to the Jigsaw 2.1 search for John's birth time at the beginning of Chapter

Four, which selected 7:31 AM from within the 7-8 AM range. This exercise only confirms what we already thought was an "A" data time and now we might consider it an even more reliable time for forecasting during Johnny's life.

Search the Secondary Progressions to Confirm Early Results

Even though we are already pretty certain of the 7:30 AM birth time for Johnny Cash, it may be of interest to search the position of the Progressed planets: Sun, Mercury, Venus, Mars and the Midheaven and Ascendant at the times of his major life events.

Table 70 Lifetime Progressed Inner Planet and Angle Positions for Johnny Cash

Progressed Angles for 7:30 AM	Progressed Inner Planet Aspect 7:30 AM	Age at event	Corresponding Life Events	Date of Event
AS conj NN	Venus sq Pluto	3	Family Moved	3-15-1935
MC sx Mars		5	House Flooded/Lost/Forced Move	4-10-37
MC sx Moo	Venus sq Saturn	12	Brother Jack died	5-20-44
	Merc conj Venus Merc conj Uran	22 ½	Marriage to pre-war sweetheart, Vivian Liberto	8-7-54
AS sq Saturn		22 ½	His band, Johnny Cash and the Tennessee Two, appeared on radio and recorded first record	10-1954
AS sx Mars	Sun sx Saturn	23	Daughter, Roseanne, born	5-1955
		23 ½	On top of country music charts	12-1-55
		23 ½	First appeared on TV/Louisiana Hayride – a big success	11-13-55
	Mars trine Pluto	24	Folsom Prison Blues/top of country charts	2-10-56
MC op Pluto		24	Arrested for spousal abuse	3-1956
MC op Pluto		24	Daughter, Kathy, born	3-1956
	Venus sq Jupiter Mercury sq Pluto	25	Appeared on Jackie Gleason Show/launched national career	6-1957
		26	Daughter Cindy born	3-1958
		26 ¼	Began heavy drug use-amphetamines (1958-1967 worst)	5-1958
		26 ½	Moved to California	7-1958

Why Are Time Twins So Different?

Table 70 continues

AS sx Merc AS sx Sun As tri Nept MC sx AS Mar con AS		27 ¼	Released 3 hit albums	6-1959
	Venus sx Pluto	29 ½	Daughter, Tara, born	8-24-61
		30	Appeared at Carnegie Hall/totally drugged out/was a flop!	5-10-62
		32 ½	Friends with Bob Dylan/ wrote protest song, Ballad of Ira Hayes	10-1964
	Mars con NN	33 ¼	Accidentally starts forest fire/ loses lawsuit/ fined $82,000	6-1965
AS sq Jupit		33 ½	Arrested on federal drug charges/ in the news/ drug use now public	10-4-65
MC con Sat	Venus incon MC	34 ½	Vivian files for divorce	9-1966
		35 ½	June Carter gives ultimatum about NO drugs, Johnny drug-free 'til 1976	10-21-67
		36	Performed live from Folsom Prison/ a huge hit/Live album recorded	1-13-68
		36	Married June Carter, his soul mate	3-1-1968
		36 ½	Friend, died in house fire while drunk, Johnny had ignored his call/ felt guilty for death	8-3-1968
AS sx Pluto	Mars sx Saturn	37 ¼	Gets his own TV show, The Johnny Cash Show	6-7-1969
	Venus tri Saturn Sun trine Jupiter	38	Son, John, born	3-1970
AS inc Moo	Sun sq Saturn	53 ¾	Father died of Parkinson's disease	12-23-85
	Mars tri Jupiter	56 ¾	Double bypass heart surgery	12-1988
		57 ¾	Again, in drug and alcohol rehab	11-23-89
	Mars conj Venus	58	Abscessed tooth removed/jaw cyst scraped off/left disfigured/in pain	1-1990
	Mars conj Uran	59	Mother, Carrie, died – she was his greatest encouragement and fan	3-1991

		61	John won $1.6 million suit against builder	3-1993
	Venus sq AS Sun opp Moon	61 ¾	Brother, Roy, died/another big fan	11-1993
	Merc tri Jupiter Mars sq Pluto	63	Overdose of pain pills/ cancelled tour	4-1995
	Merc conj Venus	65 ¾	Hospitalized for pneumonia	10 & 11-1997
	Venus inc Saturn Merc sq Pluto Mars trine Pluto	70	Pneumonia again/another album out	3-2002
	Venus tri Mars	71	June brain dead after heart surgery in May 2003/she died 3 days later just before sundown	5-15-03
		71 ¼	John hospitalized w/ peritonitis	4-24 thru 9-9-03
MC con Mer MC op Nept MC con Sun AS opp MC		71 ½	Rushed to hospital/ died at 2:00 AM	9-12-03

Mean Nodes were used

The Graphic function of most astrology software programs is quite helpful for easily spotting Progressions as well as Directions and Transits. Note that the Angles for the 7:30 AM birth time are appropriately aspected at most major events, and the progressed inner planets further described the events to provide us assurance that the 7:30 AM birth time is confirmed.

Figure 167 Secondary Progressions of Inner Planets and Angles for John Cash 1932-1967

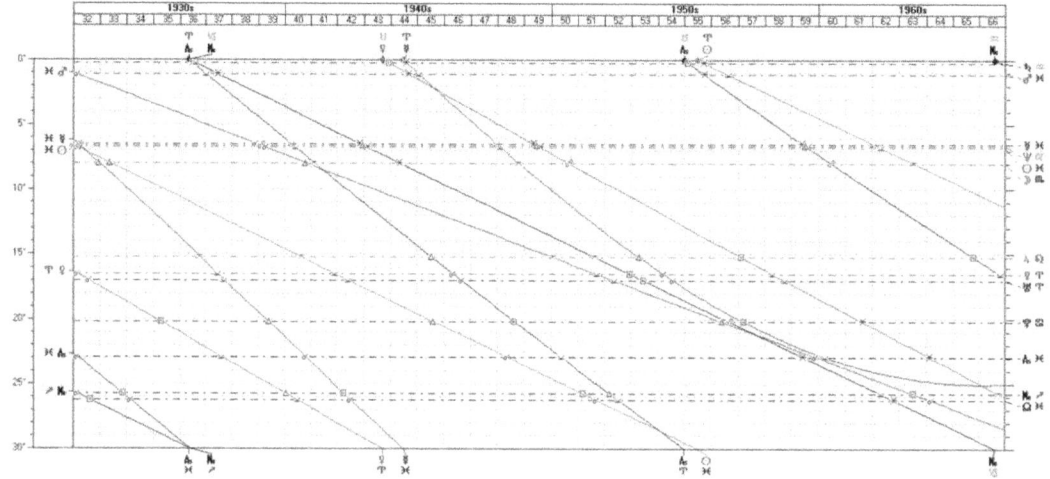

Figure 168 Secondary Progressions of Inner Planets and Angles for John Cash 1968-2004

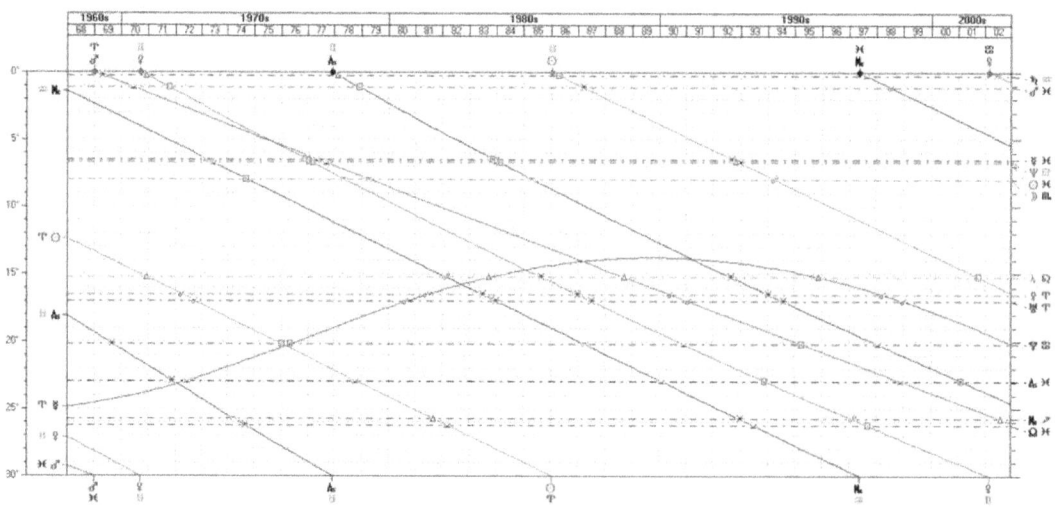

Just as we searched the Secondary Progressions to the important life events for Johnny Cash, a similar process works just as well for the Directions and Transit searches. It is interesting to compare the Progressions with Directions for key life events.

Table 71 Directed Inner Planet and Angle Positions at Key Life Events for Johnny Cash

Directed Angles for 7:30 AM	Directed Inner Planet Aspect 7:30 AM	Age at event	Corresponding Life Events	Date of Event
	Mars con Merc Mars opp Nept Mars con Merc	5	House Flooded/Lost/ Forced Move	4-10-37
MC conj Saturn		33 ½	Arrested on federal drug charges	10-4-65
	Sun sq Saturn Merc sq Saturn	53 ¾	Father died of Parkinson's disease	12-23-85
MC conj Mercury MC opp Neptun MC conj Sun	Venus sq NN Venus sq SN	71 ½	Rushed to hospital/ died at 2:00 AM	9-12-03

Table 72 Outer Transits at Selected Events Narrows Possible Birth Time Range for J. Cash

	Transits	All Times	7:25 AM	7:30 AM	7:35 AM
House Flooded/ Lost/ Forced Move 4-10-1937	16:44 Virgo 26:29 Canc 8:27 Taur 28:19 Pisc	Nept incon Venus Nept incon Uranu Pluto inconj MC Uran opp Moon Saturn conj NN Saturn opp SN			
Arrested on federal drug charges 10-4-1965	16:59 Virgo 18:21 Scor 16:51 Virgo 11:49 Pisc 7:19 Gem	Pluto inc Venus Pluto inc Uranus Nept inc Venus Nept inc Uranus Uran inc Venus Uran inc Uranus Satur in shadow conj Merc opp Nept conj Sun NNode sq Merc NNode sq Nept NNode sq Sun			
Father died of Parkinson's disease 12-23-1985	6:42 Scorp 19:00 Sag 4:15 Sag 16:29 Aqua	Pluto trine Merc Pluto sext Nept Pluto trine Sun Uran incon Pluto Saturn in shadow sq Merc sq Nept sq Sun Jupit sx Venus Jupit sx Uranus		Venus conj MC	
Rushed to hospital/ died 9-12-2003 at 2:00 AM	17:17 Sag 00:05 Pisc 3:30 Virgo	Pluto trine Venus Pluto trine Uran Pluto trine Jupiter Uran conj Mars Jupit in shadow conj Nept opp Venus opp Sun		Venus sq MC	

The Transit search confirms the 7:30 AM birth time of our previous searches, though one might make a good case for using the 7:01 AM time with a 26:01 Sagittarius Midheaven and a 23:15 Pisces Ascendant as projected by the Jigsaw 2.0 search of Progressions, Directions and Outer Transits in the 4th harmonic, which includes the aspects: conjunction, applying square, opposition and separating square. Of course, some may want to run the Transit Graphics for the 7:30 AM birth time to see the shadow areas traced by the outer planets and note where they activate the chart of Johnny Cash at key life events. The planets transiting within a shadow range while activating Johnny's natal chart are noted above. Given all of the evidence provided by our several searches, the 7:30 AM time is pretty well confirmed.

Search Solar Eclipses for Key Events for Final Birth Time Confirmation

Finally, a Solar Eclipse search can confirm any remaining doubts of the birth time. The Solar Eclipse at the time of the devastating flood that destroyed the Cash house and forced them to run for their lives activated both of John's Angles, square his Ascendant and Conjunct his Midheaven. Clearly, it was the involvement of the Angles that left such a major impression on young John. Similarly, the Solar Eclipse of 1985 involved an Angle, his Ascendant, at the death of his father. The other two events that have provided "hooks" for our searches are quite revealing, because they share the same Solar Eclipse by sign and degree. John was arrested on federal drug charges at the 1965 Solar Eclipse at 9 Gemini and died at the 2003 Eclipse at 9 Gemini. Not only was the infamous Grand Opposition of the Sun/Mercury opposite Neptune activated, but the Eclipse made an inconjunct aspect to his natal Moon – all separative influences in the life.

Table 73 Solar Eclipse Contacts at Key Life Events for John Cash 7:30 AM Birth

	Event	Event Date	Age	Eclipse	Aspect/Planet/Angle
1	House flood/ house lost/ family moved	4-10-1937	5	21:48 Sag	Square Ascendant Semi-sq Moon Inconj Pluto Conjunct Midheaven
2	Arrested for possession of illegal drugs	10-4-1965	33 ¾	9:13 Gem	Inconj Moon Square Sun Square Neptune Square Mercury
3	Father's death	12-23-1985	53 ¾	20:08 Sco	Trine Pluto Trine Ascendant Square Jupiter Trine North Node
4	Own death	9-12-2003	71 ½	9:19 Gem	Inconjunct Moon Square Sun Square Neptune Square Mercury

The examples for birth time rectification provided in these chapters should show a way into the chart for all astrologers, whether hand-calculating, using standard astrology software for computer searches, or using the advanced research features of more specialized computer software. Armed with the modern astrology techniques and whatever search tools that are available, the results of a rectification search for a birth time that matches appropriately with life events should be the same.

Chart Comparison of Time Twins: Liz Taylor and John Cash

Now that both birth times of our "time twins", Elizabeth Taylor and Johnny Cash, are confirmed by the rectification searches as appropriately corresponding to life events, the next obvious question to address is, "How can their lives and charts be so different if they were born within the same 24-hour period?" The short answer is that the 18 ½ hours difference in their birth times reveal major differences in the position of and aspects to their Moons and their Angles – the very factors that distinguish any of us from others born on the same day. Specifically:

1. 9-degrees separate their Scorpio Moons with greatly different aspects and house placements
2. There is absolutely no similarity in their Angles by sign placement, degree, or aspects
3. The latitudes of their births are so diverse that John's Midheaven and Ascendant are nearly 90 degrees apart, whereas Elizabeth's are nearly 60 degrees apart

Recognize How Location and Date Can Affect the Angles

In fact, according to Bernadette Brady in Predictive Astrology, "If two people are born at precisely the same instant in time but at different places on the globe, their planetary patterns will be absolutely identical. However, the house position of the planets will be quite different because the sign rising in one place may well be setting in another. It is the position on the Earth at any particular time which indicates the position of a planet in its particular semi-arc or house. Starting with point 3, Elizabeth was born in London, England which has latitude of 51N30. All far North or far South latitudes exhibit such skewing of the Angles due to the rapidly diminishing diameters of each latitude belt around the earth and the time of the year. Further, Rob Hand tells us that, "The Ascendant, Midheaven and Vertex are all nodes, i.e. points defined by the intersection of two great circles upon the celestial sphere." The Angles more usually form a square relationship in latitudes below 40 degrees North or South at certain times of the year near the equinoxes, and Johnny's very late February birth in Kingsland, Arkansas at 33N51 latitude confirms that to be true. Therefore, when one of John's Angles is hit by Secondary Progression, Direction or Outer Transit, the other is hit by square aspect. When one of Elizabeth's Angles is hit by any of the same moving factors, the other is activated by a sextile aspect. Astrologers all know the interpretative distinctions between the challenging square aspect and the benign sextile, and those distinctions played out in the lives of our "time twins", Elizabeth Taylor and Johnny Cash.

Not only do the latitudes of Elizabeth and John's births make it impossible to have the same Angles, and house divisions, any difference of just 4 minutes in their birth times places another degree on the Angles and House Cusps, and in winter births such as theirs, possibly two-degrees. With 18 ½ hours between their births, it would only be by accident that the signs and degrees on their Angles would have any relationship at all. Connections that might be possible are the same degree on one of the Angles, but in a different sign; however, even that is a far stretch of the imagination and reality, with only a 1 in 12 probability. More realistically, the sign on one of their Angles may echo the other by element (fire, air, earth or water), or quality (cardinal, fixed or mutable). In comparing any set of "time twins" the likelihood that even one of their Angles has anything in common with the other is slim.

Nonetheless, John and Elizabeth do share a pair of signs Angular. His Midheaven for 7:30 AM on February 26, 1932 is 25:46 Sagittarius and Ascendant 22:56 Pisces, while Elizabeth's Midheaven 18 ½ hours later for 2:00 AM on February 27, 1932 is 6:02 Libra and Ascendant 7:31 Sagittarius. They do not have the same degree on any Angle; however, they do have the same two signs (Gemini and Sagittarius) but on different Angles. Elizabeth has Sagittarius on the Ascendant with Gemini setting on the 7th, and John has Sagittarius culminating at the Midheaven and Gemini on the 4th. John's home situation was always changeable from the early moves and flood, to being constantly on the road to the extent that his children barely knew him until later years. Of course, Gemini on Elizabeth's 7th shows a much different changeability of partners and marriages. John's Sagittarius on the Midheaven placed the career greater than life, even performing for smaller audiences up until his death. Elizabeth's Sagittarius on the Ascendant suggests that she, herself, is the Jupiterian icon of greater than life humanitarian work, and not so much her career.

Elizabeth and John do both have mutable signs across the Ascendant/Descendant axis that describes their many dalliances in romance and relationships whether one counts Liz's 8 marriages or Johnny's notorious reputation for infidelity. That changeable relationship situation for both is further compounded with challenge from both having an Ascendant degree placement in the dwad degree range square to the sign. Elizabeth's Ascendant is in the 7 ½ - 10-degree range giving a Pisces dwad placement square the Sagittarius rising sign. And John's Ascendant is in the 22 ½ to 25-degree range of Pisces giving a Sagittarius dwad placement square to the Pisces rising sign. Therefore, it comes as no surprise that both Elizabeth and Johnny have fought major battles with alcohol and drug addiction, and have several times been through rehab at the Betty Ford center in Palm Springs, California. As well, both have a long history of respiratory ailments from battles with pneumonia requiring extended hospitalization and life-saving tracheotomies.

Still comparing the Angle placements of John and Elizabeth, they received very different aspects from entirely different planets. Elizabeth's Ascendant if squared within 1-degree by natal Mercury, Neptune and Sun, greatly compounding the problem with respiratory ailments and issues with pills and alcohol. Such a close hard aspect of Neptune to the Ascendant is a signal of such problems in any chart. On the other hand, John's Ascendant is exactly sesquisquare his natal Moon suggesting that he may have had more resistance to illness and personal setbacks than Elizabeth.

Both John and Elizabeth have faced image problems suggested by their Midheavens facing multiple close hard aspects. John's Midheaven is closely square the Moon's Nodes by 1 ½ degrees, which suggests major life lessons to be learned about commitment and responsibility within the realm of work. John was notorious for being unreliable to show up on time or at all for performances, and even when he did show, he was usually wasted on drugs. Elizabeth's career is less challenged than John's, but her close 1 ¼ degree inconjunct of Sun and Mercury to the Midheaven suggests that circumstances beyond her control, such as illness, frequently interfered with her work.

Compare the Dwad Placements of Angles for John and Elizabeth

Not so many astrologers even note dwads, much less apply the concept of the aspect relationship of the 2 ½ degree dwad sign to the 30-degree whole sign that contains it. Nonetheless, it serves as a useful tool in distinguishing the nuances of the more general sign placement. John and Elizabeth's charts show a Midheaven mutual reception of sorts, one with the sign Libra and the Sagittarius dwad, and the other with the Sagittarius sign and the Libra dwad. Both signs and dwads describe people who have led their careers in the public eye in a big way.

As discussed earlier, both have the Ascendant dwad (part) square to the sign (whole), which signals a restless inner tension to the personality that keeps them constantly on the go. Both "Tme twins" have their dwads of the Moon in hard aspect to their sign placement, which reinforces the emotional tension and quest for excitement in life. Table 73 provides a visual of the similarities and differences in the charts of Elizabeth Taylor and Johnny Cash that explains how "time twins" can differ so greatly.

Table 74 A Chart Comparison Close Aspects to Angles and Moon of the Time Twins:

Johnny Cash			**Elizabeth Taylor**		
MC 25:46 Sag	**AS 22:56 Pis**	**Moo 7:57 Sco**	**MC 6:02 Lib**	**AS 7:31 Sag**	**Moo 15:10 Sco**
Square NNode Square SNode Square AS	Ssq-sq Moon	Trine Sun Trine Merc Sextil Nept Ssq-sq AS	Inconj Sun Inconj Merc Sx AS	Square Sun Square Merc Square Nept	Inconj Venus Square Jupit Inconj Uran
10th House	1st House	8th House	10th House	1st House	11th House
Libra Dwad Sextile Sign	Sagitt Dwad-Square Sign	Aquar Dwad Square sign	Sagitt Dwad Sextile Sign	Pisces Dwad Square Sign	Taurus Dwad Opposed Sign

Speaking of the Moon, remember that 9 degrees separate the Scorpio Moons of John and Elizabeth, with greatly different aspects and house placements. Elizabeth's Moon and emotional nature is greatly challenged by the very close square to natal Jupiter and inconjunct to both natal Venus and Uranus, suggesting her difficulty in cultivating lasting and meaningful relationships. The excess of inappropriate mate choices and the dysfunctional relationship drama that follows each of them confirms that Elizabeth faces a life-long challenge to gain control of her Moon-ruled emotions. On the other hand, Johnny's chart reveals several very close harmonious aspects to his natal Moon, suggesting that he is much more secure in himself. Even though he is noted for countless extra-marital affairs, he remained married for many years and always came home to one wife – first Vivian, the mother of his children, then June his late-life soulmate. John's near 8-degree Scorpio Moon is trine his natal Sun and Mercury and sextile Neptune that supports a better chance to make emotional involvements work. Only the close, but minor, sesqui-square sounds a discordant note.

Outer Transits Activate John and Elizabeth's Close Natal Aspect Patterns Simultaneously

One might reasonably speculate that with similar close natal aspect patterns, wouldn't Outer Transits active them for both "time twins" at the same time, and wouldn't they experience similar events? Again, the short answer is no, because they each have the close natal aspect patterns in different houses, not to mention the connection of the Angles or the Moon to the pattern for one and not the other. For example, we know that both John and Elizabeth have a natal Sun/Mercury conjunct within 1-degree opposition to Neptune; however, the pattern is across John's 6/12 axis, whereas Elizabeth's is across her 3/9 axis. Both have the pattern in mutable houses and mutable signs, but even though the pattern would be activated at very nearly the same time by any Outer Transit, the areas of life described by the different house positions make a significant difference in how the activated pattern is expressed in the life. John's Sun/Mercury in the 12th opposes Neptune in the 6th signaling his unreliability in work stemming from indulging his personal hidden issues (drug addiction) thereby making it impossible for him to work. John's Grand Opposition pattern is complicated by a close trine/sextile from the Moon, suggesting his restlessness and moodiness as part of the problematic pattern. Elizabeth's Sun/Mercury in the 3rd opposes Neptune in the 9th signaling her unreliability of some sort in travel or with foreign locations, compounded by miscommunication and/or personal whim. Elizabeth's Grand Opposition pattern is more complicated than John's because the close square to her Ascendant is more challenging than the gentler Moon aspects that connect John's Grand Opposition. As her biography confirms, Liz's personal whims and demands along with her many illnesses, plagued nearly every performance or film she made. Producers, directors, and acting colleagues could count on long delays and films excessively over budget if Elizabeth were involved. Ironically, they tolerated her excesses and excuses because she was the "name" that drew the crowds that made money for them all.

Solar Eclipses Activate John and Elizabeth's Close Natal Aspect Patterns Simultaneously

In similar fashion, Solar Eclipses simultaneously active the charts of "time twins", John Cash and Elizabeth Taylor, but very different life events transpired. Using the same Grand Opposition pattern of Sun/Mercury opposite Neptune, two Solar Eclipses at 9 Gemini (square to the pattern) that occurred on May 30, 1965 and May 31, 2003 brought very different results for each. The Solar Eclipse at 9 Gemini squaring the 6/12 Grand Opposition activated John's 3rd house, but also made an inconjunct to his Moon. During the active 6-month period of the 1965 Solar Eclipse, John was arrested and convicted for possession illegal drugs. Thirty- eight years later at the next 9 Gemini eclipse, John died. The degree area of 9 Gemini activated Elizabeth's Grand Opposition pattern as well on both dates in 1965 and 2003; however, it did not activate her Moon. Instead, it eclipsed her Descendant, signaling another marriage and another relationship in the news. Even in the case of "time twins", the differences in the house placement of planets; the degree, aspects and possibly the sign of the Moon; and the sign, degree and aspects of the Angles describe very different character traits and personalities. Even when common patterns are activated at the same time, the life experiences, and events of each play out on a different stage according to the house position, and on different planes according to any additional connections the common pattern makes with other planets or personal points.

As in the beginning, so in the end, rectification of birth time all comes down to finding the exact position of the Angles – the fastest moving points in the chart, and for this pair of "Time twins", the degree of the Moon. Hopefully, this study is helpful to the practicing astrologer as well as the beginning student in providing a strategy for tackling one of the most complex astrological problems we face – rectifying the birth time to appropriately describe and align with life events. Clients will appreciate more accurate forecasting and astrologers will feel more confident in their forecasts with a birth time that works.

Fraternal or Identical Twins are Very Different from "Time Twins"

Rectification Example Three – Fraternal Twins, Barbara and Jenna Bush

Figure 169 Twins Barbara Bush 9:50 am CST, Jenna Bush 10:05 am CST Nov 25, 1981, Dallas, TX

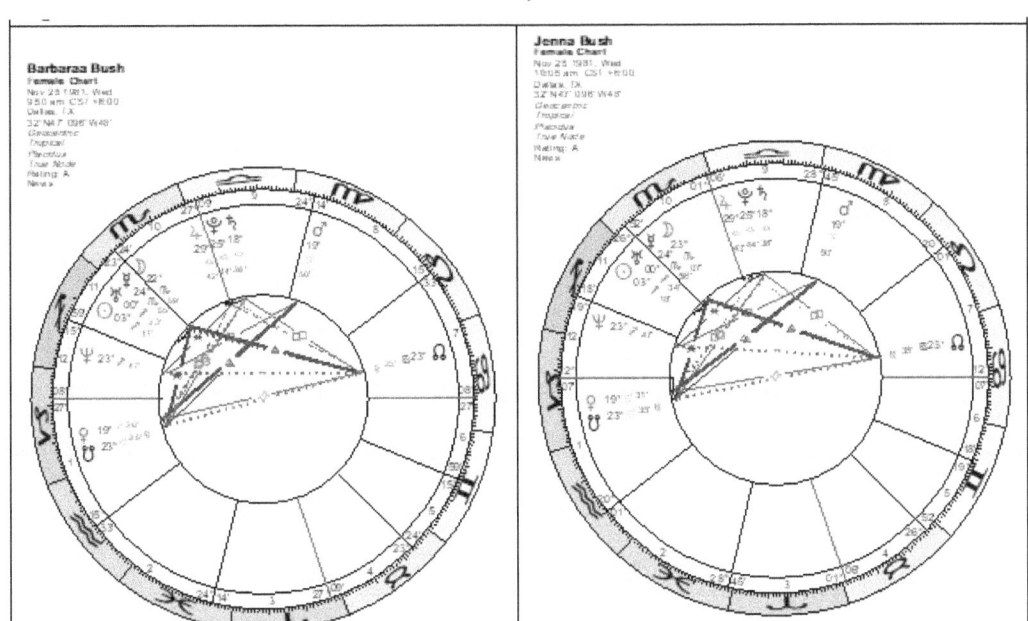

Fraternal twins, Barbara and Jenna Bush, are born fifteen minutes apart on the same date and location, November 25, 1981 in Dallas, Texas. Barbara was first born at 9:50 am CST and sister Jenna was born fifteen minutes later at 10:05 am CST. Study their charts carefully to see that all of the planets are the same with no interpretive difference, not even the Angle and house rulers. Even Barbara and Jenna's Moons are at the same sign within 1/13th of a degree. Barbara's 22:59 Scorpio Moon is within 00:08 minutes of a degree of Jenna's Moon at 23:07 Scorpio. Everything is placed in the same Placidus houses except Jupiter, which is 2 ½ degrees past the Midheaven for the more serious Barbara, but Jupiter is applying to the Midheaven by 1/3 of a degree giving more emphasis to fun-loving and light-heartedness for Jenna. The ONLY other change in the twin's charts are the degrees of a sign on the Angles and their 2 ½-degree segment of that sign, dwad, which equals 10-minutes of clock time. Since Barbara and Jenna are born fifteen minutes apart, the dwad segments for their Ascendant, Descendant and Midheaven, Imum Coeli will be the only other noticeable difference.

Table 75 Barbara and Jenna Bush, Fraternal Twins, Angle Comparison: Sign, Decan, Dwad, Ruler

Barbara	Sign	Decan	Dwad	Ruler	Jenna	Sign	Decan	Dwad	Ruler
ASC	Capric 8:27	Capric	Aries	Saturn	ASC	Capric 13:07	Taurus	Virgo	Saturn
DES	Cancer	Cancer	Libra	Moon	DES	Cancer	Scorpio	Pisces	
MC	Libra 27:09	Gemini	Leo	Venus	MC	Scorpio 1:06	Scorpio	Scorpio	Mars Pluto
IC	Aries				IC	Taurus	Taurus	Taurus	

Doing a rectification of birth time within any time range for fraternal or identical twins is, at best, a hopeful challenge because two participants must provide information and feedback. However, if the birth time is rounded to the earlier custom of every quarter-hour, the decan and dwad technique will help put them in the correct order by fitting the Ascendant and Midheaven sign, decan and dwad descriptors to the twin biography and personality traits. In the Angles descriptors for Barbara and Jenna Bush, there is a clear personality difference in their Saturn rules Capricorn Ascendants. Barbara is clearly defined as sensible, responsible, and taking action; whereas Jenna, is clearly defined as enjoying the comforts and pleasures of life and a practical edge. When the two women are compared for their image and work in the world by their Midheavens, especially important here because the signs change from Libra to Scorpio – a very different public image. Barbara's Venus ruled Libra Midheaven is courteous and diplomatic, whereas Jenna's Mars/Pluto ruled Scorpio Midheaven describes the intense party girl who is capable of flirting with trouble, even with abandon.

Years ago, the 1970's, Geoffrey Dean from Australia challenged willing astrologers to study his 30 pairs of twins, both fraternal and identical, to determine which of the two birth times fit each twin. The time range of the 30 twin pairs was from a few minutes up to a half-hour as I recall. Clearly, in that time range not even the Moon moves 1-degree, so how did our California group led by Zip Dobyns get 97% of the twin birth times correct? The only technique that worked within that narrow time range was the dwadashamsas, or dwads. I gave the details for how dwads work in Chapter 5, but again, the technique works well for distinguishing between minutes of time that are so important in rectification.

A good example are the well-known twins, Alanis and Wade Morissette. At www.astro.com there is a claim of a problem with the twins birth times. "Considering a biography" by Paul Cantin, there is some confusion whether Alanis Morissette was first (born 9:39) or second (born 9:51)." We do have good biography about both Morissette twins that is distinctive and very different which helps our astrological judgement to fit the appropriate descriptor and time for each twin. Alanis is a well-known song writer and singer, and her

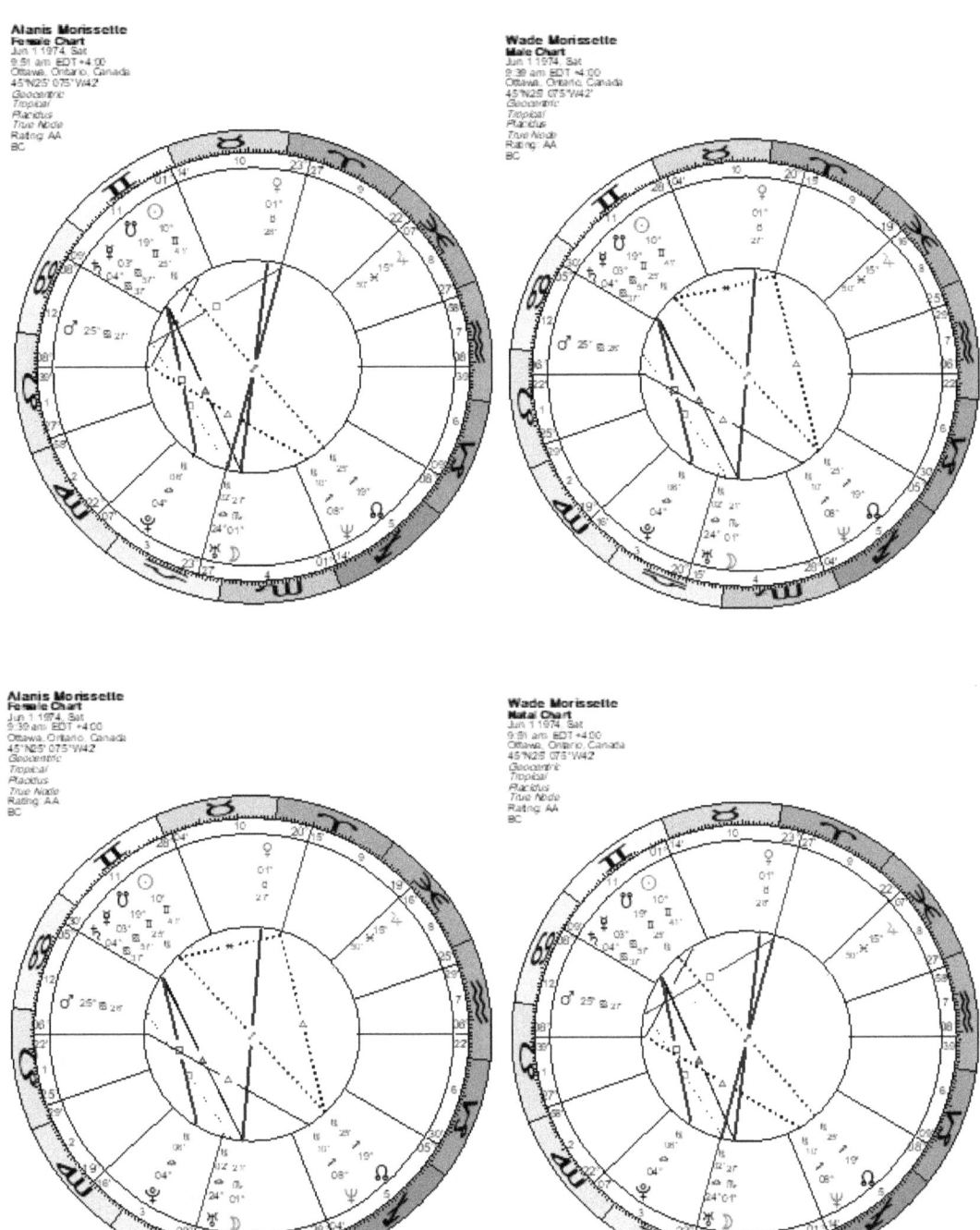

Why Are Time Twins So Different?

brother Wade is a yoga teacher and a reiki master. Using the dwads that change every 2 ½ degrees, or 10 minutes of clock time, the span of 12 minutes allows a different dwad for each twin on the chart angles.

Both have Leo rising and Leo as the first decanate, but the dwads are very different. The 9:39 am birth time has the ascendant at 6:22 Leo that lands in the Libra dwad, and the 9:51 am time has the ascendant at 8:39 Leo landing in the Scorpio dwad. This great difference clearly describes each twin, but the folk music star and song writer fits the 9:39 am birth time, and the yoga teacher and reiki master fits with the 9:51 am time.

To confirm the judgement to change the birth times of the twins, test the midheaven for each time. At 9:39 am, the midheaven is still Aries, in the 3rd decan that is Sagittarius, and also a Sagittarius dwad that best fits the biography of the folk singer and song writer, Alanis. But by 9:51 am the notable change for the midheaven is that the dwad has moved more than 2 ½ degrees to a Capricorn dwad that better fits the brother and reiki master, Wade. With rectification study, any well trained astrologer should answer such questions

Chapter 9

Why are Some Charts Hard to Rectify?

Easy to Rectify Example: Patsy Cline Has Close Hard Aspects

We already know that know that rounded birth times are most common and very easy to rectify by adding or subtracting a couple of minutes of clock time either plus or minus to align the life events with appropriate astrological descriptors. But just as easy is to hook into close hard aspects between planets that immediately catch any astrologer's eye. It's not necessarily portending disaster but rectifying a rounded birth time doesn't need the hard work of building a "Case Theory", establishing "Aspect Hooks" or using advanced software to narrow the search time range because nothing but the Angles will move 1 or 2-degrees in plus or minus 7 or 8-minutes of clock time. Not even the Moon moves noticeably.

Patsy Cline Original Birth Information

For many years, astrologers only had this rounded birth time for Patsy Cline, but after her tragic death in an airplane crash March 5, 1963, several astrologers attempted to rectify her birth time based on the following information from www.Astro.com soon after.

Of course, I was one of those astrologers who started using Ms. Cline's chart to teach rectification techniques because such dramatic events are much easier to align with appropriate astrological descriptors. And, usually, several planets and angles of the natal chart are activated for very dramatic events. It is obvious that Patsy's natal chart has significant close "Aspect Hooks" for which any astrologer would expect a dramatic event when activated by moving factors. Using the "Easy Test" of Solar Arc Direction, we can easily see that the 11:15 PM birth time does not arc to the descriptive 1-degree orb of the difficult Mars, Uranus, and Pluto square activated at the appropriately descriptive event, the airplane crash that took her life. By Direction, the Midheaven arcs to Uranus at age 51, the Ascendant arcs to Mars and Pluto at age 29, and Saturn arcs to the Midheaven at age 33 – none of which align with the major event at age 30 ½. Clearly, rectification of birth time is needed.

Figure 170: 2005 Astro.com Birth Record for Patsy Cline 11:15 PM EST

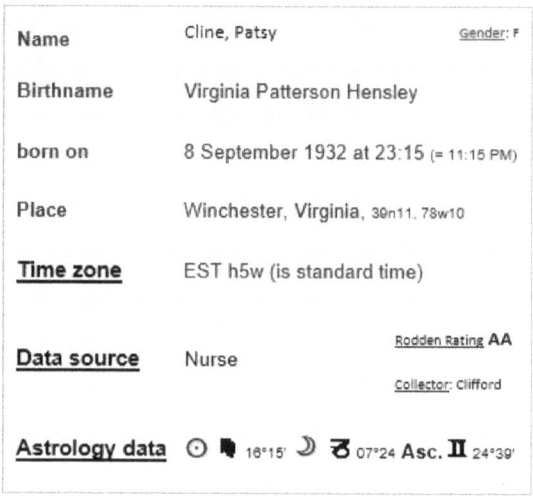

Source: From hospital records, 11:15 PM birth time was read out to astrologer Frank Clifford by staff at the Winchester Memorial Hospital in 1995.

Figure 171 Country Singer Patsy Cline - Rounded Birth Time 11:15 pm EST

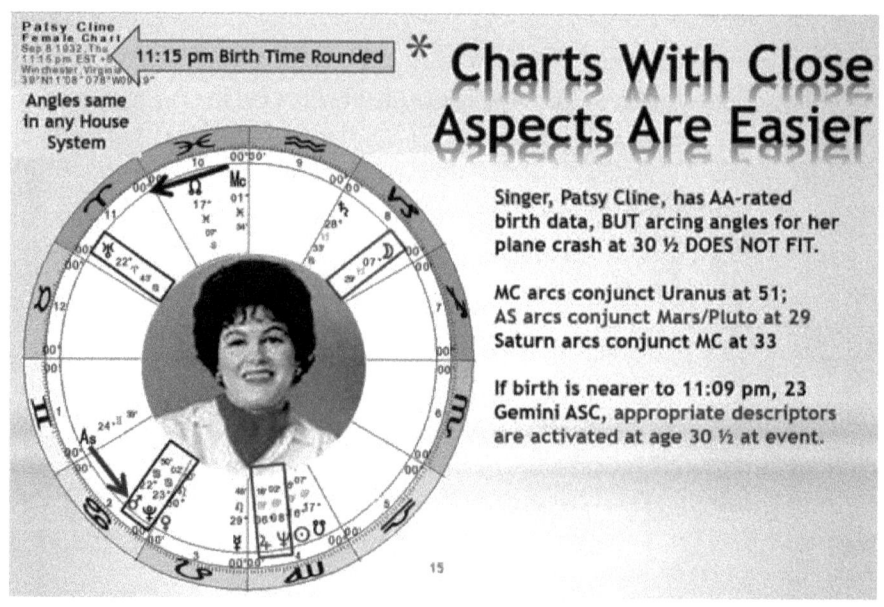

The New Complete Book of Chart Rectification

Patsy Cline's Biography:

"American country-western singer, who helped to pave the way for other female singers to become an integral part of the formerly male-dominated country music industry. In 1973, she became the first female solo performer elected to Country Music's Hall of Fame.

Born Virginia Patterson Hensley, her family called her "Ginny" until she was almost 20. Her mother, Hilda, was just 16 years old when Ginny was born, and her parents had been married just six days earlier. Ginny had one younger brother, Sam (John), and two half-siblings from her father's previous marriage, Tempie Glenn, and Randolph. The family moved shortly after her birth, and over the next 13 years, they moved about 20 times. Her father, Samuel, deserted the family when she was 15, leaving her mother, Hilda, to provide for the children. Ginny's next contact with her father was in 1956, when he was seriously ill with lung cancer; he died on 11 December 1956 and never heard her sing.

As a child, Ginny wanted to become a dancer, and she won first place in a children's dance competition; suddenly she completely lost interest in dancing and turned her focus toward music. She had no formal music training, but learned to play the piano by ear, and soon she was part of the Baptist church choir. Although working various jobs in order to help her mother support the family, Patsy… sang with local country bands… and was determined to get a recording contract. In 1954, Four Star Records signed her.

Patsy recorded 17 singles between 1955 and 1960 but only one, "Walkin' After Midnight," was a hit, making the Top 20. … By 1958 she was a regular performer on the Grand Ole Opry radio broadcasts. Once released from her original record deal, she began to record songs that she liked, beginning with "I Fall to Pieces," which hit number one on the country charts. This was a turning point in her career… Through 1961-62, she had hits like "Crazy" and "She's Got You," and her achingly romantic material was marketed as pop music, bringing her commercial success. Patsy, however, always preferred traditional country music and dressed in distinctly western-style clothing. Her last concert was … in Kansas City, on 3 March 1963.

In 1953, Patsy married Gerald Cline. They had no children. In 1956, during a performance at a local dance, she met Charlie Dick, "the love of her life," prompting her to divorce Gerald. She married Charlie in 1957, and they had two children, Julia Simadore, 1958, and Allen Randolph, 1961. In 1961, Patsy, along with her brother Sam, was in a severe auto accident. The head-on collision sent Patsy through the windshield and nearly killed her. [Two years later] … After leaving Kansas City at 6:07 PM, Patsy, along with her manager, Randy Hughes, and two fellow entertainers, Cowboy Copas and Hawkshaw Hawkins, died in a plane crash in Camden, Tennessee, on March 5, 1963[1].

---

1. www.astro.com, AstroDataBank, 2022

Life Events

- Contracted Rheumatic Fever 1947
- Marriage 1953 (Gerald Cline)
- Record Contract 1954 (Four Stars Records)
- Contacted father 1956
- Romance 1956 (Charlie Dick)
- Death of Father December 11, 1956 (Lung cancer)
- Marriage 1957 (Charlie Dick)
- Published and Released Songs 1958 (Grand Ole Opry)
- Birth of Daughter 1958 (Julia)
- Published and Released Songs 1961 ("Crazy")
- Birth of Son 1961 (Allen)
- Severe Auto Accident 1961 (Non-fatal)
- Published and Released Songs March 3, 1963, in Kansas City (Last concert)
- Death by Airplane Accident March 5, 1963, at 6:10 PM in Camden. TN
- Entered into Country Music Hall of Fame 1973

For years I have used the 11:15 PM birth time for Patsy Cline as a demonstration to students of the "Easy Test" using this one dramatic event to show how an earlier birth time of 11:09 PM works to dramatically activate the natal chart for the tragic event that ended her life at the correct age of 30 ½. In preparing this 2025 edition of The NEW Complete Book of Chart Rectification, I revisited www.astro.com and was not at all surprised to find new information about Patsy's birth – a birth certificate with an earlier time of 11:05 PM. Even though I tested only the one dramatic event, I suspect that my 11:09 PM rectified birth time may continue to appropriately align with her other life events. Remember all of the caveats about the variances of birth certificate times that are often off by a few minutes plus or minus because of the focus on caring for the mother and child first. Only astrologers are fixated on specific birth time for its importance in delineating the natal promise and forecasting activated issues for the present. Also remember that most of us have planets in hard aspect somewhere in our chart, and most of us face the challenging situation and work through it coming out wiser, and sometimes sadder. A cluster of close hard aspects does not necessarily describe death – in fact, my experience says they don't. The close natal hard aspects more often describe the life experiences we need to learn from and grow beyond our seeming limitations through understanding and compassion.

Figure 172: 2005 Astro.com Birth Record for Patsy Cline 11:05 PM EST

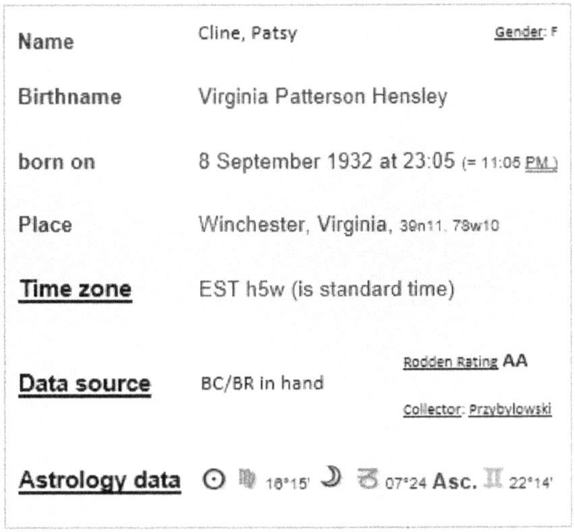

Name	Cline, Patsy Gender: F
Birthname	Virginia Patterson Hensley
born on	8 September 1932 at 23:05 (= 11:05 PM)
Place	Winchester, Virginia, 39n11, 78w10
Time zone	EST h5w (is standard time)
Data source	BC/BR in hand Rodden Rating AA Collector: Przybylowski
Astrology data	☉ ♍ 16°15' ☽ ♉ 07°24 Asc. ♊ 22°14'

Source Notes: *From hospital records, time of 11:15 PM was read out to Frank Clifford by staff at Winchester Memorial Hospital in 1995. In March 2008 Stephen Przybylowski found a copy of her birth certificate on the web stating 11:05 PM.*

Figure 173 Country Singer Patsy Cline – Tebbs Rectified Birth Time 11:09 pm EST

2. www.astro.com, AstroDataBank, 2022

Difficult to Rectify Example: Kobe Bryant Also Has Close Hard Aspects

First of all, certain facts of Kobe Bryant's birth are in dispute, akin to "Dirty Data". The NBA Register lists Kobe Bryant's birthplace as Philadelphia, but Isaac Starkman in www.Astro.com gives Harrisburg, Pennsylvania. The original source of the birth time is not known. Also, from www.Astro.com. Paddy de Jabrun rectified Kobe Bryant's birth time to 17:30, or 5:30 pm EDT and Isaac Starkman rectified Kobe's birth time to 17.10.32, or 5:10:32 EDT in Harrisburg, Pennsylvania.

Figure 174 Kobe Bryant's "birth announcement"

(shown in Ansfield biography of Kobe) This cannot be from the original birth certificate because it already reports his career.

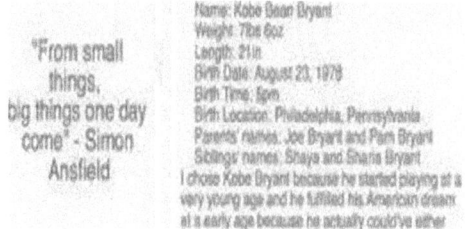

Figure 175 5:00 pm "Working Chart" for Kobe Bryant

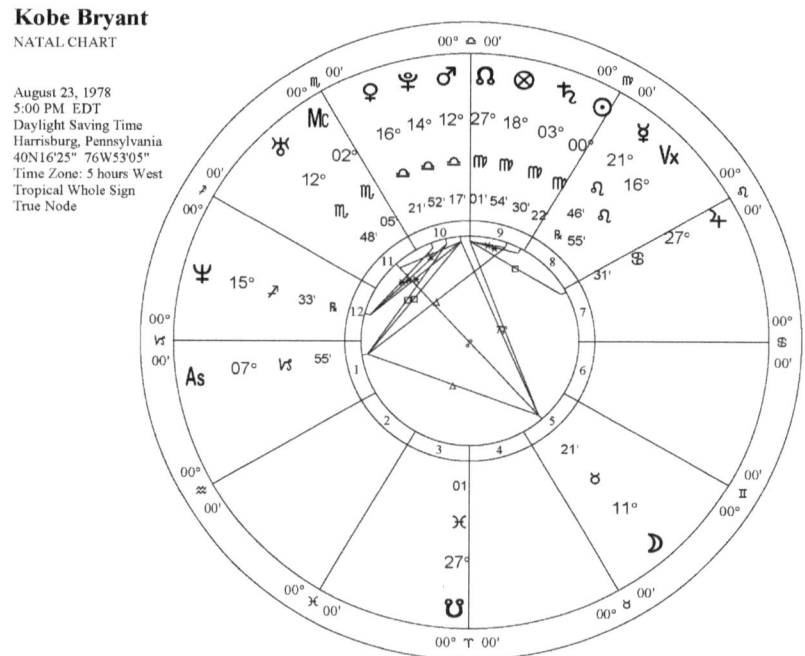

5:00 PM could be simply a rounded birth time that was fairly common earlier in the 20th century, but I doubt that was done in a large US city hospital in the late 1970's. With such weak birth time confirmation, along with other "dirty data" times for Kobe, I would start with a 24-hour search and narrow the range with the Moon sign and the possible Ascendant signs in the remaining range. In Kobe's chart, the Moon is in Taurus all 24-hours of August 23, 1978, so I cannot narrow the time range with the Moon. As well, that means that all 12 signs are possible Ascendant signs. Without the narrowing birth time "easy tools", the Moon and Ascendant signs that fit the client, the search must test all 24-hours. My preference is software with a rectification module, such as Jigsaw 2.2 and Sirius 4.1, that are built with different paradigms. Jigsaw counts the degree number of 360 for appropriate aspect hits within a 1-degree orb for each event, whereas Sirius is programmed with planetary descriptors that fit the essence of each event. For instance, a romantic date event might be described with the Moon and Venus in an ease aspect.

Test 24-Hours with Selection of All of Kobe Bryant's Major Life Events

1. Relocated to Italy age 6, September 1, 1984
2. Relocated back to Pennsylvania, Sep 1, 1991
3. Drafted into National Basketball Association June 26, 1996
4. Married despite parents' disapproval April 18, 2001
5. Birth of daughter Jan 19, 2003
6. Pending divorce March 2003
7. Knee surgery July 1, 2003
8. Arrested after claim he raped a woman July 4, 2003
9. Birth of 2nd daughter, March 1, 2006
10. Olympic gold medal, men's basketball, Aug 24, 2008
11. Wife filed for divorce, later called it off Dec 16, 2011
12. Olympic gold medal, men's basketball, Aug 12, 2012
13. Accident Torn Achilles tendon April 13, 2013
14. Shoulder surgery Jan 28, 2015
15. Birth of 3rd daughter, Dec 5, 2016
16. Oscar for Best Animated Short Film, Mar 4, 2018
17. Book, "The Mamba Mentality: How I Play" released Oct 23, 2018
18. Birth of 4th daughter June 20, 2019
19. Death by Helicopter Accident Jan 26, 2020, at 9:45 am in Calabasas, CA

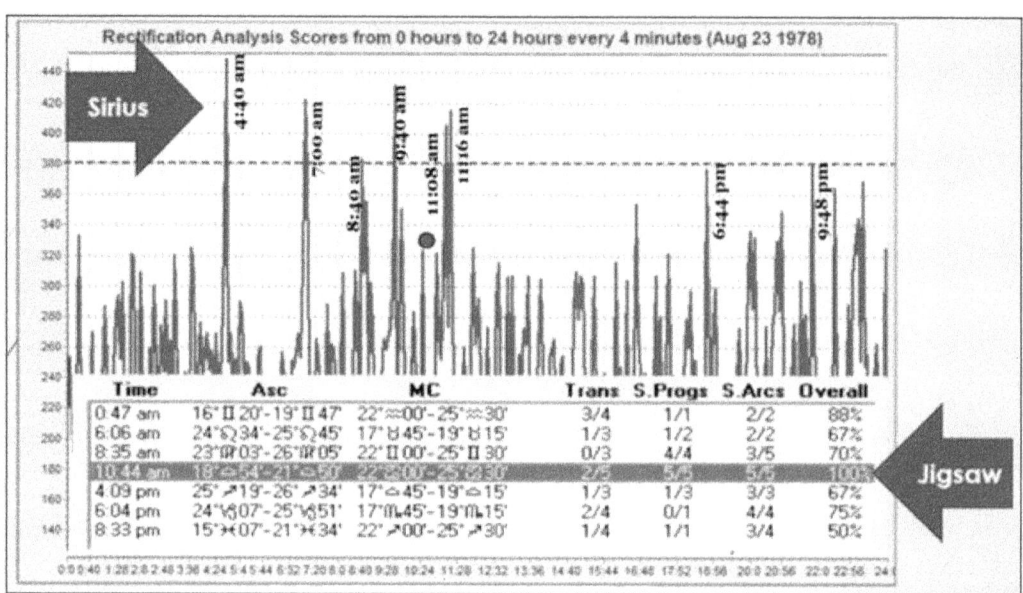

Note that Jigsaw's 10:44 am birth time for Kobe is 100%, but Sirius only rates the time as 325, very low compared to the top times well into the 400's.

Years ago, I tested 100 family, friends, and clients with certificate birth times, using a 24-hour search set for every 4-minutes of clock time that produced 360 possibilities on that date and location. Certainly, people are born within the 4-minute time range, but on average, the angles move 1-degree every 4-minutes of clock time, so it works well to set the sign and degree of the chart angles. I was astonished with the results because for more than half of the group, the software did not place their times at the top of the list. In some cases, the actual birth time was off by up to 8 minutes, possibly from rounding to the nearest quarter hour, which was common into the 1950's, but others were way down the list, though within the top 20 times. Why is that possible, you ask? Software is excellent for testing major life events to consistently align with appropriate astrological descriptors to confirm birth time, but it does not know the person's biography that fits the chart. That information is best determined by a well-trained astrologer with good biography information from their client.

* What Times Will You Choose to Test, and Why Those?

Sirius 4.1 1st choice: 4:40 am
2nd choice: 9:40 am
3rd choice: 7:00 am
4th choice: 8:40 am ⟷

Jigsaw 2.2 1st choice: 10:44 am
2nd choice: 0:47 am
3rd choice: 6:04 pm
4th choice: 8:35 am

> I would choose the top scores of Sirius and Jigsaw
  And especially any times that both formats affirm.
> Notice that all but one top time is in the AM.

* What Events Will You Choose to Test, and Why Those?

1. Fall 1984 Age 6: Moved to Italy
2. Fall 1991 Age 13: Returned to Philadelphia
3. June 26, 1996 Age 17+: Drafted to NBA
4. April 18, 2001 Age 23: Marriage
5. March 2003 Pending Divorce
6. January 26, 2020 Age 41: Kobe's Death

* Test Jigsaw/Sirius 8:35 am Birth for Kobe Bryant

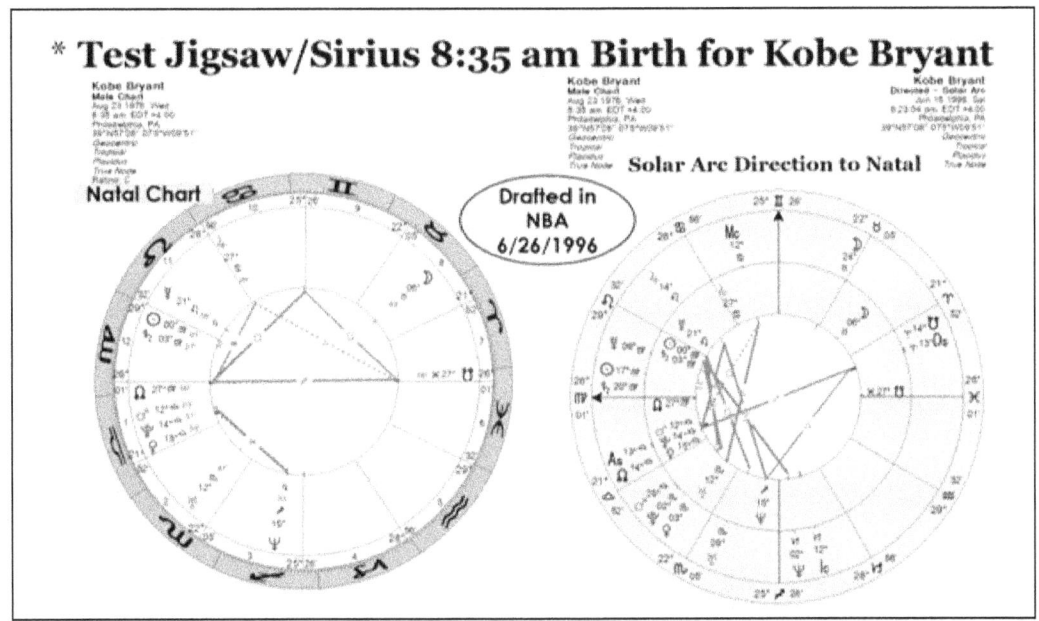

Why are Some Charts Hard to Rectify?

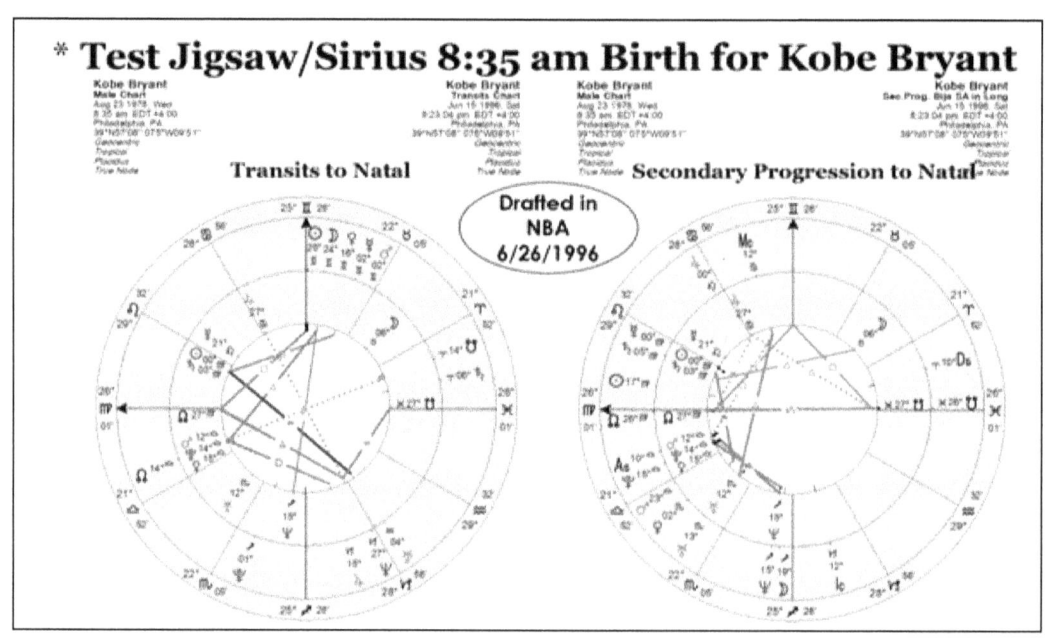

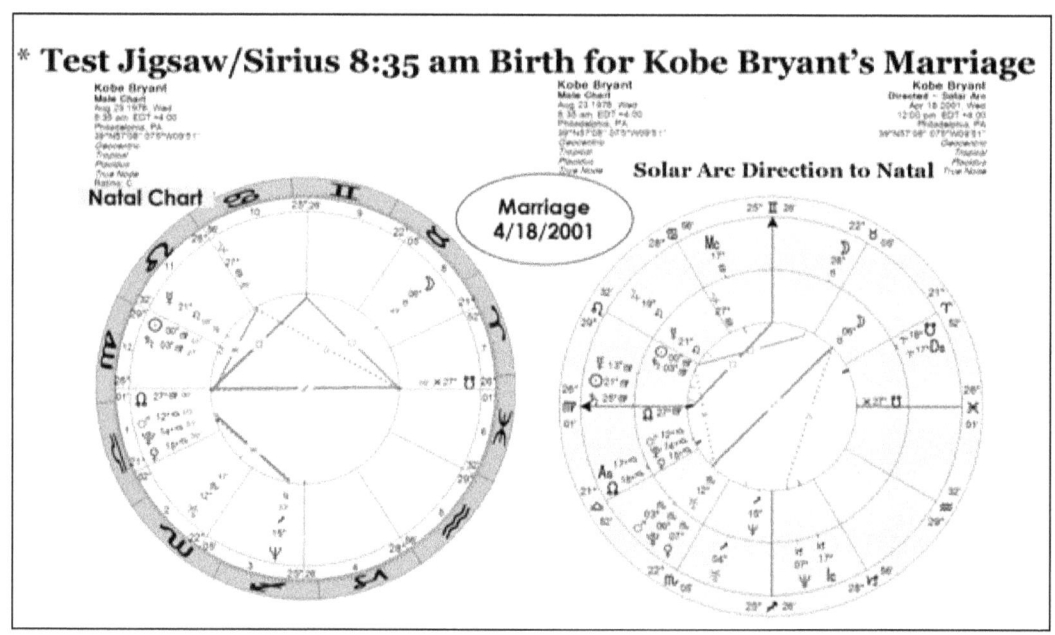

262   The New Complete Book of Chart Rectification

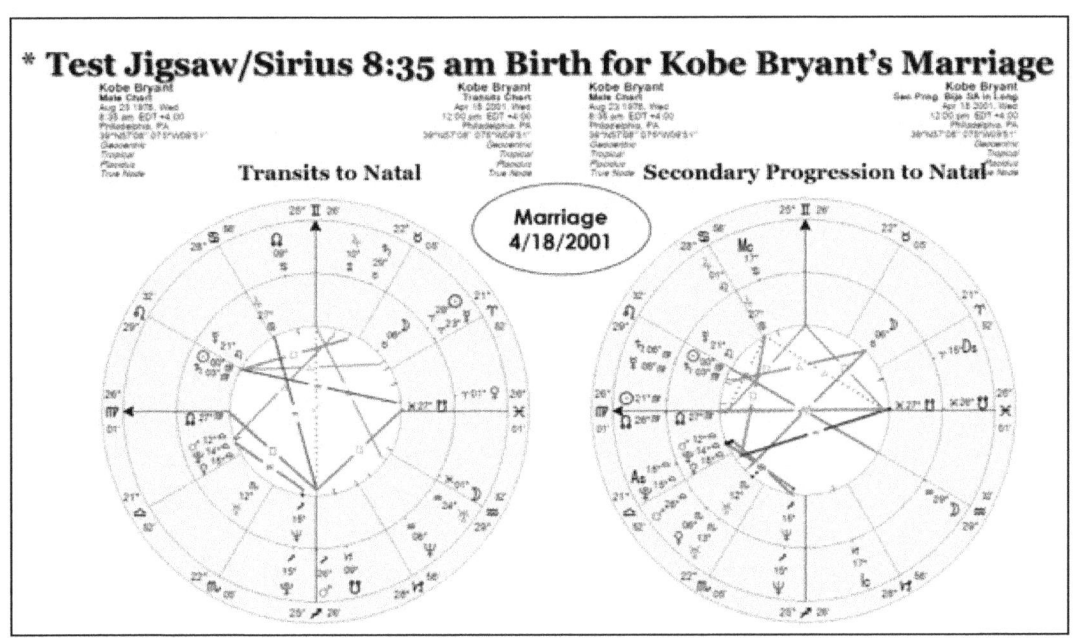

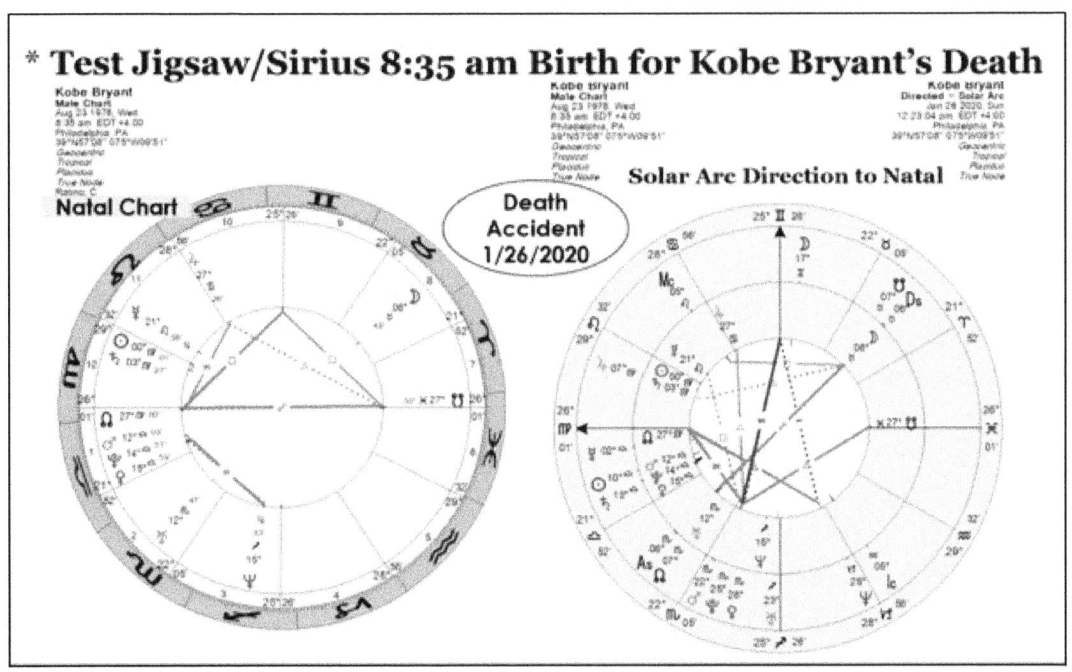

Why are Some Charts Hard to Rectify?

Test Jigsaw/Sirius 8:35 am Birth for Kobe Bryant's Death

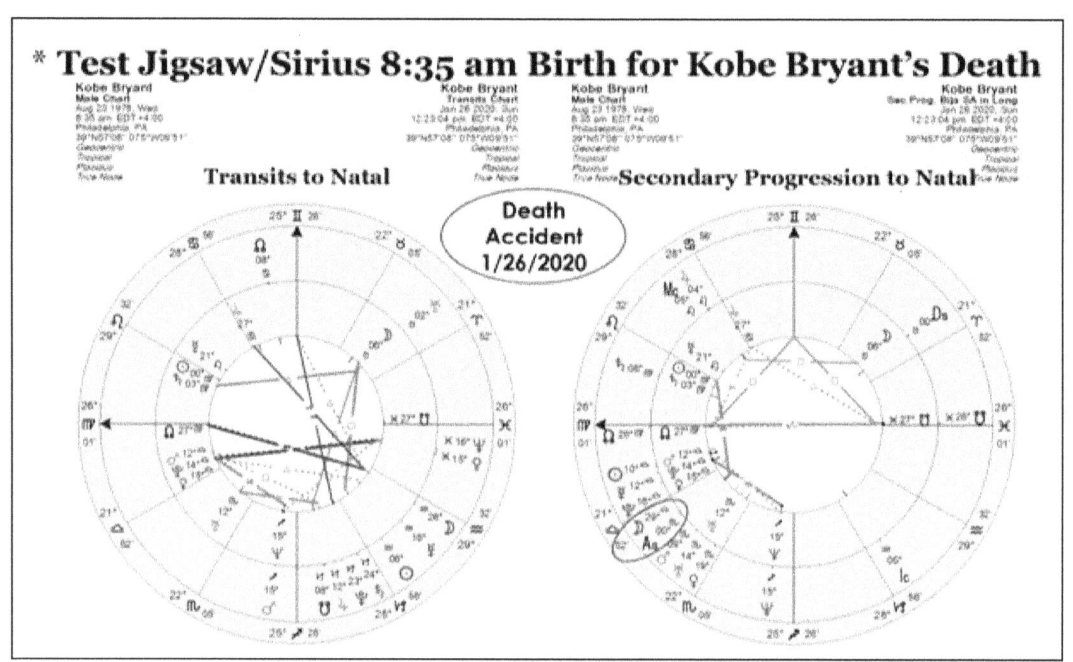

Does 8:35 AM Declination Work for Kobe's Events?

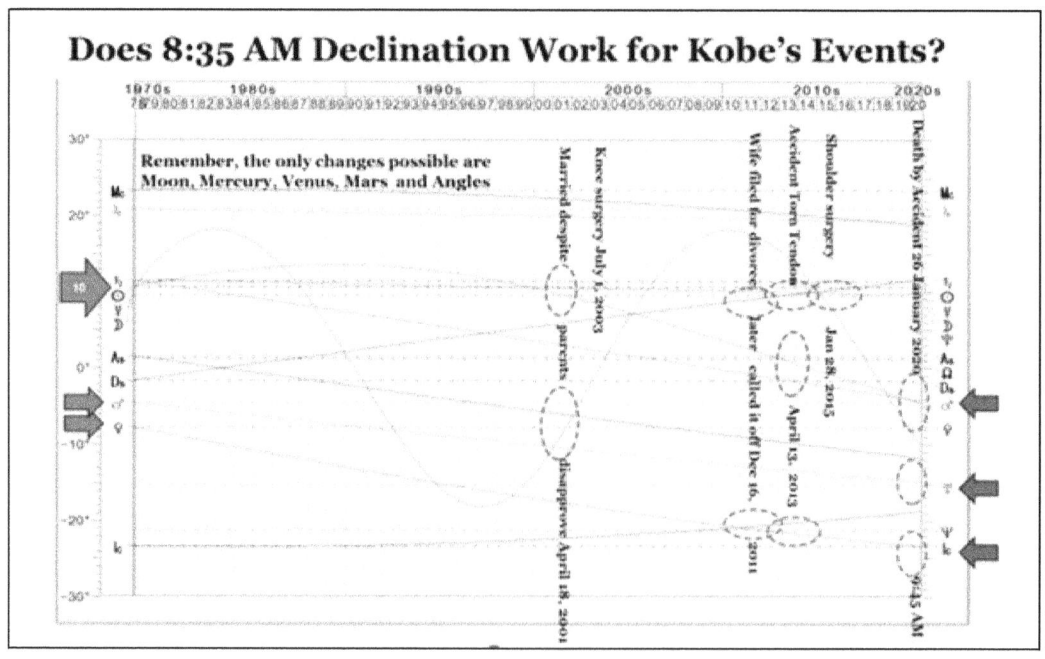

Figure 176 Kobe Bryant Chart Rectified by Paddy de Jabrun, 5:10 PM EDT, Philadelphia, PA

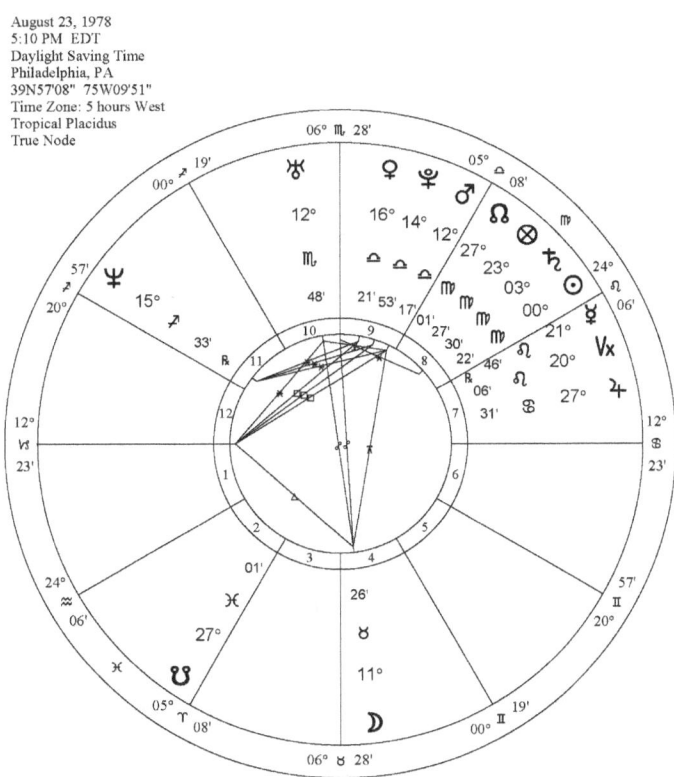

If you consider the Kobe Bryant rectifications by astrologers Isaac Starkman for 5:10 pm EDT at Harrisburg, PA, and Paddy de Jabrun for 5:30 pm EDT in Philadelphia, PA as valid, look at their rectified charts and see if the planets and rulers of each chart fit the biography of the person, Kobe Bryant.

Kobe's Capricorn Ascendant

Kobe's Capricorn Ascendant aptly describes his leadership and disciplined work ethic with ruler Saturn in Virgo in the Placidus 8th house, all suggesting that he is very particular, and even a stickler for the rules. The 12:23 Capricorn Ascendant receives a partile square from Mars and a 2-degree square from Pluto at the midpoint of Mars and close by Venus, all in Libra in the Placidus 9th house, suggesting that Kobe may have some legal trouble related to his power as applied to women.

Why are Some Charts Hard to Rectify?

As for Kobe's 6:24 Scorpio MC ruled and co-ruled by Mars and Pluto in Libra and in close conjunction in the 9th house. Further, his Mars/Pluto power structure gives a beguiling Libra surface to his famous disguise as "The Black Mamba" with the silent killer instinct on the basketball court. Kobe's 11:26 Taurus Moon enjoys the comforts and pleasures of life but its partile opposition to his Scorpio Uranus in the 10th house, and quincunx Mars and Pluto, portend dramatic emotional upheavals. He was fortunate to have a forgiving wife.

Figure 177 Kobe Bryant Chart Rectified by Isaac Starkman, 5:30 PM EDT, Harrisburg, PA

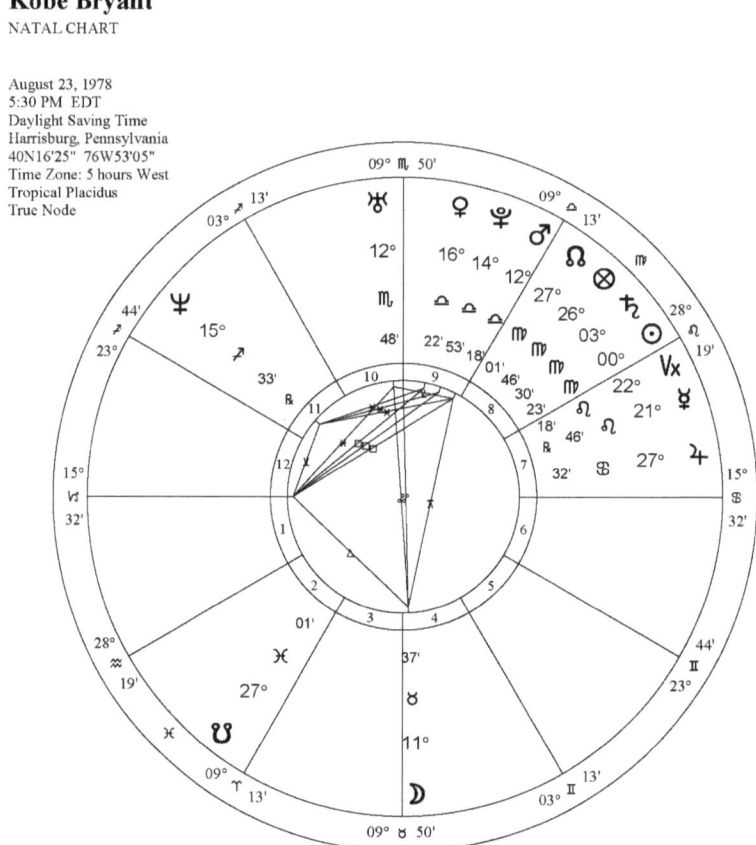

Much of the same delineation for Kobe's 5:10 PM rectified birth time Ascendant and its Saturn ruler also hold true for 5:30 PM EDT. However, Starkman brings the close Venus and Pluto conjunction to straddle the Ascendant by square, giving more emphasis to the difficulties with women. Ironically, Kobe was father to three daughters, one a teen.

The 9:50 Scorpio Midheaven now moves within 3-degrees to conjunct his 10th house Uranus and 1 ½ -degrees opposite his comfort loving Taurus Moon, suggesting erratic mood changes that bring some controversial situations public and his reputation veers from hero to villain. Neither of these rectified birth times are confirmed by the Sirius 4.1 and Jigsaw 2.2 rectification software. I often repeat, software is a great tool, but it is not better than a well trained astrologer. Trust your judgement to fit the chart to the client's biography and match the significant life events with appropriate astrological descriptors.

Figure 178
Bryant 5:10 PM Directions to Natal

Figure 179
Bryant 5:10 PM Transits to Natal

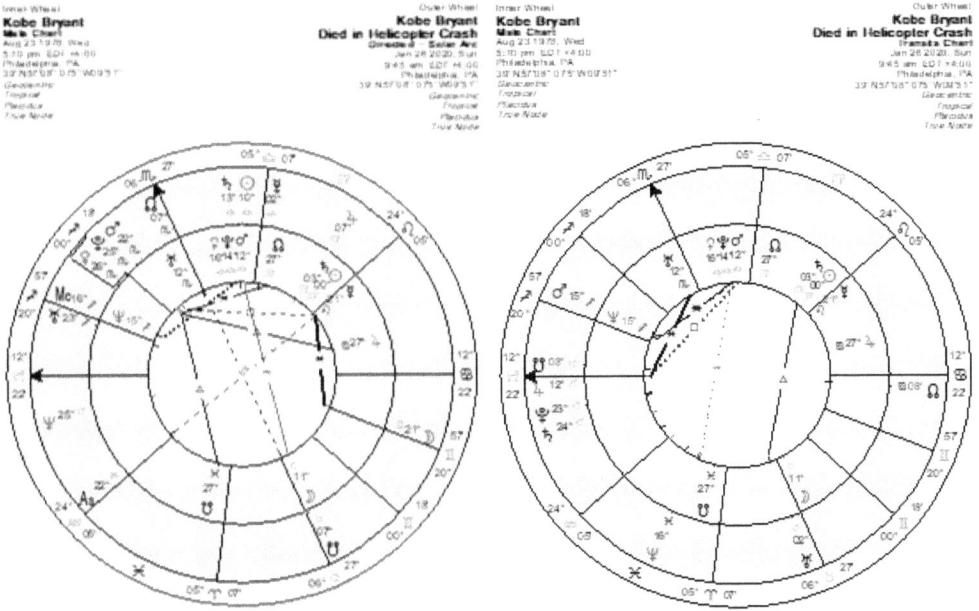

The "Quick Test" by Direction do the arcing Lunar Nodes across the Midheaven/Imum Coeli axis, elevate this 5:10 pm time over the 5:30 time where neither pair of angles are activated for this tragic event. Outer planet Jupiter appropriately transits conjunct the 5:10 pm natal Ascendant and squares Mars to a partile degree. All other directions and transits are planet to planet and true for all day during the event date.

Let's continue the "Quick Test" to see if the 5:30 pm rectified birth time is more appropriately descriptive of the sudden death of Kobe Bryant to be considered a workable rectified birth time.

Figure 180
Bryant 5:30 PM Directions to Natal

Figure 181
Bryant 5:30 PM Outer Transits to Natal

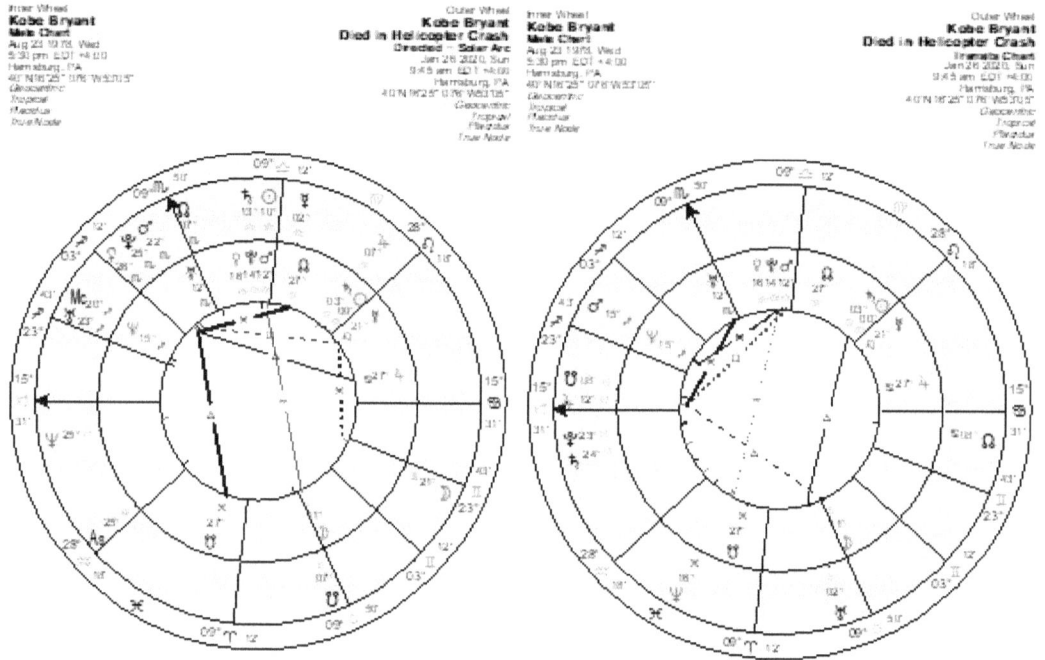

In the 5:30 pm rectified chart, none of the chart Angles are activated by Direction for this sad event, nor are the moving Angles activating anything. Similarly, the Outer Planet Transits do not activate any chart Angles. Therefore, I do not consider the 5:30 birth time a workable rectified birth time. Clearly, of the two rectified birth times for Kobe Bryant, 5:10 pm is the best.

We may not want to accept someone else's rectified birth time and want to use our software to derive an appropriate birth time ourselves. The following search results are for a 2-hour span (4 to 6 pm) with all of the events put into Sirius 4.1 and then into Jigsaw 2.2 software with the following results, none of which place 5:10 pm or 5:30 pm high on the list. This complexity is why many astrologers give up on the rectification search. However, they say that patience is a virtue. Fortunately, we do have good software to aid the process.

Figure 182 Sirius 4.1 Two-Hour Bryant Birth Time Search from 4:00 pm to 6:00 pm

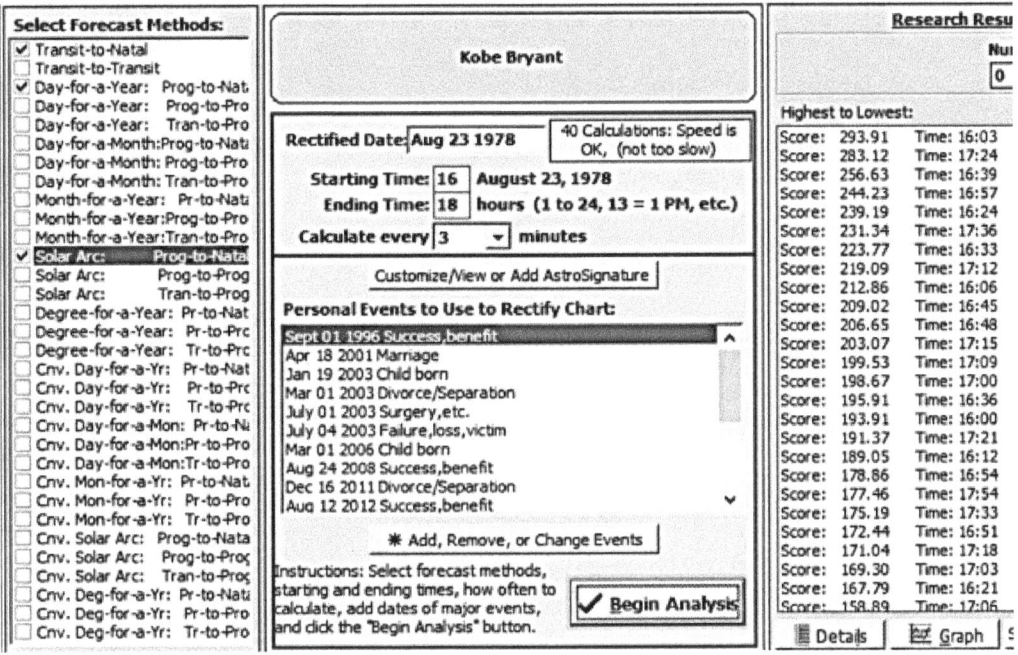

Figure 183 Sirius 4.1 Two-Hour Bryant Birth Time Search from 4:00 pm to 6:00 pm

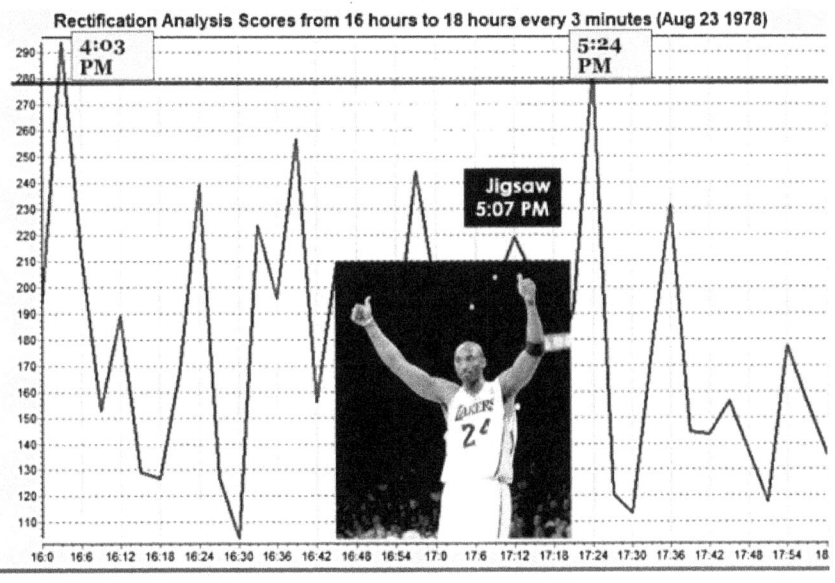

Why are Some Charts Hard to Rectify?

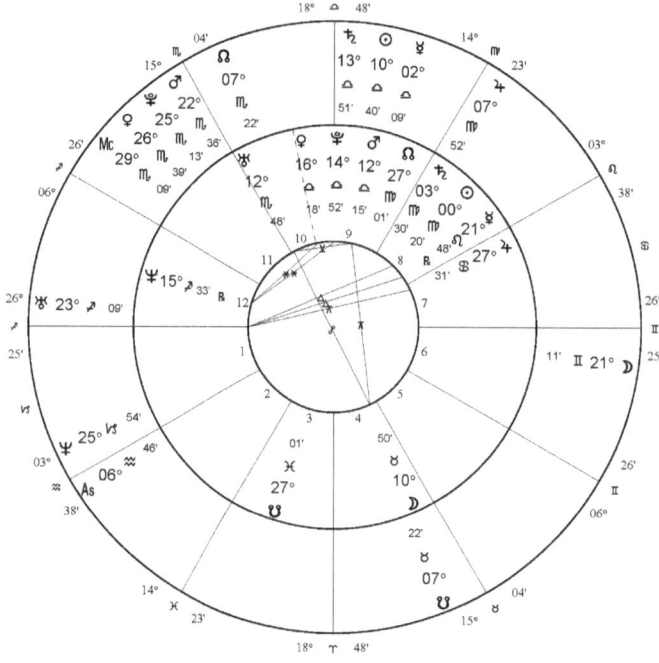

Inner wheel: Kobe Bryant, August 23, 1978; 4:03 PM, Philadelphia PA
Outer wheel: Solar Arc Direction January 26, 2020; 9:34:36 AM

Sirius 4.1 top time 4:03 PM with Directions and Transits to Natal Chart for Kobe's sudden death. Looking for planet to angle or angle to planet within a 1-degree orb.

- Directed MC/IC square Sun
- Directed Venus/Pluto quincunx DES
- Transiting ASC opposite Saturn/ IC conjunct Saturn
- Transiting MC/Mars conjunct Neptune

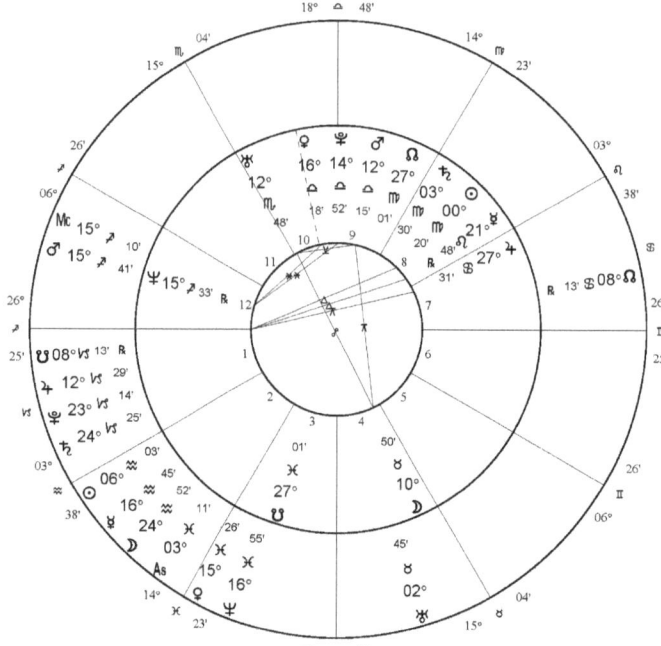

Inner wheel: Kobe Bryant, August 23, 1978; 4:03 PM, Philadelphia PA
Outer wheel: Transits January 26, 2020; 9:34:36 AM

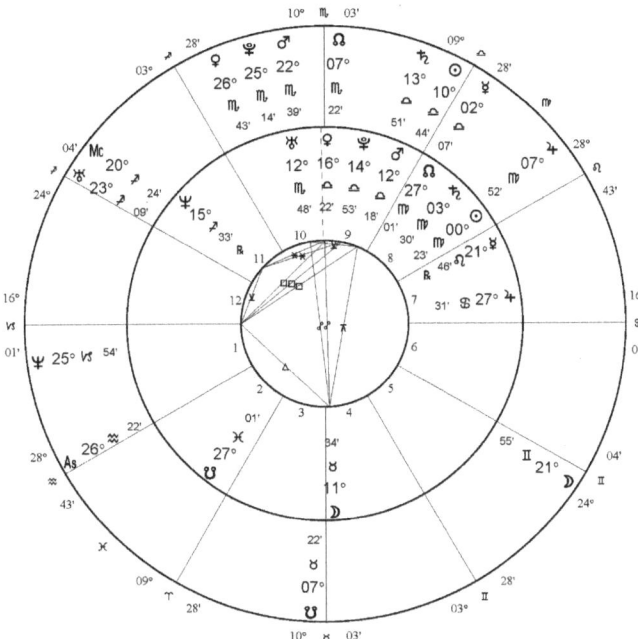

Inner wheel: Kobe Bryant, August 23, 1978; 5:24 PM, Philadelphia PA
Outer wheel: Solar Arc Direction
January 26, 2020; 9:34:36 AM

Sirius 4.1 second top time 5:24 PM with Directions and Transits to Natal Chart for Kobe's sudden death. Looking for planet to angle or angle to planet within a 1-degree orb.

- Directed ASC opposite Jupiter
- Directed MC trine Mercury
- Directed Sun quincunx IC
- Directed ASC quincunx North Node
- Transiting ASC opposite Saturn
- Transiting MC/Mars conjunct Neptune
- Transiting MC/Mars quincunx Des
- Transiting MC/Mars sextile Venus/Pluto

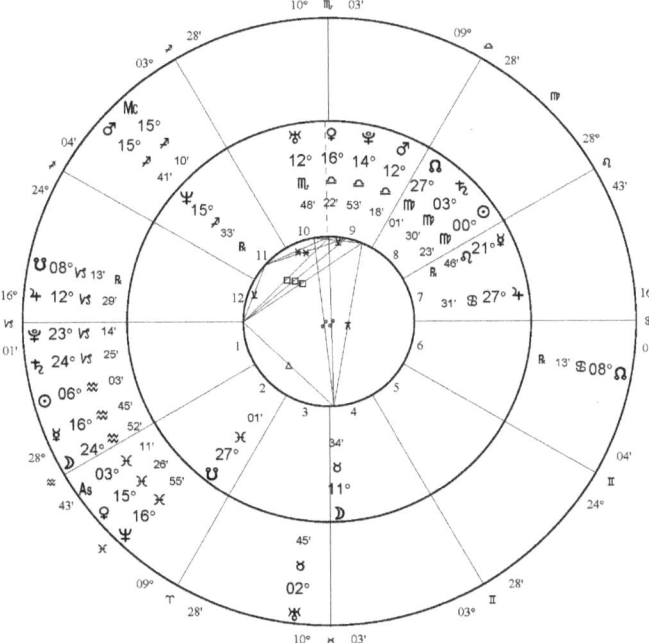

Inner wheel: Kobe Bryant, August 23, 1978; 5:24 PM, Philadelphia PA
Outer wheel: Transits
January 26, 2020; 9:34:36 AM

Why are Some Charts Hard to Rectify?

If you are skeptical, use my reliable rectification steps.

1. Narrow the time range by choosing the Moon sign that fits the client, and possibly the ASC sign.
2. Set a "Working birth time at midpoint of the search time range.
3. Develop a "Case Theory" that aligns with the biography and personal traits
4. If the search range is more than two-hours, Narrow time range with software
5. Choose the 5 or 6 best birth times to test with 5 or 6 Movement techniques
6. Begin testing Angles to Planets and Planets to Angles for each time.
7. Select the chart that best describes the client and also aligns appropriate astrological descriptors with life events
8. If in doubt, describe Ascendant sign attributes and its ruler to let the client choose which descriptors best fit

The birth times around 5:00 pm do descriptively fit Kobe Bryant, but once the search range is widened to 24-hours, it is clear to see how complicated the search becomes, and it is apparent why most astrologers will not take rectification clients beyond the half-hour search range. However, it is my experience that if birth time is rectified and fits the person's interests and biography with appropriate astrological descriptors activated for all major life events, you will have a client for life. Like a new friend, stay in touch with clients.

At this point, I must remind every reader that public charts are especially difficult to rectify, because the celebrity is most likely not a willing subject who will provide feelings and conditions of difficult situations that are so helpful to the astrologer. And once again, when the rectification comes down to a small handful of times that work, the client knows pretty well which Ascendant descriptors fit their personality and how others see them. A good rectification is more than number crunching to align events to appropriate astrological descriptors; it is also interacting with people to accept their situations and feelings as your guide to choosing the rectified birth time that fits the person's life story.

Appendix A: Frequently Asked Questions About Rectification

Rectification Overview: by Carol Tebbs, M.A.

Birth chart interpretation and forecasting is greatly dependent upon accurate birth data, the most variable of which is the birth time. Prior to the mid-20th century, it was common to round-off birth times to the nearest quarter hour, which can mean that the angles and cusps of the chart may be off by 4 degrees or more leading to an entirely different chart interpretation. Even now that birth times are recorded to the minute in most states and countries, the variation among clocks running fast or slow can still provide similar wide variation with similar interpretive inaccuracies as a consequence. Indeed, astrological forecasting based upon the birth chart can be off by as much as 4-5 years, which is not acceptable.

What can be done? The average person can do some "family footwork" before consulting with the astrologer to clarify the actual birth time by asking relatives who were present, finding a birth announcement or letter or searching notations in a baby book or the family bible. That done and the birth time still questionable, the astrologer may ask for 10-12 dates of important life events such as family deaths, job changes, marriages, illnesses, etc. to derive a birth time that more closely aligns the events with the astrological indicators. Nowadays, there are astrological software programs such as: "Sirius", by Cosmic Patterns in Gainesville, FL and "Jigsaw 2, by Bernadette Brady and Graham Dawson, through Astrolabe in MA, that aid in the rectification search. Usually, the adjustment to the birth time is only a few minutes either way; although, some countries such as Japan still do not record birth time at all. In extreme cases where a 24-hour search is necessary the rectification task becomes especially difficult, requiring much extra work. Nonetheless, once the task is done correctly, the person has a reliable birth chart forever for interpretive and forecasting purposes.

Relevant Questions on Rectification

1. In the astrology community, we hear the word "rectification", but can you explain what rectification is?

In short, the process of rectification is adjusting the birth time so that astrological indicators are activated in correspondence with actual life events. It is not uncommon that an astrologer and client feel that the astrological indicators of the birth chart and the forecasts based on the birth chart are not in timing sync with when events, situations or feelings actually occur. So to improve forecasting accuracy for the client, it may be necessary to adjust the birth time by a small amount earlier or later.

2. Why is rectification important?

Birth chart interpretation and forecasting is greatly dependent upon accurate birth data, the most variable of which is the birth time. Prior to the mid-20th century, it was common to round-off birth times to the nearest quarter hour, which can mean that the angles and cusps of the chart may be off by 4 degrees or more leading to an entirely different chart interpretation. Even now that birth times are recorded to the minute in most states and countries, the variation among clocks running fast or slow can still provide similar wide variations with similar interpretive inaccuracies as a consequence. There are still some countries, such as Japan, that still do not record birth time at all. Indeed, astrological forecasting based upon an un-rectified birth chart can be off by as much as 4-5 years, which is not acceptable to astrologers or useful to their clients.

3. Why don't more astrologers use the technique of rectification for their clients?

In the past, rectification was an immensely time-consuming process, so most astrologers avoided it. Additionally, few astrologers have trained in rectification techniques because very little has been written on the topic. However, that trend is due to change for a couple of reasons

    a)   The better astrology programs such as Jigsaw 2 sold by Astrolabe and Sirius sold by Cosmic Patterns, among others, have rectification modules whereby the astrologer may input the dates of the client's significant life events, select the astrology techniques to sort by, and a get a list of several possible birth times in a percentage of accuracy. The software takes much of the number-crunching out of rectification, but it still takes an experienced astrologer's judgment to select the best time.

    b)   Most astrologers are not taught rectification techniques and therefore are not confident in the process.

4. Why wouldn't the astrologer just pick the birth time with the highest percentage in the software search?

That is a complicated question, Jacqui, but let me try to answer it simply. Most often, a birth time close to the recorded birth time is in the list of 6-8 possible times, but it may not be first in the list because other viable times 6, 12 and 18 hours apart may show similar aspects at key life events. The astrologer must sort out which time is the most reasonable relevant to the recorded birth time. Even with the software, the astrologer may need to "tweak" the time a couple of minutes either way because the software does not evaluate the relative impact of the events reliably. For instance, death of a parent when one is age 5 is a greatly more important life event that the death of the same parent when one is age 75.

5. In the past, rectification earned a somewhat bad reputation among astrologers. Why?

I touched upon this earlier, but the short answer is bad astrologers who, prior to the Rodden Rating system for the quality of birth data, used rectified data for their research and writing. Not until the 1980's did the astrology community embrace the importance of using AA data, or when using B, C or DD data, stating so. Rectified data is not appropriate for research; however, it is very useful for astrologers and their clients to achieve greater accuracy in natal interpretations and the resultant forecasts for guidance in personal growth or for important decision-making.

6. **What can the average person do to check the accuracy of the birth time?**

The average person can do some "family footwork" before consulting with the astrologer to clarify the actual birth time by asking relatives who were present, finding a birth announcement or letter or searching notations in a baby book or the family bible. That done and the birth time still questionable, the astrologer may ask for 10-12 dates of important life events such as family deaths, job changes, marriages, illnesses, etc. to derive a birth time that more closely aligns the events with the astrological indicators.

7. **What would be the benefit of people having a chart rectification done?**

Once the rectification task is done, the person has established a reliable birth chart forever for interpretive and forecasting purposes. Instead of the "close, but not quite" feeling some may have after an astrology consultation, the client should find clarity and insight from the consultation.

Table 76 Approximate Calendar Time for Movement to Activate 1-Degree

(Describes Only 1-Degree of the Complete Cycle)

1 year+	Secondary Progression of Sun, Mercury, Venus and angles Solar Arc Direction of all planets and angles Retrograde shadow area between stations of transit Pluto, Neptune, Uranus Out-of-bounds or maximum N or S of Moon's declination
11 months	Retrograde shadow area between stations of Saturn
9 ¾ months	Retrograde shadow area between stations of Jupiter Secondary Progression of Mars
6 ½ months	Retrograde shadow area between stations of Mars
6 months	Solar and Lunar Eclipses Transit of Pluto Transit of Neptune
3 ½ months	Retrograde shadow area between the stations of Venus
3 months	Transit of Uranus Parallel or contra-parallel of Moon Declination
1 ¾ months	Retrograde shadow area between the stations of Mercury
1 month	Transit of Saturn Transit of Moon's nodal axis Secondary Progression of the Moon Stationary Period of Jupiter through Pluto
2 weeks	Transit of Jupiter Stationary Period of Mars
1 week	Stationary Period of Venus Stationary Period of Mercury
2 days	Transit of Mars (not near station or in shadow)
1 day	Transit of Venus Transit of Mercury Diurnal Movement of angles and cusps
2 hours	Transit of Moon
4 minutes	Transit of angles and cusps

Appendix B:

Frequently Asked Questions About Birth Time and Angles

RC> How can you be sure that any time is correct?

Carol Tebbs> Aside from the automatically adjusted atomic clock time that is currently in every cell phone and many clocks, you need the rectification lesson -- because clock time has so many variations when time-keeping devices were less accurate. Easily a birth time could be off several minutes from the birth certificate time, depending on the accuracy of the hospital or nurse's watch.

MB> I have two friends who have had major life events in the past couple of years and I can't find ANYTHING in their charts to reflect this.

Carol Tebbs> First of all, I assume that both of your friends do have a birth time, but it may be rounded to the quarter hour, of just recorded from memory after mother and baby were cared for. In that case, get several major life events from the person with specific dates that span the life, and you will find a consistent pattern of a bit earlier or later. Then adjust the working birth time to align with the events. That is rectification.

MB> But the birth time would only affect the angles, Moon, and houses, right?

Carol Tebbs> Yes, it is birth time that gives the angles, and conversely, we can determine the birth time if we can get the angles to consistently align to major events. It's a lot of work, though, unless the birth time is only off a few minutes. If the search time range is hours, roll up your sleeves for some really hard work because in the wider search you will find several birth times that seem to work.

Carol Tebbs> For instance, in 24-hours you will have at least four peaks that represent the angles, but then you will need to figure out which angle is which. For instance, times approximately 6 hours apart, 2:25 PM, 8:25 PM, 2:25 AM and 8:25 AM all reasonably match up with the events, but what does that tell you?

RA> Oh, MC or ASC – the Angles.

Carol Tebbs> Yes. You just don't know which one is where, so you have to test them all. In fact, you love it when your search yields 3 or 4 times that are evenly spaced, or two birth times opposite two other possible birth times. For instance, 2:25 AM, 2:25 PM, 6:15 AM and 6:15

PM are two pairs of times opposite each other, but in a different relationship to the other two. It suggests that you, again, have the angles, but the Ascendant and Midheaven are, more often than not, 90 degrees from each other because of birth location and latitude. The only thing you need to test, then, is which pair represents the MC/IC and which pair the ASC/DES.

Carol Tebbs> Basically, the first thing to test is the Solar Arc for the age of the person at major events and see where it would have to be in the natal chart in order to reach (move to or arc to) the appropriate planet or configuration to describe the event. For instance, if my client has Uranus conjunct the natal Moon possibly in very close aspect, and I know that her mother and father died within the same year of different causes, then I strongly suspect that something major like the MC or ASC was contacting that planetary pair. I would suspect a birth time that would bring the Moon and Uranus into very close orb of less than one degree. Since the event happened when she was 8 years old, I would start testing with the MC placed 8 degrees prior the degrees of the Moon/Uranus natal conjunction. Further, I would test a time with the MC placed 8 degrees after the Moon/Uranus conjunction to test the Planets arcing to the MC. This is just a beginning step.

Carol Tebbs> A good rectification is dependent upon enough major life events to build a "Case Theory" and begin testing. At least a dozen or more events that span the life is a good start, and 20 is better. It is difficult to rectify a birth time for someone with mellow life experience or someone very young. You really need the very painful life experiences to get a good handle on rectification of the birth time. You also need feedback from clients about the circumstances of the major events and how they felt about them.

RA> You mentioned that it is a challenge as to what goes where. I would think MC events are more publicly visible, and the ASC events more internal?

Carol Tebbs> Yes. Also, the Ascendant moves very fast through some signs and slowly through others, plus you have the latitude variation too – all of which make the ASC more difficult to search as a first indicator. That's why you always start with moving the MC to planets using the Solar Arc, then experiment with moving planets to the "working", or possible, MC.

CL> Let me get this clear, we SUBTRACT the Solar Arc for the event from the appropriate natal planet or configuration that describes the event, not every single planet and angle in the chart. Right?

Carol Tebbs> Right. Actually, you are narrowing the beginning search to only the close aspect network "Hook", then expand to all of the planets later, once you have narrowed to two or three possible birth times. Certainly, a computer search does sort for every planet to angle, or angle to planet contact, but I suggest that you narrow that search by first working with life events and Solar Arc increments to personal planets or the Moon's Nodes in 1-degree aspect to the other planets.

Appendix C:
Frequently Asked Questions About Transit Cycles

Carol Tebbs> In Chapter Five, Table 37 shows how fast Pluto moved for the decade in which you were born. For me, born in 1939, Pluto takes 45 - 49 years to make its first square but for you, born in the 60's, it will take only 37 - 38 years.

AM> Pluto moves fast in my generation.

PS> The opposition time will still be about the same because 180 degrees will include some slow motion as well as some fast motion, right? Still 124 years vs. the wide range for the square, I mean.

Carol Tebbs> The same time increment added for Pluto to make its opposition to my natal Pluto compared to yours, makes the cycle very different in timing for each of us because the 180 degrees of the opposition varies depending upon which part of the cycle the 180 degree encompasses. For instance, if all of the fast phase of Pluto is included in my 180-degree opposition, then that point will be reached well before 124 years. Conversely, if all of the slow phase of Pluto is included in the 180-degree opposition, then it could extend to well beyond the average motion of 124 years for opposition. The same concept holds true for the motion of the other outer planets. The difference is often great between mean motion and true motion. The lesson tables only show mean motion. You will need to search your ephemeris or do a computer search to find actual or true motion. You may also find it helpful to use your astrology software to print out a page listing the sign and degree of your chart sensitive points which includes major aspects to natal planets and angles. Sort them by sign and degree in astrological sequence.

Carol Tebbs> Anything important in the chart will shout at you in obvious ways. In the lesson I refer to a concept of "stacking up" of aspects and aspect patterns. Pay attention to that concept because it helps distinguish what is important from what is less so. Very likely any important year you choose to search for 8th and 12th harmonic aspects to your charts will reveal a "stacking up" of major transits.

Carol Tebbs> It is very important to memorize the cycle for each planet so you have some idea of how long it will be in effect (within 1–2-degree orb). Tables 30, 31 and 32 in Chapter Five gives you some idea of how long a moving factor activates the natal chart within 1 degree.

TJ> I was very surprised that the stationery period of Mercury is a whole week!

Carol Tebbs> The comparison chart in the lesson of the approximate time for the moving factor to activate one degree of the zodiac is a good ballpark estimate and is to be used as a guide only. Your software or ephemeris will tell you exactly when the transits activated your charts.

TJ> Can you explain more about the shadow areas?

Carol Tebbs> The shadow area is the entire degree span of the planet first hitting the degree area that will get activated three times – first by direct motion, then retrograde and again by direct motion. Since planets move at variable speeds, duration of the "shadow area" activation is specific to the planet. If you remember, not having to deal with retrogrades is why I recommend starting the test with Solar Arc Directions.

TJ> So basically, it's the retrograde.

Carol Tebbs> Not quite. It is the whole degree area that is activated 3 times by the planet going through its direct, retrograde, direct cycle. Uranus, for instance moves 8 degrees forward, then 4 degrees retrograde, then 8 degrees forward, and so on. The shadow is the 8 degrees that are re-traced between the two positions marking stationary retrograde and stationary direct. The shadow period extends until the transit moves beyond the point where the planet went retrograde. The whole area is considered sensitive until the planet moves beyond never to return to that spot in its current cycle. Again, I can't emphasize enough how important it is to memorize the mean motion of all of the planetary cycles.

AM> Can you explain how the shadow area affects us, Carol? Sensitive?

Carol Tebbs> Ayumi, the shadow areas are sensitive in that any moving factor hitting within that degree range can activate the planet's energy. It is similar to an orb. The closer to the planet, the stronger its message.

PS> Are the other planets as regular as Uranus (funny to say that about Uranus!) in their forward / retrograde cycles?

Carol Tebbs> If you plot out the direct/retrograde/direct periods of each planet, you will notice that they have a regular and predictable direct/retrograde cycle, but it is too complicated to memorize. Use your astrology software or ephemeris for that reference.

TJ> I'm still unclear on the shadow. Can we find one of these 11-month periods in the ephemeris such as Saturn?

Carol Tebbs> I'll pick a date randomly from 2000 because I'm not sure you all have the newest ephemeris for 2001 – 2010 or astrology software. On September 12, 2000, transiting Saturn turned retrograde at 0 Gemini 58 and continued retrograde back to 24 Taurus 0 on January 5, 2001 when it turned direct again. The entire area from 24 Taurus to 0 Gemini 58 is sensitive (in the shadow) for the duration of the whole cycle. If you think of all of the degrees within the shadow as getting hit three times during the direct, retrograde, direct motion, you can see why it is such an important marker for change. Three hits bring a re-visitation of issues that we need to deal with. The first hit brings awareness, the retrograde hit often brings action, and the final hit suggests adjustment to or resolution of the issue. So, take note of any of the outer planets making a station or hitting some degrees three times during the course of its direct/retrograde/direct transit.

Carol Tebbs> Personal example. When Uranus first transited my Ascendant in April of 1971, I began to feel stifled and wanted to get out on my own. When transiting Uranus retrograded back over my Ascendant, I moved away from my family for 17 months until Uranus again hit my Ascendant by direct motion and thankfully, I was welcomed back by my family and continued the marriage.

Carol Tebbs> Use your astrology software or ephemeris to determine the signs and degrees activated by each planet if it is between a retrograde and direct motion. That gives you an idea of how long it is active.

AM> But I am not sure what decides the area from 24 Taurus and 0 Gemini 58 as Shadow area? Was it orb related?

Carol Tebbs> In all planetary direct/retrograde/direct periods where another planet or configuration is hit 3 times, the idea forms on the first hit, action is often taken on the retrograde, and the consequence of the action are felt on the final direct hit.

Carol Tebbs> Ayumi, NO, it was not orb related. It is simply the degrees between Saturn's first activation of the degree that gets activated 3 times, which includes that retrograde and final direct motion activating the natal chart for the dates given. Every degree within that path will be hit 3 times. Don't get too caught up in retrogrades, but the 3 hits ARE the main reason why retrogrades are important in transits.

Carol Tebbs> You can see why just a single transit can become a major life phase or transition if a key planet or cluster falls within the transit of an outer planet direct/retrograde/direct degree area. Put simply, 3 hits are more important than 1, and 3 hits mark longer periods of time for the most distant planets like Pluto, whereas the faster motion of Jupiter takes only a couple of months to make 3 hits. Search your Astrology software or ephemeris for examples of how long Jupiter takes to make 3 hits, Saturn, Uranus, Neptune, and Pluto to better understand the duration of outer transits.

Appendix D:
Frequently Asked Questions About Declination and Graphs

VM> In the directions for graphing the declinations with Solar Fire 9, you said to enter 90 days. Should it be 90 years?

Carol Tebbs> The Lifetime Declination Graphic is a secondary progression based on "a day for a year", therefore, when you switch from progressing longitude to progressing declination, it is the same concept. In Solar Fire 9 software, selecting "Progressions" first is the best choice and then go to the sub-menu under "Progressions" and select "Declinations" instead of the default "Longitude". Don't forget to check the box to add "natal lines" as well.

Carol Tebbs> The Moon sometimes goes out of bounds to 28+ degrees, so the 30-degree N and S grid will do just fine.

RA> Is that the angle extent?

Carol Tebbs> It is degrees of declination that a planet can move from the ecliptic. It is not 30 degrees as in the semi-sextile of the 12th harmonic aspects measured in longitude. I liken the graphic displays of declination, progressions, and transits to a moving picture of the life, rather than the snapshot of the birth chart or the progression for a given year.

Carol Tebbs> Basically, each time that lines intersect with natal lines and/or progressed lines of other planets, you should have a corresponding event of the nature of the planetary influence. When you have a convergence of many points or planets at once, a major event is signaled. Be sure that you have selected the MC and ASC as points to be charted along with the planets. They are very helpful and select "print natal lines" as well. Do not select "background shading" because it makes the graphic too hard to read.

If you all are still young and want to only do 45 or 50 years of life graphic, that is fine. Do up to your present age, and only interpret what has happened in the past. Don't try to go into the future just yet. I want you to see the actual correspondence of crossing lines with major life events and changes.

MB> Carol, is there a way to change the colors on the graph? I just printed one out and the yellow lines for Moon, Mercury and Venus hardly show up at all.

Carol Tebbs> I don't think your software provides that option, but if you insert the chart, graph of table into a PowerPoint slide, click on "Picture Format" in the upper left of the Solar Fire 9 tool bar. There you have many options to modify the color and brightness of the image. Other software may allow a change of color within its own programming.

Carol Tebbs> On the contra-parallels, they are harder to spot, so only do those if they are obvious -- i.e., a cluster of planets converging at 15 degrees north opposite another planet at 15 degrees south. For example, in my natal chart I have a cluster of planets at 20 - 21 degrees north, so when any of the moving lines gets to 20 degrees north OR south, I know that combination will be activated. Just do the obvious contra-parallels, and all of the other crossings are pretty obvious, though I do draw in a horizontal line in ink to mark the O degree equator.

I also begin every client consultation by discussing the overview I get from the Life Declination Graphic. It is a good segue into discussing the life pattern of the natal chart, and the progressions and transits for the current year.

Bibliography

1. Boehrer, K.T., Declination: The Other Dimension, Fortuna Press, 1994
2. Brady, Bernadette, Predictive Astrology: The Eagle and the Lark, Samuel Weiser, Inc., York Beach, ME, 1992.
3. Burk, Kevin, Understanding the Birth Chart, Llewellyn Publications, St. Paul, MN, 2001
4. Davison, Ronald C., The Technique of Prediction, London, L. N. Fowler & Co. Ltd., 1971.
5. Devore, Nicholas, Encyclopedia of Astrology, Philosophical Library, New York, NY, 1947.
6. Doane, Doris Chase, Time Changes in the USA, Tempe, AZ, American Federation of Astrologers, 1985.
7. Doane, Doris Chase, Time Changes in the World, Tempe, AZ, American Federation of Astrologers, 1994.
8. Dobyns, Zipporah, Progressions, Directions and Rectification, T.I.A. Publications, Los Angeles, CA, 1975.
9. Hand, Rob, Chapter 12, The Ascendant, Midheaven and Vertex in Extreme Latitudes, Essays on Astrology, Para Research, Rockport, Mass., 1982.
10. Jansky, Robert Carl, Jansky, Interpreting Eclipses, Astrology Classics, 2013
11. Manley, Cheryl, Online College of Astrology archives, www.astrocollege.com, Astro-202 Final Exam on Rectification, submitted to Carol Tebbs, MA, December 2003.
12. Rodden, Lois, Rodden Rating system and computer software, www.AstroDataBank.com, 2007.
13. Rodden, Lois, AstroDataBank 3.0, Full Dosier, Source, "From Mother's Memory", www.astrodatabank.com, January, 1970.
14. Seaman, Ann Rowe, Swaggart: The Unauthorized Biography of an American Evangelist, Continuum Publishing Company, New York, 1991.
15. Stanley, Ena and Tebbs, Carol, Beyond Basics: Moving the Chart in Time, Bayse, VA: Online College of Astrology, 2003, www.astrocollege.com.
16. Streissguth, Michael, Johnny Cash, the Biography, Da Capo Press, Cambridge, MA, 2006.

17. Tebbs, Carol, E-Book, Beyond Basics: Tools for the Consulting Astrologer, Chapter One: Life Declination Graphics, Online College of Astrology, www.astrocollege.com, 2003.

18. Tyl, Noel, Prediction in Astrology: A Master Volume of Technique and Practice, Llewellyn Publishing Co., St. Paul, MN, 1991.

19. Walker, Andrew, Elizabeth: The Life of Elizabeth Taylor, Grove Press, New York, NY, 1997.

20. www.astro.com, Paul McCartney, Anna Nicole Smith, Barbara, and Jenna Bush.

21. www.biography.com, Michael Jackson.

www.ingramcontent.com/pod-product-compliance
Lightning Source LLC
Chambersburg PA
CBHW041238240426
43661CB00070B/2914